"KNOW THYSELF AND TI.

Handwritten: I SIMPLY VALIdate WHat's REAl! THE TRUTH i GOd! amen. 1 ST OF NOVEMBER 2022 Uncle Norris PRaise God amen!

SCIENCE of BEING

Handwritten: (uncle mike) AN KH MAN

Handwritten: 10-14-2019 MICHAEL H. NORRIS

BY
EUGENE FERSEN

Editing by Adrian P. Cooper
Author of Our Ultimate Reality, Life, the
Universe and Destiny of Mankind

http://www.ourultimatereality.com

Introduction

During the course of my quest for true nature of Reality and our own place and meaning within that Reality over the last 40 years or so, much invaluable inner Knowledge, Wisdom and Truth has been opened to me through numerous and diverse sources, and which I have since been blessed to share with readers of my books, newsletters and websites.

When I recently discovered and started reading **Science of Being** by The Baron Eugene Fersen, originally made available to a few people in the form of a series of twenty seven individual lessons, I knew at once that these are no ordinary texts. It very soon became apparent to me in fact that **Science of Being in Twenty Seven Lessons** is an extremely profound and important collection of teachings, and without doubt some of the very greatest I have ever seen on these most important matters.

Science of Being is not only one of the very first texts on The Law of Attraction ever written, if not the first, it is, in my view, one of the most profound and important texts ever written in absolute terms, written by a true Lightbearer for humanity, whose teachings reach far beyond The Law of Attraction to encompass many other fundamental and immutable Universal Principles.

It also very soon became clear to me that many of the most well known Law of Attraction and Metaphysics authors must, at least to some extent, directly or indirectly, have learned from this great teacher of teachers. No other book ever published on The Law of Attraction by any author, student of The Baron Eugene

Fersen or otherwise however goes as deeply or as clearly into these crucial subjects as does **Science of Being**.

It is now my very great pleasure to make available to you this rare collection of twenty seven powerful, profound lessons including exercises, questions and answers in the form of a single invaluable book, that all who are blessed and most privileged to read it may profoundly benefit from its valuable and indeed crucial teachings, your life thus being blessed with health, abundance and happiness, as well as further enhancing your own knowledge of the true nature of the Universe, and the Universal Principles, including The Law of Attraction, which infinitely shape our lives, reality and evolution.

Adrian P. Cooper, Author,
Our Ultimate Reality, Life, the Universe and Destiny of Mankind.

http://www.ourultimatereality.com

Science of Being

The Baron Eugene Alexandrovich Fersen
Editing and Introduction Adrian P. Cooper

http://www.ourultimatereality.com

Copyright © Adrian P. Cooper, 2008

ISBN 978-0-9799106-1-6

Published by Ultimate Reality Publishing.
An imprint of Mind Power Corporation.

Contact: sales@ultimaterealitypublishing.com

Dedication

For all Humanity and Seekers of Light and Truth.

And for the generations of Lightbearers, through whose dedication and love the teachings and legacy of The Baron Eugene Fersen are continued.

http://www.scienceofbeing.com

And in the Memory of The Baron Eugene A. Fersen, Bearer of Light and Teacher of Teachers.

Know Thyself and Thou Shalt Know All.

Table of Contents

INTRODUCTION BY EUGENE FERSEN

HEALTH, Success and Happiness are the Foundation and Aim of every human life. Health is Energy. It is your capital. The more you have of it, the better off you are.

Success is the intelligent use to which you put your capital of Energy Health.

Happiness is the satisfaction you get from the proper combination of these two, Health and Success.

The Source of all Health, physical, mental and spiritual, is the limitless Life Energy of the Universe, from which all life in Nature springs. Every human being is equipped by Nature with the physical means to contact and use that Life Force. The more you contact It, the stronger and healthier you become, thus adding constantly to that initial capital of Energy of yours with which you have to make a Success in your life. Few have done so, because few have known that it could be done, and those few have kept the secret for themselves.

"Science of Being" simply strips the mystery and uncertainty from these plain, basic Truths of life and puts you in direct conscious contact with the Universal Forces and Laws amidst which you live. It teaches you to attune yourself intelligently to the gigantic ebb and flow of those Cosmic Currents, in such fashion as to enlist their full power to help you reach your goal, instead of unconsciously opposing yourself to them.

Thus it completely re-organizes your human existence from the bottom upwards, giving you first a sound physical body through which to express your activities, then a healthy and vigorous mind to govern and direct them most advantageously and finally a ready access to the priceless and unlimited soul treasures stored within you as within every individual born to this world. You are started into a correlative growth and expansion on these three planes of your Being which results in corresponding material and intellectual rewards, not because those rewards are given to you from the outside, but because you have developed in yourself the strength of character and the ability to take them.

The majority of people today fumble blindly toward an end only vaguely seen, blundering awkwardly athwart the very Universal Laws and Powers that, properly handled, should be their greatest help. When they are flung back bruised and discomfited, the prey of ills physical, mental and spiritual, they sullenly place the blame on God, Fate, the local politician or anywhere except where it actually belongs — on their own ignorance.

"Science of Being" eliminates that guilty factor by giving you the right perspective of yourself in relation to the Universal Forces of which you are the product. It opens your eyes to the intangible elements with which you have to deal and delivers into your hands the conscious control of your own Destiny. You will know how to restore your bodily health when you are ill and how to increase your vitality and energy when you are well. You will develop your mental faculties to the highest degree. You will stabilize your emotional side, replacing fear by

Confidence, nervousness by Poise and worry by Peace and Harmony.

Achievement is a prize locked securely inside that curious and delicate assortment of complex parts which is YOU. All those parts need in order to pour forth into realization their measureless treasures of latent possibilities is the proper correlation one to another and to the Power which drives them. That is the end which it is the purpose of this Course to accomplish, so that you may be able, through the development of your own inherent qualities and forces, to experience to the full in this earthly existence the ultimate of all human desires — Health, Success and Happiness.

Cordially yours,
Eugene Fersen.

LESSON ONE

ONE of the dominant traits of modern Humanity is the desire for "Independence," Humanity is seeking it above everything else and is willing to pay the price for it, no matter how high that price may be.

And yet what is real "Independence" after all? Is it based on social position or on great intelligence, on physical strength or on money? Adverse conditions can make rich people lose their fortunes. Diseases can destroy physical strength. The most brilliant intellect may be misunderstood by people and therefore fail to bring forth the expected practical results. And social position itself is of all human powers the most unreliable and unstable.

Under these conditions something else has to be sought—a Power which will never fail you—a Power great enough to meet every emergency—a Power close enough to be right at hand whenever it is needed. It is only such a Power that can bring real Independence.

What is this Power and where is it to be found? It is within you, it is outside of you. It is the Power of Life itself. Within you there seems to be only a limited supply of it, and when that supply is exhausted you are like an engine short of fuel. From where have you to get the fuel your human engine needs? From the Great Storehouse of all Energy, of all Life—from the Universe itself.

There is an infinite supply of Power around you. All you need to do is to learn how to draw upon it and how to use it in every department of your daily life. This Power is the Life Energy of the Universe, the Foundation and

Lesson One

Apex of all Existence, the First and most Sublime Manifestation of our Great Mother, Nature Herself. It is that which always was, is, and always will be, changeless as Fundamental Power yet variable in Its Infinite manifestations, Eternal through Time, Infinite through Space with its Centre always there where you contact It—underlying, pervading, governing, sustaining and encompassing everything.

When this Power is within you, you call It life. Outside of you Its name is Primal Energy or Universal Life Energy. Because of It everything in Nature lives. It is in the currents of the earth, in the waves of the ocean, in the strength of the wind, in the heat of the sun, in the soft rays of the moon. Electricity exists because that Power is back of it. Withdraw that Force from anything and that thing would cease to be, would die. Even the Universe would collapse were that Power withdrawn from it.

This Power, known as Universal Life Energy, or simply Life Energy, as It will be called in these Lessons, is the very essence of everything there is. Not only do Sound, Light, Electricity, Radio-activity, etc., derive their power from It, but also all so-called material elements and objects are found in their final analysis to have originated from Universal Life Energy. They are known by different names in accordance with the different aspects under which they appear, although they all come from the same Source.

For instance, take steam. Super-heated steam is invisible. It possesses great dynamic power when under control. When liberated, it has the tendency to diffuse itself.

Someone who does not know through Science the different transformations which can take place with steam would never think that in another aspect this hot, light, ever-moving gas appears as a block of solid ice, cold, heavy, motionless.

So it is with that which we call Matter. Previous to the time that Science was able to show the direct relation between the invisible forces and the so-called material elements, this world was considered the battlefield where Matter and so-called Spirit were fighting their unceasing Battle. The general tendency was to side with Matter, because those who saw Creation only as a material unit totally ignored the Invisible Forces back of the so-called manifestations.

On the other hand, another part of Humanity tried to reach spiritual attainment, harmony and happiness by fighting- Matter, by suppressing their senses and even by denying their own physical bodies.

Science of Being explains the difference between those two concepts and shows impartially and impersonally the conditions as they actually are, not as they were believed to be. Under the light of this Science is revealed the Unity of Creation with its two poles, one of which is Spirit, represented by Universal Life Energy, and the other the so-called Matter.

Science of Being explains to you that Universal Energy, when in a free condition, is called Life Energy and manifests Itself through motion and vibration. Everything in this Universe vibrates, moves, even things which at first sight seem to be entirely motionless.

Lesson One

In Its primary condition of condensation Universal Life Energy forms microscopical spheres called Electrons. Electrons are considered the very Substance of the Universe, and as far as modern researches in that direction have been able to discover, Electrons underlie everything, everywhere, on the furthest star the same as here on earth. Combinations of Electrons, differing one from another by their number and mutual relations and revolving in a certain space filled with Free Energy are called atoms. Atoms, in turn, are the fundamental units which constitute Matter in its three aspects, solid, liquid and gaseous.

The more electrons, or condensed Energy, present in the atoms of a material element, the heavier, denser and more substantial that element becomes.

Those tiny electrons are in perpetual motion, rotating with an extraordinary velocity upon their own axes and revolving around a central electronic nucleus which acts as a little sun in its own microscopical planetary system.

As all elements are made of atoms, therefore within even solid matter there is a continual movement of those electrons. Everything, everywhere, moves in this Universe of eternal movement.

Your human body is formed, like all other bodies, of atoms and electrons. Therefore within your own physical body everything is in a perpetual motion governed by certain invisible yet definite Universal Laws. As long as your body functions according to those Laws, its condition will be a harmonious one, because the Laws themselves work always with perfect harmony. But if, through ignorance, you interfere with the normal functioning of those Laws, in harmony will be the result.

That in harmony may express itself through body, or through mind. In the first instance it is called disease, in the second negative traits of character; but both trace their origin to a common cause, namely, conscious or unconscious violation of the Universal Law. If this cause is removed, then all its varied manifestations — troubles physical and mental — will vanish also.

You may ask the question: How shall I know all the different and very complex operations of the Universal Laws? The answer is: Know the Fundamentals, be One with the Law in its Main Aspects and do not worry about details. If left alone, details will work out harmoniously by themselves.

Another question may be asked by you:

What am I as an individual, and for what purpose am I placed on earth, ushered into existence seemingly without my knowledge or consent?

First let us have a clear definition of what you are. In order to proceed logically let us go back to what has been explained in the beginning of this First Lesson.

Eternal Nature manifests Herself as that Universal, Infinite, All Powerful and Eternal Force called Universal Life Energy. This Force is a living Power, being the very life of the whole Universe. It is also intelligent, because it is Universal Mind. Law emitting and law abiding is this

Power, and as such it is called Universal Law. Harmonious is this Force also, and through its Law of Attraction or Love it keeps the whole Universe in a condition of perfect equilibrium and harmony.

Projections of this Universal Life Energy are continually proceeding from their source in Nature into material manifestations. These manifestations vary in degrees, details and complexity of their fundamental qualities. The strongest manifestations known to us, now, and the most complex, are called Man, or YOU, a triune being, made up of a body, a mind and a soul. You are directly related with Life Energy, which is the basis of your triune nature, through all three of these constituent parts. Consequently, you are eternally linked with Nature Herself also through the immutable and eternal part of your being, your Soul.

Therefore, though individual in one sense of the word, you are yet one with your fellow beings, one with Nature and everything in Her, because you all originated from one common Source. That is why environment is able to exercise such an effect on the individual, and the individual on his environment, either constructively or destructively. There is a kinship between you deeper and more subtle than any of blood—a community of spirit welding all things into a brotherhood no less influential because it is not commonly perceived.

Though Mind is not first as a Fundamental, being second in the Eternal, logical order of Creation, yet your human mind is one of the most important faculties you possess. Through it you become conscious of the full value of that

First Fundamental of all being, Life. You begin to perceive all Life's infinite possibilities for unfoldment and to discriminate also between right and wrong, good and evil, according to whether they will help or hinder that unfoldment. You realize gradually that the Success, or Good, in your life comes in direct proportion to your unification with Universal Forces and Laws, while the disharmonious results, such as failure, poverty, disease and trouble, are the inevitable consequences of your separation from or opposition to those Laws, either through ignorance, fear or self-will.

Never fear that you cannot do a certain thing, that you cannot bring out certain qualities from within you, that you cannot overcome obstacles on your path. Remember that all things are possible to a Power which governs the whole Universe and that you are the very embodiment of that Power. Latent within you are all those forces and qualities of yours. Your problem is to bring them out. How this is accomplished will be the subject of the following lessons.

As the closing instructions of this Lesson will be given to you two Exercises, Relaxation and Silence, which you are to start today and to practice regularly throughout the whole week. These two, together with the Star Exercise and Mental Contact which will be explained in Lesson Two, form the foundation for succeeding Exercises of a specific sort. They are to be practiced continually, not only during the period of the Lessons, but throughout your entire life. They must become a part of your daily routine, just as important and vital to your well being as the food of which you partake, the air you breathe or the care which you give to your body. The fifteen or twenty minutes a day which will be regularly devoted to these Exercises will be the best investment of time and energy you ever made in your life.

The specific Exercises based on these Four, however, are designed to suit the particular Lesson with which they are given. A new one will be added each week, but is to be practiced for that week only and then held in reserve for future use whenever you feel a special need for it.

The Science of Being is an essentially practical course, one which, if practiced daily, will bring forth all you expect from it and even more; but if you will be satisfied with the perusal only of these Lessons and then expect them to produce results without any effort from your side you will be greatly disappointed. It is a very well known fact that the more you use an organ or faculty the better it works and the stronger it grows.

All the exercises given in this course are arranged systematically and progressively, and are designed in such a way as to develop gradually all your latent qualities and powers, making them stronger and more productive every day.

These exercises are also of a sort that everybody, men and women of all ages and in different stages of development, can easily perform without the least trouble. Even children can do some of the fundamental exercises and obtain most constructive results. The ones which are most adaptable to children will be especially pointed out.

It is advisable, in fact quite important, that these exercises should be performed under the most favourable conditions, which are the following:

You choose a certain time of the day, preferably in the morning immediately on getting up, or the last thing before going to sleep. The morning is better, as one's forces are fresh after the night's rest. If possible, always keep the same hour. Try to be by yourself, with nobody in your immediate vicinity, in order that other people's mental vibrations may not interfere with your own very delicate mental work. Be comfortably seated in a chair, the body erect but not tense, with the left hand up resting on your left knee, palm upwards. and the right hand on your right knee palm down. Be careful not to cross your legs. Eyes may be kept open or closed, but preferably closed. In that posture the body is most favourably disposed both to receive from outside the Life Energy which is filling all Space and to convey and distribute it through the complex nervous system to all parts of your body, and especially to the brain.

Universal Life Energy will enter mainly through your left hand, whose palm is turned upwards, receiving the Force from above. Through the nerves of the left hand and arm that Force is conveyed to the spinal cord, and through the spinal cord to that nucleus and centre of radiation of life in your body which is called the Life Centre of it. That Centre is situated at the very base of the spinal column, and from there it radiates life vibrations throughout the whole body. That Centre was known to the ancients, especially to the Hindus, who called it "Kundalini," the Coiled or Serpent Power, because it is like a sleeping serpent coiled, resting. Using modern terminology we would say it is Life Energy in a static condition.

From this Life Centre, which it stimulates first, the current of Life Energy flows into the solar plexus, which is called solar because the radiation of the nerves which form it looks like sun rays proceeding from a common centre. The solar plexus is a reservoir where life currents are stored to be distributed to the different parts of the body according to their needs. After the current of Life Energy has filled to the brim the solar plexus its surplus is conveyed from there back to the spinal cord, passing through and purifying on its way all the different interior organs. Then it goes through the right arm to the right hand, from the finger tips of which it flows again out into Space. It is a continual flowing in and flowing out of your body of Universal Life Energy, stimulating, invigorating, purifying, developing and harmonizing it.

Not only does the Life Energy penetrate into your body through the above mentioned channel, but it enters into it, when you are properly relaxed and in the right posture, through every cell of your body. The cells inhale that Force, which then travels along the nerves to the Life Centre of the body and back again, to be exhaled by the same cells in a form of life radiation called the Aura or Human Atmosphere. In Lesson Two will be given more details on that subject.

EXERCISES TO LESSON ONE

The two exercises to be acquired by you first are Relaxation and Silence, without which no other exercise can be properly performed. Only when the body and mind are completely relaxed can you get what is called a real rest, for only then are you in the most ideally receptive condition. All the gates of your body and mind are then opened to the inflow of that supreme Universal Power called Life Energy.

When starting Relaxation do not expect it to be perfect from the very beginning. To relax at will, like everything else, needs practice. If you notice that there is any tension in any part of your body when you are seated in the chair in the correct posture, let it go. Try to feel physically as comfortable and as much at ease as you can.

The same also with your mind. Relax your brain as much as possible. Try not to think of anything, but just to sense rest, peace; and when that condition is attained, then enter mentally into Silence. That is, try to silence within your own self for the time being all impulses, desires and even thought. You will not be able to attain perfect silence within yourself right from the start, but every time you practice it you will gain something in that direction.

Practice those two Exercises conjointly for about five minutes. Later on, when you will have trained yourself in that direction, a few minutes of Relaxation and Silence will be quite sufficient to rest completely your body and mind and to open them to the inflow of Life Energy.

These two exercises are fundamental ones and though very simple and easy to perform, yet they are most helpful, constructive and necessary for your well being. It is a known fact that those who can relax properly for a few moments during physical or mental work are able to produce, with less effort, greater results than those who do not know how to do it.

Later on, when you will have trained yourself sufficiently in this direction, you will be able to relax and enter into Silence instantaneously whenever and wherever you feel the need, even in a crowd or amidst noise and disturbed conditions. In practicing Relaxation and Silence you will gradually gain such control over yourself that unfavourable surroundings will no longer be able so to influence you as to prevent you from deriving all the benefits from these two Exercises whenever you choose.

QUESTIONS TO LESSON ONE

1. What are the fundamental Principles of Being?

2. What are Forces of the Universe?

3. What are the Laws which govern them?

4. What is Universal Life Energy and where is it to be found?

5. What are its main aspects?

6. Explain vibrations.

7. What are electrons?

8. What is Matter?

9. What is Man?

10. What is Man's relation to Nature and to Universal Forces and Laws?

11. What is Disharmony?

12. How can it be removed?

Lesson One

ANSWERS TO LESSON ONE

1. The Fundamental Principles of Being are:

(1) A Primary Causeless Cause of All Being, the Great Principle, or the Unmanifest.

(2) Its First Manifestation, called Universal Life Energy, which in Its condensed condition is known as Universal Substance, or Electrons.

2. The-Forces of the Universe are:

(1) Life Energy.

(2) Its expression as Mind Force.

(3) Its highest manifestation as Love, or Soul Power.

3. The Laws which govern them are:

The Laws of Nature, which are the expressions of the One Universal Law, called the Great Law.

4. Universal Life Energy is:

The Fundamental Manifested Power of the Universe, and as such is Omnipresent, Omniscient and Omnipotent.

5. The Main Aspects of Universal Life Energy are:

Life, Mind, Law (Truth) and Love.

6. **Vibrations are:**

The rhythmic motion of Universal Life Energy. As everything in Nature is made up of Universal Energy, everything therefore vibrates, or moves.

7. **Electrons are:**

Individual units of condensed Universal Life Energy. They appear as microscopic spheres and are the smallest known particles of what is called Matter.

8. **Matter is:**

A combination of various manifestations of Universal Life Energy in degrees perceptible to our senses.

9. **Man is:**

An individualized, conscious, compound and harmonious projection of the Great Principle into its own eternal Substance.

10. **Man's relation to Nature and to Universal Forces and Laws is:**

Man is ONE with Nature, and is the best medium known through which Universal Forces and Laws express themselves.

11. Disharmony is:

An unconscious or conscious opposition to the Forces and Laws of the Universe. It is the perversion of the Natural Law of Evolution.

12. Disharmony can be removed:

By consciously uniting oneself with Universal Life Energy, the Supreme Power.

DEAR FRIEND:

Lesson Two will explain to you the relation between the Universal Life Energy outside of you and the same Power known to you as the life within you. It will give you a thorough understanding of why, until this point has been made clear and the proper means given you to overcome those limitations, you are seemingly able to use only the very limited amount of energy which is in your body.

In order to re-establish your free and open contact with the vast store of Life Energy outside of you, the first two of several Exercises contained in this Course will be explained to you. Through them you will be able to connect the life current in your body with the inexhaustible Stream of Universal Life Force, thus making yourself consciously One with a Power which is supreme among all powers.

The importance of these two initial Exercises cannot be too greatly stressed. They are Fundamental, the twin valves through which you flood your entire Being, physical, mental and spiritual, with the energizing flow of Life Force. Upon them will be built up the complete sequence of Exercises which are to be given in the succeeding Lessons.

Commencing with Lesson Three, the specific EXERCISES TO which these two original Ones form the basis will be appended at the end of the Lesson, under the heading, "EXERCISES."

Cordially yours,
Eugene Fersen.

LESSON TWO

IN LESSON ONE was explained the existence and the qualities of that Supreme Power, the First Manifestation known to us of the Great Principle, the Causeless Cause Itself, which is called Universal Life Energy. Now further details in that direction will be given.

As previously stated, Universal Life Energy is everywhere. Its supply is inexhaustible. Outside of you it is in a condition as Dynamic Life Energy. Within you, in your Life Centre, it is in a static or condensed condition.

Your problem is to make the connection between these two aspects of the same Power through certain Exercises which will be given to you in this lesson. You are to open your body to the inflow of the Universal Life Energy outside of it. The life force within, from its centre in your body, then acts as a magnet and attracts the Force from without. Your Life Centre within, stimulated by the current of Universal Life Energy from without, takes in that Force, transforms it into the life current of the body and sends this changed condition to the Solar Plexus, its reservoir or storehouse. From there it is conveyed by the nerves throughout the whole system.

As Universal Life Energy is limitless and all powerful, the more it flows into the body the stronger the individual becomes. The object of these Exercises described hereafter is to establish a permanent contact and thus secure a continual flow of Universal Life Energy into the Life Centre of your body, from where it will be distributed by a way of the Solar Plexus in a constant and increasing radiation of life throughout the whole body.

It is obvious that when filled with vitality, all the cells of the body are made to work to their full capacity, all the functions of your different organs are stimulated to the highest degree and all your qualities, physical, mental and moral, are brought out and developed to the utmost. Under these conditions you will be able to work and grow strong. Every kind of effort, physical or mental, will be easy to you because you will always have at your disposal more force than you can actually use. Work, instead of a duty or a burden to you, will become a genuine pleasure, not only because it affords an outlet for your abundant energy but because of the ease and efficiency with which you find yourself able to do it.

Investigations of the astonishing feats of strength and endurance among animals, birds and especially insects have brought to light some remarkable discoveries as to the source of their great energy. Nature itself, as a loving Mother, has provided her children with the necessary means to contact Universal Life Energy constantly and transmute it through their bodies into the startling activities which baffled scientists for many years. Animals, for instance, use the hair of their bodies as numberless wireless poles to contact this Power of the Universe. The birds use their feathers for that purpose, reptiles and fish their scales, insects their feelers and the little down growing on their bodies, plants the underside of their leaves, etc.

If it were not for that continual contact with Universal Life Energy ants could not carry burdens so many times heavier than themselves with such ease and continuity of effort. Without that power continually flowing into their bodies and sustaining them throughout their many days of migration, birds could not cross the ocean, thousands of miles in one stretch, without food, without resting, without sleeping. Even the many layers of fat which migratory birds acquire through intensive feeding before they start on their long journey would not be sufficient to supply one small part of the energy which they spend on their way. If it were not for the continual inflow of Universal Life Energy into their bodies, through their feathers, during the very process of flying, they could never reach their destination.

As we human beings are also members of the Great Family of Nature, we are endowed with the same faculty as the rest of Creation to contact Universal Life Energy directly through our body and to use it whenever we need. But because we have grown apart from Nature in the slow process of civilization, we have let that faculty sink into disuse until it has become almost completely atrophied. We became so interested in cultivating ourselves that we utterly ignored the more important job of keeping up our contacts with Nature's marvellous array of Forces — literally pulled ourselves up by the roots and thought we had grown because we stood higher.

Today we have to re-establish consciously that vital connection which we wilfully broke. We have a mind which can soar into the highest regions; but how few of the wonderful thoughts conceived there can we really bring to practical fruition! Potentially the strongest and noblest of Nature's children, we have become what we actually are now, the weakest and most helpless of all, simply because of the pride and conceit which led us to separate ourselves from Universal Powers in order that we might be self-sufficient. Our roots are dangling in the air.

The only way to restore our lost connection with those Powers is to put our roots back in as deliberately as we pulled them out, by uniting ourselves consciously with Universal Life Energy. It was on the Mental Plane that this union was first broken, through the fault of our mind, so it is on the mental plane also that the first steps must be taken to repair the damage. Therefore we start the process of re-establishing our contact with Universal Life Energy through certain mental exercises, now to be described.

Relax as completely as you can, physically, mentally and emotionally. Enter into silence as you were taught in the previous Lesson, and when you feel harmony within you as a result of that relaxation and silence, then say to yourself in a low voice the following words, "I AM ONE WITH UNIVERSAL LIFE ENERGY. IT IS FLOWING THROUGH ME NOW. I FEEL IT."

Thus you open the mental door which separates the life force within you from Life Energy without life force within, because of its inherent quality of attraction, contacts the Force from without, which begins to pour into your Life Centre with an ever increasing power and is transformed there into life currents and distributed throughout the body.

The above mentioned formula to establish the contact with Universal Life Energy is of three distinct constituent parts, vibrating to the three planes, the Soul Plane, the Mind Plane, and the Body Plane. Considered singly, the three touch their respective notes in the one chord as follows:

"I AM ONE WITH UNIVERSAL LIFE ENERGY" is an Eternal Verity. Its audible statement awakens within your Soul the realization of the eternal fact of your actual unity on the Soul Plane with Universal. Life Energy. Thus the Soul is stimulated to assert that union.

"IT IS FLOWING THROUGH ME NOW" represents the opening of the mental gates. You are a law unto yourself on the Mental Plane. To become conscious of something mentally means to give life to it, to make it real, whereas things of which you are unconscious are as if non-existent for you. To become conscious that Life Energy is flowing through you right now according to mental laws makes it so. And as your Soul has been awakened by the first statement, it will support with all its awakened power your second mental statement.

"I FEEL IT," are the closing words. This refers directly to your body. It makes you not only know, but actually feel, the fact of the contact; and that which you feel becomes very real to you. In practicing that mental contact as an exercise you must be very careful how you do it. Whenever you make those statements remember two cardinal points, namely: First, that when repeating those words you must try to realize mentally as strongly and clearly as you can their actual meaning. The more you can make it real to yourself, the better it will work.

Second, that you must consistently avoid all mere automatic affirmations. You must not try to suggest to yourself the words you are repeating, but you must actually realize them as based on genuine facts. It is this realization of the meaning behind the words that is alone of value, and not the mere unthinking repetition of the words themselves. Both affirmation and suggestion only numb the individual without producing the desired results. Suggestion and affirmation usually mean something superimposed, something painted on, while scientific statements of Fundamental Truths, thoroughly understood, develop in you that which you already possess.

When making the last statement, "I FEEL IT," you must not try to imagine or persuade yourself that you feel Life Energy flowing through you. On the contrary, you must be as analytical as possible, though not sceptical. You must take the attitude of an individual who, for instance, tries to hear far away sounds or see a distant object. He strains his senses, sharpens them in order to perceive otherwise imperceptible impressions. Similarly, when making the mental contact you must make your sense of feeling very acute in order to perceive the inflow into your body of Life Energy.

Like everything else, this is a matter of training. The more you will train your body in that direction the more you will actually feel the Life Currents entering it. If in the beginning you will not feel the flow of Life Energy through your body, do not be discouraged. The proof that it has entered will lie in the fact that you will feel stimulated and more energetic in doing any work. At first you will have to practice that contact from five to ten minutes every day. After a month or so you should be able to make it almost instantaneously.

The mental contact with Universal Life Energy is one of the easiest ways to contact that Power. You should use it continually before starting any work, be it physical, mental, or inspirational. The few moments it will take you to make the contact and the little effort required will amply repay you in helping you to perform your work without ever becoming tired. Not only will you be able thus to eliminate fatigue and weariness, but you will be able to do better and quicker work. The more you will practice the mental contact the more you will become consciously ONE with Life Energy.

When you have practiced that mental contact as an exercise for some time, you will find that you can make it instantaneously whenever you need it. Instead of audibly repeating the formula given above for making the contact, all you will need to do is to realize your Oneness with Universal Life Energy and you will become actually and consciously One with it. Because of the association of ideas the other two parts of the formula for the mental contact will work automatically.

Once the mental contact with Life Energy is properly established, remember that the Force which you will be using in your work is no more dependent on your own limited supply of it. As it will flow through you from the Limitless and All Powerful Store of All Energy, naturally there can be no end to it. Thus you will soon discover that work will make you grow stronger instead of tiring you as it did before.

After you make the mental contact with Life Energy its flow will continue until your attention has been transferred from your work. At that moment, especially in the beginning, you will disconnect yourself from Life Energy and a new contact will therefore become necessary. The more you practice that contact the better it will work and the longer you will remain each time connected with Universal Life Energy.

Before starting the slightest and easiest task always take the trouble to make the contact Why should you use your own life force, of which you have so little in your body, when there is waiting outside of it a Universal Power ready and willing to do all the work through you and fol. you, if you will only let It in. All that is necessary is for you to use the different qualities of your body, mind or Soul, as tools, through which is working Life Energy Itself.

In spite of the simplicity of the method, not everybody is at first able to use it successfully because of the doubt which some people may entertain in their hearts as to the efficacy of such a mental contact. You must remember that on the Mental Plane you are a law unto yourself. If you believe in a thing, that thing will become a reality to you. But if you doubt or fear, that doubt or fear also becomes a reality to you and prevents you from realizing the thing you want.

In order to overcome that difficulty and enable everybody, even the most sceptical and timid, successfully to make that conscious contact with Universal Life Energy, there is another method which will now be explained, a method of pure physical contact based on the operation of physical Laws. That second method has this advantage over the mental one that it does not require any faith to enable it to function freely. It works for the reason that the Physical Laws are there put into operation, and the physical contact with its Universal Energy is made not because you think or want it, but because you cannot help it. Obviously, if you also think about the Universal Life Energy flowing through you at the moment of physical contact with It, It will work all the better. Yet, if you do not think at all about It, still It will work, because It is wholly independent of your mental attitude.

This second, or physical method, is based on a certain exercise originated by the author and called by him "Star Exercise." The reason why this posture is called the Star Exercise is because the individual, when taking it, places his body in such a position that it will fit into the five points of a star. It is in this position that the physical channels are most widely open for the reception of the Universal Force. For this reason the Star Exercise is indeed a KEY TO ALL POWER, unlocking and bringing forth in Man all his latent powers and forces.

The actual contact between the Life Centre within the body and the Universal Life Energy outside of it takes place when the body is disposed as shown in the diagram. Standing straight, yet relaxed, with legs spread to a degree corresponding to the design, the arms stretched to either side on a level with the shoulders and with head erect, your body will fit into the five pointed star. Even the proportions of a normally built body will correspond to the figure of the star. The head fits into the upper point, the two arms into the two side points, the torso into the centre, and the legs into the two lower points. The palm of the left hand should be turned up and that of the right hand should be turned down. The whole body must remain erect, but not tense.

The upturned palm of the left hand receives the Universal Life Energy which is directed from Space towards the Earth. The inherent power of attraction exercised by the Life Centre within your body acts as a powerful magnet to increase the inflow of the Life Energy coming from Space. Through the nerves of the hand, arms, and the spinal cord Life Energy flows to your Life Centre, located at the base of your spine. There as stated in the previous Lesson, it is transformed into the life current of your body and is sent thus transformed into your Solar Plexus.

After the Solar Plexus has been completely filled with it the surplus flows out through the down-turned palm of the right hand and into the earth, in response to the earth's magnetic attraction. The Solar Plexus itself acts as a distributing centre from which the life force is continually sent out to the various parts of the body according to their needs, whence it is finally radiated in the form of a radio-activity called the "Aura," or "Human Atmosphere." Thus is established a current of Universal Energy flowing from the Infinite Source into the Human Body, invigorating, purifying and developing it, and flowing out of it only to return with an ever increasing power. Not only through the left hand does the Life Energy penetrate into your body; it pours in also through every cell and nerve of your body. All those secondary currents converge towards your Life Centre, which absorbs it and, after transforming it into life force, sends it out again throughout your body. Yet during the exercise the main current is received as stated above.

Shortly after you have taken the position you may begin to feel a certain heaviness in the palm of the left hand, somewhat as if a heavy ball were pressing on the palm. You will probably also sense a kind of tingling in the finger tips of the right hand. These two different sensations are due to the influx and outpouring of the Life Energy. Thus you will feel that the contact is established.

There are several other important points to be remembered in connection with this exercise. The best time to perform it is in the morning immediately after getting up, before doing anything else, and at night before going to bed.

Three to five minutes is all that is needed to perform the Star Exercise. For the first month it would be inadvisable to do it longer because of the very strong inpour of Life Energy. But later on, when your body becomes accustomed to that inflow of Life Currents, the duration of the Star Exercise can be prolonged to fifteen minutes and the exercise taken more than twice a day.

During that exercise in the morning and at night you ought to be dressed as lightly as possible, in order to leave your body free and without pressure on any part of it. The exercise should be performed in front of an open window, and if the temperature and circumstances permit, out of doors.

The Star Exercise should never be taken immediately after a meal. At least an hour must elapse between the two; otherwise a nausea and sometimes even indigestion may result, as too much Life Energy can upset digestion and produce the above mentioned effects. Deep rhythmic breathing is very helpful during this exercise because of the stimulating effects of the oxygen.

In the beginning, your arms may feel tired during the performance of the exercise. No effort should be used to keep your arms up in their proper position. Let them drop and lift them again when rested; otherwise the tension of the muscles and nerves resulting from a prolonged forced elevation of the arms will counteract to a great extent the flow of the Force through them.

If you are very sensitive you will notice a certain swaying of your body forward and backward in performing the exercise. If that swaying becomes too strong, stop doing the exercise in a standing position and take it lying on your back, on a couch or on a bed. For many people it is preferable to take the exercise in a lying position, as the swaying may be so pronounced as to cause them to fall when it is taken standing. Yet, if you can perform it in a standing position by all means do it that way.

Those who are heavily built or stout will notice in the beginning that when they perform the Star Exercise they perspire excessively. They should be not at all alarmed by that. Though rather unpleasant, it is an excellent sign, for through perspiration are eliminated from the body undesirable elements.

The points of the compass are of no importance to those who use Life Energy, which is Universal. There is no necessity for observing them in any way, as the Force will flow equally well no matter in what direction the face is turned.

This exercise works so automatically that there is no imperative need to think about the Force flowing through your body. It will flow anyway, because of the attraction exercised by your Life Centre within. Yet, as before stated, if during the exercise you mentally contact, it will work so much better, as mind and body will then cooperate to the same end.

The Star Exercise is exceedingly beneficial to children. It stimulates the entire body, especially the brain centres and those glands which play such an important role in the child's growth, and development.

The Star Exercise ought to become a part of your daily routine. It is to be carried on regularly throughout ALL YOUR LIFE, and if this is done the positive results obtained will exceed your most sanguine expectations. It is Life, in its strongest Exercise and use for the greatest unfoldment of your Body, Mind and Soul. For sometime in the beginning that process of unfoldment may be rather slow, but by persevering you will win the reward of complete success.

The Universal Life Energy contacted through the Star Exercise as Life Force will not only stimulate and invigorate you, but as it is at the same time the Intelligence and the Law which governs all Being and the Love which keeps it in a condition of perpetual harmony, it will also establish within you within you that perfect equilibrium which is the basis of real power. The Star Exercise will produce automatically the same growth and harmonization within you which the application of Universal Law by your mind will produce consciously. Working together they will achieve the quickest and best results because of, their mutual reaction one upon another.

There are various modifications of the Star Exercise by which Universal Energy can be contacted physically and yet not so obviously. Whenever you want to receive the Universal Force without making the mental contact or the Star Exercise, all you need to do is to turn the palms of one or both of your hands upwards. In that position the current of Universal Energy will flow through your hands into your body, with the sole difference that instead of flowing out through the right hand, as both hands have their palms turned upwards, it will flow out through your feet into the ground.

This second physical contact can be made while sitting, standing or even walking. As you do not need to extend your arms, the turning upward of the palms of your hands being sufficient, you can make that contact easily in the presence of people without being conspicuous.

When seated you can have your hands resting palms upward on your knees or on the side of your arm chair. When standing you can cup your hands at your sides or clasp them Loosely behind your back in such fashion that the palms will be turned up for the reception of the Force. The student can contrive a variety of other ways to make that contact, according to the occasion.

QUESTIONS TO LESSON TWO

1. What are the methods of contacting Universal Life Energy?

2. What is the role of the Life Centre in connection with Universal Life Energy?

3. What is the role of the Solar Plexus?

4. What are the advantages of the Mental Contact?

5. In what way is the Mental Contact limited?

6. What are the advantages of the Physical Contact through the Star Exercise?

7. Are there any other means of physically contacting Universal Life Energy?

8. What is the best mental attitude to take during the Mental Contact and the Star Exercise?

9. How can one grow stronger in Body, Mind, and Soul by working?

10. Do animals contact and use Universal Life Energy for their daily needs?

11. What is the quickest way to develop man's latent powers?

12. Why does Universal Life Energy establish equilibrium within?

ANSWERS TO LESSON TWO

1. **The methods of contacting Universal Life Energy are:**

   The Mental and the Physical.

2. **The role of the Life Centre is:**

   To receive Universal Life Energy and transform it into life currents which it sends by way of the Solar Plexus throughout the whole system.

3. **The Solar Plexus:**

   Acts as a distributing agent for the life currents sent to it from the Life Centre. The strength of the individual is in direct proportion to the development of the Solar Plexus.

4. **The advantages of the Mental Contact are:**

   Its quickness and its simplicity.

5. **The Mental Contact is limited:**

   In that until properly understood it must be taken on faith.

6. **The advantage of the Physical Contact is:**

   That Universal Life Energy is contacted through the use of Physical Laws which work irrespective of one's mental attitude.

7. **Universal Life Energy may be physically contacted:**

   By any modification of the Star Exercise through which the palms are turned upward for the reception of the Force.

8. **The right mental attitude to take during the Star Exercise is:**

   One of confidence and receptiveness.

9. **One can work and grow stronger:**

   By contacting and using Universal Life Energy in all daily activities.

10. **Animals:**

    Do contact and use Universal Life Energy for their daily needs, just as everything in Nature does.

11. **The quickest way to develop Man's latent powers is:**

    By the continual use of Universal Life Energy.

12. **Universal Life Energy establishes equilibrium within:**

    Because of its natural harmonizing properties as the basic Force of the Universe.

DEAR FRIEND:

In this Lesson will be revealed to you the use of Universal Life Energy in ancient times, by prophets and miracle workers, by great teachers, leaders, warriors and statesmen—in fact, by all whose achievements have won them everlasting fame in the eyes of the world which could only admire where it could not understand.

It will also give you concrete examples of how this

Power has been and is being used in modern times by men and women who have made a success of their lives and who have not only risen above the level of the crowd, but have been able in their turn to lift the crowd to a higher standard.

You can become one of those fortunate ones. You are to be taught in this Course the secret of how to use consciously that same Power which they, for the most part blindly and without knowledge of its nature, used to raise themselves to their lofty station.

Cordially yours,
Eugene Fersen.

LESSON THREE

IN the Sacred Books and the traditions of all nations are found divers accounts of people who, versed in occult knowledge, were able to perform all sorts of so-called miracles. The generally accepted belief is that either these accounts are untrue, or the ones who were able to perform those miracles were endowed with supernatural powers.

The fact is, those accounts are generally true, though sometimes exaggerated through the enthusiasm of their recorders. Only the Powers used, instead of being supernatural, were simply Natural Powers whose origin and character were not understood except by the select few who employed them. Jealously guarded throughout the Ages, the secret of how to use those Powers and Forces has been revealed to the bulk of Humanity only NOW because only Now has Humanity as a whole progressed to that stage of Evolution where it is ready to know what before it could merely believe blindly.

In times so remote that their history has descended to us only dimly through legend and myth, the knowledge of these Powers by rare individuals invested those individuals with such a transcencient glory in the eyes of the marvelling multitude that they were considered Gods descended to Earth. Thus originated the first anthropomorphic concept of Divinity.

Vishnu and Siva, the dual manifestation of Brahma, the Absolute, (the Great Causeless Cause Itself) were using the Power of Universal Life Energy continually throughout the whole of their earthly life, and the wonderful feats they were able to accomplish led their admiring followers to deify them and erect temples for their worship.

Rama, the great conqueror and at the—same time liberator of India, who penetrated at the head of his Aryan hosts into the heart of the Indian Peninsula to found there a powerful empire of the Caucasian Race, used Universal Life Energy to achieve his gigantic task. To him it was given to free the White Peoples from their bondage to the Black Race which then ruled the World, and to make them the dominant power they now are. Belonging to the great body of Druids, or Tree-worshippers, which had existed from time immemorial throughout all Europe, Rama received the secret knowledge of how to use Universal Life Energy on his initiation into that cult.

Krishna, the Great Teacher and Uplifter of Humanity, whose amazing achievements are still vivid in the racial memory of the Hindus, used Universal Life Energy incessantly and explained also to his beloved friend and disciple, Arjuna, how to apply it to the varied problems of daily life. This discourse on Universal Laws and Forces, given on the eve of the famous Battle of Kuru and on the battlefield itself, is preserved for posterity in the Baghavad Gita, one of the most beautiful and inspired records of all time.

Prince Siddhartha, during his direct initiation amid the mystic silence of an Indian jungle into the Higher Knowledge, became conscious of his One-ness with Universal Life Energy and from that moment was known as Buddha, the Blessed One, the Great Teacher and Friend of Humanity.

Jesus the Christ, throughout the whole of His earthly mission, continually used Universal Life Energy. Through it He transformed water into wine at the wedding feast, multiplied the five loaves and two small fishes for the feeding of the multitude, stilled the storm on the Galilean Sea, brought the dead to life and performed countless other miracles, among them His own resurrection.

On the Mount of Transfiguration He raised the rate of vibration of His body to such an extent that not only did that body become luminous, but even His garments glistened like silver.

He predicted the general use among human beings of Universal Life Energy as a healing and harmonizing power when He said, "The things that I do you shall do and greater things also, because I go to the Father."

He clearly stated that His Age was not ready to receive complete knowledge of this Power when He said: "Many things have I to tell you, but you cannot bear them now."

His words, "And I shall send you the Holy Ghost, the Spirit of Truth, which will teach you all things," are fulfilled NOW, in our modern times, through the knowledge which is brought to the world in the teachings of THE LIGHTBEARERS, of which these Lessons are a part. The Holy Ghost, the Universal Breath of Life, is that Universal Life Energy whose use is explained in this Course. The Spirit of Truth is the True Knowledge which now lifts from human consciousness the triple veil of ignorance, superstition and fear.

Moses, versed in the secret knowledge which the Hierophants, or High Priests of the Egyptian Temples, taught him when he was educated at the court of the Pharaoh, made vigorous and unceasing use of that Power. By directing Universal Life Energy he was able to make the waters of the Red Sea divide; with It he brought forth water out of a rock in the desert; from It also he drew the strength to hold in check those nomad tribes who persistently harassed the Israelites in their journey through the wilderness.

The proverbial strength of Samson which depended so much on his luxurious growth of hair, was due to his ability to use that same hair as a wireless station whereby to contact Universal Life Energy. The harmonizing power of this Force saved the life of Daniel when he was thrown into the lion's den, quieting even the wild beasts. Its preserving qualities kept intact in the midst of the flames the bodies of the three youths who were flung into the fiery furnace. Elijah brought back to life the son of the poor widow by directing through his body into the body of the dead boy currents of Universal Life Energy.

Invariably the progressiveness of a race or people is determined by the extent to which Universal Life Energy finds expression through individuals of that race, and especially through those individuals to whom its destinies are entrusted. Some of the great Indian chiefs, famed leaders of the Red Race, whose exploits have descended through legend and story, possessed the secret of that Power. Even the Polynesian Race, inhabiting the islands of the Pacific, was once, through its highest representatives, acquainted with the use of that Force. The Queen of Sheba, coming from the heart of Africa to visit Solomon, knew how to use Universal Life Energy. So also did Solomon, who through it won for himself an immortal renown as the wisest and richest of all rulers. Though king of a young and small nation, he was able to employ his own power of attraction to such effect that he secured the most advantageous alliances with the foremost nations of his time. The unusual energy and personal magnetism of Semiramus Queen of Babylon, was drawn from the same Universal Source of All Power, as was also that of another famous Queen, Cleopatra. Alexander the Great, Hannibal, Caesar, Napoleon, and scores of other famous men and women became great through the constant though probably unconscious use of Universal Life Energy.

In contrast to the examples cited above, we may consider the case of China. Laotzu, China's great philosopher, who lived some six centuries before Christ, was able, because of his intense love of Nature, to perceive its Universal Forces and Laws. Though he tried hard to disseminate that knowledge among his own people, he failed. Even his friends misunderstood him, because his knowledge was too much in advance of his time.

Another philosopher, Confucius, a contemporary of Lao Tzu, succeeded in giving to the Chinese a system of ethics based exclusively on mind and appealing solely to the intellect. Yet the decline and final cessation of all progress in China dates from the time of the acceptance of that system. The teachings of Confucius have ruled the lives of hundreds of millions of people for over twenty five centuries, but now at the last the infinitely greater teachings of Lao Tzu are emerging from obscurity into clearly understood relief against the dawn of the New Knowledge rising on the world through the medium of THE LIGHTBEARERS.

Evidence that a vague realization of the existence of Universal Life Energy prevailed even in the so-called Dark Ages, the period of wide-spread intellectual stagnation, is seen in the persistent search by alchemists of medieval times for the Elixir of Life. The Elixir they sought was in fact Universal Life Energy, which the limited material concepts of that age could visualize only in the form of a liquid.

In modern times, more than ever before, energy and vitality are not only appreciated but very urgently needed. The demand for them increases in proportion as the demands of our intense modern life upon the forces of the individual increase. The extraordinary capacity for work and the unusual personal magnetism of some of our present day scientists, captains of industry and leaders in all branches of human activities can be explained only by the fact that, consciously or unconsciously, they were able to contact the unlimited supply of Universal Life Energy.

In this connection a brief survey of the most prominent world figures, especially of today, would reveal the fact that almost invariably they are what is known as "self-made," born usually of humble parents, in comparative poverty and in an environment distinguished chiefly by its harshness and bleak opposition to large ambitions. Their starts in life were full of trials and handicaps of the most discouraging nature, yet their unquenchable vitality, enthusiasm and perseverance were such as to enable them to surmount every difficulty, overcome every obstacle in their path to success.

Anyone who approaches men like Edison, Marconi, Charles Schwab, Ford or the like, cannot help but be impressed by two dominant traits which they all possess in common, namely — great energy, expressing itself in extraordinary vitality of body, mind and Soul, and an unusual personal charm. Through their energy and the magnetism of their own personality they were able to attract all the necessary elements to create a wealth which brought remarkable prosperity not only to themselves but to their countries also.

Perhaps nowhere is the quest for replenishment of one's vital forces more clearly illustrated than on the stage and* in the moving picture studios of today. Experience has produced numberless devices for counteracting the tremendous nervous drain on those engaged in the art of portraying emotions, and chief among these is the remarkable stimulating power of music. For that reason, in some of the large studios, orchestras are kept whose duty it is to play appropriate music during the "taking" of a scene.

The remarkable harmonizing and strengthening effects of these musical vibrations, low as they are in the vibratory scale, are merely an indication of what can be accomplished if one is able to contact the infinitely higher and stronger vibrations of Universal Life Energy. When actors will use Universal Life Energy Itself instead of Its very feeble expression in sound vibrations, not only will the histrionic results they obtain be much better, but their own health will also be preserved and improved to an extraordinary degree. The stimulation, and inspiration, moreover, instead of subsiding at the end of the scene, will persist throughout their daily life and will advance the whole tenor of their existence outside the theatre as well as in it.

The astonishingly youthful appearance of some luminaries of the stage who, by the calendar, are far past their prime, is due to something more fundamental than "makeup." Their features genuinely reflect the youthfulness of the spirit within—a spirit kept young and buoyant through an exceptional ability to contact and use, even though unconsciously, the Universal Life Energy.

If such rewards are secured from the unconscious use of that Power, how much greater ought to be the rewards of a conscious and intelligent application of It.

The success of those individuals can be emulated by any normal persons who will use Universal Life Energy in connection with their work. All human beings born into this world are endowed with certain latent qualities which can be developed, together with the power to contact Universal Life Energy, which can be used for the development of those qualities. Therefore no matter how limited one may appear to be at the start, there is hope for anyone who will make proper use of that Force.

This holds true regardless of how humble one's condition or profession may be, or how devoid of prospects. There is no avenue of human activities in which Universal Life Energy, constantly and intelligently used, will not strike out a way to prominence.

For instance, take a street cleaner. Though engaged in what is considered one of the humblest of occupations, he is by no means cut off from ample possibilities for success. His road, like all others of a constructive nature, points up. All he needs is the energy and determination to push along it to the top.

An ordinary street cleaner who uses that Force will soon find himself growing stronger in energy, intelligence and ambition. He will begin to perceive and take advantage of opportunities to which he had been blind before. The relation between present causes and their probable future effects will become clearer to him; he will discover the larger possibilities and broader scope of his work; and by availing himself intelligently of every opening he will be able to shape an upward road to more and more responsible positions until eventually, perhaps, he will become the head of that department in his community. In such a position he cannot only improve the sanitary conditions of that city, but can also contribute in general to the well being of his fellow citizens. Thus he will become a valuable influence for progress both to his own community and to Humanity at large. As a natural consequence, fame and prosperity will be his reward.

This is a rational and very possible prospect, typical of the possibilities that exist in the most unassuming occupations. However, many obstacles may exist between the beginning and the end of the road, there is always a way to surmount them. Ally yourself to Universal Life Energy, look where your road leads and set yourself confidently to the business of getting there. With that Force to help you, nothing will be able to stop you or turn you back.

EXERCISES TO LESSON THREE

As EXERCISES TO this lesson, continue the Star Exercise, Relaxation, Silence and the Mental Contact with Universal Life Energy, as described in the previous lessons.

QUESTIONS TO LESSON THREE

1. To what basic cause must be attributed the achievements of great men and women of all time?

2. Were they conscious of that cause?

3. If any were, name several.

4. How far back in human history can the use of Universal Life Energy be traced?

5. Was this knowledge of how to use Universal Life Energy general or was it restricted to- a few individuals?

6. If restricted, why was it not made general?

7. What has been the effect on nations of the capacity of its leaders to use Universal Life Energy?

8. Was this knowledge limited to any particular countries, religions, philosophies or sciences?

9. In what human activities is the use of this Power impossible?

10. Will the use of this Power in modern times lead people to Success?

11. Has the success of prominent people ever been easily attained?

12. What is the simplest and most practical way to rise to prominence?

ANSWERS TO LESSON THREE

1. **The achievements of great men and women of all times are to be attributed:**

   To the ability of those individuals to contact and use Universal Life Energy.

2. **In most cases:**

   They were not conscious of that cause, but in some cases they were conscious of it.

3. **The best known of those who consciously used Universal Life Energy were:**

   Vishnu, Siva, Rama, Krishna, Buddha, Moses, Solomon, the Queen of Sheba, Samson, Daniel, Elijah, Christ and many other prominent but less known characters.

4. **The use of Universal Life Energy:**

   Can be traced beyond written history to times so remote that they are reached only by legend.

5. **The knowledge of how to use Universal Life Energy:**

   Has always been restricted to a few individuals until the present day.

6. **This knowledge was not made general:**

   Because the mass of Humanity has never until now progressed to that stage of evolution where it is ready to receive it.

7. **The factor that has always determined a nation's progress is:**

   The capacity of its leaders to use Universal, Life Energy.

8. **This knowledge:**

   Was not limited to particular countries, religions, philosophies or sciences.

9. **Branches of human activities in which the use of this Power is impossible:**

   There are none, of a positive and constructive nature.

10. **The use of this Power in modern times:**

    Is bound to lead people to Success now as in the past.

11. **The success of prominent people:**

    Has never been attained without hard work.

12. The simplest and most practical way to rise to prominence:

Is continually to contact and use Universal Life Energy in all one's activities.

DEAR FRIEND:

During comparatively recent years research has uncovered hitherto unsuspected Forces of Nature; mechanical science has fashioned bewildering varieties of machines of marvellous complexity, precision, speed and sensitiveness wherewith to harness and direct those Forces; but Man's utmost ingenuity has fallen far short of evolving any device that can compete even remotely with-that perpetual miracle of mechanical perfection, your physical body.

This lesson will explain to you how that wonderful physical apparatus which your Soul has constructed for the expression of its qualities and activities comprehends in itself the functions of all the machines that have ever been or ever will be made.

For instance, consider the Radio. The most recent and prominent of present day discoveries has been the Radio; yet how many people know that from time immemorial there has lain dormant and unused in the human body, but within immediate reach, a wireless station of capabilities exceeding its most completely equipped counterpart in the laboratories of today.

All this is your own, awaiting only the operating and directing energy of your own intelligence to leap to your service. By taking advantage of all the possibilities within yourself you will be able to produce the most astonishing results.

Such is the object of this lesson—to give you full control over that physical side of your nature.

Cordially yours,
Eugene Fersen.

LESSON FOUR

THE first question you may ask is: What exactly are the qualities and the different functions of the physical body? It is presumed that you already know how this physical body came into existence. The process of its development from conception and growth within the mother until it reaches full maturity is so well known to the average reader that we are not going to enter into details on that subject. But the mysterious Forces and Laws back of that physical development, governing it and emerging into visible expression through it, are of vital interest to everybody; and it is the operation of those Laws and Forces which will be here explained in detail.

The physical body as a whole represents the embodiment on this material plane of your Ego, or Soul, whose manifold activities are expressed through its different organs and members. That body is made up of millions and millions of cells, grouped according to the different functions of the body, and each group of cells having its own particular duties to perform. Moreover, every cell has an individual and independent life within it. Modern investigations have proven that even when taken from the body these cells can, if placed in the proper surroundings, not only live an independent life, but can even develop under those new conditions.

If you want to have a strong and healthy body, you must give to the cells the opportunity and possibility to function properly. Breathing and taking material food are two of the ways to accomplish this. Physical and mental activity naturally needs energy, and it is in the work of supplying this energy that all the cells of your body cooperate. You feed the cells of your body with gasses and chemicals which, being absorbed and transmuted by the cells into a form of energy, in their turn feed you. That is, they supply you with the necessary amount of power for the work you have to do.

This transmutation into energy, or Life Force, of the air absorbed through breathing and the chemicals absorbed through eating is in direct proportion not only to the amount of their absorption by your body, but also to the body's capacity for transforming them. As that work is limited the amount of Life Force stored in your Solar Plexus is therefore also limited.

Naturally under those conditions you can use these forces only to the extent of the actual capacity of your Solar Plexus. Once the Solar Plexus is drained of Life Force, you feel that there is nothing to draw upon any longer. Then you call yourself tired, because you have exhausted the supply of energy in your body.

Yet Nature, who takes good care that her children should never be left stranded at the time when they need her support, has provided various physical channels through which to replenish this store of energy by tapping the great Universal Reservoir of Power.

For instance, the hair on your body, which is developed more on certain parts of It than on others, as well as the hair on your head, is of tremendous value in helping you to recoup your physical Forces. Each hair is a tiny wireless pole contacting Universal Life Energy and conveying it into the cells and the different centres of the body. Just as those natural wireless poles are ready to function all the time, so is Universal Life Energy ready to flow through, them continually.

Another major means for contacting the Energy outside is through the fine network of nerves which send their tendrils to the skin over every portion of the body. Where these tendrils are concentrated to form a genuine mat of sensitiveness, such as in the balls of the fingers, the palms, soles of the feet, etc., the sensitised areas act especially strongly as the grid of a receiving set, the point of contact peculiarly adapted to the reception of vibrations of Life Energy from without.

With all this highly specialized apparatus already at your disposal, it would seem as if that Power ought to be flowing into your body all the time. The reason it does not is because your nerves and cells are contracted on account of the general tenseness of your body and are almost paralysed and closed up by some latent fear.

Naturally under these conditions the Life Force concentrated within your Life Centre cannot attract the Universal Life Energy which surrounds your body on every side. That is why Relaxation and Silence are such important EXERCISES TO the harmonization of the body. If human beings would live a natural life and would be in as close contact with the Forces of Nature as is the rest of Creation, there would be no necessity to contact Universal Life Energy. It would continually flow into the body, as there would be no obstacles to prevent the inflow.

The more Life Energy enters into your body, the stronger the individual cells will become. As the entire body is made up of millions of cells, it is obvious that the well being and proper functioning of that body as a whole depends chiefly on the well being and proper functioning of its component cells. Add to this clear, strong, harmonious thoughts, constructive and lofty emotions, and you have power and harmony within ready to contact the Universal Harmony and Power without.

That Power, flowing through the cells as the medium of transmission, bathes them individually and collectively with Life Energy, refreshing and stimulating them, washing them clean from impurities and building them up naturally into a healthy, strong and beautiful body, a fitting instrument for the expression of the Individuality that dwells within.

As stated previously, Harmony means Equilibrium, and Equilibrium is Power. If you want to be powerful you must achieve the Balance which Power demands for its most efficient expression. There is no better way to obtain that Balance than by bringing out your fundamental qualities.

Remember that your body is the outgrowth, the vehicle through which your Soul's Individuality expresses its activities. If the Four Fundamental Qualities — Life, Mind, Law (Truth) and Love—as explained in a previous Lesson, are given physical expression in your daily activities, they will by nature build up adequate physical channels for that expression. That is, in proportion as those Four Qualities are brought out in your own

Individuality they will be reflected in the body which is but the material counterpart of that Individuality.

Remember also there are two ways of bringing out those Qualities, each way of equal importance and each supplementing the other. The continual use, through the Star Exercise and the Mental Contact, of Universal Life Energy, whose essential function it is always to establish Equilibrium, will automatically develop them within you, promoting their growth to the point where they will blossom into your consciousness as ready for expression. Then your conscious application of them by performing every act with Energy, Intelligence, Accuracy and Joy will cultivate and strengthen them in an increasing and harmonious growth which will visibly manifest itself in the various organs and members of your body.

As your body is simply the visible, material expression of the activities of your own Individuality, naturally if those activities are harmonious their physical expression must be so also. Real Harmony, Power and consequently Beauty of body are absolutely unattainable unless Equilibrium is first established within the individual and manifested through his daily activities.

It has often been noticed that when individuals are happy, that happiness radiating from their faces makes them appear actually beautiful, though originally they may have been very plain. The explanation is, of course, that the inner sense of Happiness, of Love, is able to produce such a transformation. If that inner condition were sustained through any length of time the effect would be so radical and lasting that the body would not only appear to be transformed, but would actually be transformed and would remain so as long as the cause of that transformation continued to be active within the inner self of the individual.

The definite physical process through which such fundamental causes obtain permanent expression usually takes place more quickly with young people than with older ones. Scientific investigation has proved definitely that all body tissues are being continually renewed, with the result that everybody possesses a virtually new body at periods ranging from one to seven or more years. It is through this renewal that any change must be gradually manifested. The younger a person is the more rapidly that work of renewal generally takes place, because the plasticity of a young mind is reflected in a young and pliant body, whereas in older people a set habit of thought and ideas has expelled that buoyant physical elasticity.

Yet age must never be considered an impediment. However slowly or quickly that change may be taking place, nevertheless it is taking place every moment of your lives. Not a minute passes but what some element of the new invades every tissue of your body to replace a corresponding amount of the old and worn out which it expels. You who will honestly and perseveringly follow the instructions here given will so temper with your aroused qualities this new fabric which is being perpetually knit into your being that you will produce most astonishing bodily changes, both as to appearance and as to producing power.

Naturally the transformation of your body is so gradual that you will not notice it at first. Yet the growth from within your body is continually operating, and if you have in you a continual flow of Life Energy, as well as harmony in your thought and action, then Life Force penetrating into every cell is bound to make that physical side of your triune nature grow healthier, stronger, finer and more beautiful all the time. All you need to do is to apply the rules and laws stated before, and particularly to use Universal Life Energy continually, never worrying about the results. The very Forces and Laws you put into operation will take good care that the results manifested in your body shall be in exact proportion to the direct application of those Laws and Forces in you.

The right kind of food, well prepared but not too much of it, especially for grown people, will help a great deal in that work of harmonization of your body. Vegetarian food is by all means preferable to the ordinary meat diet. You have only to look into the great book of Nature to find there the answer to your query as to which diet is preferable, meat or vegetable. The animals which can produce the greatest continual physical effort are vegetarians, as for instance elephants, bulls or horses. Carnivorous animals can produce a great deal of energy in a single effort, but only for a very short duration of time. Sustained effort is almost an impossibility for most of them.

However, the demands of our modern life call for this sustained effort. A sufficient proof that there is already a dim realization of this exists in the increasing number of vegetarians. Eventually the whole Human Race will become vegetarians and fruitarians.

Yet as in everything else, gradual growth is preferable to an abrupt change, and for that reason you are advised to eat what you feel like for the time being. Inner adjustment will demand a different kind of a food to sustain your physical body, and then without any effort you will adopt a different diet. It will be no more a sacrifice to you, as you will have gotten into that new condition. Under these circumstances your body will be changed gradually, and will not suffer depletion or cause you any such physical discomfort as usually afflicts those who make a sudden radical change.

The same can be said in regard to smoking, drinking or any other similar habits. You will be able to get rid of them not by fighting or trying to overcome them, but through transmutation into healthy habits. There again the continual use of Universal Life Energy will be of invaluable assistance to you. Being a Perfect Power, it will by and by eliminate from your system all harmful desires and appetites.

Scientific breathing is also very helpful in the work of harmonization of your body. Most people breathe only to a partial capacity of their lungs. Under such conditions there is not a sufficient amount of oxygen conveyed into the body. As oxygen is, next to Universal Life Energy, the most important element for the subsistence of all life, it is obvious that if you do not absorb a sufficient amount of it through breathing your physical body suffers as a result of that shortcoming.

The above mentioned scientific breathing performs also a great service aside from the mere introduction of oxygen into the system. Based usually on the beats of the heart, it attunes the rhythm of the life within to the vast Rhythm of the Universal Life Energy outside. Thus it is an excellent help in establishing a quick and vigorous contact between the two.

Western systems of breathing, of which the object is only to bring about harmonious physical results, are preferable to Oriental methods, which are not so much concerned with the physical results obtained as with the development of psychic powers within the individual. There are quite a number of very good methods of scientific breathing which may be found in books on physical culture written by specialists in America as well as in Europe. A good system is that of Dr. Miller, a Swedish physicist, whose book "My System" is known all over the world.

Modern science constantly gives more and more scientific information in all directions, and in this direction also. Only by taking the trouble from time to time to keep yourself informed about the latest discoveries made along specific lines can you progress together with the general progress of human knowledge.

Physical exercises and sports of any kind are very necessary for your well being. As physical exercises the "daily dozen" by Walter Camp are excellent to keep you fit; but whenever opportunity presents itself do not despise walking, climbing stairs or any other similar effort. You will be more than amply repaid for it. Hiking, skating, swimming, rowing and all kinds of outdoor games are also excellent means to sustain the health and energy of your body.

Whenever exercising or indulging in sports, always remember two capital points. First, to make the contact with Universal Life Energy, so as to get the double benefits of the Force, and Second, to perform those activities with enthusiasm, since only then will they actually benefit you.

An exercise performed indifferently or with reluctance, at the compulsion of the will, will never bring any very constructive results, because the use of the will induces a general contraction and tenseness of the body nerves and cells which completely neutralizes the beneficial influence of the exercise itself. Under such circumstances the muscles are only wearied, not refreshed, and the individual acquires from his exertions nothing but that sudden fatigue which comes from utterly exhausted tissues.

EXERCISES TO LESSON FOUR

In addition to the Exercises given to you in the previous lessons — the Star Exercise, Relaxation, Silence and Contact — there will be given to you this week a new Exercise, **STIMULATION.**

The object of this new Exercise is to teach you to use nerves, to contact Universal Life Energy, and by the reaction of Universal Life Energy in its stimulation of all cells and tissues, to make those wireless stations function ever more strongly. This Exercise will help you also a great deal in the work of harmonization of your physical body. It is performed as follows:

When making the contact with Universal Life Energy try to feel the Force pouring in through every hair and nerve. You will perhaps perceive it as a tingling sensation, a feeling as if the hair were trying to stand on end. Think of your body as perfect, strong and harmonious. Do not try to localize or make specific that harmony, as the activities of your Individuality may not at all coincide with your idea of what they ought to be. Think harmony as a general condition, and leave it to your higher self to see that its expressions are tempered with that harmony as they emerge into and through it. That way you will discover that what comes out is really best for you.

QUESTIONS TO LESSON FOUR

1. What does the physical body as a whole represent?

2. What are the Forces and Laws back of physical development?

3. What is the best way to acquire a strong and healthy physical body?

4. In what way has Nature equipped the body for contacting Universal Life Energy?

5. What Centre within the body exercises the greatest power of attraction for Universal Life Energy?

6. Why does Universal Life Energy not flow continually into the body of every one?

7. On what does the general well being, strength and harmony of the body depend?

8. What essential qualities must one cultivate in order to build a harmonious body?

9. What are the two ways of bringing out the latent qualities of one's Individuality?

10. Is old age an impediment to the harmonization of the physical body?

11. What diet produces the most desirable results in the human body?

12. What mental attitude must be observed in performing physical exercises if benefit is to be derived from them?

ANSWERS TO LESSON FOUR

1. The physical body as a whole is:

The material expression of the qualities and aggregate activities of the Soul.

2. The Forces and Laws back of physical development are:

(1) Universal Life Energy;

(2) The Law of Attraction, or Harmony.

3. The best way to acquire a strong and healthy physical body is:

By making it an open channel for the continual flow of Universal Life Energy.

4. Nature has equipped the body with hair and with specialized nerve systems which act as complete radio stations for contacting Universal Life Energy.

5. The Centre within the body which exercises the greatest power of attraction for Universal Life Energy is:

The Life Centre, located at the base of the spinal column.

6. Universal Life Energy does not flow continually into the body of everyone because of a general tenseness and contraction of nerves and cells.

7. **The general well being, strength and harmony of the whole body depends on:**

   The well being, strength and harmony of its individual component cells, as well as on harmony of thought and emotions.

8. **The essential qualities to be cultivated in order to build a harmonious body are:**

   Energy, Mental Activity, Accuracy and Joy.

9. **The two ways of bringing out the latent qualities of one's individuality are:**

   (1) Continual use, through the Star Exercise and Mental Contact, of Universal Life Energy.

   (2) By performing every act of one's daily life with Energy, Intelligence, Accuracy and Joy.

10. **Old age:**

    Is not necessarily an impediment to the harmonization of the physical body. Constant use of Universal Life Energy will overcome the effects of old age.

11. **The diet which will produce the most desirable results on the human body is:**
The one toward which the individual feels naturally inclined, and should change with the change of inclinations.

12. **The mental attitude which must be observed toward physical exercises if benefit is to be derived from them is:**

One of joy and enthusiasm.

DEAR FRIEND:

This lesson will give you a thorough understanding of how to use Universal Life Energy in your daily life, at home as well as in your office, in the country as much as in the city, when doing inspirational work like painting, singing and playing, and in the laboratory doing research work or probing into the Universal Intelligence for new discoveries.

No matter what your activities may be, first of all and above all, you need energy without measure to start and complete your work. You need to have your intelligence operating at its best to be efficient. You need discernment, a sense of truth, in order to be able to discriminate between the right and the wrong, and you need the power of harmonization in order to adjust matters the way they should be.

All this Universal Life Energy will supply to you, as these are its inherent qualities. All you need to do is to use that all-powerful Force, never worrying about results, knowing that they are bound to be harmonious when the Power producing them is Harmony itself.

Cordially yours,
Eugene Fersen.

LESSON FIVE

You have probably noticed that one of the main difficulties encountered in your daily life is a certain feeling of laziness, especially in cases where the task to be performed is not of particular interest to you. Even when, through an effort of will power, you are able to overcome that feeling and start to do your work, you begin presently to experience a sense of fatigue which often culminates in actual exhaustion. That is the reason why work is a real ordeal to most people, with the result that they do it not because they like it, but because most often they are compelled by circumstances to do it.

The cause of this attitude toward - work as something necessary but at the same time very unpleasant is the lack of supply of Life Force in the majority of individuals. When you have drained away the very limited amount at your disposal in the Solar Plexus, the reservoir of that Force in your body, you feel that you cannot work any longer. Yet if, before starting any kind of work, you take the trouble to insure a continuous and ever increasing fresh supply of that Power by making the contact with Universal Life Energy in accordance with the methods previously described, you will find that conditions are completely reversed.

Once connected with that Great Power which will flow into you, supplying all the life force you need for the work you have to perform, and even much more than that, the thing that seemed difficult to you before will appear extraordinarily easy and simple, because of the superabundance of energy at your disposal. The sense of laziness you may have felt before starting to work will be done away with as if by magic; and as for fatigue, you will soon forget the meaning of that word, because you will realize that -the more you work with the Universal Power to back up every step, the stronger and healthier you will become. That which appeared to you before almost as an ordeal will become a real pleasure to you. Thus not only will your attitude toward your work change, but your entire outlook on life will change and broaden also, bringing you that sense of freedom, of exhilaration and reserve power which invariably comes to him who is "stepping out of the rut."

Remember, any work quickly and well done naturally commands a larger financial return. It brings advancement and increase in salary. Besides that, quick and good work performed with joy, with a pleasant smile, will do away with criticism and will invite instead that sincere appreciation which harmonizes relations between employer and employee. A good worker, no matter in what department of human life, is appreciated and paid according to the value which his work actually represents.

The reason most people receive such small salaries is because their producing power corresponds fairly well to the small financial return they receive. Time and again, whenever an individual, be it man or woman, has been discovered to do better work than others, special attention has been paid to that individual and promotion and higher salary have followed as a natural consequence. Even if the recognition of that increased efficiency does not come in due time from the organization or people who enjoy the benefit of it, opportunities are seldom lacking to place it where its value is substantially appreciated; or if such opportunities are lacking that same Universal Life Energy can be used to discover the proper opening.

Remember also that it is within your power to bring this about in your own life. All that is necessary is for you to make the contact (the Mental one is especially advisable, because it is the simplest and quickest with Universal Life Energy before you start to do anything, and then to apply yourself to your task with the serene confidence that the Force flowing through you will support and guide you to a successful conclusion. Your body will act as an engine, the propelling power of which is the inexhaustible Life Energy. And just as the engine is never tired, and stops functioning only when there is no more power to make it work, so it will be with your body. It will work untiringly while the Force flows through it.

Moreover, your body is in all respects far superior to the mechanical engine to which it is compared. An engine has its parts worn through friction; it may get out of order or even break. Your body, on the other hand, is being repaired and renewed in every portion as fast as it shows signs of wear.

The Universal Life Energy contacted by you, and which your Life Centre is constantly transmuting into the very life of your body, not only supplies that body with the energy it needs to do the work, but what is even more important, strengthens and reconstructs its exhausted tissues down to the minutest cell. That amazingly thorough and unceasing process of rebuilding so adapts the new structure to incessantly new demands that the whole of your physical system is harmonized and fortified, daily reducing to a minimum the chances of wearing or breaking down.

In other words, just the opposite of what happens to a mechanical engine happens to your human body. The engine slowly but surely grows weaker every moment. Your body, on the contrary, through the use of Universal Life Energy grows stronger and better all the time. The few seconds which it will take you each time to contact Universal Life Energy will be compensated by hours of constructive and pleasant work. Consider this as one of the cardinal points of these teachings which, conscientiously applied, will bring results far exceeding your most sanguine expectations.

For instance, take any of your daily duties at home, no matter how small or trivial they may appear to you. Perform them always with the help of Universal Life Energy. You can use that Force when dressing or reading your newspaper in the morning. It will help you in cooking and even in eating your food. Once you make the contact with Universal Life Energy before you start to eat, the assimilation of the food by your body will be more complete and perfect. When combing your hair or giving the proper care to your body, take the trouble to contact that Great Power. It will then flow strongly into whatever part of your body you are concerned with, always stimulating, invigorating and purifying it. Your hair will attain a more luxurious growth and a rich lustre. If it has become grey it will gradually regain its original colour. Your skin will acquire a finer texture and smoothness, and will be more resistant to harsh external influences. Eyes will again grow clear and expressive, reflecting undimmed the awakened emotions of your higher nature.

It is a well known fact that if you take proper care not only of the human body, but even of the bodies of animals, trees and plants, you increase their actual value and improve their physical appearance. If such results are obtained in trying to harmonize their inherent qualities by taking care of them in the ordinary way, what infinitely greater and more harmonious results will be obtained if for that purpose a Power is used which is Life and Harmony itself and which is supreme in every direction.

In doing your office work, no matter whether you are at the bottom or at the top of the business ladder, always remember to contact Life Energy first. When your fingers are running over the keys of the typewriter, let Universal Life Energy work with you and for you, while you remain the directing mental power. If your province is farm work of any kind, in the field or in the barn, in the orchard or in the dairy, caring for livestock, feeding and tending them, or handling men, take the trouble in each instance first to make the contact with Universal Life Energy, letting it flow through you into everything with which you come in contact, and you will see what wonderful results you will thus obtain through the continual use of that Force.

Remember, this Power is the very Life of the Universe. Everything in Nature, a simple seed as well as a human being, needs it, and the more you pour that Force through your body into anything the better that thing will become. The seed planted in the field will give you bigger crops. The orchards will produce larger and better fruit. Cows will give more and richer milk, and your hens will lay more and larger eggs. Cooperation from helpers will be more spontaneous and efficient. Under its magic everything will thrive, and its continual use will reduce to a minimum the accidents and diseases so common not only among animals and poultry, bur also among trees and plants.

In the matter of healing do not forget that the source, the fundamental cause, of all sickness is the same for both animal and vegetable life. Disharmonious vibrations demand expression as well in the life of a tree as in the life of a human being, and the only difference is that their manner of expression varies in proportion to the degree of development of the channels for that expression. Thus in the simple organism of a tree the range of expression is limited to comparatively few diseases, while in the highly complex and sensitive system of a human being there is apparently no limit to the kinds of ill in which disharmony is able to manifest itself.

Through the use of Universal Life Energy, whose inherent quality is always to establish equilibrium and thus bring strength and harmony, all diseases can be eliminated, whether in plants or in animals, by the elimination of the fundamental negative cause. You do not do the healing, but by making yourself the direct agent, the open channel through which Life Energy is poured into the tissues which are too sick to contact it in sufficient quantities themselves, you introduce a harmonizing Force strong enough to overcome the disharmony at the root of the trouble. And although this Force is self-governing, it will be greatly helped in its work if directed intelligently, with a clear understanding of the nature of the task it has to perform.

For example, in treating animals there are two distinct ways to proceed. One is to take them individually and, after making the contact with Universal Life Energy, to direct it through your hands and finger tips toward that part of the body which is to be healed. If the entire body is affected, send the Force into every part of it with slow sweeping movements of the hands, working from the lower joint of the neck to the tail and feet or, if convenient, from the solar plexus outward each way, but without touching. Such treatment ought to last from five to fifteen minutes actually and be performed once, twice or more each day, depending on the seriousness of the case. Continue this until the animal is healed.

The second way of healing animals is by group treatment—that is, by treating a whole flock or herd at once. In this instance, place yourself just far enough away so that the herd comes into your perspective as a group instead of as individuals. The distance may vary from twenty feet to several hundred, depending on the size of the group. Make the contact with Universal Life Energy, and when you feel the Force flowing, direct it through your extended hands, towards the centre of the herd. Then by a slow and gradually enlarging rotary motion of the hands spread it from the centre to the edges, and repeat. Continue the treatment for from five to fifteen minutes, as with individuals.

The size of the group, far from being an impediment, tends to make the treatment even more effective because of the interaction between the individuals composing that group. Each reacts to the stimulation of Life Energy, and each becomes a channel also for the transmission of that Force, so that the whole group collectively generates within itself a continually stronger flow and interchange of harmonizing Power. Thus, though it seems to be a paradox, the larger the group is the more easily it can be treated, and the quicker and more effective will be the results obtained.

The distance one may be from the group when treating it is of little importance, as space is no obstacle to the operation of Universal Life Energy. When properly directed Universal Life Energy will work at any distance.

The best times to give such treatments, individual and collective, are in the morning with the sun's rise and in the evening with its setting. In the first case the vibrations you give are attuned to the rising vibrations of the new day, and in the second to the soothing vibrations of the approaching night.

In treating any kind of plant life, from the crops in the fields to the trees in the woods, the process is the same as for animals, except in one respect. Instead of directing the Force first into the leaves and branches, start the treatment at the roots and work upwards. Thus you are in accord with the upward trend of the life of the plant, set by the flow of the sap from the roots toward the branches, whereas by reversing the process you would be needlessly counteracting that trend rather than strengthening and reinforcing it. In either group treatment or individual treatment of plants this one essential point should be borne in mind.

There is one other use of Universal Life Energy on the farm which requires mention as of special interest to farmers—crop protection. Statistics place the money value loss to farmers through insect and animal pests at billions of dollars annually, and this in spite of the constantly improved methods evolved by Science for combating that menace. Yet if, in addition to these ordinary methods, the individual farmer will apply the principles taught in this Course, he can not only cut down his yearly contribution to that tremendous deficit, but can even eliminate it almost entirely.

By charging a crop with Universal Life Energy, through the method of group treatment, that crop is made fundamentally its own protection. Universal Life Energy is a purely constructive Force; and as such is instantly repellent to any destructive influence. All parasites, on the contrary, whether insect or animal, are by nature open channels for destructive influences, since it is through destruction alone of other forms of life that they maintain their existence.

The effect of Universal Life Energy is immediately to turn that corrosive flow of destructive energy back upon itself, so that it preys upon its own channel instead of being able to vent itself in the usual manner. The parasite feels repelled, not because the crop is less appetizing as food, but because each blade and leaf has become a conductor, a "live wire," of a directly opposite and stronger Force. Therefore the destructive animus must seek an outlet somewhere else, and in search of that outlet the insect or animal goes on or turns aside.

Should your work be in the factory, there again Universal Life Energy will be an. invaluable help to you. Not only will it give you the necessary physical force to do the tasks set before you, but it will also render you more resistant to the disintegrating effect on your nerves of your disharmonious environment. By building up and preserving a harmonious condition within you, it will counteract the disruptive influence of the noise, the heat, the odours and above all the monotony which are generally the lot of factory workers. It will guard you against accident by warding off fatigue and keeping you alert and sensitive to your surroundings.

Or are you travelling, either for pleasure or on business? You know very well that there are many unpleasant things to contend with during travel. Use Life Energy continually and no matter how tiresome the trip may appear to others you will always feel rested and full of "pep," ready either to work or to enjoy travelling.

Use the Force when taking a room from the clerk at the desk. You will get a better room at a more reasonable price. The Universal Power, when used by you intelligently, will always prompt people to do the right thing, because it is Law itself. Whenever Universal Law is used in dealing with individuals they cannot help responding to its call, with the result that you will find yourself able to overcome difficulties which otherwise seem insurmountable.

Are you a musician, or engaged in painting, singing, acting or any of the arts? Are you looking for inspiration to write, or are you interested in invention or research work in the laboratory? Universal Life Energy will help you there as nothing else can. It will put soul into your music. It will introduce a new depth and richness of ideas, colours and execution into your painting, and will make your voice more expressive and beautiful when singing. It will identify you completely with the role you are playing on the stage or on the silver screen. You will be able to express greater sincerity and deeper emotion. It will impart a more original character to your writing, a more colourful and living language, a striking imagery and a stronger rhythm. It will bring the treasures hidden in the deepest recesses of your mind into tangible expression, whether on the written page or in the form of new inventions and discoveries.

Humanity more and more recognizes the value and is willing to pay the price for that which it considers pleasant, instructive and useful for its well being. Therefore the better you can give yourself to Humanity the more Humanity will reward you for that, and it is only through the continual use of Universal Life Energy that you can discover the best there is in you for the use and enjoyment of Mankind.

EXERCISES TO LESSON FIVE

The EXERCISES TO this week are again the Star Exercise, Relaxation, Silence, Mental Contact and Stimulation. You must first thoroughly assimilate them before new and more advanced Exercises will be given to you.

You should realize the importance of the Mental Contact with Universal Life Energy. Your daily life must be a continual exercise of it, in the little things as well as in the big. Remember that these teachings are above all practical; in other words they must be PRACTICED CONTINUALLY if you are to obtain the proper results.

The unimportance of a task or duty is of no significance. What counts in the building up of your character is not the size of the task itself, but HOW YOU PERFORM THAT TASK. The most trivial and ordinary of your daily occupations becomes just as great a factor in that work of self-reconstruction as the more responsible ones when put to the test of the principles contained in these lessons.

QUESTIONS TO LESSON FIVE

1. What common difficulty encountered in the performance of one's daily duties can be eliminated by the use of Universal Life Energy?

2. How are those duties most easily and efficiently performed?

3. Is it possible to work without getting tired?

4. What specifically will be the effects of the use of Universal Life Energy on the human body?

5. How may it be used on the farm?

6. In what way does the cause of diseases differ in animal and plant life?

7. What different ways are there of treating animal and plant life with Universal Life Energy?

8. What way is most efficient, and why?

9. Is the procedure always the same?

10. What effect does distance have on the sending of Universal Life Energy?

11. In what other very important respect can Universal Life Energy be of benefit to the farmer?

12. What advantages are derived from the use of Universal Life Energy in factory work?

Lesson Five

ANSWERS TO LESSON FIVE

1. **A common difficulty which the use of Universal Life Energy will eliminate in the performance of daily duties is:**

   A feeling of laziness and reluctance to enter into the work on hand, due to lack of vitality.

2. **Those duties can be most easily and efficiently performed:**

   By the constant use of Universal Life Energy.

3. **It is possible to work without getting tired:**

   By continually drawing fresh strength from Universal Life Energy as fast as your own is used up.

4. **The specific effects of the use of Universal Life Energy on the human body are:**

   To restore its exhausted energies, rebuild worn tissues, stimulate nerves and cells to expel undesirable elements and to promote strength and harmony.

5. **Universal Life Energy can be used on the farm:**

   In every direction; in the care of animals and plants, in the orchard, in handling men, etc.

6. **The causes of diseases in animals and plants differ:**

   In no way. All disease is but the expression of disharmonious vibrations.

7. **The different ways of treating animal and plant life with Universal Life Energy are:**

   Individual Treatment and Group Treatment.

8. **The most effective way is:**

   Group treatment, because of the interaction between the individuals of the group.

9. **The procedure in treating plant life and animal life differs:**

   In that a treatment given to plant life is always started at the roots and continued upward, while a treatment of animal life begins either at the top of the body and is continued downward, or at the solar plexus and is distributed radially.

10. **The effect of distance on sending Universal Life Energy is:**

    None whatever.

11. **Another very important respect in which Universal Life Energy can be of benefit to the farmer is:**

    In the protection of trees and crops from destructive insect and animal life.

12. **The advantages derived from the use of Universal Life Energy in the factory are:**

    It will counteract the disruptive influences of the noise, the heat, the odours and the monotony of mechanical work and will render the individual less liable to accident.

Dear Friend:

The uses of Universal Life Energy in business are so unlimited, even by the scope of the business itself, that only through a clear understanding of its operation in the fundamentals can you gain a sure comprehension of its workings in the more complex aspects.

The aim of this Lesson is to give you that understanding, to show you in detail how Universal Life Energy operates in the basic principles of all business—buying and selling—in order that you may be able to apply it intelligently in all directions with a distinct perception of the effects it will have and the results it will produce.

You will be shown new methods for increasing your own efficiency, stimulating sales and promoting general satisfaction. Whether you are an employer or an employee makes no difference; your chief task is, after all, so to adjust your contacts and relations with other people that such contacts will provide a wide, smooth passage for the exchanges you wish to effect. Such passages Universal Life Energy will open up for you, both through your present customers and through the many new customers it will attract.

The methods given you in these lessons have nothing to do with suggestion or the exercise of will power. Like the rest of the teachings, they are based exclusively on Universal Life Energy and the Laws which govern It.
As the Universal Power is supreme above all powers, obviously It is a far more effective instrument than those very limited human forces. Its proper use is bound to

produce always most harmonious, definite and profitable results, in every direction and for all parties concerned.

Cordially yours,
Eugene Fersen.

LESSON SIX

BUSINESS, like everything else, is now undergoing a radical change. Higher principles are brought forth as the basis of modern business. New methods are established in order to obtain results. Science throws its light more and more on that important phase of human life. Business people are- no longer satisfied to conduct business on old-fashioned lines. Business men and women of today are seeking to save time and yet produce greater results by directing and using their energies properly and intelligently.

The ever increasing number of business colleges, commercial correspondence courses, lecturers and teachers of business psychology is a proof of the growing demand for scientific knowledge of business and salesmanship. Most of the above mentioned devices are raising the general level of business ability, because they put at once into one's hand an instrument which must otherwise be acquired slowly by experience. Yet the use of that instrument, its adaptation to the peculiar conditions, depends solely on the individual himself, and for that reason it very frequently fails to accomplish all that was expected of it.

It has been found that in most cases business aspirants with a full equipment of the theory and rules of business fall far short in the practical application of those theories to actual conditions themselves. In spite of their scientific training, in spite of the great effort and intelligence they put forth in their transactions, that energy and specialized knowledge, seen is entirely wasted and unproductive of the results which they have every right to expect. Why is this?

The reason for it is not to be found in the theories, which are sound enough if applied exactly as given to conditions essentially as described, but in the individual alone. There is where the one vital element, adaptability, resides, and not in the theories. Conditions are never the same for different individuals, because no two individuals are the same, and the reaction set up between a certain situation and one man or woman differs from the reaction between the same situation and another man or woman in proportion as their own natures differ.

Consequently theories, to be effective, must fit first the one who applies them before they can fit the conditions to which they are to be applied. That is why a business man trained in the school of practical experience is generally far superior, so far as obtaining results is concerned, to the graduate of a business college or a student of business psychology. He grows his own business skin, so to speak, and it fits well.

There is another very prominent reason for the failure of a large percentage of scientifically trained young business men. Business colleges and teachers of psychology usually develop the mental side only of the students, considerably increasing their mental baggage, but ignoring entirely the executive and creative part of their natures. That is, they do not give any information or practical training in how to increase first of all the energy and power of attracting business, without which the most scientific business methods will remain valueless.

Lesson Six

As in every department of human life, success in business is in direct proportion to your energy and personal magnetism. These qualities are precisely what Universal Life Energy supplies, as they are its fundamental component factors. Therefore if properly used that Force becomes literally a priceless Power which will help you in every business transaction you undertake.

For instance, consider some of the difficulties encountered by a salesman, especially an amateur one, in approaching a prospect. The scientific methods for selling articles or putting across business deals as taught in business colleges or by teachers of business psychology, equips him with a general plan of procedure and the tools with which to work.

But like any plan or any tool, they are dead, and they live only as he supplies them with life. His must be the energy that drives the instrument at his disposal through the massed obstruction of indifference and even antagonism that he encounters in the outer office as well as in the inner sanctum. His must be the guiding hand that shapes his end from the material he has to work on, and his must be the intelligence that instantly perceives and appropriates to his own use the little personal variations that can emerge only from the direct contact and interaction of his own personality with that of the prospective buyer. If, as is generally the case, he cannot help feeling the superiority of the buyer as the individual with the purchasing power, and particularly if this feeling has been accentuated by the difficulties in obtaining access to him, the disproportion between them is thus established and felt from the very beginning.

Another point that works against the salesman is his own position. He wants to get something from the buyer — in this instance his money — and though he is ready to give in exchange the article he sells, yet that attempt to get first and to give next usually produces on the buyer (though most of the time unconsciously) the very opposite effect from the one the salesman is hoping to produce. In fact, he repels the buyer instead of attracting him, because the first instinctive impulse of anyone who is asked to give is not to do it, and the more that individual is pressed to part with his money, the firmer becomes his resolve not to yield.

That primary obstacle in the path of the salesman's argument sprouts a thorny host of others in the form of such statements as "The article doesn't interest me," "I haven't the money now," or "I have not the time," and "Come in later." The salesman has a double task to perform; he has to exert all his energy and mental resourcefulness in order to create an interest in the buyer, while at the same time persistently meeting and overcoming the many objections which the buyer conjures out of his scepticism as abundantly as a magician conjures rabbits out of a hat.

However, assuming that the salesman, after a hard fight, has succeeded in lodging a spark of interest in the rather damp tinder of the buyer's desire for his product, his hardest work is yet to come. He has to fan that dull spark into a hot flame of craving to possess.

This is the most difficult part of the whole deal. The salesman has to bring the interest of the buyer to that culminant point called the "psychological moment." At that moment he has the buyer convinced and ready to buy; but the psychological moment is but ONE MOMENT. It requires quick judgment from the side of the salesman to see it and still quicker action to take advantage of it by closing the deal instantly. The greatest caution, tact, coolness and at the same time quickness of action, qualities which are not so easy to be found together in most human beings, are required to bring the matter to a successful conclusion. Any attempt to close a deal either too soon or too late will prove disastrous.

That is the reason why good sales agents are rare and so much in demand. Yet with the use of Universal Life Energy the whole matter is simplified to an extraordinary degree, with success as an ultimate result.

Before starting to work, the salesman who uses Universal Life Energy in his business transactions ought first to relax, enter into silence, make the mental contact with Universal Life Energy and then think strongly about the article he is going to sell or the deal he intends to put over. You must realize within yourself that there is a law which is continually operating, called the Law of Supply and Demand. You have a supply to offer; therefore, according to that Law, there must be a demand for it.

Universal Life Energy, flowing through you at that time, because of its power of harmonization, will adjust your supply to the demand for it which is already in existence somewhere. Moreover, it will turn your thoughts in the direction where that demand is waiting for you. A special concern or a certain individual to whom you would like to sell your goods will assert itself in your mind, because of the guiding and attractive qualities of Universal Life Energy. Whenever you let that Force work for you it will always guide you in the right direction.

If you have some samples to present or articles to show, take the trouble first to saturate them with Universal Life Energy by directing that Power at them for a few minutes through your hands. To do this, contact the Force mentally, then hold your hands about six inches from the object you wish to sell, with the finger tips pointed toward it. Thus the Force will flow through you from Its Infinite Source into the object, exactly as electricity flows into and fills a metallic object. That Force, concentrated in the object, renders it appealing and attractive both to the sight and to the sense of touch.

The next step is to bring the article to the prospective buyer and sell it. To do this it is necessary to overcome that initial handicap of your position. There again Universal Life Energy is an invaluable aid. Since your very purpose, after all, places you unavoidably in the light of wanting to take something from your prospect, the only convincing way to correct that disadvantage, to "start off on the right foot," so to speak, is first to give him something. This you are able to do, unostentatiously and so that the buyer himself is not consciously aware of it, yet in such a fashion that he feels somehow favourably disposed toward you from the very beginning.

Before entering the office of the buyer, make the contact with Universal Life Energy. It will immediately establish a subtle connection between you and him, and will help open the way to him through those barriers of red tape usually erected against outside intrusion. Finally, at the moment when you are ushered into his presence, make the mental contact with the Universal Power. Then in a few words and as calmly as possible state the object of your visit and show the article. Place it before him in such a way that he may not only see it, but also touch it. If the article is good, as represented, and the need for it exists there, you will effect a sale. The operation is as follows:

The prospective buyer, being usually a hard working and busy man, is very apt to be overworked, depleted of vitality, impatient and on the defensive. The contact you make with Universal Life Energy on entering his office transforms you at that moment into a living radio which sends out soothing, harmonizing and at the same time, invigorating vibrations to the prospective buyer. Instead of wanting to get something, as in the ordinary business methods, you start by giving, thus putting again into operation the Law of Supply and Demand. You pour into the buyer the very thing he needs most and which is beyond any price, and that is Life, Vitality, Harmony. You replenish in him his exhausted reservoir of energy, and in an instant the whole attitude of the man has changed toward you.

Having received those intangible yet priceless gifts of Life Itself, he unconsciously feels the value of your contribution and, as the Law of Supply and Demand is continually operating, he feels indebted to you for what you have given him already. There is within him the inner urge to do in his turn something for you, and this desire to make good will be in exact proportion to the amount of Life Energy you radiate to him. The better contact you make, the more energy you vibrate, the greater success you will obtain in your sales. The articles or samples, if such are used, will play their part also through the attractive power of the Universal Life Energy concentrated in them. Then all you need to do is to let the causes you started materialize into effects—that is, the conclusion of a deal—and you can rest assured that within reason such will be the result.

Two important points must be remembered and carefully observed whenever Universal Life Energy is used in business or in salesmanship.

First, the business or the transaction must be absolutely honest and the merits of the article sold must correspond to the description of them in the sales talk, as Universal Life Energy cannot be employed in a crooked, dishonest or unfair deal. A Universal Force, which is also the Law of the Universe, or Truth Itself, cannot be perverted, and will only "back-fire" most disastrously on whoever is rash enough to pit himself against it. It will always work, but only in one direction, the right one, as anyone who endeavours to apply it in a wrong cause will learn by bitter experience. The individual who wants to obtain real success through the use of Universal Life Energy must accommodate himself to Its Law, as there is no human power that can bend that Law to its wishes. Truth, Honesty and Sincerity are the only channels through which It operates favourably, and unless one can provide that channel in himself he will only work himself harm in trying to use that Force.

The second important point is that no will power or suggestion should be used in transactions conducted with the assistance of Universal Life Energy. Whenever that Life Energy is used in transactions you must let the Law inherent in It operate on the buyer. As Its operation is ALWAYS CONSTRUCTIVE for BOTH PARTIES the result desired by you will be thus obtained. Personal will power and especially suggestion are very inadequate and limited means to the desired end, especially if, as in many cases, you have to deal with an individual of a stronger character and personality than yourself. In such instances those human resources can very often do more harm than good.

Finally, there is another advantage gained in using Universal Life Energy in business and salesmanship. That Force tends always to establish equilibrium — that is, to fill up the discrepancies in human relations. In other words, it brings everything to the mean level, equalizes them.

Therefore whenever you use that Force in meeting even the biggest and most important people you will never feel small or over-awed by their superior prestige. On the contrary, you will feel yourself naturally their equal, and they will feel the same way toward you. Life Energy, establishing Itself in perfect equilibrium in you and the other individual, levels all differences of person and station and starts negotiations off on an even basis of mutual respect, if not of perfect accord.

Remember, the power of the individual is not dependent on nor to be estimated by the number of dollars he controls or possesses, but by the amount of energy he is able to express. Money, like all material possessions, can be lost because money is only an effect. But whoever is able to contact and use Universal Life Energy controls the Fundamental Cause which is the Source of that effect, and can therefore always recoup losses and even win greater profits than ever before.

It should always be borne in mind that Universal Life Energy is an impersonal Force that works serenely in accordance with Its own Laws and not with your desires. It is Life in its purest form; therefore Its effect is always to stimulate, to emphasize the qualities of everything with which It comes in contact. If those qualities are good ones, so much the better. If they are bad, they are emphasized just the same. That is what is meant when it is said that Universal Life Energy works favourably only through positive channels. If a salesman directs It into a genuinely worthy article which he wishes to sell, It emphasizes the good qualities of that article and renders it more attractive. If, on the other hand, he directs It into a spurious article, the bad qualities of that article are sufficiently accentuated to make it repellent to the buyer at once.

Similarly, in using Universal Life Energy in your sales talk, the true intent back of your words will always be brought out in your voice. If the intent is sincere, it will lend conviction to your argument. If the intent is not sincere, that insincerity will make your talk "ring false" no matter how astutely planned it may be.

In order to attract customers and increase general business, especially in stores where the customers come into continual contact with the employees, the employee, whenever questioned about an article by a prospective buyer, must immediately make the mental contact with Universal Life Energy and allow It to act through him during the ensuing negotiations. The result will be as follows:

If a customer really wants to buy something and is not asking merely for curiosity's sake, immediately that right desire will be emphasized by the Universal Life Energy radiating from the employee. Not only will the customer know exactly what he wants, but the Force, working also in the same harmonizing manner through the salesman, will unfailingly guide him to show the customer that very thing. Thus a great deal of time and energy ordinarily wasted will be saved by both the customer and the salesman, to their mutual benefit and satisfaction.

Naturally this will increase the volume of the general business of the store and consequently the profits of the company as well as of the employee himself, for usually in large stores employees get a certain percentage on the articles they sell. Therefore it is to their direct interest to turn over this stock as quickly as they can.

If a customer, on the other hand, comes actuated only by curiosity and without any serious intention to buy, Universal Life Energy in that instance will emphasize those motives to such good effect that either such persons will feel their interest quickly evaporate and will be repelled or they will find their curiosity aggravated into a desire to possess, and will buy. In any event, a great saving of time and effort will again have been secured.

Another very important direction in which Universal Life Energy can be of invaluable assistance is in adjusting relations between employees and their superiors. How often the attitude of those in authority renders life almost intolerable to those under them, the more so as there seems to be no way to correct such condition! Yet there is a way, for what is impossible to the human being alone becomes entirely possible when you summon to your aid the Power of the Infinite Itself.

Whenever an unjust order is given, a harsh or unkind word spoken to you, do not flare up in rebellion and feel "sore." Do not even take the trouble to answer. Just quickly make the contact with Universal Life Energy and allow Its harmonizing currents to flow through you, while you meantime think strongly about the offender. Soon you will notice a gradual change in his attitude toward you. Universal Life Energy will begin to have Its effect, and without knowing it he will be prompted to be fair to you, to treat you rightly. Thus you will have won a great victory, transforming an enemy into a friend and well wisher, and sometimes a very valuable one.

Do not be discouraged if you are not obtaining complete results from the beginning. Every time you use the Force you are progressing toward complete victory. As in everything else, perseverance is absolutely necessary in order to win.

It is obvious that a store whose employees are continually using Universal Life Energy is bound to be a very successful concern, as the greater success of the employees will naturally and proportionately express itself in the success of the whole enterprise. This success also is not confined solely to the financial aspect of the business, although it is the finances that the improvements in other respects will be finally and most satisfactorily reflected. But improvements are first of all the product of subtler adjustments which involve one other factor besides employees.

To secure the best results, the employer must meet his employee half way. If he will use Universal Life Energy in stabilizing his relations with them, he will quickly reach the most profitable solution of the problem that is vexing the business world of today — the differences between Capital and Labour. Those differences, accordingly as they are great or less, cause the friction which has occasioned so much mutual wastage and loss in the past, and which threatens to cause more in the future. The inherent quality of Universal Life Energy being to establish equilibrium, It will always bring each side more promptly to an appreciation of the other's difficulties, and will induce a speedy, amicable adjustment fair and satisfactory to both.

In the final analysis, it is through the harmonizing power of Universal Life Energy alone that equilibrium can be established between the two warring factions, Capital and Labour. So it is much better to avail yourself of it intelligently, at once, rather than wait for it to force its way through your unreasoning opposition — to your own cost.

In giving instructions to employees, either directly or indirectly, the employer should take the trouble to make the contact first with Universal Life Energy. It will then lend to his words the weight and conviction necessary to secure their immediate and unquestioning acceptance. Such instructions, even if they are of a difficult nature, will be executed with pleasure and a spontaneous desire to do well. Yet if those instructions spring from an unscrupulous or unfair purpose the reaction to them will be the invariable reaction to any attempt to misuse Universal Life Energy. That Force is impartial in Its workings; if misdirected It reacts just as disastrously on the source of that misdirection, regardless of any human prestige the offender may enjoy.

The wonderful result of the continual and widespread use of Universal Life Energy in business is that eventually it will eliminate all dishonesty, not by appealing to the conscience of people, which experience has proven to be very unreliable when there is a smell of profit in the air, but by reaching them through the one guiding star they follow as instinctively as the swallow follows the bite—Self Interest. When all parties, employers and employees, Capital and Labour, buyers and sellers, see that -their greatest advantage lies in the fair and honest way, they will not have to be urged to follow that way. They cannot be stopped from following it.

EXERCISES TO LESSON SIX

The EXERCISES TO this week will be the same as for last week — Star Exercise, Relaxation, Silence, Mental Contact and Stimulation.

Next week you will receive a new Exercise based upon and developing naturally from those already given to you. It must be remembered that in these first lessons you are building the foundation of your future progress — that in proportion as you erect a solid and substantial base now you will be able to demonstrate quickly and amply the Knowledge you will obtain later on. For that reason it is vitally important that you should make slow progress in this respect in order to be thorough.

Study and practice these Exercises more diligently than ever in preparation for those to come, and bear in mind that every surrender to a tendency to slur over and neglect them enters into your foundation as a flaw that it will take much work and trouble to eliminate in the future. All that unnecessary trouble can be avoided by the exercise of a little care and patience now.

QUESTIONS TO LESSON SIX

1. What essential element in business training do commercial schools and teachers of business psychology fail to provide?

2. What qualities neglected in the teaching of the theories of business are necessary to achieve success?

3. How can they be developed?

4. Why is the application of theories to actual conditions so often a failure?

5. What are the main difficulties encountered by salesmen in approaching a prospect?

6. How can those difficulties best be overcome?

7. How can a salesman render his articles more attractive?

8. What two important points are to be observed in business and salesmanship?

9. Explain how the attempted misuse of Universal Life Energy reacts against the offender.

10. What main advantage is derived from the use of Universal Life Energy in business and salesmanship?

11. What results will an employer achieve by using Universal Life Energy in his relation with employees?

12. How does Universal Life Energy operate to attract customers, decrease wastage and facilitate business?

ANSWERS TO LESSON SIX

1. **The essential element in business training omitted by commercial schools and teachers of business psychology is:**

Personal Magnetism.

2. **The qualities neglected in the teaching of the theories of business and which are necessary to success are:**

(1) Creative ability.

(2) Executive ability.

3. **They can be developed:**

By using Universal Life Energy continually.

4. **The application of theories to actual conditions is so often a failure:**

Because theories lack adaptability, which resides only in the individual, and are unable to conform to conditions which vary always in proportion as the natures of the individuals vary. Theories must first fit the individual before he can fit them to his own peculiar conditions.

5. **The main difficulties generally encountered by salesmen in approaching a prospect are:**

   (1) Office red tape.

   (2) Disadvantage of salesman's position as one who wants first to take from his prospect before giving him anything.

   (3) Prestige of buyer as one with purchasing power.

   (4) Abundance of objections always at buyers' command.

   (5) Double task of salesman to meet objections and at the same time create interest in and desire for his article.

6. **These difficulties can be best overcome**

   By using Universal Life Energy, which will:

   (1) Help open the way to a favourable interview by subtly connecting salesman and prospect.

   (2) Radiate Life Energy to the prospect and by thus giving him something first will make the Law of Supply and Demand work in favour of the salesman.

   (3) Establish equilibrium and place salesman and buyer on an equal basis.

(4) Make salesman alert to opportunities for meeting objections and turning them to his advantage.

(5) Emphasize qualities of article as well as of salesman's talk in order to create interest.

7. A salesman can render his articles more attractive:

By saturating them with Universal Life Energy and thus emphasizing their attractive qualities.

8. Two important points to be observed in business and salesmanship are:

(1) That Universal Life Energy cannot be employed in a dishonest or unfair way.

(2) That will power and suggestion are to be wholly omitted if Universal Life Energy is to be used effectively.

9. The attempted misuse of Universal Life Energy reacts against the offender:

By emphasizing the bad qualities of the deal or the article and thus repelling prospective buyers.

10. **The main advantage derived from the use of Universal Life Energy in business and salesmanship is:**

It levels all differences of person or station and establishes negotiations on an even, harmonious basis.

11. **The results an employer will achieve by using Universal Life Energy in his relations with his employees are:**

Thorough cooperation, efficient and willing service, mutual satisfaction and increased profits.

12. **Universal Life Energy operates to attract customers, decrease wastage and facilitate business:**

By increasing the attractiveness of goods and promoting quick understanding between customer and clerk, and by eliminating those who come solely out of curiosity, either stimulating that curiosity into a desire to buy or killing it entirely.

Dear Friend:

Nowadays practically everybody recognizes the value of education. Parents are willing to make all kinds of sacrifices in order to equip their children for successful careers. Countless young men and women who lack means eagerly trade their services for the training they have not the money to buy. Even those who have already made their way in the world do not hesitate to go back to the colleges to supply a lack whose importance they have been taught by experience.

"More Knowledge" is the cry of the times, and everywhere the widening of mental horizons, brought about by the modern facilities for quick interchange of thought and ideas, has revealed to people the limitless possibilities and value of Knowledge as a Fundamental for Success.

This lesson concerns the application of Universal Life Energy in school and in college, in studies and in sports, by both teachers and students. Not only is it the magic wand which can open wide to the student the gate of Knowledge, but what is far more important, It supplies the power and the understanding that enables one to walk through those gates to the Success which is the aim of all.

Cordially yours,
Eugene Fersen.

LESSON SEVEN

THE complaint of educators today is that students pay more attention to having a good time than they do to studies. Sports and social activities exercise a greater attraction for them than books and lectures. The purpose of Centres of Learning, instead of being one-pointed, has split into two parts, and because of that division has lost much of its constructive power. The social interest not only is not subordinate to the educational interest, but counterbalances and frequently even outweighs it. Yet the blame for this unfortunate state of affairs cannot be put on the students who, on entering, are generally actuated by a commendable desire to learn. The fault lies rather with conditions which allow that desire to die from lack of nourishment.

Youth, as a rule, is very eager to know. Curiosity is a dominant trait of the young — a pathfinder which goes on ahead and pulls the individual after on a strong leading-chain of interest. If the curiosity is drawn forward on the proper road, if the desire for knowledge is stimulated sufficiently to keep the interest taut, the function of educational institutions will be restored in full force. But the trouble now is that sports and amusements provide a bait that studies do not, and the student naturally follows the pull of his own errant inclinations rather than the dusty path of duty. Thus the disproportion is established.

Anything, to be sought, must first be wanted. Make learning attractive and the whole world will be eager to learn. The Light of Knowledge must be a warm light if it is to kindle a responsive flame in others. Most teachers in schools and colleges, especially elderly ones and men in particular, although they very often have unusual knowledge and are intellectually well developed, are dry, cold and uninteresting. Even if they sometimes command admiration, they cannot arouse enthusiasm. There is no sympathetic bond between them and those whom they are trying to teach.

Mind in itself does not possess the power of attraction. The most brilliant intellect, alone, can dazzle, but it will not warm you or draw you to it. Magnetism is a quality distinct and apart from it, something brought in from without and not inborn. The mind which is non-magnetic is like an engine out of gear—no matter how quickly it turns over it does not accomplish anything. Only when the gears are meshed, when the magnetic connection between that mind and other minds is established, can its working produce results in the form of even and harmonious progress.

This connection can be established only through Universal Life Energy, because Magnetism, the Power of Attraction, is a quality solely of Life Itself. That Power injected into your thoughts will make them living, vital, impressive, so that they will command a living, vital interest on the part of your listeners. The students, instead of remaining aloof and remote spectators, will be drawn into the scheme of your argument until they become an integral part of it, actors instead of onlookers. Their thoughts will engage with yours as intimately as the cogs on a gear shaft. They will oppose only an alert, warm, flexible resistance, the intelligent resistance of active minds quick to follow your logic and ready to test its flaws, as contrasted to the deadweight of inertia that cares for neither.

The connection thus made is of a generative nature, increasing the flow of the Force and stimulating both your mind and their interest. The reaction of other minds provides the foil that exercises your own and renders it more and more receptive to the current of Universal Life Energy. That Power opens your eyes to new vistas in your work, bringing to light ever new, fresh and interesting angles. It uncovers a wealth of new ideas and enables you to present them in a striking fashion, with the confidence that comes of a sense of accomplishment. It will give a richer intonation to your voice, will make well chosen language ready to your tongue, and above all it will impregnate every word you utter with the warmth and attraction that alone can produce the desired effect.

Not only will that Universal Force be of invaluable assistance from the side of the teacher, but it will produce equally beneficial results when used by the students. Children especially are able to contact and use Universal Life Energy to an extraordinary degree, because their bodies and minds are so much more pliant and unspoiled than those of mature people. No set habits of thoughts have as yet crystallized their mental processes into a definite pattern. Their physical apparatus is fresh, sensitive, not yet hardened to a mould of custom or rusty from disuse. They are at the receptive stage, both mentally and physically, and do not have to pierce that shell of limitations which older people find it necessary to break through in order to tap the Universal Supply of Life Force.

Therefore, teach your pupils the Star Exercise and the Mental Contact, and you will obtain remarkable results. It would be advisable, before starting each lesson, for you yourself to make the Mental Contact with Universal Life Energy in order to be personally supplied with that Power. This will render your teachings attractive to your students. Then, as cooperation is necessary to produce the best results, have those whom you teach take the Star Exercise, collectively, as a class. Thus you improve both ends — the sending end, yourself, and the receiving end, your pupils. You will be able to deliver a better lecture to a more receptive class.

Whenever, during the lessons, you see the interest wane and a spirit of restlessness begin to invade the class, stop where you are long enough to have the pupils take the Star Exercise again and restore the contact.

If you have to deal with backward children, who are sluggish mentally and physically, you can help them greatly without them being aware of it. Magnetize the books they are reading and the paper they are to write upon. Thus you will render these articles attractive, so that for the first time the interest of the pupil who handles them is aroused. Once that interest is aroused, you can, by continuing the process, stimulate and develop it to the point where the children will react spontaneously and normally to subjects properly presented to them.

An example of the operation of Universal Life Energy in this respect is presented in an instance of Its use by the wife of a professor in a certain Western college recently.

Her son, a boy of about thirteen years of age, hated to play the piano. His aversion to music lessons and practicing was a continual source of distress to her, as nothing she could do seemed to diminish in any way the boy's violent prejudice against that part of his education.

Finally, after having taken a course of instruction in Science of Being, she decided to put her knowledge to the test of use. Privately she magnetized thoroughly the keys of the piano, and then asked her son to play for her for five minutes only, saying that if he would do that to please her she would not require any further practice that day.

The boy, somewhat dazed by this extraordinary stroke of fortune, hastened in to buy his freedom before his mother should change her mind. Well over an hour later he was still at the piano, and eventually, after several requests had failed to tear him away from this novel interest in a hitherto hateful task, his mother was compelled actually to order him out of doors. Since that time the difficulty has been to keep him away from the piano long enough for a healthful amount of recreation rather than to drive him to it.

Mental deficiency is generally the result of the improper functioning of certain brain centres. The cells comprising these centres are not developed as they should be, and in consequence their activities are weak, sluggish and ill-attuned. However, the centres are still there, and all they need is the proper stimulus and nourishment in order to develop to their full capacity.

This stimulus is what Universal Life Energy supplies. The obstruction that has impeded the growth of the cell's, shutting them off from a fair supply of energy and inducing the lassitude that is reflected in mental backwardness, is broken down and washed away. Probably it was a mental obstruction, a prejudice rooted in some obscure and trivial incident later forgotten, or perhaps a genuine physical defect. In either event the clogged channel is opened, the current swelled to full force and the enervated tissues restored to a normal and healthy vigour.

In handling perverse, "temperamental" children, remember that exhibitions of bad temper are simply indications of an upset equilibrium. There is an inner condition of disharmony, a distorted development of the child's nature in certain directions without an equal and counterbalancing growth in others. To meet such a condition with harsh discipline, an exercise of force based solely on authority, while it may prevail for the time being, will only aggravate the trouble within. "Like attracts like" in such a case, but in the wrong way, the negative in the child drawing out a negative response from the teacher and thus disturbing its already poor balance still more. The teacher must be the one to take the initiative and dominate the situation by promptly making the mental contact with Universal Life Energy and then gently but firmly controlling the evil traits of the offender through the exercise of exactly opposite qualities. As the positive always prevails over the negative, the display of positive qualities by you will call forth like qualities in the child, to the effect that the unruly one gradually acquires a poise that had always before been eminently lacking.

Naturally that is not a sudden process, and although the effects of such treatment are in most cases discernible at once, the full development is a matter of growth and not of abrupt change. Therefore do not be discouraged if one trial seems to accomplish little. Bear in mind that you are simply stimulating and strengthening the regular processes of Nature. Just persevere and give Nature time to do her work in her accustomed way and the desired results will arrive through a normal, healthy development.

Children at the kindergarten stage, who are not yet able to grasp the method of the Mental Contact, are very greatly benefited by the Star Exercise. Through that Exercise they are able to contact Universal Life Energy much more effectively than most grown people who have not trained themselves by long practice, and the advantages they derive from it, both physically and mentally, are in proportion.

If, besides teaching them the Star Exercise, teachers will also treat children individually, especially those that seem sub-normal, by holding them or seating them comfortably and, after having made the Mental Contact, placing the hands on the head and pouring the Force into the brain cells, they will promote an extraordinary improvement. In a number of schools and institutions for deficient children in the United States where this method has been followed the results obtained were really astonishing, a large proportion climbing up to normal in a comparatively short time.

By continually using Universal Life Energy in your teachings you will more and more break away from the dead letter and be able to bring out the living spirit. Thus you will become what every teacher should be — a friend, a guide, a Light bearer to those to whom you are to bring the Light of Knowledge. Then you will make the name and the vocation of teacher the greatest there is on earth, and will command the respect, material success and love of your students which is your due.

If you are one of those who are taught instead of teaching, and you find studies difficult and uninteresting when the sun shines outside and all Nature calls you to more agreeable exercises, quickly make the contact with Universal Life Energy, let the Force flow through you, and see how resplendently the warm sun of interest breaks through the dull fog of studious duties. All your diffused attention is sucked into the flow of that harmonious current, drawn to the matter in hand and concentrated there. The driest lecture will become easy and pleasant, because you will pick the meaty kernel of valuable information from the withered shell of its presentation. You will be able to track down unerringly the solutions of difficult problems. Logic will emerge from confusion, light from mental darkness, interest from indifference, not because of any mysterious magic instinct in the Force Itself, but because that Force, through the Laws under which It operates, can bridge the gulf separating you from your own hidden resources and can make them instantly available for your use.

When you are called upon to answer a question and you cannot remember what the correct answer is, quickly make the contact with Universal Life Energy. That Power will immediately connect your Conscious Self with your now Subconsiousness, where all impressions received by you, including all you have learned, are stored. Then, with the help of that great Power, you will be able consciously to draw from your inner hall of records the desired information contained therein. It will come to you simply and easily, without any effort whatsoever. Once the contact with Universal Life Energy is made, all you need to do is ask yourself the question you want to have answered, or thing you want to remember, and the answer will come to you automatically from your Subconscious over the bridge established between It and your Conscious Self by the Universal Life Energy flowing through you.

The reason an answer comes to you from your Inner Self is because of the continual operation of the Law of Supply and Demand. By creating a mental demand you are disturbing the inner equilibrium established by Universal Life Energy. Therefore you immediately get the supply also, which is within you and is brought out by Universal Life Energy to restore the balance.

Whenever you read a book or have to write an essay or learn anything by heart, first contact mentally Universal Life Energy. You will be surprised at the extent to which the Power will assist you in all mental work you do, not only by stimulating your mental faculties, but what is even more important than that, by rendering all mental work attractive and pleasant.

The use of Universal Life Energy, however, should not be restricted to class rooms and study hours. In the gymnasium or on the football field, in rowing or in any other kind of athletics Life Energy will again be the Great Helper. Whenever you do any exercise in the gymnasium, or take part in sports and games in the open, always start by first contacting mentally Universal Life Energy. The results obtained on the Physical Plane in increased strength, endurance and precision will be beyond anything you can ever dream. There your Human Radio, your inherent power to contact Universal Life Energy for the immediate needs of your body, will be of the greatest value to you.

Remember those migratory birds which can fly thousands of miles without sleeping, resting, eating or drinking, because their bodily radio supplies them all the time with the energy they need for their flight. So will your body continually absorb Universal Life Energy once you have established the Mental Contact with It, drawing from It all the necessary force to be used by you in any direction required at that moment. Through the continual use of Universal Life Energy you will be a better all around athlete and you will be able to achieve much finer results in the particular sport or activity you specialize in and will be able to break your own records.

If you are a coach, there you have a wonderful opportunity to employ Universal Life Energy to the greatest advantage. In fashioning a team of any sort, for baseball, football, crew and all other sports, the vital element for which every coach strives first is harmonious cooperation. The individual athletes must fit snugly into the larger plan; their minds must jump with your mind, their aim must be your aim. When a single purpose dominates all, when the physical activities of each unit of that human machine blend into a powerful and one-pointed scheme of action, then every ounce of energy is made to produce its result without waste or loss.

By using Universal Life Energy continually himself, a coach first forms the mold of a successful team by working up a right plan of campaign for the coming season. Through that Power he is able to sense more accurately the conditions which his athletes will have to encounter, and which will determine to a great degree whether his policy is right or wrong.

Then, once that plan is laid out, he has to fit his material into it — generally raw and stubborn material leavened by a greater or lesser amount of veteran stuff. That is, he has to coordinate the different units that are to make up his machine and bring them to the point where they work harmoniously one with the other and with him. In this task Universal Life Energy is of invaluable aid, because harmony — equilibrium — is Its fundamental quality.

Therefore explain in a few words to the candidates what Universal Life Energy is and the basic principles of It. Have them use It continually when training, and especially when competing. You will be astonished at the results, for you will find the usually stubborn difficulties melting away in a very short time as the Force begins to manifest Itself in their progress. They are readier to understand, quicker to respond, more adept in making muscles, nerves and brains reject waste motions and act directly for the greatest effect. They will think and work with you and for each other, and will show you that "team-work" which is the ideal of every coach and the source of victories.

Also, you can help on the purely Physical Plane by an intelligent use of Universal Life- Energy quite-as much as on the mental and physical combined. The final "kick" which so often determines which side shall forge to the lead is in that Universal Force. Those who know how to contact and use this Power have always a reserve of energy to draw upon, because no matter how fast they exhaust the supply in their own bodies more is pouring in all the time to replace it.

But if, through loss of self control or for some other reason your athletes do not contact Universal Life Energy and you see that, as they' use up their own limited supply of force, they are becoming weak, you can send them a fresh fund of energy by making the Mental Contact with the Universal Power and then thinking strongly of them. The Force will flow to them where they are along the invisible mental line thus established. And as those who have that ultimate reserve to call on, that last "kick" to bring into play, are the ones who win, you may in that way be the one who literally hands them the victory.

Finally, it should be remembered that while the immediate goal of any contest is victory, that victory cannot be bought at the expense of the body. It is the fruit of fine and healthy physiques built staunchly enough to stand the stress of winning. If in training and contests the body is continuously drained of life force, if the demands are greater than the supply, the result is destructive and not constructive. When the strain becomes too great something has to break, and the individual may suffer all the rest of his life from the injurious effects of such a trial.

But if Universal Life Energy is used all that danger is avoided, for whoever knows how to contact the Universal Force has continually at hand a reserve supply of power to draw upon. The buoyancy, the "come-back" of healthy tissues is always there, and in place of utter fatigue and weariness the individual will experience only the not unpleasant tiredness that requires nothing but the normal rest it has earned to banish it altogether.

EXERCISES TO LESSON SEVEN

The new Exercise which you are to add this week to the number of those you have already learned is called INVIGORATION.

First relax and enter into Silence in the usual way, and then make the Mental Contact. While contacting Universal Life Energy during the Silence, think about Strength, physical and mental. Bring the concept of Strength into clear focus within you; let it blot through and merge with your system until its identity as a separate concept is absorbed in your own identity. Picture yourself vigorous, mentally alert, every fibre and nerve thrilling with abundant vitality.

Perform this Exercise conscientiously and persistently, for from five to ten minutes daily, and you will find that what you began as an abstract concept becomes permanently caught in the fabric of your being. Instead of ebbing away at the conclusion of the Exercise it will, because of the driving power of Universal Life Energy, manifest itself gradually and with increasing force in both body and mind.

QUESTIONS TO LESSON SEVEN

1. What is the general complaint of educators today?

2. Is this complaint justified, and if so to what must the fault be attributed?

3. Why is it that most teachers are not producing the desired results with their students?

4. What is the reaction of other minds to a mind permeated with Universal Life Energy?

5. What is usually the cause of mental deficiency?

6. How can mentally sluggish and backward children be restored to normal?

7. To what are exhibitions of temper and perversity in children due?

8. How should they be handled?

9. What practical results will teachers obtain for themselves by using Universal Life Energy in their work?

10. What advantage will students derive from using Universal Life Energy in their studies?

11. In what way is the use of Universal Life Energy in sports and athletics particularly effective in securing the desired results?

12. What is the most important practical knowledge for a coach to possess?

ANSWERS TO LESSON SEVEN

1. The general complaint today is:

That students pay more attention to sports and social activities than they do to studies.

2. This complaint:

Is justified, and the fault must be attributed to the fact that knowledge is generally presented in an uninteresting and unattractive way.

3. Most teachers are not producing the desired results with their students:

Because they are dry, cold, uninteresting and nonmagnetic.

4. The reaction of other minds to a mind permeated with Universal Life Energy is:

Interest and concentration on the matter presented, becoming active participators instead of passive onlookers.

5. The cause of mental deficiency is:

Poor development of certain brain centres.

6. **Mentally sluggish and backward children can be restored to normal:**

   (1) By treating them individually with Universal Life Energy.

   (2) By magnetizing books, papers and other articles they are to handle, so that these things radiate an attractive power and catch the interest of the children.

7. **Exhibitions of temper and perversity in children are due to:**

   A disturbed equilibrium brought about by disproportionate inner development.

8. **They should be handled:**

   By exercising precisely opposite positive qualities which will call out a positive response in the child.

9. **The practical results that teachers will obtain for themselves by continually using Universal Life Energy are:**

   (1) They will break away from the dead letter of their teachings and bring out the living spirit.

   (2) They will elevate the vocation. of teaching to its rightful place in the esteem of the world.

(3) They will command respect, material success and the love of their students.

10. The advantage students will derive from using Universal Life Energy in their studies is:

A lively interest in their work that enables them to get more out of it and retain and use what they get.

11. The use of Universal Life Energy in sports and athletics is particularly effective in securing the desired results:

By coordinating and harmonizing activities, and giving to the athletes a permanent reserve fund of energy to call upon.

12. The most important practical knowledge for a coach to posses is:

A knowledge of Universal Life Energy and how to use It.

Dear Friend:

Poverty is a disease which, like every other sickness, is the visible shadow of an unseen inner Cause. And just as you can scrub diligently at a shadow and never rub it out, so you can spend youth and energy in a vain effort to wipe Poverty out of your life unless you know how to make it vanish by removing the fundamental causes.

Those causes, mental and physical, Lesson Eight will reveal to you. It will show you that no matter how limited you may be financially before taking this Course, that is a condition which you can change completely by putting into practical application the instructions given herein.

You have the channels within you whereby to contact and bring to your service a Power of which even a small part will suffice to wash away that inner Cause if intelligently directed. By showing you the causes this Lesson will enable you to reach them effectively with the Force whose use you have already acquired through the previous lessons.

Then you will see the spectre of Poverty swallowed up in its original nothingness under the light of the Knowledge conveyed to you in these pages, and Abundance, the true and eternal condition of the whole Universe, emerging into natural expression in its place.

Cordially yours,
Eugene Fersen.

LESSON EIGHT

MILLIONS of people are asking themselves every day the question, "Why is it that some are so rich and some so poor, some successful and others in spite of all their endeavours scarcely able to make ends meet?"

You have probably noticed that not always do those who work hardest and longest and are the most honest get the best rewards, while many who seem never to exert themselves to any degree and are not too particular of the methods they use win with effortless ease the fortune for which less favoured ones strive in vain.

At first glance that seems unfair, yet it is not so. There is always a reason for everything that happens. If there is an effect there must be a cause, and that cause usually corresponds directly to the effect. What appears to be haphazard, irrational, is in reality the outcome of the most logical natural processes; but it is only when we perceive and understand those processes that events resolve themselves into the proper perspective and assume the right proportions one to the other.

The immediate causes of Poverty are two-fold—physical and mental. The physical cause is the brain itself, the material instrument through which the qualities of your Individuality must pass to find expression. The mental cause is in that part of your three-fold being called Mind. There is a direct and intimate relation between the two, the physical cause being the projection into substance of the mental one.

Let us consider first the physical cause. There are within that human brain of yours all kinds of centres which not only control the various functions of the body, but which also act as channels through which your different human qualities are expressed. Each centre is identified with a particular quality, physical, mental or emotional, for which it is the transmitting medium. Some centres for instance, would control the expression of emotional qualities, like religious faith, love, joy, etc.; others physical qualities, such as natural aptitude in tasks requiring manual skill; and still others purely reasoning powers.

Phrenology long ago perceived the truth back of this, but though it was able, by a study of the bumps on the human skull, to estimate roughly the degree of the development of the respective brain centres underneath and consequently the degree to which the corresponding qualities are manifested in the life of the individual it never attempted to modify that development by discovering and controlling the cause.

The extent to which any centre can express the quality it represents depends wholly on its ability to contact and transmit Universal Life Energy. If the contact is blurred and uncertain that quality will trickle into only feeble expression. If the contact is sound it will be manifested to the full strength of the current poured into it.

In that respect the brain centres are comparable to so many differently collared bulbs each colour standing for a separate quality. There is only one original undifferentiated current of Life Force flowing from the Solar Plexus into the various centres, by way of the nerve systems, just as there is only one original current of electricity flowing to an assortment of collared bulbs. The electrical current produces inside each bulb the same white light; but that light, in passing through the collared film of glass enclosing it, borrows the tint of the glass and appears on the outside as a light of the corresponding colour.

So with Universal Life Energy; it becomes differentiated into powers possessing the qualities of the centres through which it flows. That is, one original power produces different effects because of the difference in the channels through which it passes, and those different effects are strong or weak in proportion as the current producing them was admitted in greater or lesser quantities.

The more any centre opens itself to the influx of Universal Life Energy the more it is able to open itself. In doing that work of transforming the Life Current into a power manifesting its own individual quality it is also stimulated and strengthened into a rapid growth by the very Force it handles. In other words, the more it works the stronger it becomes.

Every human being possesses within his brain all those various centres, but they do not all function equally well. With some of them the contact is dull and feeble, and the amount of Energy that filters in is no more than enough to keep them barely alive, to say nothing of furnishing them with strength to develop and a surplus to send on.

Such centres need stimulation from outside to awaken them from their lethargy and open them to the vital surge of the Universal Life Current. This stimulus you provide when you consciously make the contact with Universal Life Energy for them, opening them to that initial flow which enlarges itself automatically by enlarging the channel through which it passes.

The physical inability of some centres to contact that Power outside may be due to their own lack of development, to a paralysis of them by overstrain, or to exhaustion. In any event the effect is the same, since nothing can come out unless it first goes in. However, the first of these physical reasons is far more common than the others, and is less difficult to correct when once understood. Let us take, for instance, one centre – that connected with business and financial abilities. The individual who has this centre properly developed has the power of turning everything he touches into money. A sure business instinct guides him through to the profitable end of every deal. Therefore financially he is, of course, very successful.

With most human beings, however, that centre is in a very undeveloped condition. Like the collared bulb, it is there but dark, because it has not within itself sufficient power to turn-the- switch that Connects it with the main current. Obviously, under such conditions, no matter how great a supply of Power there may be outside it is of no avail to the individual, since the channel for its expression is closed. Therefore if you want to be rich you must first open that channel within you and give to the dormant centre inside your brain the power to function properly.

To do this it is necessary to go behind the physical lack of development of those nerve fibres in the brain and eliminate the mental cause back of it. That cause is Fear, and is generally the product of conditions which governed the youth of the individual.

 Most children are born into families of limited means, and are accustomed from infancy to hear their parents discussing those material limitations. The most pressing concern of the parents is to "make ends meet," and the spring of action which drives them daily to their tasks is the fear that they may not be able to do so. They are continually on the defensive, fighting to survive rather than to create. Dread of failure sets the key-note of their thoughts and tempers their conversation as well as their attitude toward life, and all this taken together naturally produces a certain negative impression on the child's mind. Because of the deadening influence of that negative mental condition the centre which controls the financial aspect of the child's nature is unable to develop normally.

Grown up under those unfavourable circumstances, the individual lacks the proper confidence and ability to make money. The desire to make money is there, but it is overshadowed by an even greater fear of Poverty and material limitations. Most people are and remain poor because their intense fear chokes off the activities of the one centre which alone can bring into their lives the think they lack yet desire with all their hearts — Abundance.

There are some who, sick at heart of leading a life of hardship and Poverty, are goaded into blind revolt and determine to break the fetters which bind them. Through many years of hard work, after countless trials and failures, they finally succeed in bursting through the wall of their limitations and emerge into the sunshine of Prosperity.

Great courage, energy, perseverance and above all an unflinching optimism are required in order to win that fight; yet how few are able to express those qualities! The majority of human beings are doomed at birth to a handicap which they seldom overcome adequately. Fear is bred into them, unconsciously, perhaps, but the more subtly for all that, until they come to accept it as a natural condition instead of recognizing it for the poisonous drug it is, slowly but surely numbing one activity after the other and shutting them off just that much more each time from their rightful contacts with the-world-in which-they live.

Mental science, realizing that this is a problem of Mind, seeks a solution by trying to change thoughts of Poverty into those of Abundance through purely mental methods, like affirmation or suggestion. Many people, those of the more advanced way of thinking, practice these methods diligently, yet they usually fail.

The reason for such failure is that Mind alone is not able to develop a brain centre which is still in an embryonic condition. Mind is a cold light; its rays illumine but they do not warm or energize. In order to be effective it requires the cooperation of another and greater Power, Universal Life Energy. That Power can flush the inactive centre clean of its constricting fear and open the channel for genuine thoughts of Abundance to flow through.

There is another reason why mental methods are most often a complete failure. The effect of affirmations as they are generally used is exactly the reverse of what people expect it to be. That is because they do not even know how to use affirmations properly.

For instance, they say, "I AM—Wealth, Affluence, Abundance, etc." This is fundamentally wrong. You are NOT the thing you are wishing to realize in your life. At best you can only be ONE WITH it; but the thing, like any ideal, must always remain outside and above you, a magnet attracting you to itself.

Finally, even those who use the right kind of affirmations—those who say, "I am ONE WITH" Abundance, Wealth, Success—they usually are not able to realize that affirmation in their lives because, the constant repetition of one statement, instead of stimulating the brain cells, tends to numb the very centre which it is supposed to awaken. Therefore very often the more an individual affirms Wealth the less he is able to demonstrate it, as that constant hammering of an unscientific affirmation stuns the corresponding centre and prevents it from developing properly.

Such attempts to gouge out the mental cause back of the physical disability are as inefficient as they are harmful. Fear is not a localized growth which can be amputated; it is a general condition which must be purged away. This Universal Life Energy is able to do, cleansing, stimulating and healing in accordance with Natural Laws instead of mangling by an unwise imposition of the human will.

That wonderful Power, properly directed to the financial brain centre through a mental realization of one's Unity with Universal Abundance, will stir it into action just as a seed in the ground, when it is touched by moisture and warmed by the sun's rays, is stirred to life. Then the more Life Energy is used the more that centre will be able to use It, the quicker it will develop and the stronger its activities will be expressed in an ever increasing power to manifest Abundance.

The first indication that the financial centre has been properly stimulated will be felt rather than seen. You will become conscious of a novel sense of Wealth, of Abundance, within you. Next you will discover that, whereas before you were scarcely able to make ends meet, now there is a little excess of earnings over expenses. Finally, that uncertain trickle of excess will swell gradually to a steady flow of Affluence expressed in various ways, such as increase of salary, better business, unexpected opportunities for making money, etc.

In this connection you must remember always that you are the instrument through which Universal Life Energy works. You cannot contact that Power and then sit idle and expect it to work for you. It gives you the physical energy and the mental alertness to perceive and take advantage of opportunities, the judgment to know the right course and the boldness to act decisively and promptly; but your own brain and body are the tools which It must use. Then when your financial centre is developed, the energies which before were misdirected will operate through it to attract Wealth and Affluence. The second of the physical reasons why that centre may be unable to function, paralysis of it from overstrain, is apt to make its appearance at this point. If the individual is impatient and, by exaggerated efforts to make money or meet demands, tries to exact from it more power than it can yield, he will produce that condition. It is much more difficult to restore a centre thus affected than to develop one which is undeveloped.

In order to obtain the best and quickest results it is necessary to let Universal Life Energy work undisturbed in accordance with Its own Natural Laws. Any attempt to force that work through personal will-power instead of accelerating the growth of the centre, will kill it. Hothouse growth is never lasting. Simply be patient, wait for the gradual and healthy development of your financial centre, and do not despise the results at first obtained. On the contrary, accept them joyfully and gratefully, thus making yourself ready to receive more. An attitude of dissatisfaction or impatience, prompting you to demand more of the centre than it is then capable of producing, spoils everything that has been accomplished so far. It is like "choking" an engine by too sudden a demand on it, so that instead of supplying the added power it stops completely.

In these rare cases where the financial centre is paralysed the same treatment as for the stimulation of an undeveloped centre, described in the EXERCISES TO this Lesson, is to be used. However, it is a much more difficult-matter and will take a longer time to restore that centre to its normal function than would have been necessary to develop it only.

The third physical cause, a centre which is exhausted or dried up, is of all three the worst because such a centre is practically dead. There is no life in it. The cause of such a condition is usually the misuse of Money Power, as by misers or spendthrifts.

Yet through the application of Universal Life Energy those sapless tissues can eventually be nursed into activity and then brought up to normal. Although the results in this instance may not begin to manifest themselves for a very long time, nevertheless they can be achieved by perseverance and the continual use of Universal Life Energy.

The physical reasons for the inactivity of any centre, and the mental causes of which they are the products, are in general the same. Their operation and how to cure them has been described specifically in relation to one centre, the financial one, as art example of how they work in other centres. The single piece partakes of the qualities of the whole and is much more easily analysed. Yet there are finer and more subtle aspects which should be understood in order to get a clear perspective. If you want to be rich you must first genuinely feel that way before its actual materialization will take place in your life. To feel rich you must also know what Wealth is.

Wealth is not money so much as it is the use to which money is put. A miser is poor because neither he nor anyone else gets any benefit from his hoarded gold. A debtor owing a million may be rich because of the use to which he puts his borrowed money and because of the things he creates to fill needs and serve others.

Money is a Power which was here when you were born and will be here when you die—an impersonal Force which you can neither bring into the world nor take out of it. In proportion as you are able and fitted to be a custodian of that Power you will win riches. You are a channel open at both ends: the stream of Money Power will flow into you at one end in exact accordance with your capacity to give it out into expression as wealth at the other end. There is a Natural Law called the Law of Compensation which says that one receives in proportion as he gives. If you want the Universal to be generous to you, first you must learn to be generous yourself. The more you are of service to others, the more the world will be of service to you with its various treasures of Infinite Supply.

Forced generosity is not true giving. In order to receive you must learn to give freely, spontaneously and joyfully, knowing that it will be immediately replaced within you. That is natural giving, and as Nature does not permit a vacuum there will always be a compensating supply.

But if you give reluctantly, with the fear that by so doing you are depriving yourself and making a sacrifice, you profit neither yourself nor others. Your gift will be poisoned by the sense of fear and limitation you put into it, and that same fear will paralyse and make void the little activity of your own financial brain centre. Thus you close the channel in you and isolate yourself from the natural Supply, so you are that much worse off than you were before.

That is why so many kind hearted people who sincerely want to help others and try to do so succeed only in impoverishing themselves. It seems unfair, and prompts one to question if giving is worthwhile in the face of such disastrous results. Yet the reason such kind hearted people are so poorly rewarded is that, though animated by a kindly motive they give ignorantly and with fear. Intelligent and joyful giving, with the knowledge that you give not of your own but of the Infinite Abundance which is flowing through you, will bring about entirely different results. The very physical channels within you, the centre through which Universal Life Energy is manifested as Abundance, will be properly stimulated and will function accordingly. Then you will become richer all the time, as the developing capacity to use money brings you more money to use.

Giving is not limited to money or material things only. You can give of your intelligence, your energy, your inspiration, your time. They are all very valuable, usually more valuable than money or material things. Give them without grudging, without limiting yourself, unreservedly, whole-heartedly, joyfully. Feel within yourself that you are giving from the Superabundance you contact. Thereby you will open to that very Abundance the opportunity to materialize Itself in your life as Wealth and Prosperity. That is what is meant by vibrating to Abundance and Prosperity.

EXERCISES TO LESSON EIGHT

This week, in addition to the Star Exercise morning and evening, you are to commence a new Exercise which will give a certain direction to the current of Life Energy contacted by you during the Relaxation and Silence. It is called the CONTACT WITH INFINITE SUPPLY OF ALL WEALTH, and its purpose is gradually to enable you to transmute more of the Universal Force into abundance by developing the physical organ in your brain for that transmutation. Perform it as follows:

During the Silence, after you have made the Mental Contact with Universal Life Energy and feel It flowing through you, think strongly of Abundance and the Infinite Supply of all you need. Realize to yourself the statement, "I am expressing Infinite Wealth; It is now flowing through me; I am one with it."

Thus you start the corresponding centre within your brain vibrating in response to your thought vibrations. The Life Energy you contact will then flow by way of the spinal nerve system to that centre, there to be transformed into vibrations of Prosperity and projected through you into material realization in your life.

Remember this point also, that you must naturally continue to strive for Abundance, for a great Supply.

Your mental work will guide you to the right source of that Supply, will discover to you opportunities for contacting it, but it is for you to take bold and vigorous advantage of those opportunities.

The familiar saying, that you can lead a horse to water but you cannot make it drink, applies here. Universal Life Energy can place you in direct relation with the Supply, but your conscious self has to draw it in. Mental work alone is not sufficient. Simply to contact mentally Universal Abundance and then not take the necessary steps to get it is useless. You live on the physical plane as well as on the mental one, and the cooperation of the two is required to produce results.

QUESTIONS TO LESSON EIGHT

1. What is the fundamental Cause of Poverty?

2. How does this Cause express Itself?

3. How can it be overcome?

4. What are the physical channels through which the qualities of the individual are expressed?

5. What determines the degree to which those qualities are manifested?

6. How does the original undifferentiated current of Universal Life Energy become differentiated in the individual?

7. What role does environment play in the development of a child, especially in relation to its financial brain centre?

8. To what three immediate causes may the inability of any brain centre to function be due?

9. Why are purely mental methods for overcoming Poverty inadequate?

10. How can Abundance be most successfully demonstrated?

11. What attitude in giving prevents the operation of the Law of Compensation?

12. What is the understanding of Money essential for
    true giving?

ANSWERS TO LESSON EIGHT

1. The fundamental Cause of Poverty is:

Fear.

2. This Cause expresses itself:

By preventing the development and operation of the financial centre within the brain of the individual.

3. It can be overcome:

Only by the -use-of Universal Life –Energy.

4. The physical channels through which the qualities of the individual are expressed are:

Brain centres, each of which corresponds to a certain definite quality.

5. The degree to which these qualities are manifested is determined:

By the degree to which the corresponding brain centres are able to function.

6. The original undifferentiated current of Universal Life Energy becomes differentiated in the individual:

By assuming the qualities of the various centres through which it passes.

7. **The role played by environment in the development of a child, especially in relation to its financial centre, is:**

Such development is largely moulded by environment, so that if the parents have a defensive and fearful attitude toward Poverty, that fear is bred into the child and prevents the natural development of its financial brain centre.

8. **The three immediate causes for the inability of any brain centre to function may be:**

(1) Lack of development, due to fear.

(2) Paralysis of the centre, due to overstrain. 3. Exhaustion of the centre, due to abuse.

9. **Purely mental methods for overcoming Poverty are inadequate:**

Because they lack the creative and energizing power of Universal Life Energy.

10. **Abundance can be most successfully demonstrated:**

By allowing Universal Life Energy to develop the corresponding centre within you in accordance with Its own Natural Laws.

11. **The attitude in giving which prevents the operation of the Law of Compensation is:**

An attitude of Fear, so that the gift is given with inner reluctance and a sense of self sacrifice which closes the physical brain centre against a compensating supply.

12. **The understanding of Money essential for true giving is:**

That Money is an impersonal Power which expresses itself through you only in proportion as you are able to give it out in intelligent and constructive ways.

Dear Friend:

Old Age is a condition of health, not a tally of years. Therefore-it is most appropriate that this last of the cycle of Lessons on the Body in relation to Universal Life Energy should show you how to ward off the attacks of Time by increasing and preserving the health of your body. A sound and harmonious physical apparatus will always defy Old Age, because it will always be able to manifest completely the qualities of the individual. Youth is chief among those qualities; therefore in proportion as we supply that immortal part of our triune being with a fitting instrument for its expression, Youth will shine through, ageless and indomitable.

Mankind loses the open contact and free exchange between its inner Self and its material body, not because it wants to, but because a long inherited habit of thinking gradually overthrows its balanced development and starts it downhill on a false course. Reliance on Self shifts to reliance on others. Fear opens the door to sickness and fatigue, the resilience of Youth departs and Old Age creeps in to ripen slowly into Death.

This Lesson will explain to you how to restore that broken contact by the use of Universal Life Energy, how to rejuvenate through It an old or tired body, and how to drive out the poisons of disease and troubles which have lodged there. Though you may not intend to use that Force as a professional healer, still you can readily appreciate the value of a Knowledge which enables you to meet and overcome every emergency of accident or illness, whether for yourself or anyone else. Self Reliance will then take the place of that increasing dependence on others, and by developing within yourself the means to remedy all shortcomings, physical as well as mental and spiritual, you will win at last the true Freedom which is the right and ambition of all.

Cordially yours,
Eugene Fersen.

LESSON NINE

To enjoy glorious health is one of the most ardent of human aspirations. The health of an individual is the measure of his ability to "live," to express himself in terms of power and achievement on this Earth Plane. It is worth more than riches, because it gives one unlimited opportunities for acquiring wealth, whereas all the money in the world cannot actually buy health.

Health-is the efficient outward Manifestation through the body of harmonious inner activities. For this a sound body is as essential to each individual as is a good instrument to a musician. A master violinist handicapped by a broken or ill-tuned instrument, cannot give expression to the exquisite melody within him, because every note is shorn of its power, beauty and attractiveness in passing through an imperfect channel. So with the physically unfit—no matter what the harmony within, it emerges only into distorted and jangled expression through the flawed channels for its transmission.

As Mankind is the sum of the individuals comprising it, the progress and vigour of the Human Race, as well as the relative progress and vigour of respective Nations, depends directly on the degree to which every one of its people can manifest their inner qualities. A healthy member of Society is able to serve Society in proportion as he is able to manifest more qualities, thus constituting a positive force for its advancement. An unhealthy person is on the contrary a burden which Society must carry and which retards it. The difference between the two marks the progress or retrogression of the people as a whole.

Therefore an equal responsibility rests on everyone to develop a healthy body, not only for their own sake, but also for the sake of their fellow beings. We have certain qualities which are there for expression, and we have the physical organs to give them that expression. If those physical organs are poorly developed the greater part of the qualities they represent will never be brought out. Thus not only does ill health result in a great loss to the individual in particular, but also to the world in general which is prevented from benefiting by those qualities.

In this connection you may recall divers prominent figures who, in spite of ill health and physical limitations, have been able to produce remarkable results in their lives, while others with every apparent physical advantage have accomplished nothing constructive at all. There are two explanations for this seeming paradox.

The first and obvious one is that those who achieved much in spite of physical limitations could have done a great deal more if they had been in sound health, whereas those whose excellent physiques did not enable them to attain any special prominence would have been much worse off if they had not possessed at least that single asset.

The second and more important one is the prevailing misconception of what Health is. Most people are inclined to judge the health of an individual by the muscular development of his body, which is in fact a very specious indication. A man may be splendidly muscled and still in poor health, because the development of more important inner centres may not at all have kept pace with the growth of visible sinews. In that case the magnificent body is an excrescence, a sort of huge wen growing out of a spindling core where all the centres except those controlling that exaggerated development are starved and shrivelled almost to nothing.

Real health is a condition which must pervade every fibre. The physical apparatus for the expression of one's qualities is like a lens, or burning glass, for focusing and transmitting the rays of the sun. If the lens is dirty or chipped and full of flaws it will permit those rays to filter through only very imperfectly, so that their expression on the other side is blurred and dim and powerless. If it is crystal clear it will concentrate the scattered rays into a one-pointed beam of such potency that the individual can say, with reason, "watch my smoke," because in whatever direction he turns that beam he is going to get action and results.

The healthy body is the clear lens—that is, not only polished on the outside, but free from dirt and faults and bubbles on the inside also. Such a body does not need to be hardily muscled; all it needs is to be clean and evenly developed throughout. Just as limpid water can be made to focus the sun's rays as effectively as a burning glass, so also can healthy tissues be made to correlate their activities and produce as good results by simply keeping them clean and wholesome.

The keystone of Health, therefore, is a balanced development, or poise. A normal individual with all his physical faculties equally developed, inside and out, is able to bring into play more power than one who has a few developed at the expense of the rest. Unbalanced powers neutralize one another, whereas balanced powers fortify each other. Observations made on criminals have revealed that their bad characteristics are very often the consequences of just such a lack of poise brought about by physical defects, especially in the brain. Once those defects are corrected, usually by an operation, the whole character of the individual is changed.

Physical culture has taken elaborate pains to evolve methods for promoting the general health of the body.

Most of these are scientifically worked out and bring excellent results if followed faithfully, but they are limited by the very principle on which they operate and the artificial aids required.

Any scheme of physical exercises proceeds on the actual theory, though probably unformulated, that by making a muscle work harder the centre controlling that muscle is naturally obliged to develop in order to supply the increased energy demanded of it. In other words, such a scheme tries to control causes by manipulating effects. Therefore it is circumscribed in the number of hidden causes it is able directly to influence by the number of visible effects it is able to handle. And while those centres which are not touched nevertheless benefit sympathetically with the improved condition of the part of the body, they are not actually developed in harmony with the others. Thus the equilibrium is only partially restored, and in cases where the exercises are not wisely chosen is apt to be even more disturbed rather than corrected.

Added disadvantages reside in the fact that most of these exercises depend upon mechanical devices or special surroundings for their proper performance. Many of them, particularly games, are a part of outdoor life and require the cooperation of others. Yet to a great number of individuals neither specialized apparatus nor outdoor life and companionship are available, so they cannot benefit as do the more fortunate ones. But for those who know how to use Universal Life Energy no such limitations of environment exist, because wherever they are that Power is there also, waiting only to have the way opened for It to enter.

The ultimate purpose of both physical exercises and the methods taught you in this Course is the same — that is, to develop a healthy and efficient body — but they go about it from diametrically opposite points of view. Physical exercises works from the surface inward toward centralized causes by as many channels as it is able to find, just as one might try to clean a clogged shower bath by squirting water back through each hole separately. Universal Life Energy works from the centralized causes outward into surface effects — a single stream spurting under equal pressure through each separate hole or channel and driving the accumulated dirt of sickness and ill health before it.

The most direct reversal of this natural process is to be found in the use of drugs and medicine, that last recourse of failing health. Although the basis of all such artificial stimulants is, after all, Universal Life Energy, since every material thing is composed of that Force in different degrees of condensation, their use should nevertheless be avoided as far as possible and then resorted to very carefully under adequate medical supervision. To obtain Universal Life Energy through your own physical channel, contacting that inexhaustible Supply in Its pure aspect of Life Force, is one thing, whereas obtaining It in a corrupted form out of a bottle is another. In the former case you develop your own inner organs for drawing in as much as you need, in quantities automatically adjusted by the requirements, and you rely solely on yourself. In the latter you not only depend more and more on a box of pills or a vial whose contents are administered through unnatural channels in quantities determined by a seldom infallible human judgment, but by introducing a supply of energy artificially you deprive the centre in your brain on which you ought to rely of its function, so that it sinks into disuse. Universal Life Energy in Its pure form contains the antidote for every ailment, and through Its inherent power of harmonization will establish Equilibrium and Health by eliminating disharmony and disease wherever and however found.

The way to treat yourself for any physical trouble is as follows: Make the contact with Universal Life Energy after seating yourself comfortably in a chair. If you are too ill to sit, lie down. When you feel the Force flowing through you place your hand on that part of your body which is troubling you. Universal Life Energy will then flow in a healing current through your hand into the diseased part. There it will by and by eliminate the trouble by throwing it off, and will restore the natural condition of equilibrium.

If there is inflammation, due to congestion, Life Energy will dispel that congestion and the inflammation will disappear. Remember that most of human troubles are due to local or general congestion of the body; therefore its elimination is one of the most important points in Therapeutics.

If there are diseased or dead tissues, as in so many so-called organic troubles, Life Energy will restore the diseased cells to their normal activities. Those which are dead will be thrown off by the living ones which will replace them, and the affected part will then assume once more its full share of the work of the body.

In its aspect of Protector against deadly microbes and the germs of contagious diseases, Universal Life Energy plays the same role in the body as ammunition and supplies play in the work of an army. Each cell of your body is a tiny soldier on guard over his own minute sector of the line, and Universal Life Energy, flooding along the nerve pathways, seeping into every blood corpuscle, stimulating and strengthening everything It touches, carries to every individual fighting cell of those massed millions the power to repel the attacks of an enemy much more subtle and persistent than any human foe could be. That Force is the ammunition whereby those soldier cells preserve an unbroken front, as well as the food which sustains them during that endless battle, and It produces a radiation of positive Life Current from the body so strong that negative assaulting units explode and destroy themselves on contact with It just like toy balloons which float within range of a bonfire. That is why a genuinely healthy individual, one whose inner supply depots and lines of communication are well organized, can go through epidemics and can associate intimately with people suffering from contagious diseases without being affected in any way by them.

Its distinctive quality of self-government makes the use of Universal Life Energy so simple and practical that anyone, even a child, can get equally effective results from It. No special knowledge of anatomy or of the disease itself is required, and no misuse is possible, because the unvarying tendency of that Force always to seek and find equilibrium is stronger than any human will to direct or change it. If you have that special knowledge, so much the better, as you will then understand exactly how the Power you use is operating. But whether you know or not It will operate just the same, flying directly to Its need, filling the diseased part of your body as rain spills into the hollows in the ground, in precisely the right quantities and carrying just the right antidote, bringing Its own peculiar quality of basic harmony to replace the disharmony It expels.

When treating others the method of using Universal Life Energy is slightly different from self-treatments. Have your patient if possible comfortably seated in a chair and perfectly relaxed. The patient does not need to make the contact with Universal Life Energy. You are to do that. Take good care to make the contact before you touch or even approach the patient, as otherwise he will, because of his exhausted condition, draw out of you instantaneously your own reserve of Life Energy stored in your Solar Plexus and will leave you in your turn exhausted. In that condition it will be more difficult for you to make the contact than if you are in your ordinary physical shape.

After you make the contact, place your two hands on the shoulders of your patient from behind in such a way that your thumbs, touching each other, rest on the seventh vertebra, which is most easily identified as the lower joint of the neck. This is the most sensitive point in the spinal column from which your spinal cord, and consequently the whole of your nervous system, can be influenced. Your other fingers and the palms of your hands are to rest on the shoulders of your patient, the finger tips directed downward over the breast bone toward the Solar Plexus.

Then all that is necessary is to let the current of Universal Life Energy flow through your hands into the body of your patient. It will pour into the spinal cord and from there be distributed by way of the nerve system to every part of the patient's body. Where a particular need for It exists, that need will act as a vacuum which sucks It more strongly to the sick tissues until the healing is accomplished and the lost equilibrium re-established.

The less you think about your patient-during the treatment the better Universal Life Energy will work. Mental effort, either through thought, suggestion or will power, produces a tension which contracts the channels for conducting the Force and thus hampers It in Its work. Thorough relaxation is what is required, and the more you are able to achieve that through a placid, open realization of your One-ness with the Universal Current, complemented by a calm and loving attitude toward your patient, the better results you will obtain.

Remember, it is the Universal Power which does the healing and not you. You are only the medium, the conducting agent through which It finds expression. Therefore put aside all personality and be as open as you can to the inflow of that Power.

The question may arise as to how long each treatment shall be continued. The general rule is to keep your hands on the shoulders of the patient until you feel that the current of Life Energy has stopped flowing through your finger tips. This indicates that the body of your patient is saturated with that Power; therefore to continue would be a waste of time and energy. At this moment gently remove your hands, for the treatment is completed.

The length of the treatment varies in accordance with the nature of the case you are treating. If the need is great it will take more time to fill it. However, from five to fifteen minutes is a reasonable space of time for most treatments to last. In some cases it may be shorter, in some longer. It is a question of developing within yourself the faculty of sensing when to stop, and that is something you can learn only through experience.

If there is some local trouble to which you wish to give special attention, you can follow the treatment described above with an additional one to complete it. Keeping your left hand on the left shoulder of the patient so that the thumb touches the seventh vertebra, place the right hand on that part of the body which you want to heal. If the affected area is very small, as in the case of eye or ear trouble, also wounds and burns, bunch the five fingers of your right hand together in order to concentrate into one ray the five streams of Universal Life Energy flowing from your five finger tips, and then direct that ray on the sick part, but without necessarily touching it. Wounds and burns so treated heal with remarkable rapidity, usually without leaving a scar. These local treatments are very strong, because of the combined action of the individual currents flowing through your fingers, and care should be used in giving them.

These instructions concerning the use of Universal Life Energy for healing purposes are of a general kind. As each case is an individual case, it is left to your own intelligence and resourcefulness to adapt the application of that Power to special needs.

Remember, the Life Force is like a current of electricity which you can direct through your finger tips in any direction you choose. By opening yourself to It more you can increase Its power; by closing yourself you can diminish It at will.

In treating yourself and others for so-called chronic troubles, you will notice that very often, after a decided improvement, there will be a sudden relapse and the condition will grow worse perhaps than it was in the beginning. Though. unpleasant, this is an excellent sign. It shows that the deep-seated poison of the disease is being driven to the surface for elimination. Naturally, this results in an intensified expression of the trouble for the time being, until the inner venom all forced out, but meantime the cure is taking place within. Such a process is called Magnetic Chemicalization. Continue to treat vigorously and soon the condition will disappear entirely, never to occur again.

Universal Life Energy can be applied not only in treating human beings, but also in treating animals and even plants (see Lesson V) which, as they are closer to Nature and less subject to fear, actually respond much quicker and better than human beings.

In a consideration of the human body and its limitations there is one other problem paramount in the interest of everybody, as it has been all through Humanity's history. That is the question of Old Age. Why is life so short? Why do advancing years batter down this fleshy temple of our souls, defacing it with the scars of Time, draining away beauty and youth and buoyancy and power, ruthlessly exposing it to every sort of disease and disappointment, and saddening with its solemn threat of death the twilight of our sojourn on this plane?

From time immemorial it has been the dream of our immortal part to secure something strong and lasting for its expression, and this secret yearning has found voice in countless legends and stories of Fountains of Youth, Mixers of Life, Magic Apples of Health and numberless other nostrums for restoring old and tired bodies to their earlier vigour. Although everyone seemed doomed to grow old, the hope irrationally persisted that sometime, somehow, someone would discover the secret of how to stop the disintegrating processes of Old Age and Death.

The indestructible Soul within the perishable human body refused to accept the material fact of growing old and dying.

The reason for this is that the cause of Old Age is not to be found in the Soul, which knows no bounds of time, but in the Mind, in our own Consciousness. Through Pride -of Mind Humanity deliberately separated itself from the Infinite Source of All Life and limited itself to the small. supply of life force in the physical body. From that moment, naturally, human beings were bereft of the only Power great enough to withstand the disintegrating influences which are continually working for the destruction of the material body. If it were not for that mental separation of the individual from the Eternal Life Principle, Old Age and Death would never have been known on this Earth.

The immediate causes of Old Age are of two kinds, mental and physical. Fear, worry, disappointment, hatred, jealousy and all other negative thoughts and emotions are the mental causes, while the essential physical cause is low vitality due to overwork, malnutrition, unsanitary conditions and habits of life and all sorts of abuses. The inability of the individual to overcome these causes accounts for the victory of Old Age.

That inability to conquer physical limitations is directly due to the interference of Mind. When the individual is young his physical growth is emphasized, while his mental development trails along in second place. It is the formative period, when all faculties are fresh and clean, wet clay for the moulding of the future man or woman.

Mind has not yet bulked big enough to thrust itself between the individual and that intimate contact with Natural Forces which is his birthright. Fear is a sinister stranger whose acquaintance is to be made gradually by experience, a sombre sprite lurking in a thousand different and unexpected guises along the road of development and leaving a raw wound to commemorate every encounter.

As years bring Youth into Maturity those encounters become more frequent, so that the accumulated scars harden and crust the Mind with a dread consciousness of its limitations. Through that tough shell Life Energy is no longer able to penetrate freely and nourish the centres within as abundantly as before, so those centres wither away or pulse feebly in accordance with the meagre trickle they are able to secure. The individual becomes more and more restricted to the pool of reserve life force in his own body, and the demands of a ripening mental growth drain that reserve day by day, often stopping development prematurely, then lowering the vitality a bit at a time until wrinkles appear, firm flesh sags, cheeks cave in, teeth drop out, and all the melancholy insignia of Old Age emerge like dry rot through the walls of that sturdy structure erected by buoyant Youth.

The tragedy of this process is that at the very time when we most need all the power we can bring to bear in order to-make every quality count to the utmost, at that time our Mind is working most strenuously to cut us off from contact with the unlimited Supply of All Power. Not only that, but it is sucking dry the reserve of energy in our body in order to feed itself. It is depriving cells and tissues of the sustenance and power they must have to carry on successfully the ceaseless war against destructive outside influences — opening the back door to disintegration and death, as it were, while squandering the defensive forces on its own selfish concerns. It is the most subtle of traitors, for while it dazzles us with the brilliance of its performance it robs us of our greatest treasure, the contact with Universal Life Energy. So slyly that we seldom realize it, Mind reverses the course of Nature so that whereas in youth the body lives on the individual, who supplies it with Power from the Universal Source, in old age the individual literally preys upon his body and eats himself into his grave.

The incursion of Old Age is definitely marked in accordance with Natural Laws. Like a light which is turned out, the glow of life sinks inward on its own centre. The skin is the first to suffer as the lustre and freshness of Youth recede from it. Then tissues and muscles fail, and arteries become brittle and incapable of carrying the blood current as they should. The heart and other vital organs next lose their powers. Finally the dimly glowing filament which is the individual himself fades into the darkness of death, and only the cold and empty shell of what he was remains.

This is briefly the sad experience through which every human being seems compelled to go. Yet Nature teaches us an entirely different story. Animals and birds, especially wild ones, do not lose their powers with advancing age. On the contrary they grow bigger, stronger and more beautiful almost to the end of their lives. Especially is this true of reptiles. Turtles and crocodiles are credited with a length of life extending over several centuries, as are also quite a number of larger species of fish and other sea animals. It is only when they have reached the so-called limit of their individual lives that they suddenly cease to develop, grow old very rapidly and die without going through that human experience of losing one's qualities and forces gradually from middle life onward.

In the vegetable kingdom this process of continual growth and unfoldment is even more clearly exemplified.

For instance trees, such as the giant Sequoias of California and the Western United States, are often many thousands of years old, but they do not give an impression of age. The impulse is always to refer to them as big trees, because their size and strength are what strikes the eye, not their age. Yet through slow centuries they have been steadily gathering to themselves the power to achieve that growth, and in their present massiveness are proofs of an unfaltering progress in the face of every obstacle, over every danger, through all limitations to an ultimate and glorious Success.

Are human beings inferior to trees? Is their latent fund of infinitely richer qualities and more varied possibilities unable to accomplish for them what an insensate piece of wood can do for itself? If a tree, an alligator, an elephant can progressively overcome outside destructive influences almost until the end of their lives, can we not do as well? Certainly we can, once we understand how.

Eliminate Fear and you vanquish Old Age. Fear is the drug which not only paralyses the expression of those positive qualities so vital for the preservation of Youth, but it also contracts and numbs every nerve and_ cell and tissue. It is a blight which withers everything it touches, cutting the individual off more and more from his contact with that life-giving Power in whose energizing current alone Youth and Strength are to be found.

Change your ways of thinking and feeling from the negative to the positive, not by a tensing exertion of will power, but through calm relaxation and a serene consciousness of your One-ness with Universal Life Energy. Abandon Worry, which is one of the most powerful disintegrating factors in the whole catalogue of negative forces. If you start right causes to the best of your ability, right effects will eventually result. Worry will not alter those effects to come in the slightest, and will very decidedly hamper you in starting more right causes now. It puts you out of joint physically, mentally and spiritually, so that those three parts of your being are no longer able to work in a correlative and harmonious manner for the expression of their activities.

Thoughts of Hatred, Jealousy and all kindred negative emotions are the implacable foes of Beauty and Youth. They are like a corrosive acid, which harms those at whom it is thrown but harms those who throw it infinitely more. Nothing so quickly scorches away the bloom of youth, and no disfigurement is so repulsive as that which it produces when it has eaten through the containing walls of flesh around it.

Love, the single antidote for every destructive thought and passion, not only heals the wounds inflicted by them, but opens the individual to the purging flow of that Great Power which alone can make him immune to them forever more. All channels, physical, mental and spiritual, which have shrunk under the bitter lash of negative thoughts and emotions until -they are-tightly closed, relax again at the vivifying caress of Love.

If you want to be always young and strong, give the positive thoughts and emotions an opportunity to help you. Preserve a loving, optimistic and joyful attitude towards life, taking it neither too lightly nor too seriously. Thereby you will attain a poise impregnable to every destructive influence and will arrest the advance of age. Nature, working normally through you as through the rest of Creation, will develop an ever finer instrument for your expression, so that you will become stronger and more harmonious in body, broader and nobler in mind, richer in spirit, until your Evolution on this plane is completed and you are ready to go on.

Old Age can and eventually will be completely overcome by those who will conscientiously and persistently put into practical application in their daily lives these Principles of Nature. This Lesson, explaining those Principles, is designed for the express purpose of enabling you to solve that problem, and the Exercises appended to it will help you to the right path by which to achieve that natural victory.

EXERCISES TO LESSON NINE

Continue as usual morning and evening the Star Exercise, also Relaxation, Silence and the Mental Contact with Universal Life Energy. Then, by means of the new Exercise described below, direct the main currant of that Force to those centres within you which govern Strength and Youth. This Exercise is called REJUVENATION, and is performed as follows:

During the Silence, while contacting Universal Life Energy, think of that Power as rising upward from your Solar Plexus, through the spinal cord into your brain, flooding every portion of it, invigorating and stimulating every centre, cell and gland. Think of It specifically as flowing to your eyes, your centres of hearing, etc., in turn. By mentally contacting a particular organ or part of your body you open the nerve channels within you which control that part to the vivifying flow of Universal Life Energy, so that the Force is for the time being concentrated more strongly there. It is the entering wedge, in a way, that pries open the narrow mouth of the centre which feeds an organ a little wider to the Supply that seeks entrance.

As the process starts from the centre and proceeds outwards, a more or less logical sequence ought to be observed in directing the Life Current. Send It first to the inner vital organs, which are nearest to the source of that flow and therefore the first in Its path. Think of It as filling the heart, spilling from there into the lungs, brimming over into the kidneys, spreading to the liver, stomach, limbs, feet, arms, hands, muscles, tissues, teeth, hair and last of all the skin. Feel it like a steady rush of wind blowing out through the pores of your skin, just as air exhaled from your lungs issues from the nostrils. And above all remember not to use will power, since the successful performance of this Exercise, like all others based on Universal Life Energy, depends primarily on Relaxation.

As the skin is the first to show the marks of Old Age, so it will be the last to lose them. REJUVENATION takes place first within, through the gradual elimination of outworn cells and tissues in favour of new and healthy ones. You will feel the change long before you will see it. As your inner organs are refreshed you will notice a sense of buoyancy and strength stealing through you like a clear stream through stagnant waters. You will take more interest in life and in your surroundings, and will be alert and responsive where before you were indifferent. Eventually every cell and fibre of your body, in muscles, bones and nerves, will be replaced and you will have been literally made over after a new, younger and better pattern.

The process reaches completion when your skin undergoes that alteration, the wrinkles melting away and a firm, harmonious contour of the features emerging to reflect accurately your changed attitude. Youth will glow again from beneath the grey ashes of years, and this time will abide with you as long as you consciously keep bright and warm the flame which before you permitted to grow dim because of lack of knowledge how to feed it.

QUESTIONS TO LESSON NINE

1. What is Health?

2. How is it related to the progress of Humanity?

3. What is the keystone of Health?

4. To what specific bodily condition are most physical troubles due?

5. How can those troubles be eliminated?

6. Should will power be used in that elimination?

7. What is Magnetic Chemicalization?

8. What is Old Age?

9. What kinds of causes are responsible for Old Age?

10. To what fundamental cause can all others be traced?

11. To what part of our triune nature is Old Age restricted?

12. How can Old Age be overcome?

Lesson Nine

ANSWERS TO LESSON NINE

1. Health is:

The efficient outward manifestation through the body of harmonious inner activities.

2. Health is related to the progress of humanity:

In that, as Humanity is the sum of the individuals comprising it, the vigour and progress of a Race or Nation as a whole depends directly on the vigour and progress of every one of its members.

3. The keystone of Health is:

A balanced development of all faculties.

4. The specific bodily condition to which most physical troubles are due is:

Congestion, local or general.

5. These troubles can be eliminated:

By dispelling through the use of Universal Life Energy the congestion which causes them.

6. Will Power:

Should not be used in that elimination, since will power necessitates a tense effort which contracts the channels for contacting Universal Life Energy.

7. **Magnetic Chemicalization is:**

The expulsion to the surface of an inner unhealthy condition, resulting in an intensified expression of the trouble for the time being.

8. **Old Age is:**

The encroachment on the body tissues of inside and outside disintegrating influences.

9. **The kinds of causes for Old Age are:**

(1) Mental, such as fear, worry, hatred, jealousy and all other negative thoughts and emotions.

(2) Physical, such as overwork, malnutrition, abuses and unfavourable environment.

10. **The fundamental cause to which all others can be traced is:**

Fear.

11. **Old Age is restricted:**

To the physical part of our triune nature.

12. Old Age can be overcome:

By consciously restoring the free contact with Universal Life Energy and thereby developing a fresh, wholesome and evenly balanced instrument for the expression of the qualities of the individual, particularly Youth.

Dear Friend:

In this Lesson you step from the Physical to the Mental Plane, where you will view the still greater wonders wrought by the use of Universal Life Energy in the limitless realm of Mind.

The creative part of our nature resides in Mind. Therefore in Mind are struck out first the lines of our respective lives. Whether those lines will be broad and daring in scope, firm in execution on the plane of our physical existence, ambitious in extent, depends upon. how well we coordinate them with material fact through the use of Universal Life Energy. The dreamer sees far, yet the dreamer is useless unless united with the doer. In Imagination is charted first the road that creeps persistently onward into the Unknown: but the Builder of that road is the one who actually thrusts back the bounds of our limited understanding and leads us into broader fields of Progress and Achievement. We must be both Dreamer and Builder.

The Science of Mind is a great Science, breath-taking in the horizonless vistas which it opens to those who even venture along its edge. It supplies a Knowledge by which you can bridge the gulf of human limitations separating you from your desires.

It provides a Power which, when properly used, constructs this bridge and brings you across it to that independence of thought and vigour of action which are the dominant qualities of a Master Mind.

Cordially yours,
Eugene Fersen.

LESSON TEN

MIND endows you with that sublime power not only to think and to know, but what is still more valuable, to be conscious of through Reason. You are conscious of your own existence and of all that is around you through the mental part of your being; thus Mind is the foundation of your active life on the Physical Plane, as well as the adjusting medium which determines your relations to the world in which you move. Therefore in order to make Mind serve you to the best advantage, it is first necessary to have a clear understanding of its nature, functions and method of expression through your body.

Mind is not produced from within the individual. On the contrary, the individual is produced by Mind. You are born simply with the faculty to think — that is, to transmit Mind currents — just as a lens has the faculty to transmit sunlight. Only Mind, the medium through which Soul manifests itself, creates its own lens for its expression on a lower plane, and that lens is your physical body.

The actual mental self behind that physical expression is but a single ray from one common independent Source, a basic Power which is one of the Aspects of Universal Life Energy and which is called Universal Intelligence, or Infinite Mind. This Infinite Intelligence contains all knowledge, all activities, all possibilities pertaining to Mind, harmoniously blended into One just as all the colours of the spectrum are blended into the one white light of the sun.

Like a central mental sun also it sends forth an infinite number of individual rays, or minds, each of which partakes of all the qualities of its Source; and these individual rays, passing through us into expression on the plane of our mental existence, are what we know as our human minds.

As Universal Intelligence has for its fundamental principle complete Unity, its expression in Cosmic Consciousness is based on complete Unity also. Our human minds, proceeding from Universal Intelligence, originally possessed that individual Unity. But now, in our present state of consciousness, where everything appears to us in a threefold aspect, the single undifferentiated ray of our mind also enters our perception split into three distinct parts, known to us respectively as Superconsciousness, Consciousness or Self-consciousness, and Subconsciousness.

Superconsciousness, the unbroken ray connecting us with Universal Intelligence, has in the brain, like every mental quality, a particular organ through which it expresses itself. This organ, the physical counterpart of Superconsciousness, is located near the base of the brain and is called the Pineal Gland.

Messages received through the Pineal Gland are of a rare and perfect nature. They are known as "Inspiration," and are conveyed directly to our consciousness without having to go through the mechanical process of reasoning. If we could register all these Inspirational Messages consciously, our Unity with Universal Intelligence would be re-established and we could then dispense entirely with reasoning. We would be omniscient. Yet because of the disturbed condition, or coarseness, of the second part of our mental trinity, we are unable to do this.

Selfconsciousness, the second of our three mental conditions, is the faculty we possess of being conscious of our own existence. It is to us what the electric light bulb is to an electrical circuit—the point where the invisible currents poured into it from our other mental states glow into visible being, illumining for us the world in which we live. Because of it we are able to say, "I am conscious of myself, therefore I know that I am." Thus it is the seat of our most precious and brilliant mental quality, the one which enables us not only to reason logically, but to be also aware of that process of reasoning, and which we call the Reason, or Rational Mind.

Also, in Selfconsciousness resides the power by which we bring that light of Reason into clear focus and hold it steadily to the purpose toward which it tends. This power we term the Will and it, together with the Rational Mind which it sustains and directs, is one of our most valuable mental assets.

Selfconsciousness has also in the brain its own physical organ for expression, comparable to the filament in the light mentioned above. This organ, called the Pituitary Body, or Telepathic Apparatus, is located at the front of the brain, and its function is to send out and receive mental vibrations in the form Commonly called thoughts. It is what enables us to communicate telepathically with our fellow beings and also very frequently to "sense" impending conditions before they actually enter rational perception.

Subconsciousness, the third member of our Triune mental nature, is the vast mental field where all thoughts, good and evil, are planted and flourish side by side until they ripen to the day of mental harvest, which is our consciousness of their actual existence. All acquired knowledge, all vagaries of thought or fancy, all things that once enter even remotely into our experience, sink into the fertile ground of this great farm of our mind, there to grow intermingled, like the wheat and the tares, till the time when they can be assorted and disposed of according to their natures. Upon the care with which this assorting is done depends primarily the quality of the crop, or record of the conscious, active life of accomplishment and endeavour of each of us.

The physical organ of Subsconsciousness is the back part of our brain and the Solar Plexus, sometimes referred to as the Abdominal Brain. The two are directly connected through the Spinal Cord, and they communicate with our Conscious Self by the process called Memory. As all impressions are stored in the Subconsciousness, it becomes in a way a Hall of Records from which almost any desired information can be obtained through the proper exercise of this Memory process.

Mind as a whole, therefore, while it is intimately connected with the brain, is not actually in it. Your brain is but the physical outgrowth, the embodiment in material flesh, of the activities of your mind; yet your mind itself is an aspect of that highest part of your triune nature, called the Soul. Each quality of the Soul, acting through Mind, constructs its own physical organ through which to find expression on the Physical Plane; all those organs together constitute the body, or outlined activities of the entire Soul; the brain, that infinitely complex and delicate instrument, with its various lobes and centres, its thousands of convolutions and millions of cells, is the wonderful unit which your Mind has built among that assortment of specialized units for the expression of its own activities alone.

Yet ideas, originating first in Mind, require a definite working power to carry them into expression through this material brain. Such power. Universal Life Energy supplies in the purely physical form of the life force of your body. That life force, flowing from its storage place in the Solar Plexus, through the spinal cord to the brain, causes it to function much as steam or electricity engine to function. Only in the brain each centre is like a tiny separate engine, to which the driving power must be distributed in proportion to its need or capacity to use it.

There is another difference, also. The life current, besides driving the engine, in addition acts as the vehicle which carries to that engine what is to pass through it. Ideas which Mind wishes to deliver to our Consciousness are impressed, as it were, into the vibratory current of life force, and are then borne by it into conscious expression through the various centres best adapted for giving passage to them.

Which centres these are is determined by the rate of vibration peculiar to each different idea. Just as the vibrations of a single note on a musical instrument may be caught up and transmitted by any material object that happens to be in tune with it, so every individual idea arouses a sympathetic response from the proper channel for its transmission in the brain.

Once ideas are thus attracted to their respective brain centres, they are there transformed into the corresponding mental currents and sent in that new form through the brain nerves to the common focal point from which eventually they must all emerge. This focal point, the organ of our Self consciousness, is called the Pituitary Body or Telepathic Apparatus, and is situated in the front part of the brain, back of the root of the nose, securely encased in a bony socket of its own a skull within a skull.

The Pituitary Body is at once one of the most fascinating, important and perhaps least known units of our physical equipment. It is one of the ductless glands mentioned in the previous Lesson, and few if any of our organs are so carefully fortified against accident or injury. There is good reason for this, as any injury to it means certain death.

Some of its functions, which are many and varied, were known thousands of years ago to the ancients, who called it the "Third Eye," the "Eye of Siva" (Mind), or the "Bump of Wisdom." That knowledge, practically lost in the passage of centuries, has only lately been re-discovered by Science, and is now brought forward as the most recent and valuable contribution to the comparatively new Science of Mind.

The Pituitary Body consists of two lobes, an anterior Or frontal lobe and a posterior or back lobe. Each of these lobes has its own special field of activity with respect to your physical body, as well as its cooperative work on the Mental Plane. In its physical department the anterior lobe, for instance, small as it is, governs the bony growth of the body, while the larger posterior lobe determines how finely organized that body may be. Those who have the anterior lobe better developed are generally very robust and hearty, while those who have the posterior lobe better developed are of a more delicate and sensitive nature, both physically and mentally.

Another physical activity of the Pituitary Body is to condense the pure vibratory life current flowing into it from the spinal cord into a fluid secretion which it sends directly into the blood stream. This fluid, circulating through the brain, stimulates and regulates its functioning. Because of this the Pituitary Body is often called the Key of Intelligence, as its proper activity determines the ability of the brain to do mental work.

Mentally, the function of the Pituitary Body is to receive and project mental vibrations, commonly called thoughts. It is the Telepathic Apparatus through which the mental vibrations sent to it from the brain centres pass out of your body. That is, it exactly repeats, on a lower octave which is within the scope of our understanding, the quick theme of ideas which is being continually improvised on the loftier scale of Mind.

The operation of the Pituitary Body in this double role as the Open Door through which all mental vibrations from within pass out, and all mental vibrations from outside come in, makes every human being the most wonderful Mental Radio that can be conceived. There is no mechanical device, even in this era of electrical marvels, that remotely compares with your own natural apparatus, for there is no mechanical device that can ever approach the power, sensitiveness and diversity of the living Human Radio. Yet in order to bring out that potential effectiveness within, the individual must conform to certain Natural Laws which govern mental vibrations, like all others.

As explained previously, the mental current, conveyed through the brain nerves to the PITUITARY BODY, is projected from it into space as mental vibrations, or thoughts. These thought vibrations, proceeding in obedience to distinct Physical Laws, spread outward from their source in all directions, exactly like light, sound, heat or any other vibrations. Therefore naturally, the further they go the weaker they become, losing power in direct ratio to the distance they have to travel. This loss of power by ordinary thought vibrations is why they are so difficult to transmit at long range. When they reach their objective, the Telepathic Apparatus of the one who is to receive them, they are too feeble and diffused to make a perceptible impression.

Yet by taking' intelligent advantage of those same Physical Laws which govern all vibrations this difficulty can be overcome. Thought vibrations can be concentrated into a single ray and directed at will, just as light or sound vibrations con be concentrated and focussed.

For instance, in order to project light vibrations at a distance, all that is necessary is to place behind the light a reflector to throw all the rays forward, and in front of it a lens to gather those reflected rays together. Thus all the power of the light will be concentrated at one point, and can be turned in any direction desired.

Precisely the same method is to be used to direct mental vibrations, with the sole difference that, instead of mechanical devices, the physical apparatus, or Mental Radio of the individual, is to be employed in the capacity of reflector and lens.

Through will power the function of the Pituitary Body, or Telepathic Apparatus, can be modified and emphasized as follows: Its back lobe can be made to act as a reflector for the projected thought vibrations, and the front lobe can be made to serve as a lens which will concentrate in one point the vibrations already collected and directed through it by that reflector. In this way the sum-mum of power and efficiency can be obtained from a thought, not by abusing the uses of Telepathic Apparatus, but by accentuating the purpose for which its structural design adapts it.

The exercise of the will to focus thought vibrations in this manner is called Concentration. Obviously those who have learned how to perform that Concentration have acquired a power which amounts to mental mastery, for they can then consciously reinforce and direct their thought in a way that will make it efficient to the highest degree. Yet in order to attain that desirable result, it is necessary to develop one other faculty without which successful Concentration is impossible, namely — Attention.

Attention is the ability to take accurate mental note of whatever comes within range of your perception. It means to have the Mind arrested and drawn by immediate - interest to anything it may contact, either directly or through the medium of the senses. The more attentive you can be in general to the world about you, the more alert you are to perceive and appraise things exactly, while the more attentive you can be to your own present concern in particular, the more power you are able to pour into that to the exclusion of all else.

When the lines of our attention are dimmed and blurred, every irrelevant thing constitutes a leak which drains away a certain amount of the energy that ought to go into the matter in hand. But when those lines are sharp and cleanly cut, everything promptly stands out in clear relief. Such Attention, applied to one thing, focuses all our energies on that thing instead of letting it seep away in a thousand different and unrelated directions.

Thus Attention is really the factor which determines how much power we are able to put into the projected thought, Our Will, through which we adjust our Telepathic Apparatus, works effectively only in proportion as interest holds our attention to what we wish to do. It is "geared" to Attention, so to say, and will enable us to produce a strong, concentrated ray of mental vibrations only as our attention itself is strong and concentrated.

Therefore each step in that procession leading up to efficient Mental Radio is dependent on its predecessor, and a flaw in one will continue through all the rest until. it emerges in the final result. So in order to enable you to control your thought vibrations completely, the Exercises for this Lesson will be for the development of the faculties which will give you that control, and which are called CONCENTRATION and ATTENTION.

EXERCISES TO LESSON TEN

The Exercises you learned in Part One of this Course have been designed to serve as the foundation for other Exercises of a more specialized nature. Therefore continue as before with the Star Exercise morning and evening, Relaxation, Silence, and the Mental Contact with Universal Life Energy. To these you will add this week two new Exercises, the first of the mental group, called ATTENTION and CONCENTRATION.

ATTENTION is developed by arousing and putting in order all your perceptive faculties. Everything about you holds its message, has a special significance with relation to other things or to yourself. In the measure that you are alert to fathom that message you will take an interest in the thing, and the more interest you take the more attentive you will be.

Try always to get a quick but complete understanding of whatever you may encounter through any of your senses. Determine in a few moments, if possible, its form, size, colour and general appearance, and then, penetrating deeper, try to discover what it stands for.

The more you practice this, the more sensitive you will become to the deeper meanings of things that before were meaningless. You will perceive and take advantage of opportunities which present themselves in your life, because you will be able to see just where otherwise insignificant events are leading. Your mind will be stimulated and clarified, your mental vision sharpened. You will find yourself thinking directly and truly, picking out your objective without hesitation or loss of time, and -striking for it confidently. And the reason will be that, by developing Attention, you have made possible the realization of that other priceless quality, the Key to all mental power—CONCENTRATION.

CONCENTRATION demands, in the beginning, at least, complete solitude for its proper performance. Choose a time and place where for ten or fifteen minutes you can remain absolutely undisturbed. There should be no distracting circumstances; the room should be quiet, comfortable, and in a subdued light.

Having established yourself in such favourable conditions, choose a mental concept of some material object of a pleasant nature—for instance, a flower—and concentrate your thoughts on it. You will notice that your mind continually wanders away from that concept of a flower, turning in almost any direction except the one you have set for it. By an effort of will power you can bring it back time after time, until finally it will stay fixed where you want it.

After you have achieved this much, try to summon up in your mind a strong, clear picture of that flower. Make it so vivid that it becomes real to you, affecting even your sensory nerves with an imagined fragrance. Then it becomes an actuality to you, and when you have done this you can say that you have done good CONCENTRATION WORK.

In choosing some concept for CONCENTRATION practice, select one of a concrete object instead of an abstract one, because it is much easier to concentrate on a thing which is perceptible to the other senses as well as to Mind. Also choose a different object each time, in order that you may develop the mental plasticity in keeping with mental strength.

CONCENTRATION is one of the most difficult and important of all mental exercises, because it requires coordinated energy, will power and perseverance in order to produce effective results.

Those three qualities are seldom found properly balanced in one individual; but as Universal Life Energy is the Fundamental Power back of them, you can bring them into the balanced relation necessary by contacting and using that harmonizing Force. Once they are coordinated and strengthened, CONCENTRATION becomes an easy task which will no longer need complete privacy and special circumstances for its performance. You can then dominate your surroundings instead of being influenced by them, and can focus your thoughts instantaneously at will, under all conditions.

QUESTIONS TO LESSON TEN

1. What and where is Universal Mind?

2. What is Cosmic Consciousness?

3. What is the individual mind?

4. How does the single individual mind express itself?

5. What is Superconsciousness?

6. What is Self-consciousness?

7. What is Subconsciousness?

8. What are the physical organs respectively through which these three aspects of Mind express themselves?

9. Where do ideas originate and how are they conveyed into our Consciousness?

10. What is thought?

11. What is Attention?

12. What is Mental Concentration?

ANSWERS TO LESSON TEN

1. **Universal Mind is:**

An Intelligent, Conscious, Creative and Eternal Power, one of the Aspects of Universal Life Energy, and is all pervading.

2. **Cosmic Consciousness is:**

The Self Consciousness of Universal Mind Itself.

3. **The individual mind is:**

A single one of the countless rays or projections proceeding from Universal Mind.

4. **The single individual mind expresses itself:**

In three distinct aspects into which it is broken by our present Triune State of Consciousness, and which are called Superconsciousness, Selfconsciousness and Subconsciousness.

5. **Superconsciousness is:**

Our higher mental self, the undifferentiated individual Ray proceeding from Universal Mind and reaching our Conscious Self through Intuition.

6. **Selfconsciousness is:**

That aspect of our individual mind through which we perceive, discriminate and live consciously, and which is the seat of our Reason and Will.

7. **Subconsciousness is:**

The undiscriminating, retentive and generative part of our mind, in which all impressions are stored and which communicates with Selfconsciousness through Memory.

8. **The physical organs respectively through which these three aspects of our mind express themselves are:**

(1) Superconsciousness — the Pineal Gland.

(2) Selfconsciousness — the Pituitary Body.

(3) Subconsciousness — the back part of the brain and the Solar Plexus.

9. **Ideas:**

Originate in mind, and are conveyed into our Consciousness through the brain centres best attuned to their rates of vibration.

10. Thought is:

(1) Ordinary — mental vibrations projected into space through the Pituitary Body, but not consciously controlled or directed.

(2) Concentrated — ordinary thought vibrations focused and directed by a conscious effort of Will.

11. Attention is:

Sustained alertness and sensibility to all impressions, induced in our Conscious Self by interest.

12. Mental Concentration is:

Modifying the action of the Pituitary Body by Will Power so that the ordinary thought vibrations passing through it are gathered together and focused into one point.

Dear Friend:

This Lesson will be to you the rift in that cloud of mystery which has always enveloped the workings of your Subconsciousness. It will open to you a broad vista of all the limitless resources within you, of all the-prodigal- treasures of human thought and experience there awaiting your command, and behind that still the golden gleam of perfect qualities and powers untainted by the touch of the humanly Conscious Self.

You will learn how you are daily sowing the seeds of your own future in the Subconscious fields of your nature, and how the experiences you reap in the course of your Conscious existence are not the whims of some fickle Goddess of Chance, but the inevitable fruit of your own thoughts and activities. You are the creator of your own Destiny, and it is only because you work blindly, with no knowledge of the end you shape, that you subject yourself to errors and misfortunes which prompt you to believe yourself the victim of a Providence that you cannot sway or alter.

You are the victim of no one but yourself. It is in your power to sow within you the seeds of whatever success your ambition may decree, and to realize that Success on the Plane of your Physical existence.

In these pages will be revealed to you the means whereby you can accomplish this, and by which you will be able, through channels which you yourself will provide, to coin into material fact all that other hidden mental wealth now latent and waiting only the right opportunity to break out into abundant expression in your life.

Cordially yours,
Eugene Fersen.

LESSON ELEVEN

SUBCONSCIOUSNESS, very often erroneously called the subconscious mind, is a condition that was created by the Conscious Self through the breaking up of the original Mind Ray. It is now that third part of your mental trinity which is, as the name indicates, below the conscious state. Its function is to accept whatever comes into it by way of the Conscious Self and from it to manufacture the-substance of most of your rational thought. In addition to this it also acts as a vehicle in which you carry the record of all human thought and experience, from your first ancestor down to his latest representative, yourself.

Most distinctive among the powers of the Subconsciousness is its ability to receive and retain everything that comes to it through the Conscious Self. Anything that once enters the field of your conscious experience, whether from Mind itself or by way of the Physical senses, is deposited in this great catch-basin of your mental nature. Nothing is ever rejected, nothing ever lost. All thoughts, all impressions, good and evil, ugly and beautiful, are accepted impartially and, after having been acted upon by the second of your Subconscious qualities, are laid away as a part of the imperishable record to be handed on by you to your descendants.

The second and most immediately important of the qualities of Subconsciousness, at least so far as your present conscious existence is concerned, is its power to increase thought. This power is called Imagination. Your

Subconscious self is not aware of that particular process of thinking, just as the ground is not aware of its activity in making seeds grow, but its abundant productive forces express themselves none the less. Yet these productive forces, while they can increase and propagate to a remarkable degree any mental matter sent down to them, are not able to create that matter themselves. Original thought is a much rarer and more precious commodity, the gift of Inspiration; but Subconscious thought is the less perfect product of something that has been admitted first by the humanly Conscious Self. This product is what ripens back into your perception as conscious rational thought.

The seeds which your Conscious Self admits to this fertile soil of your Subconscious nature are the thoughts and impressions that pass through it in the form of vibrations. You are aware of only a very few of these thought seeds because only those vibrations which proceed from your own mind activity and from your immediate surroundings are strong enough to enter your perception. Yet together with them is the vanishing flash and sparkle of an immeasurable stream from the whole world of vibrations, momently glowing across the field of your Consciousness and plunging on into the dark night of forgetfulness which separates you from your Subconscious state. Each will take root and flourish, and later will have its influence in your conscious life, but none will be traceable back to any remembrance of their entrance through your Conscious Self.

Your Subconsciousness, therefore, is a distinctly human-creation, limited by the bounds of human experience, and possessing a double function with relation to you in particular and to Mankind in general. Through your conscious state it taps the entire world of present human thoughts and activities, as well as your own, and from what it receives in this way it develops the mental matter which you harvest as rational thought. Then it perpetuates this mental growth in exact detail, like ancient forests which are sometimes found perpetuated in the rock strata of their period, and thus adds the pattern both of your own life and of the time in which you live to its preserved record of those countless ages of human existence from which you have emerged.

The interrelation of these two functions of your Subconscious Self, further complicated by the reaction with your Selfconsciousness, makes that part of your mind nature one of the most bewildering, illogical and difficult of all to understand. It is a seemingly hopeless tangle of good and bad, right and wrong, destructive and helpful, sprouting forth without any apparent reason and stubbornly opposed to any, direct control.

The fact that good does thus alternate with bad fosters the mistaken belief that Subconsciousness is the fount of all knowledge and is directly connected with Cosmic Consciousness. However, this is not the case.

Cosmic Consciousness is the pure Source of all Perfection, and all Knowledge stored in it is Perfect also. No evil or disharmonious thoughts can ever proceed from It, or from Its direct manifestation, Superconsciousness, because evil has its origin only in that lower part of your mental nature, the humanly Conscious Self. Therefore, whatever knowledge you receive from Superconsciousness through Inspiration is Perfect Knowledge and can be relied on absolutely.

Subconsciousness, on the other hand, while it still possesses latent within it all the perfect qualities of the Super-conscious Ray from which your Conscious Self cut it off, is also the receptacle into which Self consciousness has emptied all the human evil as well as all the human good of its experience. This superimposed mass of human mental matter, good and bad, all thrown together and silted down permanently on the floor of your Subconscious state, is what comprises the Subconsciousness you know, and not those perfect and infallible qualities beneath it of which you have had no experience. For this reason your Subconscious self, the imperfect product of human manufacture, has certain limitations and disadvantages.

The most prominent of these is that Subconsciousness does not possess the power of discrimination, as does the Conscious state. It takes in, rears and preserves indiscriminately whatever falls on its surface, just as the ground takes in and rears good and bad seed alike. Therefore wrong thought seeds which are admitted to that Subconscious soil receive the same care and nourishment as the good ones; like the tares among the wheat, they are given an equal growth with it and they ripen to produce wrong thinking in you just as right thought seeds produce right thinking.

That is why any direct control of Subconsciousness is so difficult, because whatever once gets into it will increase and bear fruit and be recorded as a part of the permanent record within you in spite of yourself, as it has always done. Yet from outside and above that range of activity you are still able to exercise a very effective control.

Evil has its origin in the humanly Conscious Self, and that same humanly .Conscious Self is also able to reject and destroy the very evil to which it is giving birth. The faculty which gives it this authority over its own wrong is the power of discrimination which it possesses. The Conscious Self is able to distinguish between right and wrong, good and bad, constructive and destructive, and to bar from the individual's Subconsciousness what it perceives to be undesirable. Thus evil, which is the perversion of good by that imperfect human member of our mind trinity, is able to gain admission to the Subconscious mental field only through the weakness or negligence of the Conscious Self.

The trouble with this faculty of conscious selection is its limited application. Through it you are able to determine in some measure the nature and direction of your own mortal career, because it enables you to determine the kind of thought seeds that shall be planted to grow out into your conscious rational thought. But all the wrong and destructive matter poured into your Subconsciousness by the Humanity of all preceding ages, preserved and perpetuated there as a part of your legacy from the past, is left untouched and still rebellious under the thin shell of positive thought which you lay down over it.

Therefore, the very ground out of which your own rational thought must grow is really a gigantic graveyard of all that endless throng of predecessors from whose lost life threads your own is spun. The good and the bad, the right and the wrong, the statesman, adventurer, rogue, genius and thief, all sorts and conditions of men and women with all that went to make them what they were, sleep there in solemn tier upon tier, like mummies under the Egyptian sands. But theirs is an uneasy slumber, for unlike mummies, they refuse to stay decently dead.

When the ghost of one of these departed ancestor's walks in our own conscious life, we very often call it an instinct. If it is an unusually good instinct, we are prone to associate it with Inspiration and call it Genius; if it is a bad instinct we are very apt to excuse ourselves on the ground that we are helpless victims of heredity. Neither is exactly true, for before any ghost in the whole interminable collection can rear its head, it must first be roused by our Conscious Self.

The Conscious Self admits the seed whose roots prick that drowning spectre into action. This is not a haphazard process, but one so exactly regulated that each seed seeks unerringly the buried individual in you whose essence renders it most congenial to the elements demanding growth. Through vibration the proper affinity is established, and the evil seed thrusts its tendrils into the soil whose nature makes it most fertile for that particular brand of evil, just as the constructive seed tends toward the soil which takes its flavour from a correspondingly good individual reposing in it.

Thus all the world of human experience is lying in wait to have its influence in your rational life, and because you do not exercise discrimination it secures opportunities to vent the latent wrong in it as well as the right. You never know which of those wraiths out of the past is going to bubble up in the sap of your mental vegetation and emerge once again into your conscious experience, so you regard your Subconsciousness as an unruly, treacherous, rebellious servant, as indeed it is if you permit it to be. In proporti9n as you admit to it the elements of perversity and arrogance you resign your authority over it, but the fault is exclusively your own. When you subject it to the firm and intelligent control it needs you will find it only too ready to serve you.

You have, therefore, a double problem to face—first, to prevent more evil from entering into your Subconscious soil and growing out to poison your immediate rational life, and second, to clear away that almost illimitable rubbish heap of wrong and destructive thought which has been imposed upon you by the whole erroneous thinking of all Humanity, from the beginning until now. There are two ways to meet this problem, one limited and painfully inadequate so far as the main solution is concerned, but effective in its application to your present conscious existence, and the other of a scope and power that knows no bounds and admits no failure in any department of the Subconscious field.

The first of these methods, concerning chiefly the quick growth and exchange between Subconsciousness and the Conscious Self, is the positive realization of constructive thought matter and the conscious selection of the mental seeds that shall go to make up the crop of your future rational thought. This realization and selection is exercised with the help of one of your human conscious faculties, the Will, and is therefore as limited, and fallible as that very human attribute is apt to be. Yet used as it is best adapted to be used, for the barring out of negative thought vibrations and the larger admission of positive ones, it becomes actually the means whereby you can change the colour of your whole present existence and really determine your own Destiny in this life.

The instruments which make this method possible are certain Mental Laws. On the Mental Plane negation of anything means its destruction, while realization of a thing means its creation. Therefore, if you keep yourself mentally alert, through the use of your Will, to stand guard at the door of your Conscious Self and destroy through negation all the negative thought matter which seeks entrance mingled with the good, you have started a weeding out process which will show results in the crop of positive thoughts to come.

When you have cleared the ground, so to speak, in this way, your real constructive work is to think as many positive thoughts as you can. in the activity of mind, one positive thought is the equal of one negative thought, in the sense that the positive represents a unit of constructive power which can destroy a single unit of negative power. Therefore, for every positive thought which enters your Subconscious field one negative thought is eliminated entirely from it, and in the ratio that more positive than negative thoughts are admitted your conscious harvest will be constructive or feeble.

Yet this process, thrown into tiny relief against the gigantic mass of wrong and destruction heaped clown on us by all Mankind through the uncounted centuries of its existence, reveals how utterly hopeless and beyond the remotest possibility of accomplishment the correction of all that evil would be if we had to depend on our own limited human forces. No amount of positive realization that the Conscious Self of any individual could ever be capable of producing would suffice to gnaw away even a perceptible fraction of that ponderous bulk of wrong, for no individual can hope to combat singly the resistless tide of all the ages of wrong thinking, driven on by the weight of all races and all people whose lives their minutes have measured. Therefore, if you can ever aspire to sift the treasure from that topless mountain of human experience, you need to wield a tool vastly more sure and powerful than any the faltering human mind can provide.

This tool is supplied by Universal Life Energy, whose use constitutes the second and by far more comprehensive method of purifying your Subconscious self. Universal Life Energy is the one saving Ray of Hope for Mankind in that great task, because it is both the one Perfect and Uncorrupted Power to which no Plane of our being can deny admission, and the one whose constructive and harmonizing Force no negative power is able to withstand. It is the stuff of which everything is made, and to which everything must eventually yield, and in its action is as sweeping as our conscious human forces are limited. Where negation destroys one negative thought, Universal Life Energy at a touch explodes millions, and on its larger scale accomplishes for the entire field of Subconsciousness what negation only imperfectly achieves in one small department of it.

Every time you contact Universal Life Energy, you admit It not only to your physical body, but to the Plane of your Mind as well. There It sinks into and permeates not only the active surface growth and exchange from which your conscious life derives its existence, but also the whole buried field of all preserved thoughts and experiences from which the countless lives of the whole human kind were once made up. Nothing is immune to Its healing touch, and nothing negative is able to escape or withstand the constructive power of Its flow. Just as It corrects and eliminates imperfections on the Physical Plane, so It wipes out on the Mental Plane the flaws of which they are most frequently the reflection.

The organ of your Subconsciousness, as explained in the Tenth Lesson, is the back part of your brain and the Solar Plexus, or Abdominal Brain. That is the seat in you of the Subconscious mind condition which effervesces into the matter of your rational thought, and which holds in its depths all the immeasurable ill and good, the positive and the destructive, the woe and joy and hate and love that has been ground out as the fabric of conscious human life during all the ages of mortal existence. From that sodden mountain you must let the cleansing current of Life Force wash clear the veined gold of positive thought that laces its sombre mass, and by so doing you will not only benefit yourself, but will help Mankind a little nearer to the realization of what its problem is to realize in this human phase of its evolution—the fundamental perfection of the Subconscious self.

That perfection, latent in Subconsciousness since the time when it was first split off from the Perfect Mind Ray, waits only for a way to be broken for it through the successive crusts of imperfect human thought and experience which the Conscious Self has laid down over it. Your task is to open that way by eliminating consciously, with the help of Universal Life Energy, all those negative crusts, and thus to bring the good walled up in your Subconsciousness into expression.

By filling your Solar Plexus, the organ of your Subconsciousness, with the energizing flow of Life Force, you will be able to accomplish this. It will not only destroy those monsters conjured up by the perverted activity of the human consciousness and set to guard jealously the inner treasures of your heart, but It will enrich that precious hoard still further by emphasizing and strengthening the positive thought elements within. Then when you penetrate into that treasure house of yours, you will find there everything you can want or need in superabundance.

The operation of Universal Life Energy, and the help derived from It, is due purely to Its unvarying activity in stimulating, strengthening and harmonizing. It does not create anything new to add to your mental nature because there is nothing new which is positive that can be made to add to it. All that it has possessed from Eternity, and the only aid which can or needs to be given by Universal Life Energy is the gradual lifting of all negative thoughts, impressions and habits which are buried in it and their elimination in the form of vibrations. This is done automatically each time you contact that Universal Force, because Universal Life Energy is both all powerful and basically harmonious, and disharmonious vibrations cannot prevail against It.

When you combine this use of Universal Life Energy with the method of mental negation and realization, you form an alliance which safeguards your Subconscious mental field absolutely. Through negation you prevent more negative matter from entering in to grow up and corrupt further the mental soil, and through the use of Universal Life Energy, combined with positive realization, you purify that soil of all the evil bedded in it and waiting only an opportunity to express itself.

This elimination of the negative first by the methods above cited, and not the mere covering of it by positive suggestion, is essential for the proper scientific training of your Subconsciousness. To suggest the positive without first eliminating the negative would be like putting a coat of paint on a metal object covered with rust. At first sight all will appear well, because the rust is hidden under the paint; but although the object may look sound and clean, the rust under that paint is increasing all the time through the chemical action of the air which still remains in the pores around it. Presently the paint will flake off, as it has no substantial foundation, and the rust breaking through will make the object much more shabby and disreputable than before.

Therefore unless the negative rust in you is cleaned away first, the good which you try to lodge in your Subconsciousness can get no firm hold and will not be very lasting in expression. Moreover, the destructive matter buried under that coating of good will have plenty of assistance in breaking out because of the evil which you also admit. The wrong thought vibrations which sink into your Subconsciousness all have an affinity in the wrong already stored there, and the mutual response between the two is in effect the same corrosive action observable in rusting objects. And the ultimate result is quite as unlovely as that described in the physical example above.

Finally, the constructive power of the Universal Life Energy with which you flood your Solar Plexus will manifest itself in a way that is of supreme importance to you in your conscious life—namely, by increasing your power of imagination. Imagination, as stated previously, is the power to make thought grow out and produce; but the strength of that power, the measure of its productive capacity, is the fertility of the Subconscious soil to which it belongs.

By eliminating the negative, Universal Life Energy performs the first service for Imagination, for in proportion as the Subconscious soil is corrupted by wrong thought vibrations its constructive producing power is reduced. A pure soil is the best foundation for a rich harvest, but it also needs something besides purity. It needs energy, the strength to put its clean qualities into vigorous expression through the seeds that fall on it.

This also Universal Life Energy supplies, because It is in Itself the very force and strength that is needed. So when you contact Universal Life Energy abundantly and let It fertilize that Subconscious mental ground you are doing yourself an invaluable service, for besides eliminating the negative It is enriching that very quality in you on which hinges the scope of your activities and achievements on this Physical Plane. You attract to you and bring within the possibility of realization the thing you want through the power of your Imagination; so the fertility of that Imagination should be one of your dearest concerns from day to day.

EXERCISES TO LESSON ELEVEN

In order to enrich and develop your most important Subconscious quality, Imagination, an Exercise has been designed which is to be known as FERTILIZATION. This Exercise being the outgrowth of these other basic Exercises which have been given you, and depending on them for its successful performance, requires that you shall perform those Exercises regularly, as always, before expecting to reap advantage from their product. Therefore repeat morning and evening the Star Exercise, Relaxation, Silence and Contact, together with Attention and Concentration. Then proceed with FERTILIZATION as follows:

As the object of your Concentration Exercise this week take your own Solar Plexus, the seat of your Subconsciousness. Then, after having made the Contact with Universal Life Energy, focus your thought on that Solar Plexus and picture it mentally as being fertile, strong, pure and harmonious. Know that all the perfect qualities and knowledge of your Superconsciousness are there, latent, under all the human experiences and knowledge, all the information and impressions, heaped over them. Try to reach them through the good part of that human thought matter, and not only create in your Conscious Self the concept of them as an actual possession, but be joyful at the realization of such treasures.

That whole mental treatment, applied to your Subconsciousness, will open it widely through the physical avenues of your body to the abundant inflow of

Universal Life Energy. Then do not worry about results and above all do not close yourself up by fear, because the Great Law of the Universe will take care that Life Energy does Its work properly.

In this way you will purify and strengthen the productive powers of that mental soil. Then in using Universal Life Energy continually in all your activities, physical, mental and emotional, you will safeguard that specific work by warding off all the negative thoughts and impressions which are continually seeking a way in to destroy it.

QUESTIONS TO LESSON ELEVEN

1. What is Subconsciousness?

2. How did it originate?

3. What two distinctive qualities does it possess?

4. How does Subconsciousness react with the Conscious Self?

5. What are the qualities and limitations of the Subconsciousness?

6. In what respect is it dangerous to the individual?

7. How can Subconsciousness be consciously controlled?

8. What are the two methods for purifying Subconsciousness?

9. Which of these methods is limited, and why?

10. How do Negation and Realization operate on the Mental Plane?

11. Should any definite sequence be observed in the application of the two methods of purifying Subconsciousness, and why?

12. What is the method and the result of Fertilization of the Subconsciousness?

ANSWERS TO LESSON ELEVEN

1. **Subconsciousness is:**

The third part of the mental trinity which is below the conscious state.

2. **It originated:**

Through the breaking up of the single Mind Ray by Selfconsciousness.

3. **Two distinctive qualities which it possesses are:**

   (1) The power to receive and retain permanently whatever comes to it by way of the Conscious Self.

   (2) Imagination, or the power to increase the thought matter that enters into it.

4. **Subconsciousness reacts with the Conscious Self:**

By tapping the whole world of human thought and experience through the conscious state, increasing the thought matter thus received, and yielding it back in its augmented form as the substance of the conscious rational thought.

5. **The qualities and limitations of the Subconsciousness are:**

That it possesses all the perfect qualities and powers of its source, the Perfect Mind Ray, but buried out of reach under the superimposed mass of all human knowledge, good and evil together, which the Humanly Conscious Self has dumped down upon it since the beginning of its existence.

6. **It is dangerous to the individual:**

In that it lacks the power of discrimination, and receives, nourishes and sends back to the Conscious Self the evil as well as the good which is admitted to it.

7. **Subconsciousness can be consciously controlled:**

By the exercise of the power of discrimination, which is a quality of the Conscious Self, to determine what matter shall be admitted to Subconsciousness.

8. **The two methods for purifying Subconsciousness are:**

(1) Mental Negation and Realization.

(2) The use of Universal Life Energy.

9. **The limited method is:**

Mental Negation and Realization, because it depends upon purely mental forces, principally the human Will, which are as fallible as the Humanly Conscious Self and can be applied only to the active process of exchange now going on between Subconsciousness and Selfconsciousness.

10. **The operation of Negation and Realization on the mental plane is:**

Negation of a thing means its destruction, while Realization of a thing means its creation.

11. **The sequence to be observed in the two methods of purifying the Subconsciousness is:**

First, the use of Universal Life Energy, combined with the Negation of evil, in order to clear the way for positive Realization to establish itself securely. Second, realization of positive thoughts. Unless the negative is cleared away first it will break out and make the thin shell of good deposited over it very impermanent.

12. **Fertilization of the Subconsciousness is:**

The abundant use of Universal Life Energy to destroy the evil bedded in the Subconsciousness and to increase and strengthen the positive expression of the pure matter there, thus stimulating the power of imagination.

Dear Friend:

This Lesson will explain to you those Mental Laws on which the whole intricate structure of Mental Science is based, and which govern the operation of your conscious thought. You will be shown how all the mighty streams of thought matter from outside as well as from within converge on the narrow throat of that passageway through the Conscious Self, and how, because your faculties are not harmoniously developed and adjusted, only a small trickle is skimmed off the top of this unceasing flood and submitted to them for your practical use.

An insight will be given you into your Reason, the quality of your Self consciousness which, supported by Will and Common Sense, is an instrument of almost unlimited potentialities for creative and constructive work. You will learn how to employ it for Self Analysis, a vital activity for a successful existence, and how to adjust yourself through it to the Great Law of the Universe. Evil, its origin, its destructive influences and the means whereby it can be transmitted into good by the help of Self Analysis will be presented in detail.

Fear will be analysed and traced to its source in Ignorance, and the method described whereby it can be not only overcome, but completely eliminated, together with all its negative expressions in Body, Mind and Soul.

When the ground has been cleared by uncovering all the obstacles in the way of efficient conscious thought, you will be given an understanding of the power of the liberated thought, and how to project your thought, with the aid of Will Power. Through the understanding you have gained of the Mental Laws the procedure of your thought, all its activities and effects, will be clear to you, and by applying what you have obtained from the study of these pages you will be able to make your Conscious Self at last the Master of itself.

Cordially yours,
Eugene Fersen.

LESSON TWELVE

SELFCONSCIOUSNESS is that quality of your mind which enables you to be conscious of every thought of your own, of every feeling and action of the world within and also of the world without. It is the point toward which all the numberless unassorted elements that go to make up your active life converge, there to be spun out into the compact fabric of your actual existence. Accordingly it is one of your most precious mental possessions, the seat of your conscious being.

To be conscious of something means not only to be aware of it, but to understand it appreciate it, and know just how to integrate it with other things in order to get the most effective results. You are fully conscious of only a very few of the vast flood of impressions you receive; the rest, slipping past below the level of your perception, are practically non-existent to you. Even the virgin treasures of your Superconsciousness and the great stores of human knowledge in your Subconscious field are useful to you only as they are tapped by your Conscious Self; so your limited conscious capacity prevents you from turning more than the smallest part of them into the minted coin of real fact.

Three supremely important conscious faculties form the machinery by which thought stream is partly turned to your account. Foremost among them is Reason, which selects and arranges in the most effective order what you need to meet the demands of your life. Through it you assort and analyse things with relation to themselves and to other things also, and from that analysis you draw logical conclusions. Thus you orient your individual thoughts and make them complete yet harmoniously associated units.

Your Will, the second of your conscious trinity, is the motive power whereby you drive into active and compelling expression amid the expressed thought of Humanity those mental projectiles which your Reason has made ready. Once launched at the impulse of your Will, they will bring a just return according to their force and merit. But whether your profit will be great or little depends upon how well your third chief conscious faculty has functioned.

Common Sense, that last and rarest of your conscious gifts, is the ability to see things in their true light and to judge them as they are, instead of as they seem to be. In other words, it is the faculty whose use determines the worth of the thoughts you employ as tools to help you live and progress. When Common Sense is well represented in you, the mental tools you fashion are of sound metal, well tempered, evenly balanced and without alloy. You can depend on them to do fine work for you. When it is absent, you find your mental instruments crumbling impotently against the rocky face of circumstances, and you have to be content with the correspondingly poor impressions you are able to make in this world.

These three, Reason, Will and Common Sense, therefore form the working mechanism through which your Selfconsciousness puts its qualities forth into expression. The first arms you to meet the Future, the second provides the strength to drive your weapons, and the third determines how deeply they will bite. When properly exercised, they enable you to handle your own thoughts in accordance with the Mental Laws in such a way as to make them powerful, efficient and docile instruments in your hands.

The aggressive character of these three conscious faculties, always thrusting everything into manifestation and retaining nothing long, marks Selfconsciousness as the part of the Mind Trinity which is of the male gender, in contrast to the passive, receptive, and generative Subconscious aspect, which is of the female gender.

Your brain, with all its various lobes, convolutions, centres and cells, all of which correspond to the conscious qualities of which they are the embodiment, is the complex physical apparatus built by your Self consciousness for its own expression. Just as that Conscious Self knits all its activities into a one-pointed scheme of action whose purpose is rational expression, so all units of the brain system tend toward the organ in it which represents the same purpose. This organ is the Pituitary Body, or, as was explained in Lesson Ten, the Telepathic Apparatus, which radiates thought vibrations from within and registers thought vibrations from without, making the brain a mental Radio Station.

The Pituitary Body is thus the channel through which the product of your conscious faculties emerges into active expression. The Concentration Exercise given you in Lesson Ten taught you how to modify the form of that Telepathic Apparatus by Will Power in such a way as to gather your thought vibrations into a single intense ray, instead of allowing all their force to be wasted through diffusion. Now the action of the thought so concentrated will be explained to you.

Three distinct phases mark the progress of the concentrated thought. From the moment of its conception in you it proceeds in obedience to exact Mental Laws. Over those Laws you have no control whatever; they are as impersonal as the planets in their operation; but during the first phase of their activity you are able to control the kind of thought you intend to submit to their influence.

This first phase relates primarily to the individual who sends out the concentrated thought, before that thought leaves his Telepathic Apparatus. His function is to concentrate on the subject he wishes to convey, hold it steadily before his mental eye and then inhale slowly and deeply. At the apex of that inhalation he is to think quickly for a moment of the person to whom the thought is to be sent and at that instant exhale, at the same time letting go the concentrated thought. The energy released will drive the thought vibrations from his Pituitary Body, along the connecting line established across space by the single quick thought of the one who is to receive it, so that they strike his Telepathic Apparatus and are registered there.

In this process obviously the strength and nature of the concentrated thought depend upon the sender. You are able to decide whether the thought you let loose shall be one of hate, of love, of beauty, or of anything at all, positive or negative. Also you generate the vibratory current which carries that thought, so you make it strong or weak according to your desire or ability to do so. For this reason you have to guard against certain influences which can greatly diminish the power of your concentrated thought.

If you permit fear or worry about results to enter your mind before you have projected the thought you are holding there, you spoil most of its effectiveness. Fear is a negative condition which contracts the brain cells and cripples their activity, so naturally the strength of the mental current you send out will be cut down in proportion as those channels shrink.

After you have projected your thought, fear or worry have no power to influence it further. Once it leaves your Pituitary Body it is gone beyond recall. No amount of wishing, hoping, dreading or regretting will ever catch up with it, because thereafter it proceeds serenely in accordance with Mental Laws. It will fly on its appointed course as inevitably as a rifle bullet after the trigger has been pulled, or as the vibrations of a telegraphic message when it has sped from beneath the operator's key. Both the bullet and the message reach their destination, not because of any expectation of the one who released them that they would be received, but because he put them under the operation of immutable Physical Laws; and the strength of the impression they make at the other end is in exact proportion to the power of the charge behind them. Thus the only way you can seriously detract from the effectiveness of your concentrated thought is by allowing negative emotions to clog the channels through which it must pass in you before it leaves you.

No interval occurs between the sending and the receiving of your thought. For mental vibrations space does not exist; therefore its action is instantaneous. As soon as it leaves your mind it is present in the mind of the other individual.

The second phase in the procedure of this concentrated thought has to do with the individual who receives it. He also is powerless to exercise any control over it, except that if he is in a receptive mood he may be able to perceive it consciously a little sooner. Irrespective of that, however, the concentrated thought will enter into him, and the mental vibrations, striking his Pituitary Body, will be conducted by way of the back part of his brain and the spinal cord to his Solar Plexus, or Abdominal Brain. Here the idea they embody will be registered in his Subconsciousness, the strength of the impression it makes there depending on the strength of the vibratory current which produced it. There it takes root and grows, in obedience to the Subconscious Laws, until finally it reaches its conscious goal, persistently thrusting itself into the Consciousness of the individual from below and from time to time reminding him of its presence.

This Subconscious activity of the concentrated thought finds also a reflection in the Subconsciousness of the sender. When it is released, there is what might be termed a "backfire" which looses into the Solar Plexus of the sender the same vibratory impulse that is to be registered in the other individual, where it lodges and grows in precisely the same fashion.

Sometimes you may wish to make your own Subconsciousness the recipient of the full force of that concentrated thought, instead of another person outside. This you call "memorizing," or "learning by heart," and it is accomplished through exactly the same process as for projecting the thought. In this instance, however, your Subconsciousness takes the place of another individual, and -instead of projecting the thought you inject it into your own self. At the height of your inhalation, think of that inner destination within you and, so to say, swallow the thought just before you start to exhale. Thus you put all the propulsive energy into sinking that thought into your Subconscious Self, rather than in driving it out into space, and with this added impetus it makes so vivid an impression that it is always within the immediate reach of your conscious summons through Memory.

Finally, the third phase in the progress of the concentrated thought is its continued journey after passing through the Subconsciousness and leaving a record of itself there. Those mental vibrations, once they have deposited an impression of themselves in the Subconscious mental field, do not stop there. That is the goal to which you may have directed them, but after your purpose is accomplished they nevertheless fly on into Space in pursuit of the goal decreed for them by the Mental Laws which govern them. But before attaining that ultimate goal they are destined to undergo a decided change.

In hurtling out into Space they encounter the mental atmosphere which, as stated previously, surrounds the Earth just as does the physical one. That atmosphere is composed of the disintegrated thoughts of all thinking Humanity, a vast cloud of "thought dust" hanging there and enveloping our planet. From this cloud your concentrated thought, in its passage, attracts all the floating particles which are of a corresponding rate of vibration. The further it goes the more of this loose matter clots about it, until after a time it has grown out of any semblance to its original self, like a snow-ball rolling down a long hill when the flakes are damp and adhesive.

The significant feature of this activity of the concentrated thought is that it attracts only mental matter of a corresponding rate of vibration. "Like attracts like" — if the thought you discharge into that mental atmosphere is of a kindly and constructive nature, it will gather to it only similar positive thought matter during its passage. But all the negative thoughts of Mankind are mingled with the positive in that cloud of "thought dust" also, so if you release a destructive and negative thought you unleash a wrong which will grow into a monstrous avalanche of evil before its course is completed. The vital interest for you in this fact lies in the operation through Mental Laws of another Physical Law, expressed through the Earth's magnetic attraction, which governs the progress of your mental vibrations.

This Physical Law, whether exerted on material bodies or on mental vibrations, tends to draw everything back to its point of origin. Therefore the final goal of your concentrated thought is yourself. No matter how far into Space it may proceed it must return, like an ordinary projectile, to Earth. Because it is of such a subtle nature the Law governing it is able to achieve uninterrupted expression through it, and the thought you sent out returns unerringly to you, with all that it has acquired on the way.

For this reason you should be exceedingly careful of the kind of thoughts you project, because obviously, while you can discharge harmful and destructive thoughts against others, to do so is simply to "sow the wind and reap the whirlwind." The measure of the injury you can do another individual in that way is negligible compared to the devastating boomerang of destruction which will rebound upon you. Similarly, if you send out thoughts of good, that good will return to you increased many times and will bear positive expression in your life.

Before employing the concentrated thought, therefore, be sure you have a clear perspective of its advantages and its limitations. Remember that Laws are greater than the individual; you can accommodate yourself to them, but you cannot bend them to your will. They see to it that nothing is lost in this World, and one of them, the Law of Compensation, working in this instance through the Mental Laws, insures the certain return sooner or later of everything that has its source in you. You cannot compromise, escape or evade them, and you cannot influence them to deviate from their eternally established course. Laws are no respecters of person; what you start they will inevitably finish, but whether to your benefit or distress depends upon how astutely you have called them into play in the beginning.

All abuse of these Laws comes first from within your Conscious Self and produces a certain definite effect-Evil. Therefore Evil, as was explained in Lesson Ten, is born of conscious or unconscious opposition to the Law, and it is not a cause. It is an effect only. What you call Good is also an effect, brought about by attuning yourself to the

Law and working in harmony with it, so that you enlist all its irresistible power in your support. In that case it works constructively through you, building up the positive results which spell Success. But in opposing yourself to the same Law that, rightly applied, brought Good, you pervert its operation so that it wreaks destruction through you and against you, creating Evil.

Your control over Evil lies in the faculty alone responsible for it—Selfconsciousness. The Laws themselves are totally beyond any influence of yours to change either their nature or the Power they govern. Like the beams of the sun, those remain eternally the same; the only variety is in the results they produce through you. Your conscious state is the partly collared window through which they fall upon the floor of your temple of Self, and the borrowed pattern they fling there is beautiful or grotesque, pleasing or horrible, merely as the aspect imparted to them by you is so. If you are One with them so that you transmit them pure and undefiled, which means also that you are One with their source, Universal Life Energy, you enable them to write a positive history of development, success and happiness. If you are opposed to them you simply throw before them the stained map of Evil and trouble whose reflection vexes your life.

Obviously no neutrality is possible in your relations with these Forces and Laws. Separation means opposition, so you are definitely either with them or against them. They emerge through you either clean or dirty, because there is no good nor evil except as your conscious thinking self makes it so. Therefore in your Selfconsciousness resides the power to make your life harmonious or disharmonious, to transmute evil into good, by applying your conscious faculties intelligently to the task of cleaning that window in you.

This process is called Self Analysis, and it is essential for the proper conscious elimination of everything undesirable, as well as for the harmonious development of that which is constructive and useful. Without it no permanent mental sanitation can be assured, because only through it you are able to banish the grime of negative intrusions which are always seeking to crust your Conscious Self and disrupt the nice balance of its proportions.

Self Analysis first gives you a true perspective of yourself by uncovering your faults. The Four Main Aspects of Universal Life Energy, Life, Mind, Truth and Love, supply the basic plan on which any rightly organized life must be established. By turning every facet of your nature to this Four-square, you can easily note where it measures up to standard and where the corners fall short.

The most thorough Self Analysis, which means the most complete analysis of all these various facets, can be obtained by observing your reactions to other people. Each individual is different, and each therefore tests a different strain in your character. If an unusually successful person arouses in you a sour spirit of criticism, a sense of jealousy, then you know that you possess this negative trait in you. If the society of idlers makes you feel at ease, there an element of laziness in your composition which responds to the same influence from outside. When the effect of still others is to stir up resentment and even hatred in you, there is hatred latent in your heart. Thus everyone is a tuning fork of a different pitch which will bring out the false note in you.

When you have discovered all your shortcomings in this way you have gained a capital point without which effective sanitation would be impossible. Your shortcomings are the items of immediate interest, because they are what must be handled first in weeding them out, and until you have learned to distinguish them through Self Analysis you cannot proceed with that weeding. The above process, then, puts you in a position to continue by revealing the flaws that have to be removed.

In this further work of correcting your shortcomings Self Analysis also helps. Through it you are able to counteract the demand of the negative in you for expression by summoning up the positive instead. Whenever you feel the impulse to indulge some negative inner call, school yourself to bring out instead the exactly opposite and positive quality. In so doing, you lift the weight of wrong which seeks to drag that negative trait into expression, and by destroying its influence in your life you restore the proper balance within you.

Not only will Self Analysis uncover the individual negative elements within you, but on the larger scale it will show you just which part of your human trinity of Body, Mind and Soul is the dominating factors in your life. The being which is you is composed of those three main divisions, and the division marred by the least negative is the one to whose key your theme of existence is pitched. It corresponds most nearly with the Four-square of Life, Mind, Truth and Love, being the part in which those qualities find their fullest expression, and indicates to you your task of developing to a corresponding strength the neglected corners in the other departments of your life. Also it strikes out a vista of all those turbulent currents of evil in you and traces them back to their one vast common source — Fear.

Fear, the giant hand that grips your mind and warps it from the direct course, is a condition that exists and has its origin in mind alone. Moreover, it is not a natural or even an inherited condition, but one which is acquired separately by every individual. Experiments conducted recently in different scientific institutions in America and in other countries also have revealed the fact that children Science of Being as well as animals are born absolutely fearless. Nothing is able to produce in them the reaction called Fear except a sudden very loud sound, whose vibrations naturally hurt the auditory nerves. It is only later, after Fear has been imposed upon them by maturer people in whom it is already present, that they acquire this negative condition which becomes their greatest handicap and the source of all their future troubles, barring them from Health, Success and Prosperity.

Analysis of Fear, its nature and causes, is one of the vital points in Mental Science, because in Fear is comprehended the entire problem of all the negative. When you overcome that, you kill at a blow the hydra-headed monster which leers out in the thousand and one ills and diseases of Body, Mind and Emotions. All negative springs from Fear, so when Fear is eliminated all its negative expressions vanish also.

Fear as a sensation is a conscious or unconscious feeling of helplessness and lack of power in the presence of danger. It produces as a physical reaction a general closing up, contraction and paralysis of all the nerves, cells, muscles and tissues. The effect of that closing up of your physical channels is to deprive you of the use of the very instruments by which you should most successfully combat the menace that threatens you. That is, it deprives you of the use of your conscious faculties.

Animals and plants do not possess the conscious faculties with which the human individual is endowed, so in their cases Fear performs a definite service in protecting them from harm. A turtle, when scared, withdraws into its shell. So does a snail. A porcupine rolls itself into a spiked ball. With every animal or insect the Fear impulse to shrink and contract works automatically to bring out some protective device.

Even some plants exhibit this unconscious Fear reaction to a marked degree. The Touch-me-not derives its name from it. A certain tropical bush is so sensitive to outside impressions, especially of a threatening nature, that a stone thrown at it from a distance causes it to close its leaves and shut down its branches like the ribs of an umbrella. It preserves this singular and uninviting attitude until the real or seeming danger has had time to depart, whereupon it resumes its former natural condition.

But what is a great boon to an animal or a plant which has not the mental equipment to defend itself more effectively, is a decided disadvantage to a human being who has. Your first reaction to Fear is that you cannot think. The contraction of the nerve passages in you pinches off your contact with your conscious faculties, Reason, Will and Common Sense included. The result of this severed connection is that you are bereft of motion also, as the motor impulses which drive your body to coordinated and intelligent action come also from Conscious Self.

The consequence of Fear, then, is that you deliver yourself bound hand and foot to the very danger you wished to avoid. You are paralysed mentally and physically, except when occasionally your dammed-up energies burst out in a sudden explosion or in some violent and erratic behaviour which only renders you more vulnerable. You have thrown away the conscious weapons by which you could conquer the obstacle that confronts you, and have abandoned yourself abjectly to the mercies of a power that is merciless — Fear. What, therefore, is the source of this Fear?

The cause of Fear in most cases, especially with human beings, is ignorance. A thing which baffles your understanding, which looms up before you simply as an impenetrable mask hiding you know not what terrors behind it, produces in you that overpowering sense of inferiority and helplessness. It usually "faces you down" merely by the suggestion of what may be back of it, allowing your own imagination to help it defeat you. Or more rarely, your inferiority may be genuine, and your recognition of this constitutes your Fear.

The elimination of Fear, then, is largely conditioned on the elimination of this shadow, from which it is spawned, Ignorance. Like most vermin, Fear thrives in darkness, sallying out to spread its blight in the path of ambitions, hopes, health and friendships. Every positive quality is the potential victim of this creeping poison, which sows hatred, jealousy, distrust, anger, disease—every wrong and destructive element there is, physical, mental and emotional—in order to bar you from those things that you want and to bring into your life those things that you do not want. It is the one monstrous genius of the negative which has retarded the whole of Humanity's Evolution, only because Humanity has not taken the trouble to turn a little mental sunlight into the dark corners.

Most of the methods devised for overcoming Fear limit their scope to human powers within the individual and take for their vital principle the human Will. Thereby they destroy their avowed purpose, for while the human will is an admirable weapon to turn against anything, it functions very largely as an arm to wield a weapon. Your Will is the cutting edge of that composite tool of your Conscious Self, Reason, Will and Common Sense, but the power that can drive that edge straight to the heart of the foe is something else entirely, and it cannot be left out.

The effect of Will Power used alone is the very reverse of what is expected, for Will Power, like Fear, tends to contract and close up by strain the nerve channels. Therefore the application of Will Power to overcome

Fear, while it may temporarily give you a false position of dominance, really aids Fear all the time in closing up the already contracted channels in you still further. The more you use it the more you chop away the slim prod by which it holds you up, and when you fall, it will be into a panic the more intense the more you tried by Will Power to avoid it.

Due also to this tendency to contract, Will Power must be held responsible together with Fear for bringing into your life the very things you dread. Once a thought of Fear enters into your Subconsciousness it shuts all the doors behind it. That is, the contraction produced in you by Fear shuts the thought of Fear securely in your Subconscious mental field, shielding it from any blighting touch of the positive and affording it the most ideal conditions for growth and increase. Your use of Will merely seals it in more tightly, and then when it does sprout forth, your efforts to drive it back from your Conscious Self succeed only in impressing it more vividly on your Subconsciousness. There, thanks first to Fear and then to the Will Power with which you tried to eliminate Fear, it grows abundantly under cover and gathers the strength to break out irresistibly in your conscious life.

To depend upon Will Power alone to rout such an enemy, therefore, is like sticking a sword in the path of an army and expecting it to cut them to pieces. Will Power and the other conscious faculties are not an army in themselves; they are merely the tools, the weapons, which, if properly wielded, are capable of putting your most formidable opponent to flight.

The Great Power which alone can really eliminate Fear is Universal Life Energy. That is the mighty arm in whose hand your conscious weapons fit best and leap forward to clear your way, to Freedom and Achievement. Success is yours in the ratio that you strike off the grip of Fear, no matter in what department of your human activities it may be, for until you break the hold of that paralysing force you are stricken with a sense of impotence and inferiority all the more deadly in that it chokes back any real hope of getting rid of it.

Those who use Universal Life Energy consistently in all their daily activities succeed in getting rid of Fear, putting in its place a harmonious, relaxing and constructive Power in which they know they can repose the utmost confidence because no obstacle can daunt it. To such, Fear becomes a myth, a nightmare bred in the shadows of Ignorance and dispelled like an evil mist before the dawn of Knowledge and Power brought, on the wings of that Universal Force.

In allying yourself to Universal Life Energy, it is not to be supposed that you resign all responsibility for your other faculties. You are the medium through which that Ally works, but the strength it gives you does not cancel the need for taking good care of the weapons with which you must, after all, win your fight. Reason, Will and Common Sense are still the instruments you have to use, and the stronger and better you make them the more quickly and cleanly you will be able to accomplish your task.

The development of your Will, that cutting edge within you, comes from the exercise of it, and in its training involves also the development of your other two main conscious faculties. Reason and Common Sense enable you to analyse things and weigh their true value, pro and con, so that you can come to an accurate decision. When you see your way clear to adjust that decision to the Great Law of Universal Harmony, then make it and use your Will to stick to it and carry it through to the end in spite of everything and everybody, including yourself. Thus you strengthen all your conscious qualities, and above all you temper and sharpen that all-important shearing edge of your Will.

A Will properly trained in this manner gives you the mastery over your Mental Self and increases the power of your liberated thought also. Subconsciousness, as stated previously, now plays a dominant role in your life instead of occupying the subordinate position that it should, but your Will can give you absolute authority over it. When you have acquired this control you will no longer have to be content with the fragmentary and incomplete thoughts that your Subconsciousness now yields at its own whim. You will be able to free them at once from the heavy Subconscious soil of negative matter which clings to them and drags them back, so that they are promptly liberated in their entirety. Such liberated thoughts are clear, supple, strong and creative, real genii of the Mind alert to carry out your bidding in the face of every difficulty.

Since the whole purpose in clearing out of your system that negative element of Fear is to give you undisputed control and authority over your own mind, so that you can command your thoughts at will and handle them according to your desire, the Exercise for this Lesson will be designed to help you in putting to the most effective use the control you thus obtain. When you have dissolved from your thought the Fear which shackles it, then you can send it out to carry your message and to gather to it a double cargo of profit to bring back to you. Therefore Thought Projection is one of the most valuable functions of your Conscious Self, and the one which, diligently practiced according to the method to be described, will make you Master.

EXERCISES TO LESSON TWELVE

Continue as always, morning and evening, the Star Exercise, Relaxation, Silence, Contact and Concentration, and through the practice of them prepare yourself for the effective performance of the new Exercise for this week, which is called THOUGHT PROJECTION.

In order to accomplish THOUGHT PROJECTION proceed as follows: After you have entered into Silence and made the Contact with Universal Life Energy, concentrate your mind upon a certain object, preferably one of a simple and substantial nature. When you have succeeded in obtaining a clear and vivid mental image of that object, inhale slowly and deeply to the full capacity of your lungs. This inhalation should gather in it the harmonious and rhythmic momentum of your own collected inner forces, which reach the height of their power when it reaches its climax also. Then exhale quickly and project your mental concept into Space, winged with the charge of energy which you have rallied for that purpose. After you have done that, do not think any longer about it, because further thought can have no influence on what you have sent out, one way or the other.

If you wish to convey that thought to someone, you can do so by thinking for an instant of that person at the very peak of your inhalation, just before you project the thought into Space. This quick thought establishes a connecting line that projected vibrations will follow as the line of least resistance.

Repeat this Exercise several times a day, choosing each time a new subject for thought projection. In this way you will train yourself to think quickly and strongly, with an energy and decision that will make your thought produce a convincing impression. You will also achieve variety, and will develop an alertness, clarity, precision and creative power of mind that will be invaluable to you.

QUESTIONS TO LESSON TWELVE

1. What is Selfconsciousness?

2. What are its distinctive qualities?

3. To what extent are we conscious of all the thoughts and impressions we receive?

4. What is Reason?

5. What is Common Sense?

6. What is Self Analysis?

7. What is Evil?

8. What is Fear, its causes and effects?

9. How can Fear be eliminated?

10. What relation do the conscious faculties bear to Fear?

11. Define Will Power and its development.

12. What is liberated thought?

ANSWERS TO LESSON TWELVE

1. Selfconsciousness is:

The quality of your mind which enables you to be conscious of all thoughts and impressions proceeding both from within you and from outside.

2. Its distinctive qualities are:

Reason, Will and Common Sense.

3. We are conscious of all the thoughts and impressions we receive:

To only a very limited extent, as most of them pass below the range of our perception.

4. Reason is:

The power to analyse things with relation to themselves and to other things also, and from that analysis to draw logical conclusions.

5. Common Sense is:

The faculty to see things in their true light and to judge them as they actually are.

6. **Self Analysis is:**

The accurate perception of your own qualities and shortcomings through applying to all your actions the standard contained in the Four Main Aspects of Universal Life Energy, which are Life, Mind, Truth and Love.

7. **Evil is:**

Conscious or unconscious opposition to the Law of the Universe.

8. **Fear is:**

A feeling of impotence and inferiority, caused by ignorance of the thing with which you have to contend, and it produces a shrinkage and contraction of all the physical channels in your body.

9. **Fear can be eliminated:**

By the use of Universal Life Energy.

10. **The relation of the conscious faculties to fear is:**

That unless they are supported by Universal Life Energy, Fear closes the channels for their expression and deprives you of their use to overcome adverse conditions.

11. Will Power is:

The executive and sustaining power of your Conscious Self, and it acts as the cutting edge through which the other conscious faculties put their activities into definite expression. It is developed by exercising it.

12. The liberated thought is:

Subconscious thought freed by the use of Universal Life Energy from the negative which retards it.

Dear Friend:

As your life takes its tone from the human society of which you are an integral part, it is vitally important for you to be able to pierce behind the veil of appearances and perceive the elements which are to react upon you, and to know whether their influence will be good or bad. Character reading is therefore an accomplishment whose value to you is unlimited, because it helps you to direct and control your life constructively, while its associate activity of Thought Reading is of equal value in enabling you to achieve immediate positive results.

These two, Character Reading and Thought Reading, will be the uses of your conscious faculties taught you in the first part of this Lesson. The second part will then explain to you the qualities which support and coordinate your mind to the performance of those functions, and which enable you to employ their results to the best advantage. Self Reliance, Insight, Foresight, and Common Sense emerge into prominence as you give them use, and they frame a balanced mental growth tending toward the proper expression of that basic ruling Power which is supreme over all — Truth.

Strength, Poise, Energy, and Power come only from a balanced mental machine. Equilibrium itself is the ordered product of Law, but of that perfect Law which, as an Aspect of Universal Life Energy, is known as Truth. By erecting your faculties to the standard set by Truth, in accordance with the methods and principles which will here be explained, you will win the utter Freedom and Independence desired by every man and woman, but seldom attained by any.

Cordially yours,
Eugene Fersen.

LESSON THIRTEEN

CHARACTER reading is one of your most practical and valuable attainments, because it enables you to understand the other half of that human equation of which you are only the first part. Self Analysis taught you how to discover your own qualities and weaknesses; analysis of those among whom you live will, by showing you theirs, enable you to combine the two intelligently for a positive solution of the problem called your life.

Yet to read the character of another individual is an entirely different process from reading your own. Instead of being inside that shell of the human body, studying at their source the impulses which move and guide it, you are outside trying to fathom from its appearance and activities the hidden inner qualities of which it is the sum. The conditions, therefore, are reversed; you are barred from the springs of action in other people by a wall of flesh which carries in its own conformation alone the only visible indications of what may be behind it.

Numerous methods have been devised, especially by psychologists and psycho-analysts, for estimating from these indications the character they conceal. "Humanology" has grown to be a science by itself, distinguished by some very worth-while contributions from experts in that field. The student of Humanology is now able to get a fairly accurate idea of a subject merely by observing the various parts of the face and body, with respect to their comparative development and relative values one to another.

For instance, a well developed and properly balanced forehead will mark one as of a mental type, while on the contrary a low forehead topping a sturdy and robust muscular system will indicate that the physical side is dominant. Strong, clean-Cut features betoken energy and a clear, exact mind. Determination is known to express itself in a square, aggressive chin.

Yet very often the student of Humanology is puzzled to discover that some traits written large in the features under observation are lacking in the individuals, while others only mildly represented in the flesh are decidedly active within it. Thus someone possessing no chin worthy of note frequently exhibits great energy and determination in thought and action, whereas another graced with the jaw of a bull-dog may be of a timid and vacillating disposition.

This discrepancy between appearances and fact would seem to prove the inaccuracy of the body as a means of reading the character it contains, and in a measure it does. But in reality there is no such contradiction as there seems to be, and the difference grows simply out of the omission of one highly important natural factor.

This factor is the inability of the Physical Self to conform quickly to inner alterations. The human body, after a certain age, does not lend itself readily to change. During youth it is the plastic material in which the Soul, or Ego, outlines its own qualities and activities. Therefore it becomes strong and harmonious, or weak and ill-attuned in accordance as the characteristics and activities it embodies are well balanced or feeble. But when the individual has reached his full physical development, usually between the twenty-fifth and thirtieth year, the body has set in a certain mold from which it does not easily vary.

The character within, however, is not subject to this physical limitation. It continues to grow and unfold as long as the individual possesses the necessary health and strength to keep his human machinery running properly. With some that inner development may proceed until almost the end of their lives, but in most cases it reaches its climax at a period between the ages of fifty and sixty. In any event, the inner growth completely outpaces the physical reflection of it, and the longer the individual lives the greater that discrepancy becomes.

The consequence of this, then, is that every individual becomes a sort of a totem pole carved in the likeness of a departed past. Masks, sainted or grotesque, sculptured in the semblance of those qualities which their contours once fitted, peer changelessly out from every side. Some may prove to be an empty death mask, some may still cherish the trait that formed them, some may be the cast-off cradles of a quality that has since increased to towering proportions. All are crystallized records of what once was, but may quite reasonably be no more.

Therefore while the body can be taken as a fairly accurate criterion of character until the age of twenty-five, after that time it becomes increasingly inaccurate. Circumstances may have closed down on the individual with a weak chin and compelled him to develop energy in the latter part of his life, but no outward expression of that inner change emerges into view. Clearly, then, some more constant factor than human flesh must be found to carry the true story of another person's character, a factor which will transmit to you an exact understanding of the actual Self now within.

This factor exists in the Universal Life Energy whose use you have learned. In order to analyse the character of an individual under your observation, first make the contact with that Universal Power, and when you feel the Force flowing through you, try to sense the impression produced upon you by that individual. No human being, no animal or thing, can fail to convey a certain impression to you, because everything in Nature is continually radiating its own qualities in the form of vibrations which, although hidden to our senses in general, are none the less registered by those more finely developed inner senses we possess. In this impression is summed up the real character of the person or thing from which it emanates, so your task is simply to make it perceptible to your Conscious Self.

The peculiar advantage inherent in this method is its accuracy. Vibrations cannot lie, because they are the direct essence of what produces them. They are always streaming forth fresh and new, catching on the way any slight variation in the changing forces behind them. They are marred by no scars of Time; no beauty doctor can raise or drop them as he can a face; no individual can alter them except by a genuine and thorough inner alteration first. Through them Danger shouts its name aloud to those who know how to listen, and false pretence sounds its cracked note beyond the possibility of mistake.

That is why most animals and birds, being very sensitive to that radio-activity, are often able to anticipate perils before they loom in sight. It explains also why dogs in particular are able "instinctively" to perceive the true character of individuals where human reason sadly errs.

They know how to listen in a way Nature has taught, and which human beings in general have forgotten or ignored. A wholly passive and receptive attitude is necessary to catch the desired message. Any effort to project yourself into the mind of another individual succeeds only in shutting the door in your own face, because you not only put him on his guard against you, but you also close yourself completely against the vibrations which he cannot help giving out. As those vibrations, recorded on the photographic plate of your Consciousness, are the very impressions which your Reason must analyse for the character they represent, an exertion of Will Power which closes you up like the shutter of a camera leaves you practically in the position of an unexposed film. Only by remaining calm, open and receptive can you consciously record the character map projected by the other person, and only as you pour the current of Universal Life Energy through your relaxed physical channels and so sensitise that inner photographic plate will the impressions recorded there be clear and distinct in outline.

When this process is properly employed the character of the individual in question will be reproduced in you so vividly that you will eventually feel it as a part of your own. In other words you will read within yourself the character of someone else. Knowing your own character through Self-Analysis, you will be able to distinguish between the two and to classify the impressions received from outside accordingly. A few moments should suffice for you to accomplish this work, and after several months practice, when your Reason has fully accommodated itself to that novel conscious activity, you will perhaps be able to read instantaneously the character of anyone with whom you come in contact. The one vital point to bear in mind is that you must first contact. Universal Life Energy abundantly before contacting the individual you wish to analyse.

The same accuracy secured in character reading by this method is obtained in the reading of other people's thoughts. Thought vibrations are based on those identical Laws of Radio-activity which govern character vibrations, and the process for reading them is similarly applied. In a way thoughts are more easily read, because their vibrations are like strong flashes of varying intensity, as contrasted to the steady glow of character vibrations.

In reading the thoughts of another individual, the same passive and receptive attitude is also necessary. Simply relax and remain quietly within your Mental Self, because any effort to project yourself will only result in closing you to the very thing you are trying to receive. Projection means the use of Will Power, and Will Power produces contraction and strain. Naturally you cannot concentrate on giving and expect to receive at the same time.

Then, when you have made the contact with Universal Life Energy, watch the impressions registered on your

Telepathic Apparatus by the thoughts proceeding from the other individual. Let your interest be in opening and expanding the limits of your perception, as well as in deepening your sensitiveness to the incoming vibrations by the larger admission of Universal Life Energy. Presently you will be aware of the fluid theme of impressions pulsing against that screen of your Consciousness, and you will realize in your own mind the mental processes flowing from the Telepathic Apparatus of another.

Later on, after you have developed proficiency in thought and character reading through constant practice, you can extend your range indefinitely. The actual bodily presence of the subject is then no longer necessary in order to get a true estimate of his character or to perceive the trend of his thoughts. Distance is no obstacle to vibrations, so by contacting Universal Life Energy first and then concentrating your thought strongly upon the individual with whom you are concerned, you strike out a broad avenue connecting you with him across any space. Thereupon just relax into the properly receptive attitude and let that individual virtually flow into you by Mental Radio over the line already established. The impressions received will be quite as distinct and accurate as if he were standing at your side.

While these two, character and thought reading, are the most vital accomplishments for orienting yourself in the Society of which you are a part, they also imply associate functions hardly less important. They are themselves limited in that they apply only to human beings; but there are many elements bearing upon your life which, although perhaps the product of the activity of other individuals, are not immediately traceable to any specific ones. Therefore in order to solve intelligently all the complex problems of daily life, and to profit by all the opportunities sown among these unclassified elements, it is necessary to apply analysis to them as well as to people, in the manners known as Insight and Foresight.

INSIGHT is the mental capacity to perceive the hidden causes behind manifested effects. In other words, it is the ability to get at the roots of things in the ordinary run of events, just as character reading is the ability to get at the roots of appearances and traits in human beings. Its value lies in the fact that it enables you to discover opportunities that others cannot see, and also to detect and avoid dangers to which those in whom Insight is undeveloped are blind.

FORESIGHT, on the other hand, is the ability to correlate what Insight has revealed, and through that correlation to foresee conditions or events.1 It enables you to draw right conclusions, to forecast effects which are to happen in the Future by causes which are now in process of starting or which have started in the Past. Through Foresight you can create and guide your own future destiny by starting now causes which, caught in the constantly moving film of events, will someday emerge inevitably into your life as present effects.

In the development of these two faculties, as in everything else, Universal Life Energy will be of invaluable assistance to you. That is the one Force which can carry you out of the shell of your human limitations and conduct you to the very end you are seeking.

Therefore if you desire to pierce the mystery of visible happenings and unravel the casual roots from which they sprang, make the contact with that Great Power and let its propelling Energy sweep you mentally into the unseen regions where those causes dwell. Or, if Foresight into the future is required, let your glance soar winged with the Force of the Universe far above surrounding obstacles and limitations, until the unrolling horizons fall back from the clear goal to which you aspire.

The effect of Universal Life Energy in stimulating your faculties of Insight and Foresight is repeated in Its contact with all other mental qualities. Development of one commands the sympathetic development of the rest also, because the harmonious nature of the Life Force will not permit It to tolerate an ill-balanced growth.

Therefore in concentrating It upon a particular one of your many mental endowments, you really enable it to do you an incidental service of infinitely more value than the achievement of your immediate object. It welds the varied units of your mind into a compact and well poised whole, imparting to you that mental equilibrium without which true Mental Mastery cannot be obtained.

The gradual attainment of this Mental Mastery through the operation on your faculties of Universal Life Energy is reflected outwardly in the increased efficiency of your thought processes. Not only does your thought become more clear, precise and powerful, but the logic of your Reason gains purpose and direction. The development of Common Sense, the quality which enables you to make the best use of present conditions, is fortified and adjusted in its growth by the development of all subordinate qualities which bear any relation to it. That cluster then exchanges mutual support with the neighbouring chief mental groups, which are all similarly responding to the basic stimulus of Universal Life Energy. And the whole movement of readjustment, change and increase tends toward the emergence of one key quality dominating all Law.

Law is the element which, as an Aspect of Universal Life Energy, is called Truth. Thus Law and Truth are synonymous, and although they are commonly regarded as an abstract concept, of a nature too ethical to be very substantial, they are in fact a concrete, definite Power of Universal import. Human laws are abstract until they are put into active application, but Universal Law is in operation continuously everywhere, throughout Eternity. It can function only as long as It is true to Itself, yet It is never anything else because It is One with the Perfect Power which It governs.

Absolute Truth, or Universal Law, is therefore a distinct physical Force characterized by certain results which It produces wherever It touches. Foremost of these is Order, which means that It disentangles, removes obstacles, simplifies and systematizes everywhere It goes, Whenever you contact Universal Life Energy you admit also Its Aspect of Truth, just as you admit the other three of Its Four Main Aspects, Life, Intelligence and Love or Harmony. Thus you introduce into your mind a concrete, pervasive Power conducive to Order.

The elements of order, however, are not brought in by Universal Life Energy, but are already present in an unmanifested condition. What Absolute Truth does is simply to act as an outside stimulus which calls forth a response from that corresponding truth in you. Therefore you do not impose an alien curb on your consciousness, but you do bring into expression a potential order latent there. The reorganization of your mental qualities builds them up toward the standard of order set before them, and by achieving that standard establishes your mental equilibrium.

The consequence of this is that you realize the greatest and rarest of all rare gifts, Self Reliance. Feeling that mental balance and strength within, you cease to depend upon others for guidance and you assume the initiative yourself. Instead of moulding your life to the thoughts of others, you mold others to your own thoughts. From the driven you become the driver, and in this way you acquire real independence. You merge your uncertain multiple dependence on circumstances and human beings and material things, all of which can fail you, into a single unfaltering confidence centred upon the one and only Power that you know can never fail you, Universal Life Energy. Once you have learned how to become One with It, so that Its harmonizing Current flows unceasingly through you, you have won that which is worth more than all treasures and worldly powers, because It controls them and draws them in Its train.

Everything constructive and positive derives its value from this Truth Aspect of Universal Life Energy, because only where it manifests Itself through Order can effective power prevail. Where that Great Law does not manifest Itself there must be chaos, lack of balance and disharmony. In such a state there can be no utility, no creative service to a good end, any more than there could be in the scattered parts of an unassembled motor. No matter how excellent the pieces are, they remain only a burden until assigned to their proper positions in the completed whole.

By living Truth, you are assembling the mental motor within you, imparting to it the ordered arrangement and cohesion which will enable it to function smoothly and to generate ever greater power all the time. By expressing Absolute Truth, the Law Aspect of Universal Life Energy, you are opening a broad channel for the admission of that Basic Force Itself, the Fuel from which all Power is derived. Therefore the more Truth you develop in you, and the more Law and Order you thus introduce into your mind and your activities, then the more you become a Law unto yourself above any human law, because you are One with the Great Law which is supreme over all.

Very often untruthfulness will appear to promise some immediate advantage, but if your Foresight were sufficiently developed you would invariably perceive beyond it a more than compensating loss. Disorder means confusion, first mental and then reflected in your Physical Self. Confusion must without fail result in loss of power. Thus it is evident that if you want to be powerful and successful, for your own interest you cannot afford to compromise with Truth. No matter how tempting such compromise may seem, you will always ultimately be the loser in spite of something gained at first.

Remember, no one can pervert with impunity the Great Law. It governs a Power that turns aside for no man. The choice lies with each of us either to be with It and enlist It to sweep us irresistibly on to Success, or to be against It and be just as irresistibly crushed beneath Its Omnipotent Force. No compromise can ever make that Current flow uphill, so the option is clearly in our own hands. Success or failure—with or against—they depend solely on our own relation to Truth.

Therefore be true to yourself and you will be true to others. Be true to others and the World will be true to you. Know the Truth and It shall make you free, because real Truth means strength, power and enlightenment to choose your own path in this World. Practice Truth, and thereby cast off the fetters of weakness and fear with which untruth has bound you. Love Truth, and you will gain the treasures of this World, not merely of wealth, but of trust and honour and abounding love.

EXERCISES TO LESSON THIRTEEN

Morning and evening perform the Star Exercise, Relaxation, Silence, the Mental Contact continuously in all your daily activities and Concentration. Then, having sharpened your mind through these Exercises, apply it to the new Exercise for this week, which is called OBSERVATION.

The purpose of OBSERVATION is to deepen your understanding by wiping away the_ superficial crust and thus exposing to your mental eye the interwoven array of causes behind every visible effect. In its inception this Exercise appears to be very simple, yet its results in promoting the ordered, well balanced arrangement of your faculties which expresses the Power of Truth are remarkable. It broadens your perception, stimulates your interest, strikes back the narrow walls of your conscious field and makes you an alert, efficient and powerfully active instrument. To practice OBSERVATION proceed as follows:

Select any material object within your immediate reach as the object of the Exercise—a book or a pen, perhaps. Try to perceive through that completed unit all the divers elements and forces brought to bear on its creation. Analyse its form, its parts, its general and particular aspects, the materials used, their source and how they were shaped and combined to produce that particular serviceable thing. From the point of so uncomplicated a tool as a pen stretches back a widening vista of machinery, mines, forests, industries and factories, a fertile and teeming band of wealth and activity striking deep into the complex pattern of modern life. So with everything, for after all there is no such thing as creation of something new in this world, but only different arrangements of things already here. Try to see those many things crystallized in the one compact expression of them that you have elected to observe.

Later you can extend your field of observation to the larger world of your activities. Analyse the room or office in which you work and the people with whom you come in contact. Note the changing play of life on their features, in their habits, through the creeping scheme of their actions and the little alterations in their appearance. Endeavour to get at the meaning behind things, the purpose and causes which determine their existence.

In this way you will strip the skin from life and uncover the novel and fascinating world of reasons behind what are often dull and familiar surface effects. You will not only vastly increase your knowledge of things and people, but you will scrub the rust from your interest in them so that nothing can meet your eye without casting a lively and sparkling reflection in your mind. Interest responds to action, and action resides beneath the surface, not upon it. Therefore the more you develop OBSERVATION the more interesting, vital and cheerful life will appear to you. It is one quality in which utility and practicability are superbly united with the most agreeable diversion.

QUESTIONS TO LESSON THIRTEEN

1. What is Character Reading?

2. To what extent is the body an accurate indication of the character within it?

3. Is the character subject to physical limitations?

4. What role does Universal Life Energy play in Character Reading?

5. What attitude is necessary in order to read other people's character?

6. How can one read the thoughts of others?

7. What are Insight and Foresight?

8. How can they be developed?

9. What is Self Reliance and how can it be developed?

10. What is Truth?

11. What it its practical value?

12. How can it be developed?

Lesson Thirteen

ANSWERS TO LESSON THIRTEEN

1. **Character Reading is:**

   The analysis of the qualities and weaknesses of other individuals.

2. **The body is an accurate indication of the character within it:**

   Until about the age of twenty-five, after which it loses its plasticity and does not readily reflect the character development within.

3. **The character:**

   Is not subject to physical limitations, but continues to grow and change until late in life or in some cases until death.

4. **The role of Universal Life Energy in character reading is:**

   To convey through vibrations an always accurate impression of the character of another individual, just as the character is at that moment when it is analysed.

5. **The attitude necessary to read other people's characters is:**

A passive and receptive one, so that you are open and sensitive to the vibrations emanating from another.

6. **The attitude necessary to read other people's characters is:**

A passive and receptive one, so that you are open and sensitive to the vibrations emanating from another one reads the thoughts of others In precisely the same manner as one reads characters, by remaining open and sensitive to their mental vibrations.

7. **Insight and Foresight are:**

(1) Insight is the ability to perceive the hidden causes behind manifested effects.

(2) Foresight is the ability to correlate and combine what Insight has revealed, so as to be able to foresee future effects from causes now starting or that have started in the past.

8. **They can be developed:**

By the use of Universal Life Energy in a persistent endeavour to exercise them.

9. Self Reliance is:

A feeling of mental balance and strength within, resulting in individual Initiative and true Independence in thought and action. It is acquired through the coordinated development of all mental faculties by the use of Universal Life Energy.

10. Truth is:

The Law Aspect of Universal Life Energy, one of the greatest concrete Powers of the Universe, whose invariable activity is to establish order and harmony wherever It goes.

11. Its practical value is:

That It promotes equilibrium and thereby combines all faculties and things so that each develops the highest degree of constructive efficiency.

12. It is developed:

(1) By being always true to oneself and to others in thought and action.

(2) By the constant use of Universal Life Energy in all one's activities.

Dear Friend:

The topic of this lesson will be the very aim and purpose of your life and every life—Success. You will not only be shown what Success actually is instead of what it is supposed to be, but you will see through these pages the fascinating process whereby its latent elements in you emerge, unfold and gradually lift you over all obstacles to that culminant throne of Power which is your rightful heritage.

To avoid disaster, wreck and failure in your career it is necessary for you to know, like a good navigator, the reefs and adverse currents which imperil your way. That Ocean of Life which is at present nothing more than an uncharted waste to you must reveal the dangers that lurk in its depths, ready to snatch whatever heedless bark errs from its appointed course. These dangers you will be taught how to detect from afar and how to steer your ship with a firm hand, through the channel pointed out by compass needle of the Great Law, to the desired haven of Success.

Once you have gained a thorough knowledge of the natural Laws which rule that whole vast, unquiet sea of Existence—the Laws of Polarity, of Rhythm, of Cause and Effect—the dread which looms like a menacing cloud over the near horizon of your future will roll back to reveal to you your goal. The shoals will open to let you through, and you will find yourself able to transmute at will Pessimism into Optimism, Antagonism into Friendliness, Failure into Success.

Thus pursuing your course clear-eyed straight to the goal of your desire, you will become eventually what in your heart you long to be, the Supreme Master of your own Destiny.

Cordially yours,
Eugene Fersen.

LESSON FOURTEEN

SUCCESS — what a magic word! How appealing to everyone! In its syllables are caught the hopes, dreams and ambitions of all the World. To attain it means to overcome obstacles. To possess it means Mastery, Power. It is the focus of every constructive activity, the single goal toward which all the many devious paths of human endeavour tend. That is why those who have achieved Success become leaders whom the crowd is willing to follow, because they are foremost on the road to that corn-man destination of all.

Yet success is not only a human goal. It is the natural aim also of everything in this Universe, the one ultimate Purpose to which all life aspires. In each of Nature's infinite variety of living things are bred certain distinctive characteristics which, brought to fruition, represent Success to that particular unit in the Cosmic Scheme. To an apple seed it is the tree laden with apples; to a kernel of corn it is the well-filled ear; to the acorn it is an oak. Each enfolds an unborn destiny, but between it and the realization of all those verdant possibilities within stretches a long, hard road of struggle and achievement, a road sown with difficulties, pitted with failures and whitened with the bones of those who have fallen by the wayside and yielded themselves supinely to the bitter death of despair.

For instance, consider a seed thrown into the ground in the early spring. Entombed far from air, sunlight and moisture, helpless behind the confining walls of its shell, a tiny champion locked in a stubborn dungeon of its own, it can only wait. Within it broods a Dream—tall stalk nodding under a golden burden of grain, green tresses fluttering in the breeze, strength, honour, achievement—but from the Dream knocking about in the dull brown pellet to its realization in actual fact is a long, far cry. Will the untried Knight be able to accomplish that quest?

The opportunity is soon given it to try. Moisture, seeping down, breaks with its touch the prison walls. Upwards and downwards leap two tender shoots, seeking the fresh air and sunlight above and the moisture below. The silent battle has been joined, Success or Failure hanging on the points of those two slender lances carrying forward the Cause of the seed.

The first foe to be vanquished is the earth. Every grain of sand is a barrier to be pushed aside, every pebble a fortress to be won. The fragile weapons on which the seeds have to rely are so delicate that a touch is often sufficient to break them, yet they must cope with a crushing mass of soil and stone. However, the seed does not despair, but bores valiantly onward, conquering obstacles one by one, progressing a step at a time, until eventually it thrusts its victorious crest through the final crust into a new world of freedom, sunlight and fresh air.

Then it has gained its first visible Success, because as long as it laboured underground there was no way of marking its progress in the right direction. It has broken its way into an entirely different environment, far richer in honours to be won but also far more ominous with perils to be met and overcome.

The beguiling air of Freedom and Prosperity which now caresses the young plant, and the warm sunlight glancing like a guerdon of victory from its upright blade, dissemble unimagined treachery and menace. At any moment the trailing fingers of the wind can grip with a blast of fury to rend and destroy, or the sunbeam glitter with white fire to sear, wither and consume. Then the hard-pressed warrior must be able to call on its roots to anchor it securely against the frenzy of the storm and to send it moisture with which to ward off the flame-edged sword of the sun. If the seed has fought as good a battle in one direction as in the other, establishing itself on a firm footing and tapping a constant supply of water, it will survive and flourish; if not, it will go down in defeat and find all its efforts wasted.

Assuming that it has done its duty well, the plant, through adversity, becomes tough, pliant and wise in the ways of a harsh and reckless world. Persistence and energy carry it onward to the fulfilment of its destiny, so that it ripens in the autumn of its life to the realization of those treasures which are both the reward of its endeavours and the measure of its Success. It stands strong and masterful, bidding defiance to wind and sun, tossing aloft its golden prize of grain, flaunting its victory in the face of the World. The Dream is fact, the quest achieved, the goal won. Yet even that is not the end.

The plant will soon die, but Success can never die. Through each of that numerous progeny of the original seed it will go on and on, increasing from generation to generation, because to each has been transmitted the same Dream of Conquest, the same power to overcome and to multiply. Therefore while individuals are the vehicles of Success, rising and vanishing under it in an advancing tide, Success itself is above and beyond the limitations which make its possession as brief as life itself.

Just as it is with plants, so it is with human beings. You also are born with your peculiar Dream, your own Purpose, and the power to overcome every obstacle that stands in the way of its realization. Success is an integral part of your nature, the stuff of which you are made; only, like the seed, it is hedged about and buried deep under the sodden weight of outside barriers as well as inner handicaps.

Yet with you, too, every adverse circumstance of environment or nature is after all only a foil for the development of the qualities within you. From each challenge accepted, each battle won, you rise stronger, readier for the next. No matter how difficult a step may be, it lifts you one pace nearer to the coveted goal. Every constructive effort in thought, word or deed brings you so much further out of the darkness and limitations of your present surroundings into the free, open air of sunshine and prosperity, into the broad domain of Power and Success.

Many people fail because they are prone to mistake their initial success for license to do as they please. Freedom is not license. New conditions, different surroundings, while they give a much wider scope of action, also impose corresponding responsibilities. Those who disregard these responsibilities and undertake to abuse their liberty are in somewhat the same position as the plant which has neglected to root itself firmly in the soil. The very freedom they have won tears them loose and whirls them to ruin, breaking their contact with the saving current of Life Energy and exposing them to the scorching rays of a Prosperity which they can no longer control.

To enjoy a lasting victory you must remember to stay firmly rooted in the ground of Fact, drawing from there the creative energy that thrives above. Then you will have a poise that nothing can upset or withstand. Nature is a marvellous book for those who know how to read it — a book which, opened on the page of Success, will teach you an object lesson more illuminating than all the words ever penned.

The process of achieving Success is therefore similar throughout all Nature, although the details of the struggle vary. In every path there are obstacles to challenge the development of those qualities whose full and harmonious unfoldment lifts one to the desired goal. The obstacles may differ in kind, depending on the environment and the forces that strive for expression, but all serve the same end. This disposition of affairs is the result of certain definite Natural Laws, changeless, unresting and omnipresent, discernible through as many aspects as there are lives to command them, and proceeding impersonally in the task of weeding out the weak and unfit.

The first of these Laws, the Law of Polarity, is one which works continually throughout the whole Universe. Everything in Nature has two poles, a positive and a negative one. Night follows day, cold stands as the opposite of heat, shadow balances light. No contradicts Yes. In every department of Existence a positive factor implies a corresponding negative one, like a see-saw which goes as far down at one end as it goes up at the other.

You have probably noticed the peculiar working of this Law of Polarity in your own life. You have been uncomfortably aware that whenever you make a positive statement, immediately there seems to arise from some unseen and mysterious depths the silent opposition "No!" which very frequently outweighs your positive intention and takes its place. Perhaps you have tried to dismiss the feeling on the ground that it is merely a superstition unworthy of a person of your intelligence and education, but if so you did your own observation an injustice. What you noticed was not any weird "Black Magic" at all, but was simply the very logical operation of a Law of Nature which you happened to put into action.

The expression of this same Law through other individuals does not at all appear to you as superstition; in them you heartily condemn it as Perversity. You tell a person to do something, and thereby you seem to stir up in him an invincible resolve not to do it, or even to do exactly the opposite. Mules and goats illustrate the same traits most admirably. A child, when told not to do a certain thing, is at once consumed with a burning ambition to go and do it. Among ladies secrets are notoriously hard to keep, because the solemn injunction "Don't tell" seems absolutely to drive it through their lips like a charge of explosive.

Further still, you have doubtless remarked that whenever you will pursue a definite course of action, every conceivable obstacle arises to block your path, while at other times an equally firm pledge not to proceed in a particular way is followed by a change of circumstances that practically herds you into it. An evil force seems to compel you into the course in which you especially did not want to go, and to thwart and rebuff you in every direction. An evil force? No — simply the Law of Polarity or Opposition getting in its work.

Ignorance of this Law has always been a teeming source of superstitions, from the most benighted savage to the highest civilized society. Typical of these is the singular aversion to black cats, a rather reasonable distrust of ladders, a divining significance in the set of a pin and the efficacy of wood as a de-magnetizing agent for evil influences. Why do people dislike to receive compliments on their success in business, or why do they "rap on wood" when they inadvertently assert some projected piece of work as a fact to be already taken for granted? Because they have observed that they usually have to pay the price for such compliments in unexpected mistakes, difficulties and delays in the very direction in which it was given.

They anticipate the effects of the Law of Polarity without really knowing what it is.

Yet if one understands the Law of Polarity one can avoid its negative effects in a rational manner instead of blindly trying to dodge some non-existent "evil eye." All that is necessary is to identify oneself definitely with the

Positive by mentally contacting Universal Life Energy before a statement, and then to protect that statement still more by silently KNOWING, or realizing within oneself, that with the help of the Great Law such a thing will — or will not — be done." Either of these two methods alone will give satisfactory results, because both Universal Life Energy and the Great Law are the pure essence of the Positive and as such are superior to all negative, which cannot stand for a moment against the constructive Power of the Infinite.

It is thought by some that all trouble can be avoided by being neutral in your statements, but this is an undesirable method. Neutrality means Inertia, which is a condition as barren as death. Why sacrifice the creative power of a definite, positive statement merely to avoid trouble? Rather, cast the weight always in the scale of the Positive. Cultivate optimism. Enlist the driving energy of the Positive in everything you do, because the more you attune yourself to It the more you will be able to rise above the Law of Polarity in your life.

When you have learned to rely confidently on the Universal Power instead of on your own limited human forces, you will find that there is no longer any possible opposition to what you think, state or do. Then you will have overcome the Law of Polarity so far as our present state of consciousness permits.

The second Law which sways the destinies of human beings to an exceptional extent is the Law of Rhythm, which operates in conjunction with the Law of Polarity and is in fact the same Law under another and more momentous aspect. The Law of Polarity can be likened to the second hand of a watch, ticking off the individual events of your life, while the Law of Rhythm is the minute hand which sweeps down and up in its majestic circuit, summing up in its progress all the flying fractions .measured out by its busy associate.

This generous rhythmic swing you may have observed in your own experience and that of your friends. There will be periods of long or shorter duration when everything works out swiftly and harmoniously to a splendid conclusion. Every project is blessed with favouring circumstances which boost it on its way, and whatever you undertake spins serenely up the highway of Success. On the other hand, also, there occur periods of depression when anything commenced seems doomed from the very beginning to failure. People attribute these alternations to good or ill luck, but in reality they are due to the Law of Rhythm, which on its upward trend lifts you to the heights and then drags you down on its return movement.

This Law is so powerful that human beings appear to be quite helpless before it. It pervades all Existence, manifesting itself on the largest scale just as irresistibly as it does on the smaller one. The entire progress of Evolution is charted by its ebb and flow no less than is the life of the individual. Nations, races and peoples are strung on it like so many beads on a wire, so that with its ascending movement empires are built, countries arise, dominance shines through a people, while with its downward swing glory fades and empires crash to ruin.

But although the operation of this Law on the larger scale through the human race is really beyond any control, it nevertheless can and must be overcome in the individual if Success is to be achieved. Successful people are those who, through energy and optimism, were able to master it unconsciously, at least in its negative aspect. Yet few people possess by nature the unusual strength of character and positiviness necessary to assert that mastery, and as a result the majority of human kind never see their aspirations realized in their lives.

However, one recourse is available to everyone whereby to win free from the destructive influence of the Law of Rhythm. An intelligent and persistent use of Universal Life Energy is an antidote as invincible in this case as in all other negative conditions. It stimulates your inner qualities, giving you the perception to recognize the upward trend of the Law, and the strength and confidence to take decisive advantage of it.

Then you know how to fling yourself heart and soul into every opening, and how to rise to the highest possible goal on the forward surge of the wave. You are equally quick to perceive the subsidence of that wave of Success, and are able to consolidate your gains before it falls from under you. This understanding, together with the supporting power of Universal Life Energy, renders you immune to both discouragement and failure.

The problem faced by the individual is most vividly and accurately portrayed in that faced by a swimmer in treacherous waters. The waves on the ocean are the result of the Law of Rhythm operating on the physical plane precisely in the same manner as it operates in your life.

Above is the upward and forward surge of the wave, concealing a strong movement beneath it. This reserve movement is called the undertow. It is energy which, passing below the surface of the water, lifts it to a certain height, much as a chance puff of wind might slip underneath a table covering and lift it along its length. The water itself does not move from place to place, but simply molds in a sliding ripple the wholly unrelated current of energy beneath.

Your task is to stay on the crest of that advancing ripple. To ride forward on it means to be carried to greater and greater Success; to lose it and drop into the hollow behind means failure. Steadiness of activities, perseverance, optimism and a persistent assertion of the Positive through the use of Universal Life Energy are the aids which will enable you to hold your position on top and collect the richest rewards from its forward and constructive movement.

The secret of permanent success is in knowing when to stop. Many people whose activities are of a spasmodic nature wonder why they seem only to "hit the high spots" and never stay there. They are always poised on the peak of Success or wallowing in the abyss of Failure, swinging back and forth between the two and striking a very mean average.

The reason is that while they had the energy and daring to take advantage of the upward trend of the Law of Rhythm, they did not know how to anticipate its downward sweep. They forged vigorously ahead with new projects and expansion when they ought to have devoted their talents to consolidating what they had gained. In consequence they were left hanging in mid-air, struggling vainly against the crash which was bound to come.

An intelligent adjustment of activities to circumstances is necessary for continued success. One must know when to go ahead and when to hold up, when to push an advantage and when to stop. Those who have made a Success of their lives have learned through hard experience to do this; and if they were able to succeed through sheer energy, positiveness and perseverance, without any real knowledge of the Law of Rhythm with which they had to contend, how much easier it ought to be for you who know the cause of the trouble and how to overcome it.

This knowledge of how to accommodate yourself to the Laws of Polarity and Rhythm is a wonderful help in business of any kind. Finance, salesmanship, barter of all sorts, — all are victims of these Laws of which a proper understanding opens up limitless new fields of action in every direction, because through understanding, the limiting factors of risk and uncertainty will be largely eliminated.

To most people a new project is always a step in the dark. Life is like an open grand piano with the wires exposed, and the hopeful novice, striking a key, takes a chance that the right hammer will jump out to strike the note he wants. Sometimes he guesses right, sometimes not. But if he knew the mechanics of the piano he could say with confidence, This key will transmit my blow to that particular wire and sound the note I wish," because the relation would be clear to him.

A chart of stock market quotations, real estate, commerce or any industry will trace out in black and white the operation of these Laws through them. All are subject to fluctuations that recur periodically, and all are therefore rich in opportunities for those with eyes to see and the energy to take advantage of them. Once armed with a knowledge of those Laws you are able to carve a sphere of activities as great as your desires out of your environment.

The continual use of Universal Life Energy by the student of Science of Being will strengthen him to wield that weapon of Knowledge to much greater effect. It will sharpen his perception, render all his faculties more acute, and carry to him the pulse of events so truly that he will be able to forecast unerringly conditions presently to be realized in material fact in his own affairs. Thus he will detect the upward trend of the Law in time to profit most fully by it, and will anticipate the downward plunge with the needful precautions.

Inability to perceive the rhythmic ebb and flow of these Laws is the only excuse for the modern complaint that all the good things have been snapped up." All the good things have always been snapped up, yet the human race has clambered on pretty consistently somehow.

As a matter of fact, life was never richer in opportunities than it is at present, and those who will absorb and apply what they are given in this Lesson will be able to see and grasp them. There will always be those whom repeated failure, brought on because they did not have the acumen to switch their activities at the right time, has taught them to look askance at inviting opportunities, but that timidly vanishes if you know how to pick out your course ahead.

One general rule should be observed whenever you intend to invest money. Make the contact with Universal Life Energy first, and when you feel Its Current flowing through you try to sense from It the proper course on which to proceed. Bring all the possibilities to the test of that searching Force, and ask of It the silent question, "Must I proceed thus and so or must I not?"

If you have properly contacted the Universal Power, Its effect will be to establish in you Its own perfect peace and harmony, stimulating and coordinating all your faculties and clearing away discord. Then the faint voice of your intuition, usually drowned out in the harsh clangour of your mental activities, becomes audible to you and warns you of any pitfalls or dangers which beset your path. This guiding voice, tolling you onward as it echoes ahead along the path in which it is right for you to go, is the so-called "hunch" to which so many of the great owe their success.

Those who will marshal all their ambitions and efforts behind their knowledge of the Laws of Polarity and Rhythm, who will assort and adapt their activities to the fluctuations induced by these Laws, and who will above all charge their endeavours with Universal Life Energy and point them according to the unerring voice of

Intuition, will achieve Success rivalling their fondest dreams.

The third and final one of the three dominant Laws affecting human progress is the Law of Cause and Effect. There is prevalent a belief that people are mere puppets of Fate, bunted hither and yon without being in the least consulted as to their own desires in the matter. In other words, the individual is supposed to have no free will of his own and no hand in the moulding of his future. This is the man-made theory of Predestination, which maintains that no matter how much one may strive to succeed in a certain direction, it is effort wasted if his destiny is to fail, and vice versa.

This theory arises from Ignorance of the Law of Cause and Effect, which in reality opens to Mankind the unbounded opportunity to create whatever future may be desired. The Law of Cause and Effect, working with mathematical precision throughout all Nature, decrees that for every Effect there must be a corresponding Cause, and vice versa. Therefore nothing exists in all the Universe without a reason, and the apparently meaningless chaos of visible Effects are simply the material evidence of most exactly ordered Causes, none the less operative because they are not seen. There is no such thing as Chance, no remotest possibility of a haphazard occurrence without any Cause whatever, because everything and every event has its place in the cosmic scheme too perfectly ruled to permit of the least infraction.

In spite of this there are always people who imagine that the World is in a lawless condition, and they can "get something for nothing,"—plant weeds and gather wheat. That is utterly impossible. Like invariably produces like as a direct result, whether it be seeds or actions. If you sow honesty, energy, intelligence and all positive qualities, you will sooner or later reap a corresponding harvest. If you sow negative causes you will most inevitably reap the thistles of negative effects.

Every individual is therefore the author of his own Destiny, whether he likes it or not. Through the causes he starts he shapes his future to a corresponding end, good, bad or indifferent. He can do it unconsciously and risk the result, or he can acquire an understanding of how the Law works and then take advantage of it intelligently and purposefully. That is, he can obtain a Destiny by accident or by design.

The most welcome advantage of the Destiny by design is perhaps the greater ease with which it is acquired. Knowledge of the Law of Cause and Effect strikes off the shackles of Worry and Fear, leaving you to direct all that wasted energy into constructive channels. You know that whatever Cause you have started will culminate in its own unchangeable Effect, no matter what you may do to prevent it. Therefore if the Cause was a right one you have no excuse to think further about it, while if it was a wrong one you cannot worry it a single degree out of its appointed course. All you can do is to take it into your calculations for the Future.

Therefore abandon Worry, which can only disintegrate your own faculties by draining away your energies, weakening you in every direction and making you an easier prey to the very negative you dread. Devote yourself to starting new Right Causes NOW, to neutralize the evil present effects of wrong causes out of the Past. The sooner you do so the sooner you will change your life from an unhappy, burdensome routine, full of disease, failure and trouble of every kind, into the healthy, buoyant, happy pilgrimage, full of strength and constructive activities, sparkling with interest, vibrant with power, that you actually desire it to be.

Impatience to realize immediately the Happiness to which you aspire will not hasten its coming. Remember, the Law of Cause and Effect cannot be skipped over or evaded. The negative causes of other times must come to fruition before the positive ones of today. You can clear a muddy stream by introducing clean water at its source, but the old corruption must run its course before its place can be taken by the clear current.

Very often, especially with people in whose lives the negative has been overwhelmingly present, a right action seems to bring down on the head of the individual a very unpleasant result instead of the expected positive one. It appears to be like a punishment for a right action, and it may occur a number of times, all the more forcefully if Universal Life Energy has been used in performing the right action.

The reason for this seeming contradiction is that around an individual whose life has been full of sorrow and trouble hangs a dense cloud of that negative, enveloping him completely. A Right Cause discharged into that cloud, reinforced by Universal Life Energy, causes a sudden precipitation of the evil there. Such precipitation would have come anyway, but not in such abundance; so that abrupt rain, while very unpleasant, is nevertheless a good sign. It indicates that the negative fog is being rapidly dispersed, breaking away to let in all the sooner the bright sunshine of Positive Effects from Positive Causes that have been sent out. Therefore while the use of Universal Life Energy intensifies for a time negative conditions, it also greatly shortens their duration.

If you are going through such an experience do not despair, but be cheered by the realization that the Law is visibly working in this manner to change your Destiny for the better. When you alter your own outlook in this manner, banishing the darkness of pessimism in the bright light of optimism, you have taken a great step toward the Happiness and Success you seek. "Like attracts like," and the inviting warmth of that constructive attitude in you will draw into your life the lustrous reward to which you aspire. Then failure, that bad memory of the past, will melt away like a shadow before the dawning reality of present Success. Enmity will crumble before you, indifference crystallize into respect, and even hatred will be transmuted at length into Friendliness and Love.

EXERCISES TO LESSON FOURTEEN

The performance morning and evening of the Star Exercise, Relaxation, Silence and Concentration, together with the continual use of the Mental Contact with Universal Life Energy at all times, are the usual necessary preliminaries to the new 'Exercise designed for this week, and which is called REALIZATION.

The purpose of REALIZATION is to breed a wealth of new ideas in any specific line of thinking and thus furnish you with ample material to project into constructive fact. For example, you may desire to improve and expand your business, to perceive practical ways of enlarging it and promoting a greater volume of trade. Or you may wish to improve some other department of your life, because in every aspect of human activities there is always room for improvement, accelerated progress and growth, with a corresponding increase in power and returns.

As the object of your Concentration Exercise, therefore, take this week that activity in which you want to uncover new ideas. The ideas are there in your mental ground, but in order to bring them within reach you have to dig for them. The more you concentrate on the subject in mind, and the more effectively you put Universal Life Energy behind that work, then the more you are probing into your mental soil and unearthing the wealth of new ideas lodged there. Writing these ideas down as you discover them will be a wise precaution, as otherwise you are apt to forget them.

When you have selected a sufficient number of ideas to form a creditable working basis, they must be submitted to your conscious faculties for examination of their possibilities. Those that survive the critical analysis of your Reason will be sound mental metal, constructive and of a great value both to you, and to others.

Remember, nothing commands a higher price among Humanity than good ideas. They are actual mind treasures which will be accepted at face value everywhere. Your unfailing bank account is in your head if you will only take the trouble to draw on it.

A student of the Work recently put this to the test with most satisfactory results. Through the method just described she obtained an idea for a moving picture play, which she wrote out and submitted in a prize contest of thousands. Her idea won the competition, bringing her not only a considerable cash prize, but also a large royalty on the completed picture, which became famous throughout America. Yet this student had never before done any sort of commercial writing, and she had, besides the reward in cash, the unusual experience of seeing her first attempt crowned with the most extraordinary success.

QUESTIONS TO LESSON FOURTEEN

1. What is Success?

2. Is it restricted to any special department of life or activities?

3. What purpose is served by the obstacles in the way of its realization?

4. What are the two natural Laws most intimately related with Success or Failure?

5. How can the individual perceive and take advantage of these Laws?

6. What exceptional advantage does a knowledge of these Laws confer in the business and financial world?

7. What is the Law of Cause and Effect?

8. Is the theory of Predestination correct?

9. Can man build his own Destiny?

10. Is there such a thing as blind Chance?

11. How can the negative aspects of all the above three Laws be avoided?

12. What two human qualities are essential to achieve Success?

ANSWERS TO LESSON FOURTEEN

1. Success is:

The actual realization in the life of the individual of all inborn possibilities.

2. Success:

Is not restricted to any special departments of life or activities, but is the single Aim and Purpose of all Existence.

3. The purpose served by obstacles in the way of its realization is:

To bring forth and develop by adversity the qualities through which alone the individual can achieve Success.

4. The two Natural Laws most intimately related with Success or Failure are:

(1) The Law of Polarity, or Opposition, which is that everything in Nature has two poles, a positive and a negative one, each the exact antithesis of the other.

(2) The Law of Rhythm, which is the expression under another aspect of the Law of. Polarity, and determines the rhythmic ebb and flow of life and activities throughout all Nature.

5. **The individual can perceive and take advantage of these Laws:**

    By the use of Universal Life Energy to stimulate all his faculties and make audible to him the voice of his own Intuition.

6. **The exceptional advantage conferred by a knowledge of these Laws in the business and financial world is:**

    That it enables one to eliminate risk and error by anticipating events, and thus opens to one much wider spheres of activity.

7. **The Law of Cause and Effect is:**

    That in all the World every Effect is of necessity the product of a corresponding Cause, and every Cause has its corresponding Effect.

8. **The theory of Predestination:**

    Is completely wrong, and arose only through ignorance of the Law of Cause and Effect.

9. **Man:**

    Is able to build his own Destiny, through intelligent use of the Law of Cause and Effect.

10. Blind Chance:

Is impossible, as no Effect can possibly exist without a corresponding logical Cause behind it.

11. The negative aspects of all these Laws can be overcome:

By the continual use of Universal Life Energy.

12. Two human qualities for achieving Success are:

Optimism and Perseverance.

Dear Friend:

Other Lessons have equipped you with a full complement of tools to carve out your Destiny in the stubborn material of this World, foremost among them being that marvellous instrument fashioned by your Conscious Self, the Concentrated Thought. Now, in Lesson Fifteen, will be placed at your command the Power by which this waiting implement must be thrust into the Substance of the Physical World and made creative in terms of solid fact. You will learn how to pour into constructive expression through it the Magnetic Force of Universal Life Energy, and how to make it a living centre of attraction for the very elements it needs for realization in your life.

Here also will be unmasked those foes of constructive effort which Fear sends out to bar the road between your inner domain of Mind and the outer plane of Matter. Timidity, Indecision, and Procrastination, dangerous pitfalls in the way of your pilgrim concepts, will be exposed and the methods explained for eliminating them altogether.

Finally, Suggestion and Auto-suggestion, which are so widely practiced and so superficially understood today will be analysed and revealed to you in their true light. You will perceive the moral threat they conceal so deftly behind a specious Curtain of effects, and will be able not only to protect yourself from their baneful influence, but will know how to obtain in enduring fact the results to which they simply seem to aspire.

The vital importance of this Lesson will be that it endows you with the power to exercise intelligently and with full effectiveness your mental qualities. It will bridge the gap between the mental and physical aspects of your nature, and will open a broad way for you to bring down from the distant plane of Mind into actual realization your abstract thoughts and ideas.

Cordially yours,
Eugene Fersen.

LESSON FIFTEEN

THE creative power of the Concentrated Thought is the beginning and the end of all constructive mental activity. It marks the border line between abstract concepts and their embodiment in concrete, living facts. Most people, especially the so-called mental types, do not possess the creative power strongly enough to bring down to the Material Plane their abstract concepts. Their thought is sterile, because they themselves are empty of the constructive Energy from which Mind as well as Body must draw its positive force. Consequently they are as impotent to attract on the Physical Plane the opportunity to realize their concepts as they are physically incapable of taking advantage of it.

Thought, in order to be creative, must live. Just as the body of a new born child, with all its undeveloped possibilities for growth and unfoldment, must have within it some centre of animating power which will drive those possibilities into expression, so your thought must contact some secret spring of action which will invest the listless form with life and make it an active instrument for the accomplishment of its design.

The cold ray of your Mind cannot impart to your concepts this vital current, any more than the cold light of the moon can stir a seed into growth. It can project, like shadows, the ideas which float past the lens of your Conscious Self; but the only Living Principle which can implant in those shadows the germ of life and make them real independent, magnetic entities of some consequence in the scheme of things is the one common Source of all animate being, Universal Life Energy.

Mental concepts become creative in direct proportion to the amount of Universal Life Energy with which you endow them. The more Life Force you pour into your Concentrated Thought, the greater power of attraction that thought will be able to exert in order to draw to it the very elements for its realization on the Material Plane. From mere aimless spectres drifting across your mental firmament, your concepts become fixed units of dynamic energy, thrusting out capable, searching fingers into the passing stream of events. They enter actively into the current of your life and work constructively to mold circumstances to your advantage.

Obviously, in business and in human relations in general, the individual with the strong creative thought is the one who wins. His idea is the magnetic centre about which cluster the thoughts and interests of others whom he enables to see the same possibilities through his own mental eye. As the host of that attractive concept, he becomes the focal centre, the point through which it is to be thrust out into realization, and is naturally in the position of leadership. Very frequently this normal crystallization of circumstances about one individual is attributed to suggestion or persuasion, but after all it is nothing but the natural response of less energetic minds to the stronger radio-activity of another.

Therefore whenever you concentrate your mind upon some object to be achieved, use Universal Life Energy to impregnate thoroughly the inner image conjured up by your Conscious Self. Your thought, so permeated, becomes actually a living thing, a seed which, wherever planted, will grow and produce a lasting impression. This is the secret of why the thoughts of some people impress, while those of others do not. Mental concepts, to strike with conviction, must be driven forward by that impelling Force, which can be injected into them as follows:

Relax, enter into Silence and make the Contact with Universal Life Energy. Then, when you feel Its Current flowing through you, concentrate your mind on the object you are interested in achieving. Let that Power pour strongly through your thought channels to the support of your mental activity, so that It etches out on the screen of your Consciousness a picture so vivid and distinct in every detail that you can actually visualize it.

Once you have brought your concept into clear focus, do not project it from yourself as if to impress others, but discharge it instead into your own Subconsciousness according to the method described in Lesson Twelve for learning things by heart. Remember, you are working now with a Power which functions only when relaxation provides It with adequate channels, and your purpose is to attract, not compel, the opportunity you desire. If you indulge the temptation to use your Will at this point you automatically close the channels within you and shift your reliance from the unlimited Energy of the Universe to the very limited and undependable powers of your own mind.

When your concentrated thought, charged with Universal Life Energy, is allowed to sink into your Inner

Self, it is conveyed from the brain along the spinal cord to the Solar Plexus, where it produces an impression upon the Subconsciousness. This initial impression is only the first step in a mental campaign to bring about its realization in fact. It blazes a neutral trail, so to speak, between itself as the magnetic nucleus at one end and your Conscious Self at the other. Therefore by repeating this process day by day at a certain time selected for that purpose you pour over the connecting line within you an increasing torrent of Life Force which stamps the image continually deeper in your Subconscious Field and radiates from it an ever more powerful stream.

The result of all this will be that your Concentrated Thought, like an electric magnet fed by a stronger and stronger current, will gradually extend the field of its influence so that it contacts and draws within reach all the corresponding elements for its actual embodiment in material expression. Environment and conditions will subtly modify themselves in response to the insistent pressure put upon them, and will eventually open a way for the birth in accomplished fact of that inner concept working through you.

Yet the creative thought itself, although it can produce the right combination of circumstances, cannot proceed further by its own initiative. Its function is completed when it has brought within your reach the opportunity to realize it on the plane of Matter. It cannot skip from the Abstract into the Concrete without any intermediary process, any more than you can think a ten dollar gold piece into your pocket. You can think of a way to earn a ten dollar gold piece, but between you and your possession of it stands a barrier which you cannot dodge or jump — Work.

Work is the activity of giving physical birth to a mental concept. It consists of welding the elements and circumstances attracted by the concept into its image and likeness on the Material Plane. The thought of a building is habitable only when it is erected in brick and stone. The thought of a bridge will carry you dry-shod across a river only when it is wrought in steel and iron. The thought of a political speech will sway a nation only when outlined in sound or ink.

The individual, therefore, has two opposite shores to his nature from which he must build out simultaneously in order to span the gap between. On the Mental shore stands the concept demanding expression; on the Physical shore stands his own body. The warm sun of Universal Life Energy, shining equally on both, expresses itself through the concept in a magnetic and harmonizing Power which flings out to mid-stream a semi-arch of Opportunity. Through the body it emerges as constructive activities which go out to meet that waiting Opportunity. The two are joined in the middle, and the keystone of the entire structure is Work.

From this will be perceived the fallacy of depending on either the Mental or the Physical Plane alone for the attainment of ambitions. Those who believe that by desiring a thing strongly they can obtain it without any physical effort whatever are doomed to certain failure. Also those who strive valiantly but without intelligence can never gain any appreciable headway. Achievement and Progress result only from a proper combination and cooperation of the two.

All the obstacles and difficulties which hinder this fruitful cooperation come from a lack on one plane or the other, or both, of Universal Life Energy. The Body is an alert and responsive tool of the Mind only as it is animated with an abundant current of Life Force. The Mind is able to wield that tool easily only as the same Power endows it with the capacity to do so. Lack of physical vitality makes the individual a weak and ailing victim of all negative influences. Lack of vitality on the Mental Plane generates most of the negative influences of which he is the victim.

Characteristic of these are Timidity, Indecision, Procrastination and all associated weaknesses. All are in effect merely the flabby yielding of an enervated mind to the force of circumstances, and all are comprehended in the single term, Fear. As stated in Lesson Twelve, Fear is a feeling of helplessness or lack of power in the face of adverse conditions. Therefore it is the fundamental cause of the specific symptoms now under consideration.

The cure for these symptoms naturally lies in the cure of their cause. Those who know how to contact an abundant supply of Universal Life Energy are never cowed by any situation which confronts them. They possess a poise which nothing can disturb, and which' they obtained not as the result of a laborious and complicated process of bolstering up the weak places one by one, but through a sweeping elimination of all together. There is no room in them for Fear, because there is no inner vacuum from which it can exert its paralysing pressure.

Occasionally a superabundance of Energy may impel one to "jump at conclusions" and perhaps come to a wrong decision. The upward surge of Vital Force through every available channel is so strong that it must burst into expression one way or the other. The individual, far from hesitating, is literally driven into taking a decision which the outcome may give him reason for regret.

Such circumstance is an error on the positive side, yet is infinitely preferable to the negative course of avoiding any decision at all. Failure to decide means Inertia, a condition as barren of results and as unsusceptible of change as Death itself. Any activity, even though wrongly directed, is better than that, because not only will mistaken action be in any event an instructive experience, but it is always subject to modification from wrong into right.

The reason why even this somewhat excusable error is less common than the greater crime of Inertia is because of the most subtle and pervasive of the three negative influences previously mentioned, Procrastination. This is a sort of mental safety valve through which any surplus steam you might generate leaks away unused. It means putting things off until some future time when, supposedly, you will be better qualified to do them. "Tomorrow" is its watchword, and "Tomorrow," as everyone knows but seldom bothers to admit, never arrives. Neither does the decision.

Therefore whenever you are confronted with a task to which you think you are not equal at the moment that is a challenge which you cannot afford to ignore. Make the

Mental Contact with Universal Life Energy and proceed to master the situation without further delay, because if you yield to the temptation to "put it off" you are beaten before you know it. You have at your command ample Power through which to assert once and for all your dominance, yet if you fail to make use of it when the time is ripe you will find it increasingly difficult to gain victory later.

Much is written and taught today of the Power of Suggestion as a means for overcoming not these limitations, but all others of a physical and emotional nature as well. Therefore Suggestion deserves a critical analysis from the point of view of the Knowledge imparted to you in these lessons, and as a result of that analysis should henceforth be left severally alone.

In the first place, Suggestion is a purely mental exercise, and is therefore subject to the same limitations and disadvantages as Mind itself, and in the same degree. The instrument through which it works is the human Will, and it is strong or weak in proportion as the Will is strong or weak. As a cure for ailments which result from the weakness of the same Mind on whose strength it must depend for its own efficacy it is therefore totally inadequate, yet as a temporary alleviation it is sometimes as miraculously effective, and as dangerous, as a powerful drug.

Suggestion consists of the imposition of one Mind upon another through the force of the Will. Auto-suggestion is the same process applied to one's own Subconsciousness by his Conscious Self. Both are mild forms respectively of hypnosis and self-hypnosis. The mechanics of their operation is through affirmation or repetition, whereby the desired thought is pounded into the Subconsciousness of the individual until he automatically reacts to it.

The singularly vicious and destructive nature of this process is apparent when you consider that it completely paralyses the department of Mind through which every individual achieves his own independent expression, the Conscious Self. That is, it robs one of his own identity and implants in him a false one fashioned in accordance with the desire of the operator. Instead of disclosing as through a clear glass the true inner Individuality which is himself, the victim reflects like a mirror the false image flung there by someone else. He is no longer a free, self-reliant entity, author of the particular Destiny that is his, but is a mechanical puppet jerked by the strings of another person's promptings to do that other person's Will.

Your whole independent existence hinges upon the three conscious guardians of your Subconscious Mental Field, Reason, Will and Common Sense. When your rational mind rebels against the intrusion of alien ideas, those ideas are jammed past the opposition of your Will by the stronger and more determined Will of the operator. Your defences are broken down, and instead of you planting the seeds of your own activities in your Subconscious soil, the other individual plants the seeds of activities conceived by him. In other words, through the unguarded door of your Mind he sows the crop that you will grow and reap for him in your life.

Therefore of all moral offences Suggestion is one of the worst, because it robs people of their most valuable rights, personal freedom and self determination. Yet unconsciously it is employed all the time throughout the whole structure of human relations, and is even deliberately urged as a desirable means to achieve your ends. You can probably pick out of your own experience numerous instances where you have succumbed against your will to the stronger mental influences of another. Often you have done things which you otherwise would have refrained from doing, and afterward have hated both the other individual for putting forth the suggestion and yourself for yielding to it.

Your supreme interest should be always to preserve your mental freedom. Station your conscious faculties, forewarned with Knowledge and forearmed with abundant Life Force, securely at the door to your Subconscious Self, ready to bar from entry every thought which your Reason condemns as unfit.

This does not mean to develop an antagonistic and suspicious attitude, which is simply a cleverly disguised form of fear and betrays you into the very condition you wish to avoid. Everything has a right to demand an audience with your Rational Mind, but your Rational Mind must have the poise and Discrimination to estimate truly its value or fitness to obtain admission. Only by exercising that power of Discrimination can you bring forth its associate activity of Self Determination, thereby establishing the moral independence which is your right. The more you use and strengthen these conscious servants of yours, the broader and freer you will become mentally, and the more efficient and powerful you will be in life.

Auto-suggestion has effects quite as undesirable as Suggestion itself, and its continual practice is bound to reduce very materially the efficiency of the individual. Repeated affirmations which do not bear fruit in realization by the Conscious Self eventually deaden the Subconsciousness, just as an incessant series of blows will numb into insensibility any portion of your body. The cumulative effect of that persistent hammering, always falling in monotonous repetitions on the same spot, is far more destructive than one severe shock which would stun, but not kill.

This effect is very noticeable in those who have become confirmed addicts to this mental drug. It is a well known fact that subjects of Suggestion or Auto-suggestion are mentally sluggish and lacking in the buoyant alertness of a healthy and normal Mind. Dependent as they are on that unnatural stimulant, they require an increasingly powerful dose of it each time in order to react at all. The dose they take may flog them into temporary activity, but it also flogs out of them a measure of the strength and resistance they have left.

That is why Suggestion invariably fails to effect a permanent cure of physical or mental ailments. It feeds on the energy of the individual; so that as it gets stronger and more pronounced in its reaction, the individual himself gets weaker and less resistant to the trouble which he is trying to cure. Thus every convalescence induced in this way is merely an easy stepping stone down into the grave.

Clearly, therefore, positive suggestion can never actually eliminate a trouble of any sort. It can suppress a negative condition by laying over it a thin shell of positive statements, but that negative condition, like water under ice, will grow in power as it is fed by the springs of evil below. Soon or late it will burst in a turbulent flood through the wall that can no longer restrain it and will spread its accumulated poison throughout the life of the individual.

Sometimes this process may take years to come to a head, but the penalty it will exact for the delay will be great in proportion. Evil not eliminated is evil growing in strength, a magnetic centre of disturbance into which pours all negative matter of a similar nature. In the end it must break out, the more acute as it has been longer postponed. It would be much better to take troubles as they come and let them run their course as they trickle into your life than to build a barrier behind which they can collect and pile up affliction for you.

Suggestion and Auto-suggestion, therefore, are both superficial and dangerous. Sometimes, especially with weak characters, they produce instant and seemingly miraculous results, yet those results are very temporary and bought at a heavy price. But through scientific mental methods, which are based on the Eternal Fact of Mankind's Fundamental Perfection and possession of all Powers and Qualities, though usually in a dormant condition, the genuine permanent cures of which these interesting tricks of the Mind can conjure up the appearance, can be obtained.

Every human being is endowed from birth with the full measure of Strength, Wisdom, Health, Wealth, Success and Happiness. They are ingredients of that Perfection to which your life is dedicated. But in order to bring them out you must first realize their existence as inherent Powers within yourself, and then take logical steps to transmute them into actual accomplished Fact in your life.

Creation of something new, in the literal sense of the word, is not within the power of any human being. You can alter the arrangement of existing things in a way that will react to your own advantage, and unite them in any new combination your ingenuity may devise, but you cannot add one atom to the Material Cosmos. It is already complete and perfect. Similarly, by developing your inner qualities and powers you uncover more and more of the perfection within you, thereby obtaining a better perspective and a broader view of the Material World in which you live. The possibilities you are able to see, and the use you are able to make of them, will be determined by the corresponding degree of development and enfoldment in you.

Your problem is therefore to thrust back the curtain of human limitations which hides from you all but a small section of your inner perfection. Those limitations are human products, manufactured out of perversions of the Truth by your human mind, and are self-imposed negative restrictions. Yet no negative can withstand the invincible strength of Truth and its pure essence as an Aspect of Universal Life. Energy.

Use Universal Life Energy in realizing the boundless wealth of qualities within you, and send into them the vitalizing current of that Positive Force. Let It pierce the veil of negative behind which they slumber, startling them into life and sweeping them into an irresistible natural development which nothing can stop. With that Power surging up within, pouring into an ever more abundant expression through the qualities It awakens, you are borne forward over every barrier to that great Heritage which is yours from Eternity, as it is the Heritage of every mortal being.

You, like everyone else, are at present the victim of a gigantic conspiracy built up by Humanity against itself from the very beginning. That conspiracy, the first evil fruit of Mind, is the suggestion that you are a creature apart, that you are separated from the inner perfection which is in reality yours and that your salvation now lies through Mind alone. The whole environment into which every generation is born is ribbed with this erroneous belief, so that they conform to it as to a mold and accept it as an established truth. Thus they rob themselves of the very qualities and powers which only a free and natural development can unfold.

As the whole limited state of Mankind is therefore due to that one false suggestion, obviously you cannot hope to win release from it by clouding your intelligence with further suggestions. It is necessary to get rid of that initial suggestion in the first place, and stay clear of any new ones in the second. Complete mental freedom and liberation from all kinds of evil can be achieved only if suggestion in all its forms is completely avoided.

Universal Life Energy, freely used and intelligently directed, is the sole Power which can and will bring into realization in your life the boundless fund of hoarded possibilities within you. Abandon mental narcotics which, while they stimulate for the moment, sap your strength and betray you to certain defeat and disillusionment. To rely on suggestion is to rely on your fallible human mind; to rely on Universal Life Energy is to rely on a Power to which Mind is subservient, and which does not permit error. A positive suggestion can be negatived by a counter suggestion which will cut away the ground from under you and leave you bereft of whatever results you may have obtained. But any constructive achievement, any positive result obtained through the use of Universal Life Energy is permanent and impregnable to the assault of any negative, because it is sustained by the One Supreme and Positive Power which governs All.

EXERCISES TO LESSON FIFTEEN

The regular performance morning and evening of the Star Exercise, Relaxation and Silence, together with the continual Contact with Universal Life Energy and Concentration, will comprise the basic preparatory activity which will be poured into the channel of the new Exercise for this week, VISUALIZATION.

VISUALIZATION is the process of so emphasizing the particular object of your concentrated thought that it glows richly out into a convincing semblance of reality upon your mental vision. From a transparent and ghostly outline it must condense into a clear, full image, distinct in every detail and warm with a lustrous fund of abundant life, which burns it into your Consciousness like a thing of fire. In order to visualize, proceed as follows:

After concentrating your Mind upon the particular object or design which you wish to realize, try to construct it in your thought so that you actually see it with your mental eye. Bring it into focus so clearly that it becomes distinct and vivid in every detail. Etch it out on your Consciousness with such precision that you could describe it in all its particulars. You must perceive it mentally with an exactitude no less striking than that which characterizes a tree seen in winter against the pale disc of the moon. Each twig stands out stark and black across the white field which illumines it, asserting its peculiar identity just as each item of your concept must assert its own on the shimmering screen of your Conscious Self. This singular clarity of mental vision, in which the individual parts stand out boldly without detracting from the harmonious strength of the whole, it absolutely essential for proper VISUALIZATION.

The Universal Life Energy poured into this work will not only wash into vivid relief your mental concepts, but it will also help you to perform a further function in that connection. You must make this concept live. See it in its brightest and strongest colours, not as perhaps it would be in reality, but as it could be. Court extremes in your imaginative process, and invest that inner image with an abounding vitality that bursts from every feature in a warmly diffused radiance, like light from a burning ember. Then you will be ready to start it on the next step of its journey into material realization with every assurance of complete success.

In VISUALIZATION there is no limitation to objects merely of a visible, tangible nature. The abstract details of a mental work, such as the policy of a business organization or the plot of a story to be written, are just as subject to that process as is the concept of a marble statue in the mind of a sculptor. His goal is the same, although the materials he works with are of a more solid nature. With hand and chisel he has to reproduce in clay and rock the image in his fancy. With words and ink the business man has to mold events to the shape he perceives as desirable. In both the single aim is Expression, and though the materials each works with are different, the process of modifying them is essentially the same.

Those whose tasks lie in the Realm of Thought are really less limited than those whose vocations confine them to physical mediums of expression. In Mind there is infinite variety, unfettered by rarity or price, bounded only by the elastic borders of Imagination. Ideas do not have to be crammed within the confines of the material scale, but cover the whole unexplored area of Mental as well as Physical Fields. They are the most plastic and subtle of all the clays from which Mind fashions its ends, instant to change and adapt themselves to the infinity of combinations that need may demand or ingenuity suggest.

Universal Life Energy, all-pervading and omnipotent, will snatch from the unfathomed depths of Universal Consciousness the mental materials you may require just as effectively as It will attract on the Physical Plane the elements for the realization of desires. Being an intelligent as well as an energetic Power, It will not only invigorate you in the act of transmuting thoughts into fact, but It will reveal to you the best way to perform that work. Through Universal Life Energy you will erect a structure of achievement not only imposing in bulk, but nicely coordinated and joined in harmonious proportions that insure its permanence no less than they enhance its loveliness. The precious and desirable qualities of all things emerge into so pronounced expression at the impulse of this Power that the more you use It in your daily activities the more impressively will be borne upon you the recognition of Its priceless worth.

QUESTIONS TO LESSON FIFTEEN

1. What is Creative Thought?

2. How is Concentrated Thought made Creative?

3. On what does the measure of any individual's Success largely depend?

4. Are Progress and Achievement products of the Creative Thought alone?

5. What is the medium through which the Creative Thought actually embodies itself in material expression.

6. What important advantage results from the proper cooperation between Mind and Body?

7. What is the cause of Timidity, Indecision and Procrastination?

8. How can they be eliminated?

9. What is Suggestion in its various aspects?

10. What is its main effect upon the individual?

11. Are Affirmations effective in curing negative conditions?

12. How can mental qualities be best developed?

ANSWERS TO LESSON FIFTEEN

1. Creative thought is:

Thought which possesses the constructive energy necessary to attract the elements for its actual realization.

2. The Concentrated Thought is made creative:

By injecting into it Universal Life Energy.

3. The measure of any individual's Success largely depends:

Upon the amount of Universal Life Energy he is able to use in the realization of his mental concepts.

4. Progress and Achievement:

Are not products of the Creative Thought alone.

5. The medium through which the Concentrated Thought actually embodies itself in material expression is:

Physical work and effort.

6. The important advantage resulting from the proper cooperation between Mind and Body is:

Poise.

7. **The cause of Timidity, Indecision and Procrastination is:**

Lack of power, or Fear.

8. **They can be eliminated:**

By the use of Universal Life Energy to supply that lack and abolish Fear.

9. **Suggestion in its various aspects is:**

The imposition of one Mind upon another through Will Power.

10. **Its main effect upon the individual is:**

To deprive him of his most valuable rights, Independence and Self Determination.

11. **Affirmations:**

Are not effective in curing negative conditions, although for the time they can suppress them.

12. **Mental qualities can best be developed:**

By exercising them, together with the continual use of Universal Life Energy.

Dear Friend:

In this Lesson you will be introduced to a Friend whom you have often dealt with but never known — Money. It is the first, and greatest of the Powers on the material side through which you achieve your active existence, yet the one perhaps most warily regarded, most unwittingly repulsed and most completely misunderstood.

Often, through this misunderstanding, the question arises, Is it right to desire to have money? Is not Money after all one of the evils of this World, though a great power?" Some of the greatest Minds of ancient and modern times have turned the light of their intelligence upon this problem, and from various angles have built up logical contradictions that seem beyond the scope of human knowledge to upset. Through the theme of their arguments march the crimes, the wrongs and the virtues associated with the name of Money, a patchwork pageantry of good beginnings and evil ends which at the last lead nowhere.

Where then does the solution lie? Why do some love Money, some hate it, as it seems in turn to be a blessing or a curse to them and to the World? Is not the answer to be found in the mental cause within, in your own imperfect Consciousness from which Money is engendered and by which it is wielded as a tool, rather than in the bare Effect called Money itself? Unquestionably it is, and that answer is what will be discovered to you in this Lesson, so that you will not only appreciate Money for the true and ready Friend it is, but will also understand how to take full advantage of its proffered help.

All Great Powers become at some time the victims of Ignorance and are subjected to abuse. Money also, like all the rest, has been forced to bear the blame for human shortcomings and has consequently come in for its share of undeserved condemnation. The purpose of these pages, therefore, is to reveal what Money actually is, what it stands for, how to attract and control it through the Money Consciousness of the individual, and finally, how to employ it in such a way that it remains always a faithful servant to you instead of an uncontrolled and irresponsible tyrant. To be able to make Money is a great achievement, but to know how to use it properly is a far greater one.

Cordially yours,
Eugene Fersen.

LESSON SIXTEEN

THE reason why most people find it so difficult to make Money is because they do not know what Money really is. They perceive it as an Effect only, something outside themselves which holds the equivalent of any specific wealth or advantage they may desire. In its terms are condensed the differing values of all things; therefore the obvious way to obtain possession of any particular thing is to acquire first the sum of Money which represents its value. But while the relation between Money and what it will do is very clear to everyone, that is after all a very superficial aspect of something deeply beyond Money itself — of Power.

Money is actually coined Power, a materialized Force. It is the expression in substance of a strength which has its origin in the individual. To spend Money means to trade the crystallized efforts of human beings for an object worth that amount of work. To earn Money means to exert through your own inner qualities a measure of power which commands a corresponding recognition in the material World. To fail to accumulate Money is to allow those qualities to lie idle and unused except to the extent of bare necessity.

The individual, therefore, is like a mill across a river The stream of Universal Life Force is the Source of its own energy and activity, the motivating power which makes him function. In proportion as he scoops that driving Energy from the passing current, transmits it along the various rods and pistons of his nervous mechanism, and stamps it finally through his distinctive qualities into the raw stuff of the Material or Mental Worlds, he will contribute to the Pool of all Wealth an added quota whose value must be returned to him in the impersonal form of Money. Yet unless he does really make such a contribution first, no amount of ulterior scheming or activity will avail to bring him the cash reward he covets.

This is why the majority of those who make the acquisition of Money the main object of their lives usually fall far short of their aim, while others to whom Money is of only secondary importance beside some other dominant interest often reap its richest rewards with no apparent effort in that direction at all. The former see only Money, and are blind to the Mint within themselves by whose operation they can obtain it; the latter are exclusively concerned with operating their Mint without any perception of what it produces. Neither have quite enough vision to link the Cause with the Effect and discern the infallible Natural Law which through their business of living is transacted.

That Law, which governs all the exchanges whose sum makes up the existence of the individual, is variously known as the Law of Exchange, the Law of Supply and Demand, or the Law of Compensation. It determines that whatever an individual gives to the World of constructive personal effort, no matter in what department of life, the World must return its value to him in the aspect of that wholly impersonal Power called Money. In other words, the individual stands midway between the vast Undifferentiated Tide of Universal Life Energy and Its Manifestations as Material Wealth. He is the channel through which It passes from one condition into the other, and in the ratio that he contacts It and thrusts It into expression through his activities, Its equivalent in cash is returned to him.

Ignorance of the Law of Compensation, and consequent failure to make oneself an open channel for it, is responsible for the failure of most people to become rich in any degree commensurate with their desires. Such individuals make the mistake of concentrating their efforts upon the Effect instead of contacting the inner Cause of which that Effect is only the reflection. They are, so to say, trying to argue with an image in a mirror, which has every appearance of being the real thing but is in fact simply an aspect of it. Only when the fundamental Cause the Power generated through the development of inner qualities, is changed will the reflected aspect as Money move and grow.

The channel within the individual through which the Law of Compensation achieves expression is called the Money Consciousness of that individual. Its physical organ in the brain is a cluster of nerve fibres known as the Financial Centre. The proper development of this Centre, and the resulting expansion of the Money Consciousness, is in effect like the opening of an inner door between Power in its primary condition as Universal Life Energy and the same Power in its diverse material aspects as Wealth.

In the new surge of creative force flushing through this Centre once it is properly opened, old barriers are washed away and one is swept past restricting mental limitations into a true perception of his relation to Money, the visible expression of Power, and the invisible Power transmuted through him into that expression.

That is to say, one's vision is enlarged so that he no longer sees just Money alone, but also sees the Source from which it springs and realizes at last the one essential truth on which the ability to make Money is conditioned.

This truth is that Money is most readily acquired, not by taking, as is generally believed, but by first giving. The individual must create Wealth within himself and pour it into expression before he can obtain the equivalent of that Wealth in Money. The wider he opens the inner door of his nature and the richer the flood of Power that he pours through his various qualities into constructive activities, the greater will be the cash return which measures its value.

Every human being is able to give, no matter how destitute he may appear to be in the beginning. He is born fully equipped with all the necessary qualities into a limitless ocean of Power in Its purest form as Universal Life Energy. All that is necessary is for him to admit that raw material, Power, transmute It through his qualities into whatever kind of Wealth his aptitude may suggest, and pour that Wealth through his activities into the brimming bowl of All Wealth. Its corresponding value is bound to spill back upon him in the impersonal form of Money. But unless he is first willing to take the initiative and generate the actual Wealth within that alone can command a response, he will strive and plead in vain for the financial recognition he is not qualified to receive.

The activity of Giving is what develops the capacity to give and to receive, because the greater the tide of Wealth one pours into manifestation the greater must be the riches showered back upon him. Yet very often some people seem to give a great deal without receiving any Money in exchange for it. Their apparent generosity goes unrewarded.

But there is a vast difference between merely seeming to give and actually giving. The virtue of a gift lies not within the gift itself, but in the individual who makes it. The thing given is presumably only evidence of some imponderable shifting of the weights within the giver, some change by which a corresponding part of himself is diverted into the interest of the recipient. Only the one who gives knows in his heart whether his gift is an empty shell or something of real worth, whether the change really took place or whether his donation was merely a mask to hide one of the two chief negative influences which destroy its value, Fear or Pride.

Fear, the first of these, is perhaps the most common. It imposes a sense of limitations or sacrifice, so that the individual gives reluctantly, as if from a sense of duty or at the compulsion of circumstances. A gift so made is not a gift; it is simply tribute yielded to your own weaknesses, a bribe to buy your temporary immunity from some tormenting voice within yourself. Its effect will be not only to bring you no return whatever in Money, but to work distinctly to your disadvantage, because if you pay tribute to a foe you naturally increase his strength in the same ratio that you diminish your own.

If you cannot give from the fullness of your heart, freely and with joy, it is much better not to give at all. This is one of the difficult lessons that human beings have to learn, yet until it is learned the path of progress will remain a steep and rocky way. The impulse to keep one eye on the gift and one eye on the selfish advantage it will bring is a barrier that the Law of Compensation cannot hurdle, and it will vanish only when the individual has developed himself to the point where he is. able to give from his Heart instead of from his Mind.

Know what true Giving is, be ready to give abundantly, spontaneously, and there will be no need to worry about the returns. You will receive in proportion, no more and no less; but the balance where the exchange is measured lies within yourself alone.

Pride, the second of the reasons mentioned, is a less frequent but no less effective impediment to the operation of the Law. It afflicts those who despise Money as something too sordid to measure the value of the gifts they give to the World. Therefore when they give of their highest qualities, and the World in the natural course of events returns to them a Money equivalent, they are offended and resent the implication that their genius can be reduced to mere material terms. Their extreme sensibility, which is simply a subtle form of Pride, impels them to withdraw and hold their qualities aloof from their fellow beings lest it should be said of them that they are selling those qualities. They prefer to avoid entirely the stigma of Commercialism.

But this attitude is not correct. However much an individual may loathe the idea of trade, he cannot consistently live and stay clear of it. Life itself is the activity of exchange between the individual and the

World of which he is a part. Money is a medium through which that exchange is made more easy, but there is no logical reason why resentment should be focused upon it any more than upon Life itself. Therefore to despise Money is pure conceit and succeeds only in hurting the one who indulges it without in the least disturbing the rest of the World.

The natural and normal function of every individual is to express, to give out that which he possesses within himself. In so doing he inevitably becomes a benefactor to Humanity, but he has no right and in fact no power to prevent Humanity from expressing and giving out in return. The Law of Compensation, which is one of the Immutable Laws operating constantly throughout all Nature, works also through every human being. Each one is a channel, a specialized mechanism of qualities into which Power floats at one end and out of which it is poured in another aspect at the other end. If Fear closes the outlet so that the channel is choked, or if Pride stops up the inlet through which the motivating Energy is contacted, the result is the same — Inertia, leading to limitations and ultimate Poverty in every direction. Nobody has the right to give without being ready to receive, and nobody should expect to receive without being first willing to give. To violate these proportions is to transgress the Law of Compensation and incur the unavoidable consequences of that transgression.

Those who obtain Money by stealing or cheating do disturb those proportions, and although for a time their activities seem profitable they always suffer the penalty soon or late. Their prosperity is a specious show, because having snatched from the Pool of All Wealth values for which they have given no equivalent in constructive efforts, they have no appreciation of the real worth of the Money they acquire. Instinctively they feel within themselves that they have no right to it, as they actually do not deserve it. Their enjoyment of what it brings them is superficial, and their hold on it is very uncertain. "Easy come, easy go" is their philosophy, the light froth of a genuine Poverty within which no amount of Money can relieve.

Almost invariably such individuals fall at the last into a material Poverty as deep and barren as the actual inner poverty which they have created for themselves. Also, because Money represents all to them, though they never understood or rightly valued it, they feel their deprivation far more acutely than the poor man who never had it to lose. They have nothing else to depend on, because they have never developed the personal qualities which would make them self-reliant. Therefore to lose their Money is to lose something more important to them than their lives.

Outright thieves and cheats, however, are not the only ones who fail to understand Money. They are extremists, perhaps, in whom the misconceptions more thinly spread throughout the rest of Mankind come to a head. The fact that they prey largely on the avarice, the envy, the carelessness and other faults of law-abiding people is proof that the majority of their victims are not wholly without taint. These little flaws, so common in the righteous armour of everybody, have led to many a financial crash and stirred up clouds of argumentative dust beneath which Humanity has gladly lost sight of its own ignorance of the real nature of Money.

This ignorance has bred the idea of Money as an evil power — the "root of all evil," the source of crime, tragedy and wrong. No error could be more complete. Gold, the emblem of all Wealth and the standard international basis of Exchange, cannot carry a curse with it. It is a Fundamental Power, and like all Fundamental Powers is wholly impersonal, devoid of prejudices and incapable of producing any evil of its own.

The only source of Evil is the human Mind which uses Money as an instrument. The same impulse which prompts an individual to kick a chair after he has stubbed his toe on it in the dark prompts him to unload upon Money the blame for his own abuse of it. Neither the chair nor the Money are able to protest their innocence; they are both equally impersonal and entirely indifferent to the right or wrong of mundane things; therefore it is only human," as errors are often very aptly characterized, to dump the burden of guilt where it can readily be borne with no inconvenience to the one responsible for it. That accumulated dross of human evil is the supposed "curse" carried by Money.

Money is neither evil nor good. It is simply there, a neutral Power crammed with dynamic possibilities, ready to unleash its prisoned force in the service of any end to which the individual applies it. Like Electricity, it is an impersonal aspect of Universal Life Energy; spun out of the original Power through the dynamo of the individual and held available for whatever use the individual may design for it. We do not call Electricity an evil force, yet electricity is used with equal facility to light a church, heal a disease or execute a criminal. It carries messages across Space without discrimination, the good as well as the bad, the helpful as well as the vicious and destructive. Similarly with Money, it is a concentrated Power that borrows good or evil only from the hand that wields it, but it cannot justly be made to bear the blame for those human weaknesses and follies of which it is so frequently the victim.

Eventually Money always seeks its own level, in spite of the artificial barriers erected by human Society to restrain it. To make Money is one thing, to keep it is another. When the capacity of an individual to employ constructively decreases, the amount he is able to command decreases accordingly. Misuse of Money through applying it in a destructive and wasteful manner, as previously described, does decrease that capacity by closing up the channels in the individual. The result is that the volume of its flow shrinks to accommodate itself to the narrower channel, leaving the individual much worse off than he was before. On the other hand, those who are constantly enlarging their capacity to handle Money properly get the benefit of what others lose.

Unfortunately, very few human beings know how to use Money properly, especially if it has come to them through no special effort or merit of their own. The cynical observation that it is "three generations from shirt sleeves to shirt sleeves" is founded in fact, not because the son of a rich man is necessarily less endowed with the natural ability to handle Money, but because he has never been obliged to exert his own qualities in payment for it. Consequently his capacity to handle it is not developed; he is blind to its value because he cannot see its constructive uses through himself; and like a leaky faucet not worth the trouble to repair he lets it spurt in wasteful extravagance through every vent but the right one, meanwhile justifying his folly with the selfish contention that the Money he flings away is his own.

But he is wrong. Nobody really OWNS MONEY, although it sometimes seems to be a personal possession. Individuals are simply trustees appointed to look after its proper use and distribution. Their term of office commences with their first responsibility and expires with their last, and the trusts bestowed upon them are in proportion to the worth they prove. If they fulfil their duties intelligently and honestly, a greater Power is placed at their disposal. If on the contrary they are vain and foolish, and fail to measure up to the demands of their position, they are doomed some day to see their authority drain away like an ebbing tide, leaving them stranded on the bleak shore of Poverty. This applies not only to the spend-thrift, but to his counterpart, the miser, as well.

Since Money comprehends all the Wealth of the Two Worlds of Mind and Matter, it is the golden key at whose touch every door within those precincts flies quickly open. Therefore many of timid vision are dazzled by it and worship it as the Supreme Power on whose altar they are willing to sacrifice their dearest possessions, even their own Souls. Such an attitude is utterly wrong.

Money can never be the Supreme Power, because there is one door which it can never unlock—the Door of Love. The clean and perfect part of our triune nature, where our higher spiritual qualities are enthroned, is beyond its reach once and forever. Those who abandon their true allegiance and place Money in its stead bow their heads to false gods and invite their own destruction, because they put in the place of mastery that which is meant to be a servant to them.

The rightful place of Money is the seat of honour at the foot of the Throne, not the Seat of Authority on it. Money is a secondary Power, which will serve you as nothing else so long as you direct and guide it to the satisfaction of your needs or ambitions. But the moment you give the sceptre into its hand, you submit your neck to a yoke of slavery that will grind you mercilessly into the dust, because you will have deprived your higher qualities of the control which they alone can exercise.

Just as vermin breed in the dark, so will all negative emotions breed when you close the Door of Love through which your higher nature should pour its cleansing light. To despise Money, or to envy it in others, will never bring it to yourself. Contempt and envy are simply different forms of hatred. Hatred repels and destroys. Therefore to hate anything is to build a wall of consuming fire between it and yourself. You cripple your own ability to obtain it, because it withers at your touch. So, if you want to have Money, you must learn first how to appreciate it, how to love and value it, not as a god or master, but as a faithful servant always obedient to your control.

A proper development of Money Consciousness throughout all Mankind would make utterly impossible the tremendous contrasts between Wealth and Poverty so prevalent today. The ideal of an equal distribution of riches, which some extremists urge should be imposed forcibly upon people wholly undeserving of it, would then emerge naturally, because through a more even development of the Money Consciousness of everyone the discrepancies between their capacities to handle Money would be wiped away. Reforms start from within, not from without. The only way to get two quarts of water at once into a one-quart measure is to reform the measure first.

To a degree that reform has already started. The standard of living, especially in America, exhibits a marked improvement over similar standards of a few years past. People enjoy better houses, better and more varied food, wear better clothes and travel more from place to place. Comfort and even beauty have become the rule instead of the exception, and life is much more full and complete for the majority than it used to be.

Simultaneously with this growth upward into a larger and wider sphere, the class distinctions which once differentiated so sharply the wealthy and non-wealthy fade gradually away. The good things of this World are no longer regarded as the peculiar privileges pertaining to the fattest purse, but are now subjected to the bold and calculating scrutiny of people who are more inclined to make their desires regulate their purse rather than let their purse limit their desires. Such is the effect of the slowly expanding Money Consciousness of the mass of

Mankind, releasing them from the bondage which they had acquired the habit of tolerating for so long.

For the most part this evolutionary process is an unconscious one. Clumsily, blindly, people are reaching out and claiming things to which they dimly feel they have a right. Because they are claiming it they are getting it, since they are unwittingly putting into operation the Law of Supply and Demand. But to let go voluntarily the safe anchorage to which they have so consistently clung and venture forth on a tossing sea of Chance, as it appears to be, is no easy task. Ignorance makes them pay an exorbitant price for their gains.

But that disproportionate price is neither demanded or required. The growth of Money Consciousness is promptly responsive to the two chief aids which it is within the scope of everyone to give Knowledge and Power. Through a thorough understanding of the Laws involved, the unfoldment can be intelligently directed into the channels appropriate for it, and all the confusing obstacles erected by uncertainty, timidity and apprehension can be avoided with no unnecessary expenditure of energy. Then, having thus simplified and made easy the process itself, that process can be hastened into a bounding growth by feeding it the Power that it needs.

This Power, the Universal Life Energy to which everyone has full access, is the Basic Universal Force from which every subordinate power, every separate aspect of the whole Mental and Material Worlds, is derived. Money Consciousness, like the rest, is merely a sort of offshoot or bud depending on it for sustenance. The more Life Energy you are able to direct into that bud, therefore, and the more raw material you give it to transmute through its constructive activities into the aspect called Money, then the more you stimulate it to a growth that will enable it to handle that increased flow. Its development is full and sound, resulting from a natural adjustment to the greater stream of Power floating to it for expression, and is not a forced enlargement through Will Power, with nothing to sustain it.

In order to turn the current of Life Force into this channel of your being it is necessary to follow the instructions given in Lesson Eight on how to vibrate to Abundance. Those instructions, followed perseveringly and supplemented by the simple rules here given you, will inevitably bring about satisfactory results.

Remember, the key to Power in any specific direction is the same as the Key to All Power in its unadulterated form of Universal Life Energy. The Four Square, represented by the Four Aspects of Universal Life Energy, is the standard to which each Centre in your Mind and Body must conform. When Equilibrium is established in any organ or quality, that organ or quality then coincides with the Harmonious Force to which it is to give passage and becomes an unobstructed channel for It to flow through. Just as a chord struck on a lower octave will draw a richly sympathetic response from the higher scale, so the right combination struck in your inner development will open a clear contact with the lofty Plane of Universal Power. But there can be no false note.

Therefore in all your life, in whatever direction you may turn your energies, whether financial or otherwise, take the measure of your goal first through the lens of the Four Square and mold your activities to that. Let every deed and every gift come joyfully and from the heart. Actions driven by Energy and Joy, winged with Intelligence and pointed with Honesty, or Accuracy, fly straight and strong to the mark.

So when those actions spring from your Financial Centre, be sure that your Money Consciousness is not a warped and twisted instrument which will impart its faults to what passes through it. Establish Equilibrium there, and in so doing you will unite it with Power that knows no limit. It will begin to function properly and to grow and unfold constantly and without end. Thus eventually you will be able to obtain all the Wealth you can ever wish to possess. Yet from the crest of that accumulated Money Power you will always have to keep guard against the dangers which threaten your supremacy, because, like ripe fruit, it is only too ready to fall into the sudden decay of unwise spending.

You must remember that Money is a living Force, and that having been brought to a climax it cannot be held there indefinitely without stagnating. If it is not kept healthy by a constructive and refreshing flow, it will most certainly dissipate itself in an unhealthy and destructive riot of self-consuming negative action. Movement forward is Life, and Life is the only - assurance against the decay of Death. Consequently your task is to keep the Money over which you have control in constant circulation, so that it does not pile up behind the dam of your neglect and turn your healthy Money Consciousness into a poisonous morass. You must regulate its outpour to its inflow.

Moreover, that outpour will always reappear in corresponding effects in your life. Therefore it cannot be simply an indiscriminate waste, an impatient gesture to rid yourself of something superfluous with the sole object of relieving the pressure. It must receive intelligent and constructive direction, becoming the source of an ever new and increasing crop of constructive works. To spend Money foolishly is to misuse a great Power which automatically exacts its own revenge, bringing destruction upon the one who spends it as well as upon the one on whom it has been spent.

Those who hoard Money learn eventually an even more difficult lesson. A miser is the poorest of men, because being a slave to his love of Money, he cannot let a penny go without the most excruciating mental anguish and suffering. He not only stops up his outlet as completely as he can, but he thereby cuts down his income which he prizes above life itself, until it is the merest trickle. At both ends, therefore, he unwittingly inflicts upon himself as much moral agony as possible, and between the two he lets the little stagnating pool of his unused wealth rot him into a pauper grave.

The inevitable result of the misuse of Money, whether in hoarding or in spending, is that sometime you will be bereft of the Power which you did not know how to control and employ properly. In devious fashion it will find its way at length into worthier hands, leaving you only the realization of a Poverty which is not a matter of

Money alone, but of something within which Money cannot touch.

You who have accumulated Wealth, whose Money Consciousness is well developed and who read these Lessons with a glow of conscious satisfaction at the realization of it, you have doubtless felt the chill shadow of this Poverty more than once and in your Secret Soul dread its approach again. It is a Poverty of the Soul a hunger that no riches can appease and no diversions completely banish or dull, because it cannot be reached from without. You yearn somehow to give more, to burst invisible bonds and pour into abundant expression a part of yourself which you feel but do not know.

The satisfaction of that hunger also does not lie outside. It rests within, ready and waiting only to be found. Most people who are rich do not take the trouble to search for it, but rely on the advice of others to provide a proper outlet for what they vaguely define as the "best" of themselves. Yet no eye but their own can ever penetrate to the corner where the "best" has its abode.

Do not make the mistake of thinking that you can buy that "best" with Money. It is not on the bargain counter. Money reaches outward with a long arm, but it cannot probe within where your most precious treasure is. That must be sought out by yourself alone, but when discovered it will bring to you a Wealth of Contentment and Joy that is beyond the measure of the Wealth you know.

Use your imagination when it comes to dispensing the Money entrusted to your care. Charity as practiced today is the excuse of laziness, an insult and an injury generally to the recipient of it and a very real harm to the one who gives in that way. On both sides the effort which should stamp its worth is lacking; the weak are made more weak and the strong acquire a flaw which is an open avenue to moral dry rot.

Real charity consists, not in helping others to that which they do not earn, but in helping them to help themselves. The little personal care and effort which enables them to knit into their characters just so much added strength and self-reliance, which props open a bit wider the inner door through which they live, is a far greater and more permanent contribution than the alms flung heedlessly through the narrowing crack. Happiness, the goal of rich and poor alike, is not an attribute of cash; it is the reward of endeavour only, and it must be earned.

Very often rich people are notoriously dull. Wealth seems to have drugged their imagination, while those whose wits are sparklingly clear seldom have the Money with which to realize their desires. Both are in a wrong condition, because each lacks the complementary power which would render useful the power that he has.

Fortunately such a condition can be adjusted if the individual will simply take stock of his fault. and proceed sensibly to correct it. A sluggish imagination can be nourished and developed without losing Money, and Money Consciousness can be perfected without any sacrifice of the keen Mind which can make it most useful. Both can achieve Completeness by rounding out that side of their respective natures which has been neglected, and can thereby establish that Equilibrium which is the basis of the greatest efficiency.

One other responsibility of tremendous import devolves upon the wealthy — the transmission to their children of the ability to handle the fortune left to them. You must teach them the real value of Money, not only as you learned it yourself through the vivid experience of making it, but also from the higher point of view as explained in these Lessons. They do not actually start at the bottom as you did; the circumstances and environment into which they are born and with which they have to deal are entirely different; yet the intrinsic qualities on which they must depend to conquer that environment are the same.

You prepared the environment for them; you must in all fairness prepare them to meet it. They will start from the Money you made as from a foundation from which to build higher. Therefore they must learn how to make Money, but in a manner adapted to the altered conditions rather than by doing your work all over again.

So do not judge by the standard of your own life, and do not expect your children to know by instinct the things that were pounded into you by hard knocks. The little pop-gun of an opportunity with which you started your career is scarcely comparable to the high-powered financial rifle which you place in their inexperienced hands. Guard against casualties by teaching them its use with the same intelligence and skill that you employed in making it, and you need not worry about them becoming a credit to your name. They will.

Finally, avoid the mistake of thinking that schools and educational institutions can perform this task for you. College can at best only partially develop your children and equip them with something_ to use if they know how, but can never produce that complete and rounded development of Body, Mind and Soul which will enable the individual to fulfil the higher and more difficult duties imposed upon, him by the Money entrusted to his care. That is something that Money cannot buy.

You alone can properly explain what Wealth actually is, where its value lies, how it is acquired, and how it is to be spent. You know, because you have built it into the very stuff of your nature and character. That is the really valuable heritage in your power to leave; and the crowning success of your life is the success with which you impart it to the new generation springing up from you. Give them, not the evidence of what you have been able to do, but the intrinsic strength by which you have been able to do it, and you will provide a legacy that will outlast and insure all the others.

EXERCISES TO LESSON SIXTEEN

Morning and evening continue to practice the Star Exercise, Relaxation, Silence, constant Contact with Universal Life Energy, and Concentration. Then, as the new Exercise for this week on whose performance these others will be focused, proceed as follows to the process known as MATERIALIZATION.

After you have entered into Silence and made the contact with Universal Life Energy, concentrate your thought on Money. By so doing you will direct the flow of Life Force to the Financial Centre in your brain through which your Money Consciousness finds expression. You will start it out of its lethargy, stimulate and strengthen it in its growth and exert through it an ever more powerful and far-reaching attraction for the object of your Concentrated Thought—Money.

In this procedure be clearly conscious of what Money really is. Know that it is a world power flowing to you and through you continually. Let your realization of its true nature dictate your perception of it. Feel your Oneness with it, your identity with the limitless supply of Abundance and Wealth. Do not pray or beg for Money, or indulge a subservient attitude toward it. Experience rather the joy and certainty of Possession, the sense of your right to it as one of the inherent Powers to which you are born. Recognize and develop your capacity to control it, and be confidently ready to receive it in proportion.

Let no Fear or Doubt enter your mind in connection with what you are doing. The invariable effect of Fear in any of its aspects is to paralyse and close up, and its influence on your Money Consciousness will be to contract its organ, the Financial Centre, and pinch off the vitalizing current of Life Energy. As you have nothing to lose and everything to gain, there is no excuse for Fear. Simply know that the thing you want you already have. Be securely conscious of it, and it will be so.

Practice this new Exercise until results show that the desired unfoldment has started. Then continue to practice it diligently in order to promote that growth with ever greater vigour. Your Money Consciousness will so develop that Realization will always more promptly and more richly crown your endeavours, because you will have trained yourself to a greater capacity for handling and attracting Money. In the end, as you render yourself a wider channel for its flow, you will overcome all the limitations which vex and restrain your ambitions, and will emerge into an untrammelled Prosperity.

Do not hasten or try to force conditions by forcing issues. Will Power is not a friend to permanent achievements. The best and only lasting growth is the natural one. Impatience is a barrier to any Force of Nature, so when Universal Life Energy is used one must dispense with it if the Laws of Nature are to take their course. Patience and Perseverance are the two qualities which insure solid, ordered improvement, and by exercising them you are bound to win.

QUESTIONS TO LESSON SIXTEEN

1. What is Money?

2. How can it be acquired?

3. What is the Law of Compensation?

4. Through what channel in the individual does it operate?

5. On what initial activity is the ability to make Money conditioned?

6. What two negative influences are mainly responsible for neutralizing this activity, and how do they act upon it?

7. Define true Giving.

8. What fundamental cause of Poverty can be avoided by conforming to the Law of Compensation?

9. Explain the "evil power" of Money.

10. How should Money be regarded by the individual?

11. What is the crowning heritage that a rich man should impart to his children?

12. What fundamental Power determines the scope of all the activities described in this Lesson?

ANSWERS TO LESSON SIXTEEN

1. Money is:

Actually coined Power, the expression in Substance of a strength which has its origin in the individual.

2. It can be acquired:

By pouring into constructive expression through one's inner qualities a corresponding amount of Power in its pure state as Universal Life Energy.

3. The Law of Compensation is:

The Law which governs all exchanges whose sum makes up the life of the individual, and which determines that whatever the individual gives out to the World must return its value to him in the impersonal form of Money.

4. The channel in the individual through which it operates is:

The Money Consciousness of the individual, represented in the brain by its physical organ called the Financial Centre.

5. The initial activity on which is conditioned the ability to make Money is:

The activity of Giving.

6. **The two negative influences mainly responsible for neutralizing this activity are:**

   (1) Fear — which paralyses the Financial Centre and Consciousness.

   (2) Pride — which deludes the individual into deliberately closing himself against the operation of the Law of Compensation.

7. **True Giving is:**

   A spontaneous and joyous expression from the heart, born of a super-abundance of Wealth within and entirely above any sense of duty or any expectation of recompense.

8. **A fundamental cause of Poverty which can be avoided by conforming to the Law of Compensation is:**

   Inertia, which leads to limitations in every direction.

9. **The "evil power" of Money:**

   Exists only in the human Mind, which is the single source of all Evil and has laid the blame for its own misuse of Money, a wholly impersonal Power, on that Money itself.

10. Money should be regarded by the individual:

As an honoured and respected servant, always obedient and effective in that capacity, but utterly destructive when uncontrolled.

11. The crowning heritage that a rich man should impart to his children is:

The ability to handle properly the Money entrusted to their care.

12. The Fundamental Power which determines the scope of all the activities described in this Lesson is:

Universal Life Energy.

Dear Friend:

Foremost among the benefits conferred upon you by that most versatile of all your servants, the Mind, is its healing power. As old as disease and trouble itself, because it is the original source of every negative condition which afflicts Mankind, it contains also the perfect antidote for every ill to which the flesh it governs is heir. This amazing Health Laboratory is what will be flung open to your view and use in the present Lesson.

Just as the aeroplane is lifting war from the Earth into the Air, so the discovery of Mind's relation to Body is lifting Medical Science from the Plane of Matter to the unbounded Mental Plane. Hitherto the Art of Healing has been a tremendously complicated affair of finding specific physical remedies for the infinite variety of specific physical effects known as diseases. Today Science has penetrated to the World of Causes from which sickness, as destructive germs and negative conditions, springs. At once the cumbersome structure of minute detail resolves itself into one clear and simple scheme which every individual, can distinctly understand.

When you perceive your physical body as it is, a changing cloak perpetually knitted anew from the vibrations poured forth from your Mind, you will see how to correct all physical disharmony of any sort by correcting the mental disharmony of which it is only the reflection. Through knowledge of how to accomplish this you will render yourself independent of outside aid, and will be able to overcome physical ailments without the help of another person.

Self-Reliance in any direction is an asset of vast worth, but Self-Reliance in the matter of preserving your Health is of a value that cannot be overestimated, because on Health depends your efficiency in every aspect of your life.

Cordially yours,
Eugene Fersen.

LESSON SEVENTEEN

TWO thousand years ago the ideal of healing was very simply formulated and expressed in the words As a man thinketh, so is he." It has taken Mankind nearly twenty centuries of bitter toil and struggle upward along the path of Evolution to arrive scientifically at the same conclusion. Yet today the attention of Medical Science is shifting bodily from the well exploited field of physical research to the comparatively new field of Mind, not because of any blind religious faith in the above principle, but because the facts uncovered by physical investigations prove it beyond dispute to be true.

There was a time when Knowledge did not penetrate beyond the outward physical symptoms of disease. All efforts were concentrated on eliminating those symptoms, of which the cause remained a profound mystery accounted for only by crude theories. Bleeding and leeches were once the common remedy for most ills, being supplanted only gradually by drugs as experiment revealed the greater efficiency of the latter. Discovery of germs and microbes as the first known physical cause behind destructive physical effects was a gigantic upward stride, rolling back narrow mental horizons from the whole vast world of Materia Medica.

From then on progress was rapid. Drugs were succeeded by serums, which in turn yielded precedence to the drugless methods now in use, typified by the so-called "Nature cures." Up-to-date physicians prescribe plenty of sunshine, fresh air, exercise and relaxation as the 'best medicine for their patients, while pioneers in the profession, analysing the healing virtues of Natural

Forces, are more and more introducing into modern Therapy vibrations of every sort, such as those of sound, light and colour.

This had led naturally and inevitably to the consideration of mental vibrations in relation to physical ailments. Suggestion and mental healing, the opening wedge in that direction, have brought about such remarkable revelations that even yet their significance is not wholly grasped. Just as the discovery of germs marked the transition of medical knowledge from outside the body to the minute and teeming world of physical causes within it, so the discovery of mental vibrations has brought Humanity to the verge of another far greater transition — the transition from the Plane of all Material Effects to that of the Mental Causes behind them.

Physicians are only now beginning to realize the absolute mastery of Mind over Body. Experiments have proved with complete certainty that the physical self of an individual is utterly at the mercy of the mental tyrant who rules it. Like a chameleon which always assumes the colours of its surroundings, so the human body always reflects accurately the mental conditions of which it is the host.

Disease and ill health, therefore, instead of being due exclusively to destructive physical organisms, as was formerly thought, have their source really in the Mind of the individual. Germs themselves are simply the material manifestations of negative influences which originate in Mind. A healthy Body is the accurate expression, the projection within the range of our perception, of clean and harmonious vibrations. A sick Body is the equally accurate expression of the disharmonious thoughts and emotions, such as Fear, Worry, Hatred, Jealousy, Envy, etc., which lodge in our mental spring and pour their pollution into the harmonious stream of vibrations emanating from it.

Science, experimenting in laboratories to determine if possible the extent of this reaction between Mind and Matter, has made some startling discoveries. For instance, the saliva of an individual has been found to exhibit to an extraordinary degree the effect on it of various mental attitudes. Samples procured when that individual was in a normal undisturbed mood had no effect whatever when injected into the blood of a guinea pig. Other samples obtained when he was under the influence of a strong negative passion, like anger or hatred, caused the guinea pigs inoculated with them to die quickly in terrible convulsions. Again, saliva taken from the same individual when his higher emotions were in the ascendancy, so that he felt loving and kindly, acted as a stimulant to the guinea pig on which it was tried, promoting the activity of the body cells and thus hastening any healing process, such as of wounds or sores.

These experiments show conclusively the thorough control exercised by Mind over Body. The saliva, transmuted from a neutral fluid into a virulent poison or an active stimulant, according to the mental condition prevailing at the time, is merely typical of a change that pervades the entire system. Evil thinking imparts its bitter taint to the entire material shell that harbours it; positive thought works into corresponding harmonious expression through every cell and tissue. A sick Body mirrors a corrupted Mind; a healthy Body is the visible evidence and direct result of mental cleanliness and poise.

In Nature, most readily observable perhaps in dogs, this intimate relation and obedient response between the mental and physical aspects of the animal becomes one of its chief weapons in maintaining its existence. The bite of an angry dog is dangerous, very apt to fester and not infrequently inducing death by blood poisoning. The bite of a mad dog is fatal unless treated promptly. Yet a dog cures his own wounds or the wounds of his mate by licking them, bathing them in the same saliva that under different conditions becomes a poison. All wild creatures instinctively take advantage of a fact for which they need no scientific explanation, making their own medicine as they need it simply by altering their mental attitude to suit the circumstances.

The same instinctive recognition of the mental factor in ill health has often strayed remotely through the thoughts of many an invalid, but until very recently has never been brought out squarely into the open. Now disease is being more and more traced directly to its source in wrong mental concepts. The physical disharmony, which drugs and medicines are able to combat but never wholly conquer, is seen to be rooted in negative centres of disturbance in Mind which feed and sustain it. Therefore modern Therapy seeks to eliminate from the Mind everything which is not positive and constructive, as the essential preliminary to enjoyment of a strong and healthy body.

One invaluable ally enlisted by this new phase of the problem is Self-Interest, which is after all the governing motive in the lives of most people. A patient can no longer throw the burden of responsibility on his Doctor. His state of health is decidedly a personal matter, and it is up to him as the author of it to change it by ridding himself of the destructive mental cause. Doctors can help, but genuine physical improvement is conditioned solely on mental and moral improvement first, which cannot be administered in doses by someone else. It must come from within.

When human beings realize that to entertain unfriendly thoughts of any kind towards others is to let loose in themselves an enemy to ravage and destroy, they will be less ready to admit Hatred, Avarice, Anger and all other negative emotions. The individual who discharges evil thoughts at an enemy strikes a double blow at himself, because not only does that disharmony permeate first his own system, but the destructive mental vibrations he releases, controlled by certain Immutable Laws, must return greatly augmented to their point of origin. Ordinary self-protection therefore dictates avoidance of all unkindly thoughts and desires towards our fellow beings, since each is sure to rebound most violently on its author.

Ignorance and a very natural desire to dodge unpleasant consequences often leads people to imagine that they can circumvent these Natural Laws. They believe that they can think, say or do evil to others, yet somehow escape paying the price for it. Even religions have been corrupted in deference to this attitude. Many a Christian, while he prays devoutly "Forgive us our debts," finds his enthusiasm wane when he comes to the words, "as we forgive our debtors."

But Laws of Nature, the just and omnipotent Expression of the very Power to which you address your pleas, distributes the emphasis more equally. Impersonal and Immutable, they operate serenely according to their kind, firm against any human will to sway or alter them, and exacting to the utmost farthing satisfaction for every transgression. Everyone knows that if he steps over a cliff he will fall, or if he plunges his hand into the fire he will be burned, no matter how hard he prays or begs the Law of Gravity or any other Laws to be indulgent in his case. Similarly, the greater Laws of which these are merely lesser aspects demand inevitably the exact penalty their transgression merits.

There is only one way to meet the demands of these Laws which govern Existence, and that is by correcting any errors which your opposition to them has created. No matter how urgently an individual may beg, implore or entreat, his words are as an idle puff of wind against the iron weight of evil he has deposited in the negative scale of his life. But when that evil is corrected, when an equal measure of positive, constructive action is heaped up to counteract the depressing burden of wrong, then the balance creeps back to normal. He alone can do this; it cannot be accomplished by proxy.

Until human beings have learned to understand this clearly, they will continue deliberately to breed the devastating hosts of diseases and ills which assail them on the Physical Plane. The tendency to evil, and the false optimism its easy prospects inspire, are too strong to be lightly discarded and too tempting to let the eye stray beyond to the price that must be paid. Some strength more sure than the faltering Will, some vision more keen than the short-sighted eye of Mind, is needed and is ever at hand for those who will use It — Universal Life Energy.

Against this supreme Essence of all that is Positive nothing of a negative nature can long prevail. Evil passions, destructive thoughts, perverted fancy — all the mental vermin spawned in the dark places of the human Mind lose their grip in the cleansing blaze of that Power and vanish like the shadows that harbour them.

Often people resort to sheer Will Power in an effort to dissolve the film of evil thinking with which their own Mind has polluted its abiding place. Yet the best they can accomplish by this method is but superficial, because while they may, if they are of strong character, clean up that which already exists, they cannot get rid of its source. Their life is a never-ending struggle, a prolonged effort to choke back something that presses ever more violently for expression the more it is repressed. The constant watchfulness, the sustained effort, demands so much of their time and energy that little is left for real constructive work and positive enjoyments.

This is too high a price to pay for the results achieved. Something repressed is not eliminated; it is merely aggravated by being cut off from adequate expression. The individual who resorts to Will Power tries in effect to sit on the safety valve of a mental boiler instead of extinguishing the fire under the boiler. His task becomes more difficult every moment, and when at length the growing pressure under him exceeds his strength to hold it back, the explosion will be vastly more destructive than if he had fumed his way through life letting off the steam of his temper and disposition a little at a time.

The only effective way for killing once and for all the menace of that boiler in your Mind is to kill the negative fires under it. The one Power which negative cannot withstand is obviously the Power of the Positive, or Universal Life Energy. If you make the contact with that Force whenever you feel the rising heat of rebellious emotions, drenching in Its cool stream those inner fires of evil, you will extinguish them utterly, leaving yourself calm and free to cope with the situation that confronts you. The energy that would have been burned up in destructive vibrations aimed against yourself is then transmuted into positive vibrations that arm you more completely against the condition you must meet.

Universal Life Energy also accomplishes a work of far more deep and lasting significance to you than the mere transmutation of negative vibrations into positive ones. People of an inflammable temperament build that characteristic into their physical constitutions. Nerve channels are modified to fit that trait. They establish within themselves a predisposition to negative passions, just as a confirmed toper creates within himself a weakness for drink.

These channels, open doors for the disharmony you are seeking to wipe out and only too ready to admit the evil ever seeking entrance, are gradually closed by constant use of the harmonizing Universal Power. This process, of course, like any other natural process of growth or healing, is not a sudden one. Change in Nature is never abrupt, and change in this respect also is no exception to the rule, however strong may be the Power you use. It will be proportioned to your capacity to absorb Universal Life Energy; but to expect a rapid transformation of so fundamental a thing as your character is to expect the unnatural if not impossible.

Two ingredients are essential in the prescription you fill from the Laboratory of Nature—Patience and Perseverance. The negative condition fostered by a life time of indulgence requires a reasonable measure of time to be undone. As your improved State of Consciousness molds the stiff clay of your physical apparatus to its altered contours, the distortions which once served so well the disharmony demanding expression through them will dwindle away, conforming to the mental Peace, Harmony, Health and Power that reign within.

Recognition of the dominant role played by Mind in controlling the physical body will bring about a new and truer perception of all organic troubles. They will fall naturally into two classifications, those originating in the Mind of the individual himself, and those winning access from outside through the Mind's weakness and inability to repel them.

In the first instance, where a mental condition produces an organic disturbance, the Body is made the direct victim of the Mind. There is no intervening agent between the two; the physical cloak simply molds itself obediently to some mental disfigurement. This is in contrast to the second instance, where the Mind, through depletion of its forces, lacks the power to protect its Body against the intrusion of destructive influences from without, such as uncongenial atmospheric conditions, germs, microbes, poisons, etc.

The most common of these two sorts of affliction are those arising from the Mind's lack of power to protect the individual from outside influences. The reason diseases make such headway is due to the fact that they themselves induce in the patient a mental atmosphere favourable to their growth. They produce a Subconscious mental reaction of Fear which not only cuts off the vitality of the patient, but thereby renders his mental ground an ideally adapted field for the cultivation of that negative impression planted there. If that negative impression could find no favourable conditions to nourish it, diseases caught from some outside source would remain simply irritations, readily overcome by the individual's own normal supply of vitality.

But disease germs are the embodiment of negative, drawing their animating power from destructive vibrations. The negative impressions produced by these vibrations on the patient's Mind is the spring which feeds them, corrupting the very energy which should be used to combat them into a vicious stream to sustain and promulgate their growth. If this ruinous reaction continues until the natural fund of health of the individual is overbalanced, he becomes the sure prey of the disease. If on the contrary the reserve of health is strong enough to turn the tide eventually, the positive flow will gradually re-establish itself, the Fear will be slowly eaten away, and the disease will be driven out as the body cells resume once more their proper function.

In every case Fear is the presiding genius under whose banner sickness makes its raids. A strong, well balanced Body governed by a healthy Mind is practically impervious to the attacks of all negative external influences. The positive radiation from the body cells is a wall that no destructive forces can storm successfully. But once Fear enters, it chokes off the fount of energy within. The wall crumbles away as its support is drawn off, and is no longer a defence against the invaders.

So also when the organic disturbance has its origin in the Mind of the individual, Fear in some aspect is the giant root which anchors it there. Everyone has at his disposal the power to purge his Mind of the negative condition that is reflected in his Physical Self; but a deep seated conviction to the contrary prevents most people from taking advantage of it. Once that conviction is really broken, the root of the trouble is also broken and the disharmonious condition fades quietly away.

Obviously, therefore, the problem of prevention and cure of all physical ills centres upon Mind. Organic troubles which have their source in Mind must patently be corrected in Mind, while diseases which come from outside can gain access only if the Mind of the individual is not performing its function properly.

Knowing this, diagnosis of all ills, and their correction by combined Mental and Magnetic treatment, becomes comparatively easy. Universal Life Energy is a harmonizing agent which penetrates at once to every disharmonious Cause, no matter how deeply rooted it may be, and with intelligent direction through Mind Force It accomplishes what physical remedies never could — restoration of harmonious conditions both on the Material Plane of Effects and on the Mental Plane of Causes. Two aspects of treatment by this method are to be taken into consideration, self treatment and treatment of others, but both start from one and the same basis — Universal Life Energy.

It is therefore absolutely essential to make the Mental Contact with Universal Life Energy before undertaking any further step in a treatment. Then, whether you are treating yourself or someone else, you have at your disposal from the very beginning that Great Healing Power, and you also derive one other exceedingly important advantage — Self Protection. A strong flow of Life Force, pouring out through every cell, forms about you an aura or atmosphere of positive radio-activity which is impervious to all negative vibrations. Thus, especially if you are treating a person with a very pronounced negative condition or disease, you shield yourself completely from any transference of that condition to yourself.

When treating others, have your patient comfortably seated in a chair. Then take a position behind him and place your hands on his shoulders in such a manner that the two thumbs rest together on the seventh vertebra, or joint of the neck, while the fingers of either hand repose lightly and naturally, collar fashion, on the shoulders. But if the patient's condition confines him to bed so that this disposition of the hands is inconvenient, simply take his left hand in your right one and pour the Life Force through that point of contact. In cases where the patient cannot be touched, direct the Force into his body by extending the hands with the finger tips pointing towards him. Space is no obstacle for Universal Life Energy, so the magnetic treatment can be just as effectually administered in this way, although it is perhaps a little less comfortable for the operator.

The physical aspect of the procedure thus taken care of, there is the more important mental aspect to be considered. You have established the communicating channel through which to deliver the medicine, but the size and consistency of the dose you wish to administer will be determined by your mental work. You must achieve the proper mental attitude towards your patient and thereby attain a State of Consciousness in sympathy with the harmonizing Power you use before It will respond abundantly.

Therefore try to feel loving. Cultivate relaxation with its attendant sense of Peace and Confidence. Give free rein to the expansive, positive emotions which measure their strength by the absence of strain and effort. As the tension lapses in every direction, so also does every nerve and fibre become constantly more open and sensitive to the influx of Universal Life Energy.

Do not let Fear creep in to interrupt this process. No matter how serious the case may be, you have no excuse to doubt your ability to cope with it. Understand that you are merely an impersonal agent, a connecting channel between the patient and that harmonizing Power which no negative can resist. Remember always that it is this

Power, supreme and invincible, which does the healing work, and not yourself. To fear for It is not only presumptuous in the extreme, but it promptly cuts you off from contact with It. You cease to be a channel, and your patient, instead of tapping through you the Great Source of All Harmony, taps only the disharmony which Fear has created in your own Mind. Also, never permit yourself to make a reality of the disease you are treating. That is to say, never let your vision stop at the bare fact, the physical effect, of the disease itself. See always the mental cause, the negative condition implanted in the Subconsciousness of the individual, of which the sickness is simply the visible manifestation. Your concern is not with physical Effects; it is with the Cause back of the Effect, which you can eliminate through the proper use of Universal Life Energy.

This perception of Causes defines the difference between combined mental and magnetic healing and magnetic healing alone. No knowledge of the trouble is required in using Universal Life Energy by Itself. That Power has the quality of seeking out flaws and adjusting disturbed equilibrium automatically. But that process is accelerated if, through a knowledge of the fundamental Cause of the disharmony, the operator is able to awaken in his patient an understanding of how he has erred from his own basic harmony, thus rendering him more receptive to that Healing Stream which will correct the fault.

In order to discover these Causes, you will diagnose the disharmonious vibrations proceeding from them. Therefore use Universal Life Energy to render yourself as sensitive as possible to all outside impressions. Let It so stimulate your perceptive faculties that, like a photographic plate, you register instantly and accurately all the negative vibrations continually emanating from the centre of disturbance in your patient. Put yourself en rapport with him, and presently you will begin to perceive consciously in some way those negative vibrations.

Exactly how they will be sensed will depend on the nature and disposition of the operator. Some contact them sympathetically as physical pain in the same part of the body; others will record them mentally, just becoming aware of the kind, degree and location of the trouble. All will realize within themselves, beyond possibility of doubt, when they have properly analysed the condition.

But diagnosis of the physical condition is not enough. By the same method, try to push your investigation further, penetrating deeply into the Subconsciousness of your patient to the mental or emotional conflict there. This will be more difficult than discovering the physical symptoms, but of incalculable value in the work of healing. Practice will gradually develop within you the ability to diagnose negative conditions, until later you will be able to do it in a few moments or even instantaneously.

There is one contingency to be carefully guarded against during process. When you open yourself to the negative vibrations coming from your patient for the purpose of analysing them, so that you feel within yourself for the moment the ailment which you wish to cure, do not let yourself fear that the condition has been transferred to you permanently. It has of course been admitted temporarily, but if, during the brief time it is within you, you allow Fear to close up the channels by which it entered, you will lock it securely within yourself. Just retain full control of yourself and let the negative impression be expelled in the natural way, fading out as easily as it crept in.

After this analysing process has been properly accomplished, the operator is fully armed and ready to go further. His problem now is to break down the negative wall which the patient has built between himself and the supply of Life Force. The operator might be said to act as a siphon over that wall, an emergency contact through which Universal Life Energy is poured into tissues starving for lack of It, while at the same time attacking the obstruction which prevents the patient from maintaining his own contact with it — Fear.

Fear of his illness is the invalid's yoke of bondage to it. Your problem is to strike off the burden of that conscious or unconscious dread. Therefore give to the vibrations you send forth a mental edge that will bite deep into that negative emotion of which your patient is the victim. State silently that there is nothing to fear, that Peace, Confidence, Strength and Harmony are supreme in the Body under your ministrations.

Once you have broken the deadening grip of that Fear, your battle is more than half won. The barrier behind which disease and disharmony have flourished undisturbed is razed away; the negative condition is exposed to the healing Force you are able to supply. Taut nerves relax, fresh life surges along their length, interest and hope revive, as your patient slowly opens himself to the invigorating stream of Harmony from without. This is the favourable moment to hasten matters by starting the scientific treatment.

Realize as strongly as possible within yourself the fundamental perfection of your patient. Pierce beneath the crust of his imperfect human nature and perceive clearly his true, eternal status as the visible manifestation of the Great Causeless Cause Itself, the One Source of all Harmony and Power. Know that you link him for the time to this Universal Force from which he has erred and that It is pouring through you into his Body, there to be absorbed by a thirsty Life Centre and distributed richly to the diseased organs or tissues. In this work do not try to visualize perfect body organs in place of the diseased ones. The Body is merely an Effect, while your concern is with the Cause back of that Effect. See the physical self of the individual as it really is, an aggregation of vibrations which have entered within the range of your perception, and which are now marred by the intrusion of some destructive vibrations which it is your task to eliminate. This you do by re-establishing within your patient a consciousness of his own eternal identity with the Infinite Harmony from which he came, and of which he is a part.

Do not try to use Will Power in treating a patient. No one can be hypnotized into permanent health. As soon as the suggestion imposed by your stronger Mind upon the Mind of another is allowed to relapse, the negative condition which your sustained effort was able to subdue bursts forth worse than before. You cannot force a sick person into a permanent state of health, any more than you can lift a rock into the air and expect it to stay there of its own accord when you withdraw your hand.

Your function is to supply what your patient has lost — a realization of his own eternal, fundamental harmony. The shell of negative beneath which he is wilting away, like a plant barred from sunlight by an ever grimier pane of glass, is, after all, a very brittle obstruction. Within your patient is still the Harmony that will always be represented as long as there is one healthy cell left. Outside is the measureless tide of all Harmony. If you sound again, and strongly, the note of that Harmony, the Law of Vibration determines that it will draw a corresponding response from within your patient. The contact established, that vibratory chord will swell in volume until between the two the film of discord is shattered and swept away.

It is apparent, therefore, that your mental work does not heal the individual directly, but stimulates him to heal himself. It arouses his Higher Self, gradually driving off the Fear which he has allowed to close his inner doors and restoring him in a natural fashion to his normal contact with Universal Harmony.

This method, which merely promotes and emphasizes definite processes of Nature, is the only scientific one which can be safely and unreservedly applied -without any danger of hurting your patient or trespassing on his moral rights. It has the advantage over all other methods of being thorough and permanent, securing its results by building up in the individual the natural channels through which those results should be obtained. Thus it develops in him the strength to maintain the Health you were instrumental in helping him to achieve, and is for that reason alone incomparably superior to such artificial devices as hypnotism, suggestion or auto-suggestion.

Next in order if not in importance in considering the question of mental treatments is healing at a distance. Frequently the patient whom one wishes to help is not within reach, yet that is no obstacle where mental and magnetic vibrations are concerned. Distance is easily and effectively overcome in absent treatments, which can be administered in two distinct ways.

The first of these, and the one most commonly employed, is as follows: The operator first establishes a connection or rapport with the distant patient by thinking of him very strongly for a moment. The activity of the Concentrated Thought in linking the two principles across space, as explained in previous Lessons, provides an ample channel over which vibrations can be sent. By means of this connecting line, the mental treatment can be delivered just as if the patient were actually present, the vibrations in the form of healing thoughts proceeding from the Telepathic Apparatus of the operator and reaching the patient over any distance, there producing their constructive results.

This method of absent treatments is the one generally used and most widely known. Yet while it is a good method, it exploits only half of the possibilities open to those whose interest is broad enough to include the Source as well as the Effects of Mental Power.

Mind alone is a battery whose strength diminishes with use. But Mind connected with the Dynamo of Universal Life Energy is a battery whose power is increased the more it is drawn upon. Therefore by combining the mental and magnetic treatments the operator is able to accomplish far more, and do it much quicker, than if he uses the mental treatment only. Such a combination can be effected in the following manner:

Take some material object which will serve as a substitute for the absent patient, preferably a pillow. With this seat yourself comfortably in a chair, relax, enter into Silence and make the Mental Contact with Universal Life Energy. Then, when you feel the Force flowing through you, direct it with the following mental activity into the pillow:

Holding the pillow on your knees, grasp it at one end so that a corner projects like the head of an individual, with your hands disposed below it as if resting on a human neck and shoulders in the usual way. Then think very strongly of the patient whom you wish to treat, but do not think of him as absent. Think of him as being right there under your hands. Imagine the pillow which represents him to be actually his physical self, a living presence of flesh and blood and sinews. The more vivid you are able to make this concept the more completely you will succeed in dissolving the identity of the pillow into the thought image of which it is the nucleus, and the better will be the treatment. Then proceed exactly as if you were treating a present patient.

The results of this process will be as follows: The invisible mental line which you first established by your thought of the patient will form a connecting link between him and the mental image of him which you have invested the pillow in your hands. Over that mental line will flow not only the vibrations of Universal Life Energy, but also all the different vibrations peculiar to the physical as well as the mental constitution of the patient. He will literally pour himself across Space, spilling into that mental image of himself represented by the pillow just as electricity spills into a light bulb.

But as each corresponding centre of vibrations is established in the mental image, that centre retains its direct connection with the original part instead of using the one communicating channel over which it first came. In other words, that first magnetic line splits and multiplies into millions of separate lines, everyone with its own distinctive rate of vibration as determined by the particular organ or centre from which it emanated. Thus between the mental image represented by the pillow and the distant patient himself grow up numberless mental lines, so that to all intents and purposes the image becomes really an extension of the individual, a living personality differing from its source only in that it is not encased in flesh and blood.

Therefore you have actually under your hands, not a pillow, but the patient himself. The pillow is simply a material object whose purpose is to help you build around it and to offer the resistance necessary to stimulate your sensory nerves.

Now when you pour the Healing Force into that pillow, you really pour It directly into your patient, because each of those millions of connecting lines acts as an open channel carrying It to him direct. You are no longer restricted to one mental link between him and you, as is the case when mental healing alone is used, but you are treating him across Space just as richly and fully as if you were in immediate physical contact with him. In this way you can treat at any distance, with results that will surpass your greatest expectations.

Not only are such combined mental and magnetic treatments just as effective as present ones, but they possess one decided advantage that makes them in a way even better. There is no necessity, when treating across distance, to use part of the Healing Power of Universal Life Energy to protect yourself. The negative vibrations of your patient, while sufficiently strong to be represented and to form a communicating channel between him and your present mental image of him, are not strong enough to invade your own field of healthy vibrations. Therefore, instead of employing some of the current of Healing Force to shield yourself, you can pour the full amount of Physical and Mental Power at your command into him. The destructive influence of the trouble you are trying to eliminate from him is reduced to a minimum, while the constructive energy you are able to bring to bear to counteract it is increased to the maximum.

In another respect also such absent treatments tend to have the advantage over present ones, due to the fact that you cannot see your patient. Very often, especially in acute cases, the sight of suffering and physical anguish so impresses a sensitive healer that he unconsciously begins to dread the trouble he is supposed to overcome. The moment he entertains Fear of the trouble he makes a reality of it, thus cancelling the very basis on which the whole treatment is conditioned. The evil he is trying to eliminate must become unreal to him before he can treat it, to say nothing of correcting it altogether.

But in treating an absent patient through a mental image of him as represented in a pillow, all the visible evidence of the negative that afflicts him is avoided. Physical agony and suffering does not and cannot impress the healer, no matter how sensitive he may be. This, together with the absence of any necessity for protecting yourself, gives the combined mental and magnetic treatments just so much more of a positive margin over the same treatments delivered to a present patient.

All that has been said so far has been of a specific nature, dealing with instances where Negative present in all Mankind has come to a head and broken out into physical manifestation in some. Yet if it is necessary to protect yourself against the destructive influence of one individual in whom the negative is more pronounced, it would seem as if there was a real need to protect yourself against the lesser but more constant negative vibrations emanating from all people among whom you live. This is in fact the case.

Every individual is continually bombarded by all kinds of thought vibrations proceeding from those with whom he comes in contact. This is particularly true when a certain number of people are gathered together. None may be conscious of those mental intrusions, yet each one is to a certain degree affected by the different thoughts coming from the Telepathic Apparatuses of the rest and each one affects the others with the thoughts sent out by him. A distinct mental tone tends to emerge, the average of all the thought vibrations contributing to it. These thought vibrations, penetrating through the Pituitary Body to the Solar Plexus of the individual, produce there an impression on the Subconscionsness. If they are of a high quality, coming from people of a high, thinking type, that impression will be a constructive one. If, on the contrary, they emanate from a lower mental type, they are seeds of evil weeds that will someday grow out and cause you considerable trouble.

The general level and quality of thought among crowds is usually not high. Therefore it is advisable, when in the vicinity of people whose thought is of rather dubious quality to you, to take measures to protect yourself.

Make the contact with Universal Life Energy and then know that its positive radio-activity is an invulnerable barrier to negative thought vibrations of any kind. Build a sheltering wall of constructive Life Force through which no destructive mental intruders can penetrate into your Subconsciousness. Open yourself to that protecting Power and pass serenely, unscathed, through whatever evil fogs of thought beset your path.

By all means do not fear, in establishing that mental self-protection, that it will not work. To admit Fear is to prevent it from working. Universal Life Energy is impelled by Its own Laws to perform Its function strictly in accordance with those Laws, regardless of any human interference. You have the choice only of opening yourself to It by attuning yourself to the same impersonal Laws, or of closing yourself against It by opposition to those Laws.

Fear is the enemy who cuts you off from contact with that Power. You are like a light bulb set amidst encroaching shadows of evil which drift down from every side. A long as you remain open to the Current of Universal Life Energy, so that it glows into positive expression through you, those shadows can never invade your life. But when you let dread of them contract your nerve wires and break the connection, they throng ever more closely on the heels of the receding radiance, until finally they close in darkness over the last fading glimmer.

When the shadows are deepest, your light should shine most strongly and constantly. Epidemics which sweep through the ranks of Mankind periodically gain their momentum from the terror that heralds their approach. Yet those who are able to retain their balance, to remain cool, calm and collected during these crises, are also able to retain their own health as well as to restore the health of their less fortunate fellow beings. Use the same method of self-protection, during these times, that you use in treating any cases of contagious diseases, and you will have no need to worry. One development consequent upon combined mental and magnetic treatments may alarm you if you do not know its cause. This is, that after a marked improvement at first the condition you are treating will seem suddenly to grow much worse. Yet this is so only in appearance. As a matter of fact, this development is direct evidence that the trouble itself is being successfully eliminated. The mental treatment, combined with Universal Life Energy, has penetrated and broken up the negative crust within, stirring it up as one might stir up filth that has settled to the bottom of a pool. It is pushing that inner evil to the surface in the process of elimination, so that while it is more acutely in evidence superficially, this is only because it is being correspondingly cleared up fundamentally.

Such a phase of the mental treatments is called Mental Chemicalization. It is on the Mental Plane precisely what Magnetic Chemicalization is on the Physical one. It is also the test period for the healer himself, because at that moment the battle reaches its crisis and demands the utmost exertion of mental forces in order to win the victory.

Therefore do not be alarmed. You have reached the point where you have pricked the negative into the open and have it fighting desperately for its existence, just as anything will fight when cornered. If you let yourself be influenced, if you weaken and lose the firm, cool control of the situation that your knowledge should give you, then you court failure. It is never a kindness to have mercy on something destructive, especially at the expense of its victim, and to let the evil live is to let your patient die by just that much. The negative has to be destroyed. If the patient suffers a little during the process it is for his own good. Therefore it would be foolish to inflict that suffering and then fail to attain the object for which it was imposed, particularly when the goal is within reach.

Remain firm during that period of Chemicalization, without fear and confident of Success, and you will inevitably prevail in expelling the negative condition. Whether the trouble is a disease, an obsession, or any other form of disharmony, it will vanish eventually into its native nothingness, leaving the individual entirely sound, clean and healthy in every respect.

EXERCISES TO LESSON SEVENTEEN

Practice Relaxation, Silence and the continual contact with Universal Life Energy as the usual necessary steps leading to the new Exercise for this week, called INVIGORATION.

INVIGORATION is accomplished as follows: During the Silence, as soon as you feel the contact well established and the Force flowing strongly, concentrate your Mind on It as Energy. Perceive It vividly as the quick and living current which forms the life of all things, the unseen Power whose touch transmutes inert Matter into something moving, sentient, able to act, achieve and create. Realize that without It your physical mechanism would be unable to stir, that sight, sound, vision, thought and all would fade like a waning ember into impenetrable night.

Then see your relation to this energizing Power. Understand that you are a single unit continually bathed in It as in an ocean, and that you are drinking It in through a certain especially adapted point of contact in your brain known to you as the Pituitary Body, or Telepathic Apparatus. Think of that tiny ductless gland as the mouth which feeds your whole Body, pouring into brain, heart, trunk and limbs the vital fluid which glows forth through them as thoughts and activities. Know that the strength and degree of every move made depends ultimately on how well your Pituitary Body functions, because the secretions it puts forth, manufactured out of the Life Force it takes in, stimulate your brain first and through the brain your entire system. It is the switch through which the current of your life pours in, strong and bright or weakly dim, according to how well you contact It.

Therefore be concerned to contact It well. Open yourself to an abundant flow. You will feel invigorated, buoyant and at the same time rested. Your thoughts will become clearer, your thinking more direct and assured, your actions prompt and decisive. Remember, you are contacting Energy, which demands expression in motion, and which will not be content to dissipate itself in dreams. if the connection between thought and act has been more vague than it should have been before, it will become clear and strong now. All blurred edges will be trimmed away; ideas will be living things to be done instead of misty pictures to be admired.

The benefit of this Exercise is most pronounced when you are mentally tired. That fatigue is caused by congestion of vibrations in the Pituitary Body and the front lobes of the brain. Your receiving apparatus is clogged so that you can neither send out nor receive thought vibrations properly, and is unable to coordinate them for clear thinking. The dispersion of this congested field can be helped if, in addition to the mental Exercises, you also direct the Force to it through your hands. Place your finger tips lightly touching at the centre of the forehead where the Pituitary Body is located, hold them there until the Magnetic Contact is well established, then move them with a brushing motion, slowly and gently, towards the temples on each side. Continue in this way until in a few minutes you feel that the pressure is relieved.

QUESTIONS TO LESSON SEVENTEEN

1. What significant change is now taking place in the diagnosis and treatment of diseases?

2. What is the relation of Mind to the material Body?

3. How can physical disharmonies of any sort be eliminated?

4. What is the danger of entertaining unkind or destructive thoughts?

5. How are physical troubles classified in relation to Mind?

6. What is the chief obstacle to overcome in healing all troubles?

7. What is the treatment whose application in various ways is most effective in correcting ill health?

8. Describe briefly the principle of mental diagnosis of diseases.

9. Can Will Power, in the form of Suggestion or any other way, cure diseases permanently?

10. In what respects are absent treatments superior to present ones?

11. What does mental self-protection accomplish for the individual?

12. What is Mental Chemicalization?

ANSWERS TO LESSON SEVENTEEN

1. **The significant change now taking place in the diagnosis and treatment of human ills is:**

   The shifting of attention from the Plane of Physical Effects to the Mental Plane of Causes.

2. **The relation of Mind to the Material Body is:**

   That Mind governs the Body completely, the Physical Self being merely the aggregate of vibrations emanating from Mind.

3. **Physical disharmonies of any sort can be eliminated:**

   By eliminating the mental cause which is the source of the disharmonious vibrations.

4. **The danger of entertaining unkind or destructive thoughts is:**

   That such negative thoughts planted in the Subconsciousness of their author not only corrupt first his own system by the disharmonious vibrations they send forth, but those vibrations, governed by the Law of Vibrations, are bound to fall back greatly augmented on their point of origin, thus multiplying there the evil of which they are the product.

5. **Physical troubles are classified in relation to Mind:**

As those originating directly in the Mind of the individual, and those penetrating from outside because the Body lacked the normal vitality to repel them.

6. **The chief obstacle to overcome in healing all troubles is:**

Fear.

7. **The treatment whose application in various ways is most effective in correcting ill health is:**

The combined mental and magnetic treatment, consisting in the use of Mind Force to aid the work of Universal Life Energy.

8. **The principle of mental diagnosis of diseases is:**

The use of Life Energy to sensitise the perceptive faculties of the operator, so that he is able consciously to register and analyse the negative vibrations proceeding from his patient, and the discovery through this method not only of the physical symptoms, but of the Subconscious mental Causes of which they are the Effects.

9. **Will Power, in the form of Suggestion or any other way:**

Can never cure diseases, although for the time it may suppress the evidence of them.

10. Absent treatments are superior to present ones:

In that the operator does not need to employ part of the Healing Power to protect himself, but can pour the entire amount into his patient, and also in that the operator is undisturbed in his work by the sight of physical suffering and anguish.

11. Mental self-protection:

Wards off all outside negative influences, such as destructive thought vibrations of other people, which might otherwise intrude into one's Mental Field and there become a source of trouble to him.

12. Mental Chemicalization is:

Expulsion to the surface of the negative bedded deep within the Subconsciousness of the individual, and the consequent accentuation of the trouble until the worst has been eliminated.

Dear Friend:

This final lesson in the series on Mind will give you access to the highest plane of knowledge. It will bring you out of the subterranean wilderness of Subconsciousness, up through the narrow shaft of Consciousness and into the undimmed, horizonless glory of Superconsciousness, that pure beam piercing into the boundless Source of All Knowledge, Cosmic Mind.

You will be shown the opening in your Chamber of Consciousness which connects you with that clear Fount of Wisdom, and which is called Inspiration. How to develop that channel of Inspiration, how to make it serve you and bring you at will all the Knowledge you desire, will be explained in detail. The real nature and function of Intuition, that marvellous Sixth Sense you possess, will be revealed, together with how to cultivate it and use it practically in your daily life.

Finally, the ultimate factor which gives to all knowledge, all qualities, the value they possess will be brought forth. One instant of time, and that instant NOW, is one of the most precious and least appreciated of all the gifts with which Mankind is endowed. Few people have ever recognized the tremendous import of this ever present NOW, few have learned to regard it objectively as something capable of direction and study. Yet it is a messenger laden with greater treasures, greater happiness and greater woe than can ever be estimated until the end of Time.

An understanding of these points, and practical application of them, will carry you automatically to that summit of mental achievement toward which every ambition tends—Mental Mastery, the possession of a Master Mind

Cordially yours,
Eugene Fersen.

LESSON EIGHTEEN

ROVE the human mind, dominating it and forming the Source from which it derives its existence, stands Universal Intelligence, or Cosmic Mind. This, the Second of the Four Main Aspects of Universal Life Energy, is the beginning and the end of everything that has been, is, or ever will be known. It includes all Knowledge, not only of the Past and Present, but of the Future also. It is Limitless, unrestricted by any bounds. It is Perfect, free from the taint of any wrong or error.

The human Mind, on the contrary, is like a garden patch staked out in the middle of this virgin mental soil, limited by the bounds of human experience, ignorant of all except what grows within its borders and foul with the evil drainage from uncounted centuries of corruption by Mankind. This dubious garden patch is called Subconsciousness, and from it people live almost exclusively, raking up the morsels which they feed to their Conscious Selves and in return planting there indiscriminately the seeds of impressions which come to them in their stale fare.

Yet all great ideas, all inventions and discoveries which add to the sum of human knowledge, come invariably from Cosmic Mind, never from Subconsciousness. Everything within the present limits of Subconsciousness is second-hand; it has been chewed up and digested and modified countless times since its discoverer first put it there; but it has never shoved back the bounds of human experience any further, opening up new territory for exploitation. Something new can come only from the untapped resources of Universal Intelligence, and when it does come it is fresh, perfect and unspoiled, because imperfection cannot exist above the level of the Conscious Self which manufactures it out of perversions of True Knowledge. These new additions are prized above all things on Earth; they bring Fame to poet, artist, musician, scientist and all alike; they are called — Creative Thought.

The reason so few people are channels for Creative Thought is not because they lack genius or some rarely bestowed talent, but because under ordinary conditions it is very difficult to contact consciously Universal Mind. Genius is not a peculiar quality imparted by the grace of God to specially favoured individuals; it is a faculty knit into the mental and physical composition of every living being, undeveloped in most but present in all. It consists of the ability to contact Cosmic Mind and is called in its mental phase Inspiration. The physical organ through which Inspiration functions is located almost in the centre of the brain, as was explained in Lesson Ten, and is known as the Pineal Gland.

The Pineal Gland, therefore, is the seat of what is commonly termed Genius. That is to say, it is the skylight in the narrow chamber of Consciousness, opening out on the Superconscious Mind Ray which links you directly to Cosmic Mind. In contradistinction to the trap-door of Memory, through which you fish out the preserved knowledge in your Subconscious cellar, Inspiration gives you access to the fresh Supply of All Knowledge at its Source, without the necessity for going through the tedious process of learning it. Learning is a function associated only with Subconsciousness; ideas derived from Superconsciousness are never extracted by learning, but pour down richly of their own volition.

The more strongly your Inspirational channel is developed, the more illustrious, fine and great will be the thoughts that come to you through it. So-called accidental discoveries, such as those made by renowned scientists, are not at all the fortuitous happenings they seem to be. They came as the inevitable result of a procedure by which the Law of Supply and Demand, which works instantaneously on the Mental Plane whenever it is given the opportunity, was successfully put into operation. The individual was eager to know a certain thing, creating the Demand; Superconsciousness held the answer, or Supply; the channel of Inspiration between the two was open and the answer poured in. That individual may not have known that his Inspirational channel was so well developed, may not realize that he has ever done anything to develop it and may therefore attribute his sudden information to accident, but it was an "accident," very logically and certainly brought about by himself.

The discoveries made in this way are few and far between because they are seldom sought intelligently. Human beings as yet know very little about that marvellous mechanism of their Mind, whose mysteries are just beginning to unravel. The purpose of vital mental organs and centres has hitherto been obscure, and only now has that obscurity been dissolved in an understanding of how to handle properly the mental instruments which project, receive and control thought vibrations. "If you know, you can", a clear comprehension of the purely mechanical aspect of thinking will enable you to contact Universal Intelligence whenever you need or desire it. The process by which this contact is established is as follows:

When you enter into Silence and make the Contact with Universal Life Energy, think very strongly of the thing you want to know. Concentrate your Mind on it, so that the problem demanding solution occupies all your thought and attention and glows forth in commanding relief above everything else. Make it the focal point of your keen interest and desire to receive the information you lack, and invest it with intense life through the realization "I need that answer. Therefore because of the Law of Supply and Demand I shall, with the help of the Great Law, have it."

Then lapse into a still and receptive attitude. Be serenely passive, relaxed and open to the silent with Superconsciousness that your initial activity has established. Above all do not let Will Power intrude upon that confident Stillness, and do not admit any annoying doubts or fears. Only through complete relaxation, absolute harmony with the Perfect part of your mental nature, can proper results be obtained; and complete relaxation cannot exist unless all personal influences are utterly in abeyance.

If that procedure has been effectively carried out, you will presently discover that the very knowledge you seek has come to you. The vacuum in your Consciousness has been filled. The answer may burst suddenly in a blaze of light, or it may glimmer dimly forth at first. Nurse that faint glimmer, help it along mentally, until soon it burns ever more strongly and clearly.

Moreover, do not be discouraged if you fail to get results at once. Perfect relaxation is not an easy thing to achieve. In fact, it is the most difficult of any mental feats, because Mind is volatile, quick, full of aggressive activity.

Contact with Universal Intelligence requires stillness, passivity, a rich sense of harmony within. Yet as in everything else, practice and training will develop the necessary poise in the most unruly intellect, and no price you can pay in patience and perseverance is too great if it brings you the power to contact at will the Eternal Source of All Knowledge.

Your conscious perception of what comes to you from Cosmic Mind through Inspiration is known as Intuition. It is that marvellous quality you possess which enables you to sense things and know them to be so without going through the ordinary process of reasoning. Your Reason is part of the filtering system between your Consciousness and your Subconsciousness. It strains the good out of what you get from that tainted Subconscious supply and retains it for Conscious use. But the Knowledge received from Superconsciousness is already pure; it does not need to be filtered; it is poured in fresh and sweet through the pipe line of Inspiration and the open tap of intuition.

Intuition is constantly functioning; it is the "still, small voice" within you which whispers what to do and what not to do; but unfortunately its advice is delivered in a tone which is below the level of ordinary perception. Few people listen to it, and fewer still heed its promptings, because their Reason clamorously refuses to acknowledge as right any information received through Intuition.

Reason is the very valuable faculty on which we are accustomed to rely, because we live for the most part on what Reason strains out of Subconsciousness. Yet Reason in its present state of development is very limited. It deals only with that which is already known, for which there is a precedent somewhere in human experience, and abhors originality. All that comes from outside the scope of Reason is beyond its control; Reason cannot get a leverage on it and therefore rejects it. Yet reason itself is prone to error, often wrong and often balked in its task.

Where Reason fails, Intuition succeeds. The solution which your Rational Mind could not patch up out of the problem submitted to it exists rounded and complete in your Superconsciousness and will drop neatly into place if you let it. Promote cooperation between Reason and Intuition and you will have a combination that is infallible. Learn to know the so-called "hunch" when you meet it; distinguish it from the subtle imitations your Reason may try to palm off through your too impatient desire; give it the place it merits in your esteem. The more you develop harmonious relations between your Reason and your Intuition, the more abundantly you will realize that dominant feature of a Master Mind which is called the "Sixth Sense," and toward which Evolution is gradually lifting Humanity.

One attribute of Intuition which emphasizes sharply its contrast to Reason is Promptness. Delay and Indecision are associated with the cumbersome rational processes; what comes from Intuition is instantaneous. Time is an element which does not enter into it, because there is no laborious progress from one conclusion to another, from one fact to a suggested hypothesis which may be wrong and throw you off the track. The information and ideas are delivered complete, fully formed and ready for use.

This attribute is one that should be, but often is not, woven by ties of action throughout the whole scheme of your mental and physical existence. Too often people allow themselves to become snarled in a web of fruitless reasoning, hopeless of finding a solution but still aimlessly plucking at the tangled strands. Or they swerve aside from the task in hand to dissipate time and energy in building air castles of easy fancy, instead of laying the practical bricks which will make that fancy a fact.

NOW, the Eternal and Ever Present NOW, is one precious asset which you cannot afford to squander. This instant, capped with action, becomes a coin of real achievement; this instant, sunk in inertia, is a loss that can never be redeemed.

You live only once, and that once is NOW. All your energies, all your qualities, all your faculties, are centred upon the present moment. It is the vital point, the single hot and living tip through which you can burn your whole life record of constructive activity into the stubborn fabric of Mankind. The Past is gone, you cannot alter it; the Future is to come, you cannot touch it. But the Present is HERE, and you can score strong and deep in it.

Except in mortal existence there is no Past and Future. Divisions of Time varnish outside of limited and divided Minds. Eternity knows no such division; it includes both Past and Future and is itself simply an eternal and ever present NOW. But the human Mind, inside the self-erected mental walls which made it human, cannot comprehend Eternity and has enslaved itself to the very limitations which it fashioned. It possesses only the moment to tie to its lost heritage, and only through the proper appreciation and use of that moment can it win back something of what it has lost.

Yet how few people realize the value of that intense and living NOW in which their lives are packed! Some lag in the burned-out Past, indulging fond memories of what has been once but is no more, which is beyond their reach and out of their control. Their energies are wasted blowing on cold embers; the spark has fled far on before and will not pause for wishes or regrets. Their one resource is to speed after it and use it while they may, yet they linger amid the melancholy ashes of recollections which can never warm them again.

Such individuals waste the only profit to be derived from the Past. They rake together their little hoard of experiences, treasure and fondle them one by one, but never put them to the practical use for which they are intended. Experiences are lessons to teach you how to do better, fuel to be poured on the flame of the living NOW so that it blazes ever more fiercely and effectively. But fuel which is never burned is no fuel at all.

The most dreary and unhappy Past is a mine rich in tinder for those who are wise enough to perceive and courageous enough to take advantage of it. The greater an error the more vividly it stands out; a Past sown thick with troubles, limitations and disharmonies, is a Past crammed in invaluable lessons for the Present. Each mistake carved in bold relief there points a flaw to be avoided, a lack in your character to be corrected.

But mourning over the mistake will repair neither it nor its cause. Once made, it cannot be unmade. It can only be counterbalanced. Idle regrets and self-pity are futile; they merely blind you to the profit you might have and beguile you into wasting more of the precious, fleeting Present. Action is the only corrective for error. Your errors are meant to serve you; make them do it. Refuse to sympathize with yourself -over them; analyse them critically and intelligently for the cause in yourself, and thus make them stepping stones to Strength and Efficiency.

A happy and successful Past, on the other hand, is a stimulus, especially if your present condition is in contrast to it. What you have done once you can do again, but you must DO it. Face yourself squarely, pick out the weak and rotten spots that have invaded your character, and set actively about getting rid of them.

In either event, the key to the situation is immediate ACTION. Wishing alone never achieves anything. You have three tools at your disposal — an inexhaustible supply of Energy, a certain array of Faculties, and the single incandescent point on which they all converge,

NOW. That point in action expresses all the rest. Idle, it represses them.

Those who live in the Future, on the contrary, are in an even worse plight than those who live in the Past. The latter have at least something substantial, even if they never use it, but the former have nothing at all. They dwell in a world of dreams, a pleasant fiction piled up out of the silent vacancies of their Imagination and planted like a mirage in the midst of an arid desert of daily routine.

That soft world is far more enticing than the harsh monotony of the real one; it is the drowsy lotus-land of weak desire, steeped in enchantment, murmurous with promise, bright with easy adventure and costing never a pang in effort expended or enterprise shattered on the rocks of failure.

But to succumb to its charm is to transfer all your energies gradually into its non-existent bounds. This is the living death. Asylums are full of people in whom this process has been carried to the ultimate extreme; they are mere clods of flesh from which all conscious life has been drained away. They are immune to pain, indifferent to food, blind to their surrounding and incapable of voluntary motion. Needles thrust into their flesh produce no reaction; sustenance is forced into them through a tube to keep them from starving; their eyes are blank and lustreless. Their bodies exist here, but they are elsewhere.

Such people are simply at the far end of a road partially traversed by many. "Where your treasure is, there will your heart be also." If your heart is in the activities of your present everyday life, if you see the joy of achievement and the virgin gold of opportunities, if your eye sparkles with the wine of Strength and Power, your treasure will also be in the deeds you do and the things you accomplish. But if your heart sits in a remote and airy palace of dreams, withdrawn alike from the challenges of actual life and the constructive activities they inspire, your treasure then will be in the unsubstantial coin of dreams and naturally of no material value to you.

To live in the Future is to pour your energies into a bottomless pit which they can never fill. The precious stream plunges down out of sight, out of sound, forever lost in the Unknown which swallows it. There is no more absolute waste of power than to hurl it to utter extinction in a Future which does not exist. Dream? Yes. But know it for what it is, a dream, a shadow. Never let it fasten upon you the illusion of reality and drink up the only energies which could ever make it real in fact.

Great men are all dreamers of dreams, but never that alone. They are supremely men of action, ready to let their imagination shadow forth that which would be desirable only that they may use the shadow as a pattern on which to erect a fact. What points their life is not their Past, flaring like the luminous tail of a comet far behind over their course, nor the Future, that dark illimitable void into which they cleave a fiery way, but the brilliant, flaming, vital NOW, boring magnificently onward, concerned only with itself and heedless of all that of which it is the focus. Very often the criticism is made, especially of this present age and its prominent representatives, that it is too practical. No loftier commendation could ever be bestowed upon any era or any individual. To be practical means to put a thing into practice, to apply it, to rear a dream in Matter. It means to do, to achieve, to construct, which is after all the only thing that counts in human life. That is the purpose for which we are here, the reason why we are fitted together and armed with the living spark of the immediate NOW. When we are practical we use that spark, we fulfil that purpose. When we ignore it we slight the Power Who created us, all prayers and protestations to the contrary.

Therefore NOW is the single instant on which all things from every plane converge. It is the soaring pinnacle from which you survey Past and Future, to which you gather the far-flung threads that you weave into the fabric of your mortal career. The Past is not useless; each cause sown there is still connected with an Effect to come. The Future is not a void alone; it holds the Dreams from which those Effects will be born. But the myriad threads which unite the two through the eye of one needle, yourself, and those threads you can see and control. This is the Law of Cause and Effect whose operation, consciously or unconsciously directed, governs every life, but on which conscious, intelligent direction can be exercised only through the EVER PRESENT NOW.

Success in any case is a product of the living NOW. The opportunities from which great things are unravelled flash by within reach only within the limits of that moving instant. Grasped and traced to their conclusions they sum up the margin that differentiates the great from the little men. Allowed to slip past untouched, they spell failure and barren mediocrity.

Just as you brand your character on life through that one sliding instant, NOW, so life in its turn spurts through to have its effect on your character. Strength, Efficiency and Self-Reliance are developed by adversity, by meeting and conquering the obstacles that oppose your progress. NOW is the only time you can reconstruct and fortify your inner qualities, because NOW is the one and only opening through which you can reach them. They do not exist anywhere else, Past or Future. They exist only in you, and you exist only NOW.

Therefore pour all that you are, all your energies, all your thoughts, all your activities, into the present scorching instant. Make NOW the vital nucleus about which everything else is erected, to which everything else tends. Estimate all values first in terms of NOW, be alert to perceive and grasp your advantage NOW, and above all decline to waste time and effort in worry about the Future. The Future will take care of itself because of the Law of Cause and Effect; you cannot reach it and you cannot modify it except through the present living NOW.

The Four Square of LIFE, MIND, TRUTH and LOVE on which these Lessons are based form the Frame in which the blazing lens of NOW is encased. If it is lop-sided, short cornered and faulty, the ray of yourself projected through it will be lop-sided, short cornered and faulty. You will have a correspondingly perverted and untrue perception of whatever you undertake, and you will perform it in the same way.

But fundamentally your Consciousness is laid true and perfect to the Four Square. The reason it appears imperfect is because of the successive films of evil, limitations and false concepts which you have permitted to collect like grime upon it. Bring your activities to the test of the Four Square, detect and wash away one by one those clogging films of grubby fallacies, until gradually, as each wrong concept is sluiced off, the perfect proportions of the Eternal Reality back of them begin to emerge. Then will the poise and equilibrium that is the keystone of Power return to you. You will look with clean eyes, confident and sure, upon a new World of Freedom, Strength, Beauty and Success.

Finally, the question has often been asked, "What shall I do to become a Master Mind? How can I equip myself to solve all problems, to perceive true motives, to understand and appreciate rightly everything and everybody? How can I attain Wisdom, that topmost peak of mental accomplishments?"

The answer to that query lies in yourself. Infinite Power, an inexhaustible Supply, is at your command. All Wisdom, a Limitless and Perfect Store, awaits your touch. Within you are the doors through which to unite them into expression. Open those doors.

These Lessons have revealed to you this Power, Its nature and how to contact It. The Lessons on Mental Force have furnished you with a complete understanding of the mechanics of Mind, its departments, their contents, their relations one with another and with you.

Study those Lessons. What. they teach is clear and simple and requires no special training to assimilate and digest them. They are adapted particularly to meet the general public demand for plain, practical information which will enable the great untrained majority to obtain higher and greater knowledge.

Then PUT THEM INTO PRACTICE. What you have been told is useful only as you use it. The knowledge imparted here is the most advanced of all knowledge, but those who never try it out will never realize that. Yet the results obtained by students who really assimilate it and put it into practical application NOW are beyond the most convincing descriptions.

EXERCISES TO LESSON EIGHTEEN

Continue to practice the Star Exercise morning and evening, together with Relaxation, Silence and continual Contact with Universal Life Energy. Then, as the new Exercise for this week, train your aroused faculties for efficient contact with Cosmic Mind through the process known as POLARIZATION.

POLARIZATION means to adjust and integrate yourself with something, to attune yourself to such sympathetic accord with it, that it becomes one with you. Your separate identity melts away like ice in water, and the two become single, undivided.

In this instance you are to polarize yourself to Universal Mind, the Harmonious and perfect Source of all Knowledge. The way to proceed is as follows:

During the Silence, after you have made the contact with Universal Life Energy and feel the Force flowing strongly, concentrate your thought upon Universal Mind. Perceive that Mind in Its real Aspect, not as limited, perhaps restricted to this planet and to human beings like the atmosphere, but as Unlimited, Universal. Realize that It impregnates all Space, all Matter, a limpid Essence in which the stars swim and Infinity reposes Appreciate the unbroken Harmony, the faultless unity of All Knowledge, which comprises that Essence. Reflect It in your own Mind as a clear pool might reflect a pure, fresh sky. Lose yourself in It, understand your Oneness with It and your ready, sensitive response to Its clear melody of silent perfection.

The more you attune yourself in this way to Cosmic Mind, the more strongly your Pineal Gland, the wireless station of your Superconsciousness, will function. It will catch the vibrations from Above and pour them in increasing abundance into your brain. Presently, having sensitised your brain sufficiently through the flood of Universal Life Energy with which you are constantly drenching it, you will become aware of those higher mental vibrations which ordinarily are too subtle to be registered consciously.

Take care not to force yourself into the desired condition by Will Power. The temptation is great, but to yield to it is fatal to your purpose. All the Energy possible must be directed into that Exercise, but it must be directed through the Law which governs Universal Power, not by Will Power which opposes It. The benefit of this Exercise is not restricted to your Inspirational channel alone.. It spreads through all associated activities, primarily Intuition. Not only is that invaluable Faculty developed, but it is coordinated with its most active enemy, Reason. The two are brought into a harmonious relation which brings forth in you that "Sixth Sense" previously mentioned, and which is the goal toward which Humanity is struggling in its Evolutionary process.

QUESTIONS TO LESSON EIGHTEEN

1. What is Cosmic Mind?

2. How is it distinguished from Subconsciousness?

3. Through what channels, mental and physical, is it connected with Consciousness?

4. What Law is put into operation in contacting Cosmic Mind?

5. What condition must prevail in the individual to enable that Law to function?

6. What is Intuition?

7. Define its relation to Reason.

8. What is the EVER PRESENT NOW?

9. Of what value is the Past?

10. What is the danger of the Future?

11. How are Power and Greatness achieved?

12. How is it possible to become a MASTER MIND?

ANSWERS TO LESSON EIGHTEEN

1. Cosmic Mind is:

The Universal Source from which all knowledge is derived, the Second of the Four Main Aspects in which Universal Life Energy manifests Itself.

2. It is distinguished from Subconsciousness:

By the fact that it is Limitless and Perfect, in contrast to the limited and imperfect Subconscious supply of knowledge, corrupted by Conscious perversions and confined to the bounds of human experience.

3. The mental and physical channels connecting Cosmic Mind with Consciousness are:

Inspiration, whose physical organ in the brain is the Pineal Gland.

4. The Law put into action in contacting Cosmic Mind is:

The Law of Demand and Supply.

5. The condition that must prevail in the individual to enable' that Law to function properly is:

A condition of absolute tranquillity and harmony, free from any stress that might interfere with complete relaxation mentally and physically.

6. **Intuition is:**

    Conscious perception of information received from Cosmic Mind through Inspiration.

7. **Its relation to Reason is**

    Reason opposes Intuition, unwilling to accept new knowledge for which no confirming precedent exists in Subconsciousness.

8. **The EVER PRESENT NOW is:**

    The single and only instant of actual life.

9. **The value of the Past is:**

    To reveal the flaws in character responsible for errors, thus showing the individual how to guard against similar mistakes in the Present.

10. **The danger of the Future is:**

    The dream it holds, which, uncontrolled, may dominate you and drink up energies and attention meant to be expressed in constructive activity NOW.

11. **Power and Greatness are achieved:**

    By ACTION, to which dreams, memories, faculties and powers are all coordinated and directed.

12. It is possible to become a MASTER MIND:

By clearing away, through your knowledge of Mind and the constant intelligent use of Universal Life Energy, the successive films of limitations and false concepts which obscure the fundamental perfection of your Mind.

Lesson Nineteen

Dear Friend:

In this Lesson you are brought over the border of that Mental Realm to which the Second of this Triune Series was devoted and are introduced to the last and greatest of the Three Planes of Being which it is our privilege to explore.

The Soul, that unseen Foundation of your Identity and Existence, will be perceived and examined through its manifestations in yourself. Its origin, veiled in mystery and enveloped in a misty fog of theory which has steamed up out of the human Mind to obscure it as vapours rise to hide the sun, will be revealed to you through the clear lens of Science. You will see its boundless wealth of qualities and powers spread lavishly before you, waiting to be brought within the sphere of your life and used there by you.

How the Soul pours its bounty into expression through your Mental Doors and through your Body, flooding you with its own limitless Strength, Knowledge and Harmony if you only open the way, will be explained also. You will discover how to pierce the narrow human walls which hem you in and gain ready access to that vast treasury which is rightfully your own.

The understanding you obtain in this Lesson will give you the perspective of which have always felt the lack, not only in relation to the world of your fellow beings but, what is more essential, to the greater World out of which you have been born. You will know how to search out and recognize your own Identity and

Individuality—how to "find Yourself." Once you have found that Real Self, you have accomplished one of the primary aims of every individual on the Plane of Existence, the Purpose which dictates the activities of all blindly seeking Humanity.

Cordially yours,
Eugene Fersen.

LESSON NINETEEN

SUPREME POWER—PLANE OF HARMONY—SOUL
MANKIND have speculated about their immortal Souls
ever since a dawning Human Consciousness first blotted
out their direct knowledge of that Perfect Part of their
Being. Religions have fostered a blind belief in its
existence, great teachers have lit the fires of impassioned
faiths to serve its ends, the voices of a thousand peoples
in a thousand times have clamoured down the ages their
defiant assertion of its supremacy. Yet, far and clear
above this emotional tumult born of a steadfast
conviction in the hearts of men, echoes still the challenge
of a Mind that cannot help but doubt—"Is there a Soul,
and what is a Soul?"

Humanity, in this Material Age, is not satisfied merely to
believe; it wants to know, to have irrefutable proofs that
certain things are as they appear to be and not otherwise.
Material Science has made astonishing discoveries on the
Physical Plane. Mental Science is unearthing priceless
information on the Plane of Mind. But Metaphysicians,
vainly essaying the loftiest Plane of our being, have
produced only clouds of elaborate theory conjured out of
an unverified supposition that there is a Soul, iridescent
bubbles of floating logic which burst and vanish at the
query of an analytical Mind demanding "Prove to me
that the Soul exists, show me that unbroken transition
from visible effect to invisible cause, so I can know
definitely."

As Metaphysics deals only with what is beyond physical
perception, it cannot exhibit actual proofs of that which it

teaches. However well its reasoning may hang together in the abstract, there is no concrete fact to anchor its argument within reach of the practical rational Mind. It becomes therefore the task of the scientist, the physicist, to overbridge the hiatus between the two, correlating unseen Causes with visible Effects and extracting a satisfactory solution of the problem of the Soul's existence.

Starting therefore with the Physical Body, let us examine and classify what is apparent there in order to obtain a clear understanding of the nature of the unseen Cause behind it. Analysing yourself as a Human Being, you discover four fundamental qualities out of which your whole complex life structure is erected, each retaining an identity peculiar to it alone yet all fused into a single unified expression, like the component elements in a clear drop of sea water.

First of these four qualities is Life. Without that the rest are dark and void. When you live, you are; when Life goes, you are not. It is the flame on the human wick which draws all other qualities into luminous expression. Your body, living, proves your existence.

Second comes Mind. Life manifests itself through you in a conscious way. You are aware that you live, and you know that you are aware of it. You have the power to think.

Third in the sequence is Law. You see it working through your Physical Body, the automatic functioning of which is based on Law. Your Conscious Life also is not haphazard. You are able to think and act consecutively for your own greatest advantage. You perceive the Natural Laws within whose bounds you exist, and you realize that you must conform to those Laws in order to progress. Transgression of them, conscious or unconscious, must inevitably result in a corresponding measure of trouble, disease and disharmony of every kind, so your constant endeavour is to attune yourself to them to the best of your ability.

Finally, the quality that holds all together in that coherent Unit which is the individual is the power of Attraction, or Love. You do not disintegrate physically because the magnetic pull exercised by this Force glues cell to cell and flesh to bone. You seek to gratify desires because you are attracted emotionally to the thing you want by Love. Attraction is the more comprehensive scientific term for a Power that is often regarded in only one application when spoken of as Love.

These Four, Life, Mind, Law (Truth) and Love, indissolubly knit into one Unit, conscious of itself and emerging into perceptible manifestation in the Physical Body, constitute the unseen Cause which is called the Soul. Though the Soul is perfect, its projection into expression is through the impure lens of the present State of Human Consciousness. Therefore that expression is never perfect; Life among mortals is not eternal, Mind omniscient, Law harmoniously observed or Love serenely flawless; yet these perfect expressions in the Physical Body bring within your human perception the proof of the Eternal Cause from which you emanated and to which you are eternally connected by your Soul.

The amount of sorrow and discord that enters the experience of everyone corresponds to the degree of their lapse from a standard set by these qualities' in perfection.

Your Soul, the real "you," is thus the basis of your Existence and Identity. Its physical embodiment on this Material Plane is perishable and imperfect, but not the Soul itself. That uncorrupted Ray proceeding direct from the Sources of All Life, All knowledge, All Power, eternally sustained by It and connected with It, possesses all those powers and qualities also as inherent in its nature. Universal Life Energy is Eternal; the Soul born of it is Eternal. Universal Life Energy is Infinite Mind; the Soul possesses all mental qualities. Universal Life Energy is basically harmonious and perfect, entirely devoid of the disharmony which we know as Evil; the Soul is equally harmonious, perfect and clean of wrong. However faulty may be its human expressions, the Soul is and remains untainted, an individualized, self-conscious, harmonious and eternal projection of Universal Life Energy into its own Universal Substance. The real "you," sharing all the qualities and powers of its Original Cause, individual, perfect and eternal, is indeed the "Image and Likeness" of that Cause.

Yet a human being is not the only thing that possesses an Identity of its own. Throughout all Nature, animate and inanimate, the numberless elements comprising it are individual and distinct, segregated from each other by characteristics which may vary in degree but never in kind. A horse is always a horse, whether big, little or indifferent; a cow is always a cow; each evolves along its own particular line and neither ever lapses into the other. Similarly with plants and minerals; gold does not degenerate into lead, nor pines into gooseberry bushes. Therefore the question may logically be asked, "What imparts to these lesser members of Creation their special Identity? Do they also have Souls which are manifesting through them?"

The answer is—Yes. Everything in Nature has its Soul. Beginning with the most simple elemental yet perfect Souls and going up link by link, through the Mineral, the Vegetable and the Animal Kingdoms, with each link becoming more complex as it offers a wider avenue for expression, all the members of that vast composite Nature manifest Souls, but everyone only within its own specific limits. All modifications and all improvements, such as are apparent in Evolution, occur within those limits.

Thus the arrangement of things in Nature is comparable to the numerical scale in Mathematics. In that scale each number retains its own peculiar identity and place in the mathematical scheme, no matter in what way it may be indicated. Five can be written in any number of styles that ingenuity may suggest—large, small, plain, fancy, etc.---but it remains always and immutably Five. It can never of itself become Six, nor can it lapse into Four. It includes Four, and one unit in addition, just as it in turn is included in Six, yet lacks one unit that Six has. But it is distinctly and unmistakably Five.

If this were not so, if each number did not preserve eternally its own identity and refuse to lose that identity in some other number, the whole elaborate structure of Mathematics would instantly collapse. Similarly in

Nature, if the physical expressions of Souls were not self-contained, changing and developing only with their own respective walls and refusing to merge into one another, the whole superbly ordered Natural Structure would collapse also.

The culminant point in this hierarchy of Nature is the Soul of Man, the most complex and comprehensive of all. It includes and expresses all the qualities of other lesser Souls in Nature, and something more besides. Like the highest number in the numerical table, it embraces all the less advanced numbers which dwindle into a central core of Unity and to them adds the final margin of its own distinguishing shell. That is why Man is to have dominion over the rest of Creation; he contains all the characteristics of others and is therefore greater.

The evidence of this exists both in the material composition of the human body and in the human character, and in many instances is strikingly apparent. All material elements — all gases, all minerals, such as gold, lead, silver, etc. — are present in the chemical makeup of the individual. Various characters exhibit as dominant traits the qualities that observation has taught people to associate with certain animals. In describing other people, they are often shrewdly identified as foxes, lions, weasels, rabbits, skunks, and less savoury representatives of our natural life. Even vegetables are not ignored as an aid in cataloguing fellow humans. All are latent in everyone.

Finally, what is the added unit which elevates Mankind to his position of dominance? It is the fact that Man is conscious of his own Soul, while his lesser brethren are not conscious of theirs. The Soul of Man is not fundamentally more perfect than the Soul of anything else; all have their common origin in the Great Causeless Cause, which projects them into expression through the one common medium of Universal Life Energy; but the sphere of expression is more ample in subordinate forms. Other things can look consciously up to Man; Man looks consciously up to his Original Cause.

There is thus a fraternal bond uniting all Nature. Every human being has something in common with everything else. The Souls of all emerge from a single Source and are embodied in a single Universal Substance, which Science calls Electrons. Only the arrangement is different. That is why, as the children of one Father-Mother, peace, cooperation and mutual help should be exercised throughout the teeming members of that Great Universal Family instead of fighting and destruction. And on none does the responsibility rest more directly than on Man, because he, with his gift of Consciousness, KNOWS.

The argument may suggest itself that all things do not manifest Soul qualities. An inert lump of mineral substance exhibits no perceptible evidence of Life, Mind, Law (Truth) or Love. Yet if you believe that you are very much mistaken.

All substance, mineral, vegetable or animal, express these Four Qualities unconsciously in the very stuff of their composition. All are made up out of the same Universal Substance called Electrons. Different combinations of Electrons produce the atoms of -the various forms of Matter. Human perception cannot discern Electrons or even atoms; it can see agglomeration of them as a whole, and that agglomeration appears motionless, inert. But within the atom, in the electronic units which comprise it, is an ordered intensity of action that the human Mind is too coarse to enmesh in its concepts.

But this action, while it expresses all the qualities of the Soul, is not aware of itself. Life is in the incredibly swift motion of the Electrons, Intelligence and Law in the exact plan they follow, and Love in the magnetic attraction that keeps the spinning constellation within its atomic walls. Yet there lacks the one factor that distinguishes every other agglomeration of Electrons and atoms from that which is known as Man—Conscious Expression.

The primary purpose of human existence is to transmit into as nearly perfect and abundant expression as possible on the Material Plane the perfection of Qualities in the Soul.

All Knowledge, All Success, All Joy, All Power wait thereto be uncovered and put into practical application in your daily life. in proportion as you render yourself a clearer lens for their richer and more unsullied transmission into positive activities you fulfil the Law of Progress. In proportion as you fail to groom yourself toward that flawless ideal you transgress this Law and incur corresponding consequences.

Your opportunity to derive the fullest advantage from the Law of Progress lies in the intelligent development of the channels connecting you with Superconsciousness. That is the door through .which your Soul pours in its treasures with a lavish hand when the door is open. Only as you mold yourself, through the conscious and constant use of Universal Life Energy, in every department of your life, to the dominant Four Square of Life, Mind, Law (Truth) and Love can you achieve the Poise, Harmony and Power within that will attune you to the Perfect Source of All Power. But when that sympathetic accord has been established, the door of your Superconsciousness will be open wide and through it you will welcome consciously those perfect qualities and powers which your Soul has already possessed and held in readiness from Eternity.

Human mental force cannot accomplish this. Will Power strikes a far harsher note than the harmonious one with which you are trying to get into communion. To use it is to contract yourself physically and mentally, closing the very door you desire to open. Universal Life Energy sounds the only note that corresponds with Universal Life Energy, represented in your own Soul, and It cannot be bullied or driven. You have no choice but to accommodate yourself to Its Laws if you want It to work through you.

Understanding these Laws, realizing the Fundamental Principles which they outline, you can build those Principles into your life according to the methods described in these Lessons. Do so, and you will find your patience and perseverance rewarded by gradual growth into a Power that will exceed your most sanguine expectations.

Last and most comprehensive of the material questions implied by a study of the Immortal Soul is the question of Death. If the real "you," the core about which the physical individual is constructed, is eternal and imperishable, why is it that every mortal being must inevitably die? Why must trees decay and metals corrode and rocks at length crumble into dust—like the rest of us?

Modern Science, investigating this matter on the Physical Plane, has discovered that, from a scientific point of view, there is no such thing as actual death. There is a change, but never complete annihilation. You change radically when you die, so far as the physical aspect of the case is concerned; your Body undergoes rapid dissolution, disintegrates and sheds its material identity as a Body. But although the constituent parts of that structure of flesh and bone abandon their relation one to another, relinquish the close association which they preserved while "you" were inside, they still exist as particles of dust, gases, minerals, etc. Every particle is itself a cluster of atoms, and every atom is a spinning cosmos of indestructible Electrons, still whirling headlong in their appointed orbits, still manifesting the qualities of the Universal Power from which they were born, still unreeling their tiny destiny, quite indifferent to what goes on outside.

In other words, Life did not die; it simply dispersed when the Soul which attracted it into that association withdrew. The process was like switching away the current in an electric magnet; once the attractive power receded, the clinging bits of matter let go and fell apart. Yet the current itself, the individualized Ray of All Power, the Soul, which collected about itself that material crust, not only exists itself, but exists as a Conscious

Entity which has already attracted a suitable medium for its expression on the loftier Plane where it now resides. It merely discarded the Material Body which was no longer adequate to transmit the qualities it was ready to unfold and built another one which was.

Human life is but one step on a long upward road of growth, evolution and unfoldment. The very same process that the Soul experiences on the large scale is apparent on a smaller scale within the limits of the Material Plane. Your physical Body is continually "dying" and being renewed around you. Skin, hair, cells, bones, everything inside and out is eroding and crumbling away only to be replaced by new structures. Every few years, in fact, sees you entirely remade from cover to cover without you being in the least aware of it, except, perhaps, as the melancholy evidences of advancing age betray an unnecessary slowing down of the process.

Looking lower in the scale of life, the change becomes more sharply defined the further you go. Animals moult seasonally, birds shed their plumage for new at the mating period, snakes and various other reptiles abandon their last year skins almost in one piece. But it is among the insect life that the transition is most completely and vividly illustrated.

Consider, for instance, the life history of a caterpillar. Between that crawling, earth-bound worm and the exquisitely collared, elusive butterfly whose domain is the Air there seems to be no common bond of relationship. Yet through some amazing necromancy the dull worm appears to reconstruct itself and blossom forth into that winged marvel of a butterfly. What is the connection there?

The caterpillar, like everything else, is the imperfect material shell of a perfect Soul. That Soul has in it all the distinctive qualities of both the worm and the butterfly, but it unfolds them in logical sequence from the bottom up. When the lower, fundamental qualities have received the necessary development in an appropriate environment, they are ready to give birth into expression the finer qualities which outline themselves in the form of the butterfly. Therefore the caterpillar is simply observing the Law of Eternal Progress when it creeps along its career into the caterpillar destiny of a chrysalis.

Once entombed in its chrysalis, the caterpillar has experienced what we, in our evolution, call Death. That is, it has died as a caterpillar, yet the Soul still remains in the "dead" body through which it has ceased to express its former activities and quietly prepares itself for the expression of finer qualities which the old material shell was not adapted to transmit. The living chrysalis in which the Soul dwells during that period of rest gradually molds itself to the form of the soaring nature now demanding expression, until the day when the same Soul bursts forth in its entirely new aspect of a butterfly.

There within the limits of a Physical Plane is repeated what the human individual goes through when he steps over the border of that Plane, out of range of our perception. From the discarded shell of the old Body rises a new Being, one which embraces all that the other has been but differs completely by virtue of what is now added. The Soul, finished with expression through its human number of Five, devotes itself to ampler expression through the next higher number of Six.

Because the caterpillar and the butterfly demonstrate so well this transition, the butterfly has been taken from early times as the emblem of the Soul liberated from its material prison. It sums up most concisely a Lesson written large throughout the whole Great Book of Nature for those observant ones who care to read — that there is no Death. There is only continual change, evolution from one condition into another and usually a better one, according to the Natural Law of Evolution or Unfoldment from the lower into the higher.

Nature does not countenance any divergence from this upward trend of all things. The reverse process, Involution, is a direct abuse of that Natural Law, resulting in degeneration in every direction, Involution, if it could be carried to an ultimate extreme, would culminate in the utter annihilation of real Death. The Soul would swallow itself," so to say, as the barriers to expression turned it constantly in on itself. Yet in order to do this, the process would have to run out the small end of Infinity, which of course has no end, so even there "Death" is impossible.

Progress is the Law of Eternal Existence. Life based on Laws of Nature and lived according to those Laws cannot go backward. Death is a step forward, a transition into a wider sphere of activity; the only terror connected with it is the dread spawned from ignorance of its real character. The greater part of agony and suffering attendant upon leaving this Material Plane is bred of that

Fear and is a total waste, as the sufferer will discover to his astonishment once he has died out of his Physical Self and into his new and finer condition.

The new shell which the Soul assumes on the next higher Plane is just as much a Body to it as the old one it discorded, only constructed out of the medium peculiar to that Plane. Human beings cannot perceive that Plane; the rate of vibration there is too high for our coarser faculties to register consciously; therefore the Bodies which Souls acquire there are invisible to us under ordinary circumstances. Yet the Mortal Being, encased in his physical senses, while he cannot break through the lid of his limitations to perceive what is above him, is perceived readily from that Plane.

The particular advantage this confers upon those who have stepped out of our human sphere is that it teaches them definitely the non-existence of Death. Mankind, in their activities, are always accustomed to proceed from the point of view of Matter as a perishable thing, including themselves. They traverse the Material Plane at a single stride, yet do not perceive where their next stride is going to take them.

That is because their lower rate of vibration does not render them sensible of the higher rate of that Invisible World into which they are forging ahead. They cannot see beyond the horizon which their creeping process unrolls only gradually from the unexplored Future into which they advance. But all behind them, all that they have once passed on their course, is known territory, and from the loftier eyrie they attain on the other side of mortal bounds they are able to survey the whole human field they have left. They are able to see human beings still living in physical bodies, because the higher rate of vibrations they have achieved includes and surpasses the lower rate which prevails in the Visible World; yet those in the Visible World, limited by that lower rate, cannot perceive them.

The higher the rate of vibration, the more abundantly the Soul is able to express its qualities through them and the more powerful the individual becomes in every direction. The World beyond this Physical World is thus one of far broader scope, of richer knowledge, finer qualities, greater power and quicker realization. It is a World stripped of the clumsy limitations which hamper one here.

Death is still the Great Enemy of Mankind, as it has always been, because of the Fear of it which erects it into an ominous reality in human Minds. But some day Knowledge will strip from it that funereal mask; people will see it as the fresh, vital experience it actually is, the kindly adventure thrilling with the surprises that will greet them on their awakening. They will approach it with something of the spirit that animates aviators rocketing through Space at a speed never before attained, or putting their winged mounts through breath-taking stunts in the middle of vacancy. Confidence, absolute and serene, sparkles through their daring; they know that a strong apparatus under them, guided by a clear Mind, a steady heart and a firm hand will mock the dangers that lurk in their antic course.

When knowledge of so-called Death as simply a milestone marking the way into a continuation of the life here, but on a higher and incomparably richer Plane, becomes a part of the mental fabric of Mankind, the Fear of Death which now gives it so bitter a flavour will be wholly banished. The sting will be removed, the old prophecy fulfilled. Death will be swallowed up in Victory, the Shadow dispelled from human Consciousness by the brilliant Light of Knowledge.

Mankind prepares now for that not far distant day when the whole condition of life on this Earth will entirely change. People will not need to die in their physical Bodies, like a caterpillar, in order to reach a higher state of Consciousness. They will merge into that new state as naturally as ice melts into water, merely raising the rate of vibrations which now manifest themselves in a corresponding physical Body until that Body fades out of the perception of their Fellow Beings and assumes the finer aspect of their next and higher expression.

All the needless sorrow, pain, suffering and regret now associated with the departure of loved ones from this Plane will then be eliminated. Translation into another Plane of Existence will be achieved without a pang and without loss even for a .moment of one's Consciousness and memories of the Past. And just as the harsh edges will be rubbed from the far limits of the human career, so also will the distress that stands ward at the portals through which we enter into this life be avoided. The present method of being born to the Earth will then also be outgrown; the confining walls which imprison mortals on this plant will be razed before and behind, so that access is no less easy and free from difficulties than departure.

EXERCISES TO LESSON NINETEEN

Practice as usual, morning and evening, the Star Exercise, Relaxation, Silence and the continual Contact with Universal Life Energy. Then apply the coordinated stream of your forces in the channel of the new Exercise for this week, MEDITATION.

MEDITATION implies a deep and placid consideration of the world within, a seclusion from storms and squalls that blow down out of your environment to ruffle the delicate calm of your reflective mood.

Therefore choose a time and place suitable to your purpose, and comfortably withdrawn from all likelihood of unexpected intrusion. Then proceed with MEDITATION as follows:

Select for the object of the Exercise a sufficiently lofty and appropriate subject, in this particular instance your own Soul. Then, after you have entered into Silence and made the Contact with Universal Life Energy, concentrate your Mind strongly on that highest and deepest part of your Being. Perceive it in its untarnished aspect as a pure Ray from its Eternal Source, imbued with all positive qualities of Strength and Power. Understand it as the Inexhaustible Spring of its manifestations in you as Life, Mind, Law (Truth) and Love. Let your concept of it overflow distinguishing material barriers and search out its brotherhood with other Souls throughout all Nature, both in the basic Universal Substance of Electrons into which all are projected and in the common Source from which all emerge. See yourself as its embodiment on this Material Plane, expressing but not obscuring its qualities.

Your process of thinking during MEDITATION should be slow, unhurried but deep. Let your thoughts sink into yourself like tiny motes sinking into the clear, bottomless depths of a quiet mountain lake. Drown your Conscious Self in the crystal Light of your Inner Self, allowing it to dissolve from you the irritating crust of disharmonious memories and experiences. The further you are able to penetrate in this way, the more satisfactory and refreshing your MEDITATION will be.

Guard against the improper use of Will Power in this Exercise. The subtle temptation to probe with that human instrument is always on the alert to spoil anything that requires patience, mental and physical repose and relaxation. You cannot rush to your destination by your own wilful strength; you can penetrate only gradually and steadily into that remote inner chamber of your Being.

Extraneous thoughts from without will probably insist on flashing through your Mind in the beginning when you practice MEDITATION. Be equally firm and insistent in dismissing them and bringing your Mind back to the subject designed for it. Cultivate the necessary calm, unflurried attitude of utter restfulness, and as you improve that you will obtain better results.

Through MEDITATION you will wipe away the discordant films which obscure expression of the Soul's higher qualities through your human channels and will promote an extraordinary development and accord in every direction. It is one of the most valuable methods for obtaining the Poise and consequent Power so indispensable for Success in life.

QUESTIONS TO LESSON NINETEEN

1. From what point of view has the Soul generally been regarded?

2. Why has this explanation failed?

3. What perceptible proofs of the Soul's existence and qualities exist in the human individual?

4. Define the Human Soul.

5. Is the possession of a Soul restricted to human beings?

6. What position does the Soul of Man occupy in relation to the rest of Nature?

7. What differentiates the Human Soul from all others?

8. In what respects does Universal Brotherhood become apparent?

9. What purpose does the Soul represent in Material Existence?

10. What is Death?

11. What is the Natural Law governing all Life?

12. How will Death eventually be eliminated?

ANSWERS TO LESSON NINETEEN

1. **The point of view from which the Soul has generally been regarded is:**

   From the point of view of blind Faith, unsubstantiated by definite proofs.

2. **This explanation has failed:**

   Because the practical Rational Mind demands proofs, the unbroken transition from visible Effects to invisible Cause, before it can accept conclusions.

3. **The perceptible proofs of the Soul's existence that are apparent in the human individual are:**

   The Four Fundamental Qualities of Life, Mind, Law (Truth) and Love out of which his whole life structure is erected.

4. **The Human Soul:**

   Is the individualized, self conscious, harmonious, compound and eternal projection of the Great Causeless Cause through Universal Life Energy into Its Own Eternal Substance.

5. **The possession of a Soul:**

   Is not restricted to human beings, since every material manifestation is but the expression of the Soul behind it.

6. **The position occupied by the Soul of Man in relation to the rest of Nature is:**

The position of dominance, including in itself the qualities manifested in all other Souls and something more besides.

7. **The Human Soul is differentiated from all others:**

By the fact that it is Conscious of its own Existence.

8. **Universal Brotherhood becomes apparent:**

In the Universal Substance, called Electrons, through which all Souls are projected into material expression, and in the common Source, Universal Life Energy, from which all are immediately derived.

9. **The Purpose which the Soul represents in material existence is:**

The perfection of qualities for which Mankind strive in order to make themselves an equally perfect medium of expression.

10. **Death is:**

A continuation of the One and Only Present Life into a higher and greater Sphere of Activity which is beyond the ordinary range of human perception.

11. The Natural Law governing all life is:

The Law of Progress, or Evolution, which decrees the logical unfoldment of Soul Qualities from the lower into the higher.

12. Death will eventually be eliminated:

By expanding the narrow bounds of Human Consciousness sufficiently to include and demonstrate, by conscious raising of one's vibrations, the continuity of Life.

Dear Friend:

In this Lesson you will perceive in detail the exact relation between your Soul, the unseen Source of your physical being, and the material shell of your Body, which it builds for its expression on the Earth Plane. The precise correlation of your various organs with the qualities behind them, of which they are the outgrowth, their delicate adjustment and interdependence on each other, their cooperative functioning, what they symbolize individually, in groups and as a whole, will be explained to you.

You will understand how to remodel and coordinate your complex array of physical instruments in the most advantageous fashion to pass into abundant, vigorous expression the boundless treasures of qualities and powers in your Soul. Superconsciousness, as the connecting link between the humanly conscious You and the complete real YOU, will be definitely assigned its place in your comprehension.

Most important, perhaps, will be the explanation of how the Soul builds and governs its Material Body. The information conveyed in this study will open to you a wealth of fascinating sidelights on matters that have long been a subject of scientific dispute, as for instance Heredity with its annoying discrepancies to flout any cut-and-dried theories. The vital bearing of the attitude of prospective parents toward each other on the kind of children they will introduce into the World will be made strikingly clear.

Finally, you will learn how to transform your Body in accordance with your own desires. A weak, unhealthy or unsightly Body is not a permanent affliction; it is an unfortunate Effect that can be thoroughly modified by correcting the Cause behind it. By the development of the Soul's qualities it can be made as you wish Strong, Healthy and Harmonious.

Cordially yours,
Eugene Fersen.

LESSON TWENTY

"KNOW thyself and thou shalt know all" was said, not of the Body or the Mind alone, but of the Soul. All Knowledge, all qualities, all powers contained in the Great Causeless Cause and Its First Manifestation, Universal Life Energy, are poured into that Core of your Being to be expressed by it. There is no end to the treasures it contains; it is an inexhaustible mine whose ore becomes constantly richer the deeper you penetrate into it; but as in everything else, this wealth must be sought. Energy, effort and perseverance are required to unearth what otherwise will not sift down into your conscious grasp of its own accord.

As it is not an easy task, under ordinary circumstances, to unfold the qualities latent in the Soul, most people try and after a few unsuccessful endeavours lapse into a sort of coma of resignation or wistful expectancy. They pin their hopes to some happy chance, some lucky conjunction of circumstances, that will someday accomplish for them at one effortless stroke what they failed to do themselves. This period of waiting usually extends itself undisturbed into the grave, because circumstances seldom conform of their own volition to the idle wish of one unable to mold them, or if they do happen to arrange themselves favourably are not recognized as the long desired opportunity.

The one way to develop into vigorous expression the wealth of qualities in your higher Self is through Opposition. That is the natural foil against which the human metal must whet and temper itself for ever greater responsibilities. Soul qualities are above all strong; they cannot express themselves through lassitude and weakness any more than the master swordsman can exhibit his flashing skill against the sluggish blade of a novice. A greater demand than any that has been met before is needed to call forth the added margin of response which represents Progress.

Life continually supplies all the excessive demands by which Soul qualities can be exercised into an ever ampler expression. Situations are continually cropping up which challenge you directly into a form of activity new and strange to you and wholly beyond the bounds of your previous experience. Most people, measuring their inner strength against such demands, are dismayed by their apparent lack of sufficient power to meet them. They shrink from the task that circumstances have put in their way, accepting defeat before the test in the words that should be forever barred from your dictionary — "I cannot."

Yet this absolute surrender is evidence only of an untrue perception of the facts. The individual who says "I cannot" is one who does not take into consideration his greatest resources, but allows his decision to be dictated by a stationary view of the matter. It is like assuming that dripping water can never fill a glass, because the one drop you see at a single hasty glance is so extravagantly small compared with the emptiness which engulfs it.

Your own supply of strength may be as that drop in contrast to the appalling demand you see yawning before you; but like the drop also, it is no sooner swallowed in the hungry vacancy awaiting it than its place is occupied by another ready to follow. Behind each drop is a shore-less Ocean of Supply from which more will come, and in a rich flood if you will only open the tap within yourself.

That supply is the Universal Life Energy Whose Essence, comprehending all qualities and powers in limitless abundance, forms your own Soul. The reason you sometimes feel that you are unable to cope with a problem is because you allow that positive current to trickle only very feebly into evidence through your Human Consciousness. You are sensible of the resulting lack of power and helplessness, elsewhere described as Fear, and through the paralysing effect of this Fear you shut off still further the expression of qualities from your Soul which would have copiously satisfied all demands. Such a self-devouring inversion is what flaunts itself finally in the gloomy assertion "I cannot."

You will never encounter a problem that you have not the possibility to solve. The fact that the Great Law allows it to block your course indicates that you are capable of overcoming it, because the Great Law is above any possible perversion that could definitely cut off all Progress. Therefore if you do not find within your humanly conscious reserves the power to meet it do not be discouraged. Open yourself through the contact with Universal Life Energy and plunge whole-heartedly into the work ahead. With the help of that invincible Force, carrying to you the very Soul qualities of which you then stand so sorely in need, you will conquer one by one the obstacles which rise in your path and will fulfil all requirements as circumstances fashion them in front of you.

Humanity has so long been accustomed to let their Consciousness obscure rather than transmit the qualities latent in their Soul that it is no quick or easy task to correct the habit. Victory does not come at a snap of the fingers; it must be earned. Yet the apparent defeats that you may suffer at first are defeats only if you accept them as such.

To go down fighting, with fire in the blood and victory in the heart, only to rise anew, is never a failure, even though your immediate object may have escaped your grasp. You step to supremacy over disasters and successes alike; but as the disasters pry open your inner channels for tapping your Soul powers, failures will become less and less frequent. Your inner Success will express itself outside as Success in your activities.

Every time you overcome a difficulty or an obstacle, you unfold a corresponding quality of your Soul. That much is added to the sum of your knowledge, strength and power, and by the measure of that increase you have advanced just so much in your Evolution. Each gain is a permanent gain, a base from which to progress further, and each forward step is accelerated by an intelligent use of Universal Life Energy. By this is meant the correlation of activities with the Soul qualities they are designed to express, so that they conform to the balanced Standard characteristic of everything above the Plane of Human Consciousness.

This Standard, represented by the Four Aspects of Universal Life Energy, Life, Mind, Truth and Love, is perfectly sustained in everything that makes up the individualized Ray which you call your Soul. Therefore the only sort of action capable of passing into equally perfect expression the qualities of the Soul is that in which Energy, Intelligence, Accuracy and Joy are manifested to a corresponding degree.

Your vital concern is to build those Four Cornerstones into your life by building them consciously and scrupulously into every act of your life, the small and seemingly inconsequential ones as well as the great. None are more important than others so far as developing your character is concerned.

All secondary qualities are contained within the scope of these Four Main Aspects, so if they are properly manifested all the numberless details erected out of them and dependent on them will automatically adjust themselves. For that reason the intelligent application of Universal Life Energy with the distinct purpose of bringing out those Aspects in each action you perform sharpens all your perceptive and executive faculties alike. You are alert to detect the right course to follow, quick to anticipate the thing needful to be done, keen to sense every twist and pitfall in your path and vigorously resourceful in overcoming them.

The strength you draw from that Universal Power is then not blind strength alone; it develops in you the skill to direct and use It most effectively and with the least waste. That natural development is a complete and all-around one, giving you equal poise and confidence in whatever direction you may turn instead of merely overdeveloping your ability in one specific direction alone.

Very often people perceive some particular. lack or weakness in themselves which they wish to correct, and they focus their energies on cultivating the special trait that has aroused their concern. Perhaps when that one is stimulated into an excessive growth it exposes by contrast the comparative weakness of an associated trait, which then becomes the object of attention. That leads to another, and so on interminably, until the individual' is involved in a furious campaign of self improvement, jumping from one little facet of his nature to another only to run into an endless chain of flaws beyond. To fall a victim to details in this manner is a tragedy, because it means a desperate amount of hard work with never any satisfaction at the end of it.

Such an individual has lost his perspective. He is struggling in a mass of details which are legion, instead of concentrating on the Four Fundamentals from which they all spring. It is like trying to solve a complicated problem in Mathematics by adding up the 'units one by one on your fingers rather than by simply multiplying in one short process; you may get there at last, but at a ridiculous expenditure of time and effort.

The direct and obvious way to adjust disjointed details is to adjust the Fundamentals on which they rest. Solve the problem first in its basic aspects and the details will ravel out in natural and logical sequence. That is the advantage of developing in your life the Four Fundamental Aspects of Life, Mind, Truth and Love, because on them everything in your life is based. If they are brought into a strong and harmonious relation, all accessory qualities will blend obediently into corresponding accord.

Therefore remember always to retain your sense of proportion and values as one of the basic conditions for successful achievement. The more you tangle yourself in details the more you lose your perception of all parts in relation to themselves and to the whole. You are opening the channels within yourself for the expression of your Soul qualities only when you survey from that lofty vantage point of your Being the whole broad field of your specific activities. When you descend from this clear perspective and limit your vision to within your Conscious Walls, the maze which envelopes you will swallow energies, purpose and all in a busy industry which leads to no visible end.

Mental vision is obtained from the highest part of your Mental Trinity, that Aspect which you call Superconsciousness and which forms the connecting link between your Conscious Self and the Great Causeless Cause.

Through Superconsciousness you become aware of all the other qualities and powers that the Great Causeless Cause pours into your Soul for expression, but particularly do you attain through its access to Universal Intelligence. Your problem, if you wish to achieve the poise and sure, far prospect essential for Success, is to rub away the crust of conscious limitations which divides you from Superconsciousness and to establish your oneness with It. Once this is accomplished, your Oneness with all Universal Forces and Powers, which also express themselves through your Superconsciousness, is inevitable.

Your instrument for doing this is the ever available Power of Universal Life Energy Itself. The more you direct that Force to the promotion of a fuller contact with your own Superconsciousness the better you will develop your inner channels for bringing it within your conscious reach. Your Pineal Gland, the organ of Superconsciousness in your brain, will develop and function with growing ease, strength and efficiency as constant use and the invigorating current of Life Force give it the exercise it needs.

As it has been explained before, that Gland is the physical door through which all the Infinite Knowledge and Power in your Superconsciousness, all the wealth of Soul qualities backed up behind it and all the boundless reserves in the Great Causeless Cause also are admitted to your Conscious Self and introduced into the Plane of your Material Existence. Therefore the more often and effectively you perform the Exercise of Polarization described in Lesson 18, the wider becomes this avenue for your Soul treasures to flow down into sumptuous expression in your life.

We know that the Soul is an aggregation of qualities, each of which manifests itself in a corresponding physical organ. The activities of all these qualities, clustered together and outlined in material form, constitute what is called the Body. The Body, therefore, is but the outlined expression of the aggregate activities of the Soul. Yet the activities of the 'Soul continually vary as its qualities are gradually unfolded and brought forth by the demands of a constantly modified environment.

As the activities change, so also does the Body, at least until the limit set by the individual's own conscious Fear "freezes" that plastic clay at about the age of twenty-five or thirty. If the material shell were immune to the influence of this Fear, it would continue to change as it did in Youth, keeping pace with the qualities unfolded through it. Also, if the Soul did not function on the Material Plane, it would not require a material medium for its expression and that most vulnerable and sluggish part of your triune nature would be dispensed with entirely.

But the activities of the Soul must always be outlined in a corresponding Body. Those activities are not restricted to the Soul Plane, as in that case they would be outlined in the medium peculiar to that Plane and wholly imperceptible to our coarse human senses. Neither are they exclusively mental; their embodiment then would be a mental one, as invisible as thought itself. The Soul, in our present state of Human Consciousness, functions through these two rarer atmospheres, emerging ultimately on the Material Plane where it requires a material vehicle for its expression, the human Body. The building of this physical Body by the Soul is called Incarnation, or Involution of the Soul into Matter.

Three distinct phases mark this progress — Conception, Gestation and Birth. The first of these, Conception, is of paramount importance in that it constitutes the selective act by which a particular Soul is admitted into material expression through the prospective parents. The Soul, ready with countless others for Incarnation and ripe with the urge to break into physical manifestation, awaits the summons from the Physical Plane which alone can open the way for it. That summons is supplied by the future parents who, during their physical union, when all their qualities and characteristics are fanned into an intense activity, discharge into Space. a wave of vibrations compounded of all their traits in general, tempered by their special physical, mental and emotional attitude at that moment.

This wave, possessing its own distinct vibratory rate, strikes an instant response from the corresponding Soul, which promptly rushes toward the prospective human Mother and overshadows her. It does not enter into her, but sends down a ray of its own life which penetrates through her Pineal Gland and Spinal Cord to the human seed deposited in her womb by the father, the nucleus from which it must erect its own habitation. The real Conception is consummated when this ray of the invisible, immaterial Life of the Soul becomes one with the material, visible life kernel through which it is to achieve expression.

Gestation is the initial period of preparation before Birth. The Soul, unaccustomed to material surroundings, can at first manifest its activities only very feebly and imperfectly in constructing its own Body, pouring itself gradually through the connecting shaft of Life projected from itself and working its way by degrees into the physical prison which it must shape to fit itself.

For that reason the human embryo goes through all stages of development, from the most primitive form characteristic of the simplest qualities to the most complex. Between the original microscopic human seed and its fruition in a human Body all the lower stages of animal life are represented successively, the physical shell changing as the Soul, becoming acclimated, is able to unfold more and more of its qualities and activities. That process culminates at last in the completed body, the intricate vehicle which the Soul has created for its expression on this Earth Plane.

Once it has built the vehicle for its expression on the Material Plane, the Soul is ready to occupy that vehicle independently. Through Birth it frees itself from the maternal surroundings and thenceforth works out its further development directly, without the intervention of some other human medium. It steps out into the World for the first time as an individual Being, a condition to which it at once proceeds to adjust itself. It breathes and takes food, learns to control its activities, to see, hear, smell, touch and taste. It explores outward into its environment through its five senses, and presently extends its range by learning to walk and talk.

As it throws itself more and more on its own resources, it becomes increasingly conscious of the fact that it is an independent and individual Being, and under the stimulus of that realization it unfolds its qualities ever more richly and vigorously through the physical Body which keeps pace with this growth. When full physical development, or the limit dictated by the present State of Human Consciousness, has been reached, the Body ceases to grow, although mental and spiritual improvement continues unchecked.

This physical halt occurs usually between the twenty-fifth and thirtieth year, from which time until the fiftieth or, more rarely, sixtieth year the physical apparatus remains about the same. Then it wears into a gradual decline, at first slow and almost imperceptible but hastening with the passage of years toward the final dissolution called Death. Yet Death, as we know, does not mean extinction, it simply indicates that the Soul, in obedience to the Law of Eternal Progress, has raised its rate of vibrations to the point where they pass above the level of the Material Plane. Consequently it loses hold entirely of the Material Plane and therefore of its own Physical Body, whose component parts disintegrate once the attractive power that garnered them together is withdrawn. That dissolution is merely evidence of one more step forward completed in the march of Evolution.

The correlation of each individual member of the Body with the Soul activity expressing through it spreads out an exactly detailed map of the relation between the two. Every respective organ, the outgrowth and product of the particular quality behind it, possesses a symbolical significance which, when read, teaches you the natural Purpose to be achieved and where you have failed to achieve it. All together, these integral parts of a complete whole compose a vivid picture of the general trend of your Being, with the strong and weak points etched in bold relief.

For example, just as in your Soul the Four Main Aspects of Life, Mind, Law (Truth), and Love embrace all secondary qualities which must express through them, so in your Body the physical manifestations of Life, Mind, Law and Love form the alliance of vital organs on which all secondary ones depend. Without the blood stream and Life Centre cooperating to carry Life to every remote cell and muscle you would wither and die; without a healthy brain to coordinate and direct your actions you could not unfold your Soul qualities into material expression; without the complicated system of glands through which Law governs the automatic functioning of the various organs, those organs would fall into ruin; without the heart, the Magnetic Centre of Attraction or Love, to pump the sustaining Life Current on its unceasing journey, you would cease to exist as a Human Entity. These Four Corners are the foundation of your Physical Being; when one crumbles, the whole intricate structure erected upon them topples to destruction.

Within their bounds are piled up the specific units to be analysed for the lesson they teach. The Soul thinks; you have a brain which acts as a switchboard, the place where all connections between the Physical, Mental and Emotional parts of your nature are concentrated. Understand the Laws which govern you so you can make the proper connections to take the utmost practical advantage of them in daily life, think rightly, strongly and harmoniously, and you will develop your brain into an ever more refined and vigorous instrument to help you work out your Destiny. Its marvellous centres, uniting in a powerful accord, will merge in one clear focus their conscious beams and illumine far ahead the road which leads to greater Success and Happiness.

The Soul perceives people, things, conditions; you have eyes. Cultivate a keen sure perception and you will be astonished to find how your eyes improve as the Soul quality behind them is burnished to a more lustrous expression. They become bright and clear and seem to burn away any film that blurs or -distorts your vision. The more fundamental harmony you are able to distinguish beneath all the superficial disharmony, the more striking will be the change in them. They will become more beautiful and attractive, especially in colour, will be luminous, expressive, supremely alive and alert.

The Soul has the power to discriminate; consequently you have ears. Cultivate that power by training yourself to differentiate instantly between the right and the wrong, to pick out the false notes in the orchestral harmony of your life, no matter how subtly concealed they may be, and your sense of hearing will become correspondingly more acute.

The Soul is able to express, to voice its thoughts and feelings; hence your mouth, lips, tongue and vocal cords. Develop the ability to express your thoughts and feelings strongly, harmoniously and accurately and you will discover that the progress made in this respect will be reflected physically also. Your mouth will become firm and well shaped, while your voice becomes powerful and "carrying," yet pleasantly melodious.

These lessons written in the head alone are typical of others carved in every organ of the body. Your shoulders imply the faculty of the Soul to carry responsibilities, a burden which grows with its unfoldment. Learn early in life the sense of responsibility, and your shoulders will become correspondingly well proportioned, broad and strong.

The courage of your Soul, its readiness to face boldly all kinds of opposition and difficulties in life is manifested in the chest. A sturdy chest indicates a willingness to forge grimly onward in the face of any criticism or obstacles.

Your heart, whose rhythmic beat sustains the life and harmony in your Body, clearly expresses the capacity of the Soul to love. The Rhythm of Love is back of Life's harmony, gathering it into concentrated expression, keeping it going in the channels where it works best and serves most. A stimulation of the Love vibrations in the heart brings the expansive feeling of Joy, an abuse of them a bitter negative contraction. You experience them directly in your heart and consciously register and appraise them in your brain.

Closely associated with these two major activities is a third represented by the lungs, in whose maze of air pockets the blood stream trades its impurities for clear oxygen. The lungs are therefore the purgative organs, embodying the faculty of the Soul to purify its own vehicle for expression, clarifying the Life Current of the Body and thus sustaining it in a harmonious condition by drawing on the finer forces of Nature, the gases.

Descending to the next sector of your physical engine, you find an interesting assortment of digestive organs— the stomach, assisted by kidneys, liver and bowels. There is embodied the Soul's power to assimilate and digest everything of .a positive, constructive nature that may be submitted to it, and to eliminate undesirable elements. Cultivate that Soul quality by being fearless in your life, immune to worry, always ready to meet and absorb boldly every new element and condition that arises before you, and you will have no cause to anticipate trouble in your digestive tract. Your liver, kidneys and stomach will function perfectly. Then be equally ready to eliminate waste and undesirable matter, that which you have outworn or outgrown, or which you wish to reject, and your bowels will supplement the activities of the rest with complete satisfaction.

The freedom of the Soul, its ability to move about at will, emerges into physical evidence in your legs. The ease and suppleness of that movement is represented in the joints of the Body, but particularly in the knees and feet. There the swiftness, strength and poise of the Soul, the fundamental factors of its standing on the Physical Plane, where you now live, are manifested.

Your Soul's Self Reliance, its capacity to grasp, hold and handle whatever it may come in contact with, the Independence it is meant to have in this World, is conveyed in your arms and hands. Exercise that Independence, strengthen your faculty of handling capably on the Three Planes the affairs that present themselves to you, and your increased efficiency in that direction will be reflected in shapely hands, strong and muscular arms.

In analysing yourself for the particular weakness and flaws to be corrected, do not lose sight of the dominating Standard set by the Four Main Aspects of Life, Mind, Law (Truth) and Love. All secondary qualities must manifest themselves in the terms of these Four Fundamental Ones. Therefore make them the starting point, the central eminence, from which you conduct all your operations in any specific direction. Remember that they are the common denominator, the simplest figure to which all problems reduce, and concentrate your efforts on expressing them and emphasize them, realizing that when they are properly established all the dependent associate items will fall neatly in line.

Except in youth, change is never rapid in the human Body. It is more noticeable in early years than later, but though it is continually taking place it cannot be expected to produce an abrupt revision of your fleshly domicile. Several years of diligent and careful effort will give the Soul an opportunity to re-fashion gradually its physical shell, in proportion as its qualities are brought into greater expression, because during that period the entire Body will have been made over inside and out as old and outworn cells are replaced by new ones. In the course of that reconstruction the former lines are bound to be modified to outline the alteration in the qualities they manifest.

As you live now on the Physical Plane, a proper recognition and appreciation of that fact through the right sort of physical exercise will help materially in promoting those changes. It will render more plastic and impressionable the clay which your Soul, as the Sculptor, must mold to the form of its ever stronger and finer inner concept. In that way you will hasten the process of eliminating old structures and stimulating the constant growth of fresh ones in their place, an interchange which otherwise would not be so quickly and easily effected although it would eventually be accomplished.

The general arrangement of your body organs blocks out before your eyes a plain illustration of the scheme that should dominate all your activities Cooperation for Progress. From first to last you are an assortment of complementary parts, two halves demonstrating respectively the Male and Female Principles, paired off against each other and each supplementing the work of the other throughout your entire system. At the apex Mind, cold, aggressive, vigorous, ruthless, ruling from its seat of power the physical domain under it, represents the Male element as opposed to the Female element, Love, which enthrones itself in the heart and holds that domain together to be ruled.

This division holds true all down the line. It is apparent on the large scale as a visible seam beginning in the skull and seeming to split your body longitudinally down the neck and back. On either side of the line it suggests are the brain lobes, the two eyes, the paired lungs, two kidneys, two arms, two feet, etc. Every member of that compound body has the power to act individually and independently, yet in order to obtain the best results they must coordinate their activities. For this reason are the two halves welded together in a complete and inseparable whole.

The Purpose to which this coordinated action should be applied is manifested in the placing of all the most important organs. They are located in the front part of your Body and have a unanimous forward trend. Eyes look to the fore and are hinged so that they can also perceive to either side, upward and downward along the path. You have no eyes in the back of the head because you are not meant to contemplate eternally the course already traversed, and the necessity for an occasional glance to get your bearings is provided for by your head, pivoted on its neck. Similarly with most other organs, even those which, for the sake of greater protection, are most deeply buried — they are marshalled in an order that tends ever to Progress, onward and upward.

Altogether, your Physical Being sums up in itself a Response from which can be read the great Need which called it forth. That Need is for practical individuals whose feet firmly tread the solid ground of fact while their heads pierce the higher spheres — well balanced, capable people who can see far and clear yet retain a true appreciation of values. Mankind must learn to appraise rightly the material life which has been set before them to be lived. If they were only meant to dream, to ignore and despise the physical environment in which their lot has been cast, to enjoy a loftier estate than that to which they have been born, they would not be weighed down with a Material Body. They would probably be built of some ethereal substance to which wishes alone are wings, enabling them to soar into higher regions.

Give the world in which you live its due. Appreciate, enjoy and use constructively in every way the Material Plane to which you have been sent to work out your human Destiny. Accept this Lesson which your own Body teaches, proceed with your feet strongly, yet lightly and swiftly carrying you over the firm ground of established fact, your body forging courageously onward above them, your head poised and alert, lifting you to view far horizons, to perceive obstacles, to understand

and take account of all dangers from every side and to govern your Progress accordingly. Then you will be fulfilling the Purpose for which you were put on Earth and which you must learn to fulfil before your Evolution will carry you into the nobler condition to which you aspire.

EXERCISES TO LESSON TWENTY

Continue with the Star Exercise, Relaxation, Silence and the continual Contact with Universal Life Energy. In addition to these, proceed this week with the new Exercise, which is called EXTERIORIZATION.

The purpose of EXTERIORIZATION is to promote the unfoldment into material expression through you of the wealth of qualities and powers which your Soul, as a Concentrated. Ray of Universal Life Energy, possesses in itself. In order to perform this Exercise, proceed as follows:

After you have entered into Silence, make the Contact with Universal Life Energy and establish a strong, rich flow of that Power through you. Then focus that Current on the task to which It is to be applied by concentrating your Mind on Exteriorizing, or bringing out into manifestation through the lens of your Physical Self, all the lavish abundance of qualities compacted in your Soul Ray. Perceive your relation as a material entity with the invisible Shaft of Universal Life Energy, your Soul, of which you are the outgrowth. Understand the exquisite symmetry and perfection of those qualities which it pours down on you for expression, their absolute identity with the Standard of Life, Mind, Law (Truth) and Love which is manifested without flaw in them. Try to feel that these qualities are expressed and outlined with equal nicety of proportion through your physical shell.

Be aware of your Life Centre as the Spring out of which the Current of Universal Life Energy wells up fresh and untainted, sparkling with Its clear essence of Strength, Eternal Youth, Mental Vigour, Joy and Beauty and all the qualities native to It. Sense that refreshing Stream spilling from the core of your being outward along every nerve, filling you as water fills a bowl and brimming over through your skin itself. Feel your plastic flesh and muscles, the tissues of your Body, responding to the Strength and Harmony of which they are the conductors, moulding and adapting themselves subtly to the perfect qualities carried into them for expression on the persistent Tide of this Force.

The more you promote the expression of your Soul qualities through your Physical Self in this manner, Exteriorizing them through their corresponding material medium, the more they will modify the shape of that medium to suit them. The outline of your features and Body is bound to change as it accommodates itself to that of which it is the vehicle. You deal with the Cause, concerned mainly with passing your Soul's qualities into manifestation as nearly perfect as they are fundamentally; the physical reflection takes care of itself. Thus you are able to achieve a dream that has always entertained the longing fancy of Mankind — to uncap the Fountain of Eternal Youth in your Body, rejuvenate it with the Life Energy of the Universe and make it always stronger, more harmonious and beautiful.

QUESTIONS TO LESSON TWENTY

1. What is necessary to develop the stronger physical expression of Soul qualities?

2. Where is this to be found?

3. Why do people often shrink from meeting problems that confront them?

4. Will you ever encounter a problem that you have not the possibility to solve?

5. Of what does Progress consist?

6. Of what importance in the development of secondary qualities are the Four Fundamental Qualities of Life, Mind, Law (Truth) and Love?

7. What purpose does Superconsciousness serve in this process?

8. What is Incarnation?

9. What determines the sort of Soul to be born to prospective parents?

10. How are the Male and Female Principles in your Soul indicated in your physical Body?

11. How can the physical Body be modified in form and outline?

12. What dominant Purpose is suggested by the general arrangement of the Body organs?

ANSWERS TO LESSON TWENTY

1. **What is necessary to develop the stronger physical expression of Soul qualities is:**

   Opposition, to challenge the greater exertion of those qualities through their material channels.

2. **Opposition is to be found:**

   In the situations and problems that arise voluntarily in life without being especially sought.

3. **People often shrink from meeting their problems:**

   Because they consider those problems only in relation to their own limited store of forces to meet them and fail to count on the Limitless Stores of Universal Power to which they have access.

4. **Problems that cannot be solved:**

   Will never be encountered by you, because the very fact that the Great Law permits them to confront you indicates that you have the possibility to solve them.

5. **Progress consists of:**

The margin of effort in excess of any that you have made before, exerted in response to a greater demand, and by which you unfold that much more of your Soul qualities.

6. **The importance of the Four Fundamental Qualities of Life, Mind, Law (Truth) and Love in the development of secondary qualities is:**

That through the exercise and development of those Four Fundamental Qualities all the secondary ones erected out of them and dependent on them are automatically developed and correlated also.

7. **Superconsciousness:**

Opens out for you a clear perspective of the myriad details in which you are hopelessly lost as long as your vision is limited within the bounds of your Human Consciousness alone.

8. **Incarnation is:**

The Involution of the Soul into Matter.

9. **The kind of Soul to be born to prospective parents is identified:**

By the rate of the vibrations those future parents discharge into Space during their physical union, and which attract a Soul of a corresponding rate.

10. **The male and female principles in the Soul are indicated in the physical Body:**

    By its distinct division into two halves and the consequent pairing of organs in it—two eyes, two hands, arms, legs, kidneys, lobes, etc.—each, of which must supplement the activities of the other if the best results are to be obtained.

11. **The physical Body can be modified in form and outline:**

    By cultivating a more harmonious and vigorous expression of the Soul qualities of which it is the vehicle.

12. **The dominant Purpose suggested by the general arrangement of the Body Organs is:**

    Progress, to be achieved by the cooperation of all parts for a sure and steady advance toward a forward goal.

Dear Friend:

Your own True Self will be revealed to you in this Lesson, that Inner Being whose Presence you have vaguely felt in the noble impulses, the daring visions, the soaring aspirations which now and then break like flame through the dull crest of convention and habit in which you live. This True Self, your Individuality, is the foundation and backbone of your character; but ignorance of the tremendous possibilities it contains prevents most people from realizing practically the treasures it conceals.

Personally, the disguise behind which your Real Self lies hidden, is an outer mask which you yourself have constructed to represent you in the eyes of the World. That mask is illumined by the Individuality behind it, but usually shows a false version of the Soul Light within it. A human device, it vanishes when the Light is withdrawn, because all its radiance is a borrowed radiance coming from the Soul qualities which it dissembles. You will discover how to fashion that Personality so that it serves as an accurate medium of expression for that inner Individuality where all the genuine intrinsic value is waiting to be manifested.

Your Purpose in life is to realize in fact the perfect Individuality within. Personality is the door through which the real YOU can emerge. Self knowledge, an intelligent understanding both of yourself and of the World outside, is your key to open the door.

Here you will be shown how to find that key, how to analyse yourself, how to sift out the distinguishing characters that form your particular Identity, and how to assert that Identity once it is discovered. When you have done this you will have taken your greatest stride toward achieving your Destiny; you will have FOUND YOURSELF.

Cordially yours,
Eugene Fersen.

LESSON TWENTY-ONE

EVERY human being has in effect two selves, a Real Self and an apparent self. The Real Self is that mysterious Soul Quality within you in which is condensed all that you could be — the ideal "you" whose possibilities you try to realize in your life. The apparent self is the aspect under which you reveal that Real Self to the World. The one is genuine and sincere, an incorruptible Ray of Soul Fire proceeding straight from its Infinite Source and wholly beyond your power to change or modify it. The other is artificial and variable, a mask deliberately fashioned by yourself to hide what you actually are. Your Real Self, the naked Flame within the human lamp, is called your individuality. The painted mask which it throws into visible relief is your Personality.

Personality, therefore, is the surface part of your nature which comes in direct contact with the World, the outward appearance which can be seen, analysed, appraised. You can alter it as often and as radically as circumstances demand, just as an actor can dress himself out in the roles of whatever characters he wishes to portray. But underneath that disguise is always the one unchanging Individuality on which it is super-imposed, the single constant factor which you may exhibit through a diversity of aspects, but which you can never modify in the slightest degree from what it already is. Others are aware of your Individuality only as an inner glow which brands your Personality on their perception; you alone can see it in its entirety as the precious secret flame cupped within that outer masquerade and illumining its carefully wrought contours.

The problem which confronts everyone is how to build up a Personality which will pass into active expression the Individuality behind it. Individuality can never conform to a standard pattern, but Personality, its humanly designed envelope, can and most often does. In all Nature there are no two Individualities exactly alike, just as there are no two Souls alike. Each is a direct projection from the Great Causeless Cause and Its First Manifestation, Universal Life Energy, and these two Primary Factors from which everything is derived have never repeated any combination that has issued from them. They are Themselves supremely Individual, Unique, and They stamp Individuality into the whole endless variety of expressions of which They are the Source.

Thus every human being has within himself a priceless "something" which no other possesses or has ever possessed—a "something" which, if he can adapt his Personality to express it, will single him out from all the rest of Creation. But if, as is usually the case, his Personality is erected after a standard pattern, the aspect he presents to the World will not differ in any salient detail from countless others everywhere. The really valuable part of his Being will be hidden, so of course no value will be placed on it.

The unique combination of qualities which forms your Individuality implies a correspondingly unique place and duty for you in the Cosmic Scheme. There is just one line of endeavour, one environment, where your Individuality will fit to perfection and empty itself into unreserved expression in all your activities. Every faculty will leap joyously to the challenge, every thought and move will knit itself into the smooth river of purposeful action, every resource will be ready to your hand in meeting the demands of that occupation. Your work will bear the mark of Originality, the impress of those distinctive qualities which guide the mental and physical tools that you supply. You will achieve the maximum of productivity, coupled with the greatest ease, pleasure and interest.

In the wrong environment, where the demands do not accord with your peculiar talent to satisfy them, the contrary will be true. You are then pulled against your own inclinations, a misplaced cog meshed in a gear of routine. Your Individuality does not fit in with the machinery around it; there is constant friction, irritation and difficulty. Perhaps in the end you will be worn down so that you churn in that place, but you will never be happy there. It is not what you were meant for; you cannot contribute any forward impulse because your Individuality is barred from expression; you simply fill a gap.

Yet in the Machinery of Life there is a right place for everything and everyone, a place where the respective Individuality fits in with the Law, Order and Harmony that govern the Universe. The reason most people are discontented and feel that they are more or less "in a rut" is because they have not found that place. They do not like their work or their surroundings, because their Individuality has no opportunity to exert itself freely. As soon as such people are transferred to the position for which their nature adapts them, an extraordinary change is at once apparent. From indifferent and incompetent automatons, they become living founts of energy, interested in their work and putting their whole weight, Body, Mind and Soul, into furthering it. They have found their Vocation, the road at the end of which they can see Success and Happiness, the common Goal of all; they have "found themselves."

In spite of the importance of getting one's Individuality located in its proper place, few people do so except by accident. No intelligent plan of action is devised to bring about that highly desirable result deliberately, because no intelligent study has been made of Individuality to discover its needs. The bulk of Mankind trust to a blind, haphazard, hit-or-miss method to juggle them eventually into their right environment, and trust usually in vain.

Understanding of the requirements of your Individuality is essential before you can hope to satisfy them. This understanding can be obtained only through Self Knowledge. The time you devote to study of your own Real Self will lavishly reward you throughout the whole of your life in the expansion, unfoldment and progress to which it is the key. Therefore face yourself squarely and frankly with the question "What am I? What are my qualities and shortcomings, my inner abilities and the faults that blunt them?"

It is futile, in this analysis, to look at yourself through rose-colored spectacles. You are the only one who can see the bare, unvarnished Truth, and you are the one to benefit from it. Therefore there is no excuse for self-deception; by indulging it you merely destroy your own purpose. Your interest is to view yourself as you actually are in order to discover where your best advantage lies. By trying to soften the blow you simply introduce the same insurmountable obstacle which has hitherto barred your road to Health, Success and Happiness.

The basis from which to proceed if you intend to get a true estimate of yourself is the Four Square of Life, Mind, Truth and Love. Energy in prosecuting the search, combined with Intelligence in directing it, will carry you along the main lode, so to say, while a genuine desire to realize on those inner treasures will sharpen your perception to discriminate the true from the false. The Four Square is the sieve into which you pour the mingled good and evil of which the human "you" is the product; what is sifted out of that composite is the pure metal of Individuality which you seek. Especially will you be struck by the amount of negative which you will uncover in that search. The rare gleams of wholesome aspirations and desires, latent ambitions of which you were never aware before, will seem poor pay for the precious quantity of dross in which they are buried. Yet they are the precious particles to be gathered together and brought out. The deeper you penetrate the more thickly sown they will be; you Will be surprised at the unsuspected traits of character you turn up, and as the sum grows you will have ample cause to consider your perseverance richly rewarded.

Therefore do not be discouraged or unduly impressed by the negative your first efforts unearth. Remember, that negative has no part with the Individuality you are trying to separate from it. Individuality, like the grains of gold scattered through the sand, is from the beginning pure and perfect, however completely it may be covered up. So while it is necessary to handle and expose all the evil dumped into your Subconsciousness by your Conscious Self and by teeming ages of perversely thinking Humanity, this procedure is inevitable if you want to get rid of it. Negative must be brought to the surface to be eliminated; the more thoroughly you perform that inner sanitation, the more your Individuality, that Eternal and Incorruptible Quality of your Soul, will shine into evidence.

Once you have discovered your Individuality, you have discovered that distinctive mark which differentiates you from every other mortal being. This is the first reward of the time and energy you have spent on that study, as well as the first step toward bringing your innermost distinguishing qualities into outward manifestations. So long as you did not know you possessed those qualities, you felt your inferiority to others who expressed theirs. You held yourself cheap because you appeared to be one of many, with nothing to contribute that thousands the world over are not contributing just as well.

But when you have found your Individuality, then you shed the sense of inferiority that has oppressed you, because you perceive in what way you are unique, able to supply something that no one but you can supply. You know that intrinsically, as an individual Ray of the Great Principle Itself, you are of equal worth with the Greatest, and from that knowledge you derive the self-respect and dignity that will help you to realize in fact the potential Greatness within.

If, on the other hand, you try to assert a dignity and importance not founded on a sure knowledge of the inner ability that can justify them, you are guilty of conceit. You pretend to something you do not deserve, because you cannot give out your Individuality to the World until you know what it is.

False pride, which prompts you to think the World is in error for not appreciating you, will only make you ridiculous. If you are a Ray of the Great Cause, remember that everyone else is also; you are not so super-perfect that you can afford to look down on perfection. Your Individuality, your peculiar talent, will win recognition only in proportion as it is expressed in definite reality. That is the only ready cash that Mankind can see and appreciate; it is a question, not of telling how much you have, but of proving it by putting it into circulation.

As Individuality is the Sum of Soul Qualities, the more you manifest it the more emphatic will be the expression of all the Qualities which comprise it. You will unfold and develop in every direction, profit others and yourself by your expansion through all associated channels as well as through the main one which represents your dominant interest. Each activity, also, each separate trait that you thrust into evidence, will express in its workings the distinction imparted to it by the supporting Individuality. No matter in what channel you direct your energies, the things they accomplish will bear the brand of yourself.

As Individuality is unique, the only one of its kind, you can never hope to bring out your own by copying someone else. However much you may admire some of those brilliant stars who stud the firmament of Humanity, remember that they shine so brightly because they stand alone. They serve as an inspiration to you, a proof that if you unveil your own Real Self it will gleam with no less a lustre in its own peculiar place and way, but it cannot usurp the place of another. There was one Washington, one Lincoln, one Shakespeare; no other existed or ever will exist, and no matter how admirable each may have been, you can only lose by trying to warp your own Individuality into the pattern stamped on History by theirs.

Be true to Yourself, focus all your endeavours on being Yourself and not somebody else, recognize the fact that you must be a pioneer bent on discovering something entirely new to Humanity, and you will be pursuing the course that has led great men before you to their respective pinnacles of Fame. They succeeded by being true to themselves; do you therefore heed their example by being true to your own Real Self, but not by attempting to drape over your bones their garment of renown.

A false human concept of values very often intrudes to confuse and obscure the way for the expression of Individuality. The demands and problems of Modern Life are infinite in their variety and complexity, but some are invested with a dignity that is not attributed to others. Thus teaching or preaching are considered activities of a lofty character, while street cleaning and similar occupations are despised. To the human eye, constrained to judge by appearances, it naturally seems great to be at the head of a country and mean to toil as a common labourer. Yet the human eye, if it could penetrate to the Causes back of visible Effects, would find itself very much mistaken.

The position one occupies is of consequence only as it provides a suitable channel for the expression of the Individuality directed into it. A man whose particular qualities fit him for clearing streets or performing manual labour works out his Destiny just as nobly along that line, advances just as far in his own inner unfoldment, as the man whose talents equip him to govern a nation. But reverse the positions, let the borrowed glory of a crown illuminate the brow of him who is by nature a labourer, and a shovel burden the hand born to wield a sceptre, and one will be no less unhappy and incapable than the other. The soaring intellect withers at the end of a spade, the lusty arm fumbles the delicate threads of diplomacy and intrigue.

It is never the office which makes the man, but the man who exalts or debases the office. Enlightened ones perceive the real king in him who perfectly controls the Kingdom of his Inner Self, whether his outward dress be patched overalls or royal ermine. The slave enthroned, commissioned to rule others yet ruled himself by his own evil passions or the evil influences around him, is no less a slave for all his outward pomp and authority. He has experienced less actual Independence than the humblest and most law-ridden of his subjects, though he does not recognize the laws himself.

Independence consists in the sublime faculty of availing oneself of the humanly constructed machinery of civilization. Man is born into a world of Existing Laws, both social and natural and circumscribes activities; it is a tacit admission of the superiority of Man-made rules to the immortal Soul. Only when Individuality pours itself into the established channels and adapts those channels to its expression, makes use of them to manifest itself, is it really free. Otherwise, when it is choked back and overwhelmed by Laws, diverted into wrong channels, it is a weak slave.

Real brotherhood between men and nations will come only when Humanity understands this and dissolves in the light of that knowledge the social barriers which now distort and obscure their vision. National pride will crumble as personal pride melts away; individual dignity will stand up in place of conceit, prejudice and envy; peace and good will, born of growing mutual respect, will prepare the way on Earth for the reign of Love. A nation is the sum of the people who comprise it; this ideal cannot be imposed upon it from without, but must take form in the individual hearts and understandings, before it will emerge into evidence as an accomplished fact on the large scale.

Realizing that when you have found your Individuality you have found your Independence, never be afraid to stand solidly for your convictions. Never compromise with that which you know and feel within yourself to be wrong. To deviate in any 'degree from the direct line, to flinch, pretend or falter, is to sacrifice by just so much the respect and confidence of others. Love is based on respect, the unconscious appreciation and desire for something better, but it can only be inspired by showing that "something better." Give your best to the World and the World will give its best back to you.

However great or humble may be the people with whom you come in contact, however debased or honoured among men, their outward dress of mingled good and evil buries one perfect core, one pure Soul Ray from the Infinite Itself. Like attracts like; all aspire, even though dimly, to the highest, and all respond with that better part of their Being to the highest manifested through you. Therefore under all circumstances, wherever you go, whomever you meet, let your Individuality shine frankly forth by observing the single vital principle it implies — to be whole-heartedly, sincerely and joyously YOURSELF.

Humanity, in the present period of its development, is manifesting the two opposite poles of Standardization and Individualization. Standards — ideals expressed in a uniform fashion — rule in nearly every aspect of modern life. Standard time, standard measurements, standard laws, rules, manners, automobiles, houses, clothes, etc., strip human existence of much of its complexity and spread abroad advantages which might otherwise be restricted to their originators. It is always the best forces of the World that produce these Standards and establish them as definite patterns to be accepted and lived up to by the great mass of the people.

This tendency to warp natural individual traits into a common mould seems to work directly against the expression of Individuality, yet that is not so. Standardization is a necessary step in the Evolution of Humanity, a human device by which the majority are helped upward along the difficult road of progress toward their respective goals. The ideal conceived and achieved by one who has advanced farthest serves as a mile post for those too hampered by limitations to set up a similar mark for themselves. Whether on the Plane of the Spiritual, the Mental or the Physical, the Standard struck out by the pioneer represents an ampler boundary to be striven for, a loftier eyrie to be attained, a broader and freer outlook to be won. It is a rest station built by those who have gone before to attract those who will come after and to be then a base from which they will launch into the next stage of their journey. Only through such a process of Standardization can the bulk of Mankind be drawn as a whole higher and higher in the Scale of Eternal progress.

Yet under cover of this harsh and stilted method, so to say, Individualization is going on in each of those swarming millions to whose progress Standards impart simply a general trend. An education, though standard, lifts them out of the dark morass of wrong concepts and superstitions and enables them to see unobstructed vistas on every side. Better living conditions and material means teach them that still better ones wait within reach a little further on. They demand more and receive more, enjoy an increasingly greater mental freedom and cultivate a keener appetite for improvement the more they improve.

Progress, even though artificially stimulated in this way, unfolds the qualities latent in Individuality, just as natural unfoldment of Individuality is bound to result in Progress. Like cranking an engine, Standards simply start a movement that, once going, will continue under its own power. Slumbering forces begin to awaken and stretch, long dormant ambitions stir out of their age-old lethargy and a distinctive Identity grows out of level monotony as stars out of the darkening sky at evening. The Soul is at last coming into its own.

The wide-spread emergence of Individuality throughout the mass of people today is apparent in the disquiet that has broken like a rash over the whole face of the earth. Human beings are so unruly, so difficult to manage, so unwilling to bow their heads to sheer force, because their awakening Individuality is no longer content to drowse peaceably in the shade of established conditions. The Great War pricked it into action first, opened its eyes to nobler perspectives ahead which now beckon it on. One of the great signs of Modern Times is this unrest, because it signifies — Progress.

Yet a danger also lurks in that new Freedom. Very often, when obtained, it is misused because those who have won it let their aspirations outrun their knowledge. To desire something which is beyond one's knowledge how to handle, and to use Freedom as a club to get it, changes that Freedom from a blessing to a curse. It becomes license, tyranny, oppression, anarchy, anything but Freedom and anything but good and constructive.

Freedom means unfettered constructive activity, complete liberty in everything that is RIGHT and that therefore does not infringe on the rights of others. Real Freedom cannot harm anyone else. It cannot be obtained at the expense of others. It can help others by pulling them sympathetically out of their shell of limitations and up to its own unrestricted level, but it does not depend on them for its own existence. It springs only from a strength developed within, never from authority conferred from without. The formula for Freedom is conformity to Natural Laws. The Law of the Universe, called the Great Law, from which all subordinate expressions are derived, is the Essence of the Positive. To govern oneself according to It is to advance always toward Unlimited Power; to oppose it is to manufacture your own limitations. The Great Law represents what people have to live up to if they want to attain perfect Freedom. Human laws represent the tools which that Freedom, once attained, enables them to use constructively in their activities.

Ignorance of Laws, human or natural, is no excuse for their violation. The legal machinery which different countries, governments and organizations build to direct and control the body under them are the expression — though sometimes perhaps crude and clumsy — on the Physical Plane of Laws already functioning on the Higher Planes. To transgress them is merely proof that you are incapable of fulfilling the greater Laws behind them. You can reach the highest only through a natural process of growth through the lower conditions leading up to it.

Therefore observe human laws to the best of your ability and you will be working your way along the only right road to the real Freedom they imply. Observe them intelligently, making use of them when necessary as well as submitting to them, and you will have taken your first great forward step. You will learn that your Individuality dominates outside rules and laws that would otherwise appear to limit it, that you are the stronger because you adhere to and use them, and you will understand that this lesson applies equally well where the Great Law also is concerned.

Individuality is the abiding place of Freedom. The more strongly you manifest your Individuality, the greater will be the Freedom you will experience. You will achieve through your Individuality the success and happiness which form the Purpose of your Existence, and you will inspire love and respect the more successful you become. People value Freedom above all else; no more magnetic power of Attraction could exist than the sense of Freedom which your Individuality radiates from all your Being.

EXERCISES TO LESSON TWENTY-ONE

Practice as usual the Star Exercise morning and evening, with Relaxation, Silence and the continual Mental Contact with Universal Life Energy. Then proceed with the new Exercise for this week, called MANIFESTATION, in the following way:

As soon as you have established a strong and harmonious flow of Life Force by means of Relaxation, Silence and the Mental Contact, concentrate your Mind on your own Soul. Look within the heavy human crust and perceive that Source of your mortal Being in the full glory of its perfect qualities. See it as the Avenue through which the Great Principle pours Its Limitless Powers and Forces to you for expression. Try to understand the boundless resources of Strength it brings to you to be used on every Plane, realize the measureless scope of Universal Forces which it focuses on you to be translated through your activities into actual manifestation, penetrate the deceptive shell of your Personality and discern within it the pure Essence of your own Soul. Then be happy in the knowledge that you have found your Individuality and that you can rely confidently on its abundant and invincible strength.

Having found your Individuality, the next step is to project its distinctive qualities into expression in your life.

The World is the problem you have to meet with the tools that your Individuality supplies; therefore turn your gaze outward upon that World and study it no less carefully than you did your Inner Self. Feel your unity with it, your identity as an integral part of it, and be willing to contribute your best to it. Let your sympathy with it be genuine and helpful, enabling you to perceive and understand faults without condoning them, and not merely a sentimental pose which prompts you to look only for good and be blind to the evil. Both positive and negative comprise the environment into which you are to project yourself, and your object is to acquire a distinct comprehension of the situation you have to face in order that you may handle it intelligently and with the greatest practical results.

Once the two sides of the equation are clear in your Mind— your Soul with its qualities drawn up against the conditions it must meet in putting those qualities into expression—your task is to establish a working connection between the two. Give unreservedly of Yourself, feel the Life Force flushing through every channel of your Being to pour from you to that which is outside of you. Know that your Soul qualities respond and stir to the surge of that Current, melting and fusing to radiate harmoniously from you in a pulsing tide of constructive energy. Let the Stream of Life Force draw your Soul with it, into its own act of expression, carrying the real YOU out through the skin of your Personality into direct contact with the World itself. Thus gradually your Individuality will glow warmly forth, its fire deepening as the latent qualities of your Soul break ever more richly and strongly into manifestation.

Mind alone, with its human tool of Will Power, is not sufficient to push your Soul's Individuality into expression. Mental powers, however compelling they may be in their own or in the physical domain, have no influence on the Spiritual Plane by whose sufferance alone all else exists. A greater Power, One which pervades all Planes equally and unites them through Its own Force of Attraction, is required. That Power, flooding into your Soul, your Mind, your Body, carrying the qualities stored in the first into ultimate manifestation through the last, is the very Universal Life Energy you have been taught to use.

QUESTIONS TO LESSON TWENTY-ONE

1. What is Individuality?

2. In what vital respects does it differ from Personality?

3. How can Individuality be best developed into expression?

4. What is the essential first step in seeking out the right environment for your Individuality?

5. How is self Knowledge to be acquired?

6. How can the example of great men help others to bring out their Individuality?

7. How is the value of the position occupied by any individual determined?

8. Of what does 'Independence consist?

9. When will the ideal of real Brotherhood between men and nations be possible of achievement?

10. What is the purpose served by Standardization in relation to Individualization?

11. What is Freedom?

12. How can Freedom be obtained?

Lesson Twenty-One

ANSWERS TO LESSON TWENTY-ONE

1. Individuality is:

The unique combination of Soul Qualities which constitute your Real Self.

2. It differs from Personality:

It is a direct, immutable and immutable projection from the Great Causeless Cause Itself distinctively unlike every other Individuality and wholly beyond any human power to change it. Personality on the Contrary is a humanly constructed mask, often designed after a standard pattern, alterable at will, and ceasing to exist as soon as the Individuality which Illumines it is withdrawn from the plane of human existence.

3. Individuality can be best developed into expression:

By consciously bringing about and balancing the fundamental qualities of Energy, Intelligence, Truth and Love, and by using Universal Life Energy to stimulate and emphasise the distinctive qualities of Individuality through the terms of those four.

4. **The essential first step in seeking out the right environment for your Individuality is:**

   To analyse yourself for the distinctive Individual qualities you possess, discovering first your needs there, and then with the help of Universal Life Energy to attract from outside the proper opportunity for satisfying those needs.

5. **Self Knowledge is to be acquired:**

   By using the Four Square of Life, Mind, Truth and Love to sift out of your composite human self the Real Self within it.

6. **The example of great men can help others to bring out their Individuality:**

   By serving as established proof that it can be accomplished, not by imitating someone else, but by simply BEING YOURSELF.

7. **The great value of the position occupied by any individual is determined:**

   By the degree to which that position challenges the exercise of the particular Individuality which fills it.

8. **Independence consists:**
   In the inner strength imparted by Individuality to make constructive use of existing Laws instead of evading or violating them.

9. **The ideal of real Brotherhood between men and nations will be possible of achievement:**

When Man's individual and fundamental Freedom will be understood and respected.

10. **The purpose served by Standardization in relation to Individualization is:**

That it draws the bulk of Mankind to a higher common level from which they can launch more easily into the development of their respective individual traits.

11. **Freedom is:**

Unfettered constructive activities in accordance with Natural Laws.

12. **Freedom can be obtained:**

By developing into ever stronger expression your Individuality.

Dear Friend:

This Lesson will explain to you that outer envelope of your Being which you call Personality. It is so to say, the border line across which the real inner "You" passes for the first time into the sphere of material expression, the present medium through which the Individuality of your Soul struggles more or less into evidence within the bounds of human perception. It marks the battle front where the assortment of qualities comprising Yourself breaks into conflict with the outside influences of your environment, the surface level which reacts first to other people and things with which you come in contact.

Therefore your vital concern is to develop a fine, forceful, and magnetic Personality which will accommodate all that flows into it to its own positive standard of Strength, without yielding place to any other influence. The more you reconcile your Personality to the Individuality it is meant to express, the more you invest it with that Strength. Your treasures of powers and qualities reside only within your Real Self, but your ability to bring them out into practical realization depends solely on the extent to which you adapt the channel of your Personality for their transmission.

The value of Personality is recognized today as never before. People perceive it as their main hope and reliance in their great Life Race, the instrument by whose help they can win to the front or through neglect of which they drop hopelessly behind. Every normal being naturally desires to lead rather than be led, to be strong rather than to have to submit to strength. Qualities of leadership are the most highly prized of all assets that anyone can bring into any walk of life, because the World today is desperately in need of leaders of the right kind.

You, and all people, have within you these qualities of leadership. You have before you the possibility to bring them out. It remains only to adjust the channels for their expression, to clarify and develop the Personality which will let them shine forth unobstructed in their full vigour. This you can do, because Personality is within your reach and subject to your conscious revision as well as responsive to the constructive power you are able to bring to bear upon it. The object of the following pages is to give you all information necessary for doing it intelligently and well.

Cordially yours,
Eugene Fersen.

LESSON TWENTY-TWO

Extraordinary changes which are taking place in all walks of Modern Life, but particularly in business and in trade, reflect a growing appreciation of the value of Personality. Merchants are no longer content merely to have goods for sale; the goods must sell themselves. For instance, there is a vast difference between a stock of fruit dumped in a slovenly heap, and the same fruits attractively arranged to display their qualities to the best advantage. The alert tradesman perceives that he cannot simply keep articles to sell to those who need them; he must dress out and exhibit the intrinsic virtues of his wares, creating the demand for which he cannot afford to wait. In other words, he must make his goods cooperate with him in their sale by investing them with a pleasing Personality.

What is true of the goods is exactly true of the individual behind them. Your Personality is the manner in which you present to other people the array of intrinsic qualities comprising your Individuality. A deft and well ordered display of the positive endowments within you constitutes an attractive Personality. An inappropriate display or careless neglect of them results in a disagreeable or weak one. In the former instance, you capitalize the "difference" in which resides your genuine value. In the latter, you simply let that value lie unused, of no profit either to you or to anyone else.

Obviously, therefore, if you want to realize practically on your own peculiar inner talents, or Individuality, you must provide them with an adequate Personality through which to emerge into expression. Very often people with a less striking Individuality than others derive a far greater actual value out of it by taking full advantage of what it offers, equipping it with a Personality through which that value can break forth into evidence. Many potentially strong individuals, on the contrary, whose inner treasures of Individuality are far more rich, allow that waiting wealth to remain uselessly buried beneath a shabby Personality, simply because they do not appreciate the need of exploiting deliberately what they have. They look on Personality as a mere by-product, desirable but not worth wasting conscious thought or effort on, which will ooze out of them as naturally as perspiration. This is a great mistake.

Personality is an effect of which Individuality is the inner basic Cause. Between the two is the channel of physical, mental and emotional machinery comprising the Human Being. If the channel is free and open, permitting the Law of Cause and Effect to function unimpeded through it, the Personality projected into expression will correspond to the Individuality behind it. But if the channel is choked by Ignorance, Indifference, Sloth, etc., the activity of the Law is so blocked that only a distorted and feeble Personality glimmers into evidence. The Effect, in other words, does not translate into equivalent expression the Cause from which it sprang.

Yet Personality borrows its value solely from the accuracy with which it manifests the distinctive qualities of your Real Self. The more your Individuality is warped and shrivelled from its original lines in transmission through your human machinery, the less it is worth in its exteriorised aspect as Personality. That is why the majority of people are born, live and die in obscurity; they never let their Real Selves out enough to stamp their identifying mark in the Material World in which they live. The environment molds the individual to its own monotonous pattern instead of the individual carving his unique destiny out of the environment, and whenever that happens the result is invariably mediocrity.

Strength, poise and power measure their degree by the extent to which Personality strikes an even balance with the Individuality it represents. You are the fulcrum across which the Law of Cause and Effect must work. Until Individuality transfers itself past the pivotal point into equally weighty expression you do not secure that equilibrium so vital for effective exertion of your powers and faculties. Therefore your interest is to see that the transfer does take place completely and that the proper balance is established.

In promoting this adjustment, your attention and conscious efforts are necessarily focused upon the Effect side of the equation. The Cause itself, your Individuality, is utterly beyond your reach to modify in any way. From the beginning it has been nothing less than perfect and harmonious; it sets a standard which its expression as Personality has failed to maintain. But Personality, the outward manifestation where the lapse occurs, is within your reach and subject to your manipulation. There you can eliminate the disharmony that has crept in, emphasize and draw out the qualities that have been shut back, remodel, develop, adapt and bring up to the particular standard existing for it in its source the whole top-heavy structure.

In this process you start, so to say, at the bottom and work upward. Your Personality asserts itself through the three Planes of your Being, the Physical, the Mental and the Spiritual. As the Physical Plane is the very foundation of your human Existence, the one into whose terms the activities of the other two must be fused for ultimate expression, that is where your work of reconstruction must start. In proportion as you make your material surroundings receive the stamp of your Individuality, manifesting the basic harmony within your Real Self, you eliminate the flaws and distortions in your apparent self, or Personality, which stands between.

Your inner harmony, in flowing out, will touch first its nearest environment. Therefore it is in your physical appearance and your home that your start should be made. Even the way you dress yourself, though it seems to be a trivial detail in comparison with the greater object in view, is in reality a quite effective barometer of your whole progress. There is nothing in the exterior world of Matter nearer to you than your own clothes; they enwrap the focal centre from which the harmonizing influence spreads outward, like ripples from a stone dropped in a placid pool; so in the taste manifested in their selection and arrangement your inner sense of harmony first breaks into evidence. Through them it widens swiftly into the home and beyond, until eventually it laps the far shores of your material existence and activities.

The richness or poverty of the surroundings on which you are to impress your Individuality is of no consequence. Material elements have a limited secondary value proportioned to their rarity, but their primary worth is borrowed from what they wear of one's Soul qualities. A simple plate of copper etched by the master hand of Benvenuto Cellini to the lines of one of his concepts will fetch thousands of times its weight in gold, while the value of a golden plaque wrought by the hand of an uninspired artist does not stir above the market price of the metal. The loveliest fabrics can appear cheap and tawdry under the handling of a cheap character; the poorest stuff can mirror the nobility of the nature it adorns. Similarly with every material foil which challenges the exercise of your qualities; it bears thereafter the stamp of greater or less worth which you imparted to it through the seal of your Personality.

Once you begin to harmonize your direct environment, you feel impelled to modify your personal attitude and conduct to suit it. The visible outward improvement reacts as a stimulus on the other Planes of your Being, a back-surge spilling over into your manners and ways of dealing with people and inaugurating the second step in your development.

In these more subtle channels of expression also it must be borne in mind that Personality is simply an agent to carry your Individuality out into evidence. It cannot do this by merely conforming to cut-and-dried rules of behaviour; it must fit etiquette to you and not you to etiquette. Strength of character, naturally and harmoniously asserted, is the formula for true gentility, which can never be acquired by pruning away your distinctive qualities to the plan of an established and conventional pattern. A strong, well balanced individual, though ignorant of accepted forms, will instinctively do the right thing at the right time. Such a one is what the world calls a born gentleman—gentle in his ways, yet invincibly firm and direct in nature.

Many people, misunderstanding what Strength really is, imagine that rough, domineering manners are the sum and substance of a strong Personality. They try to assume the appearance of what they feel emanating from those who are genuinely superior to them, to "put on a big front," as it is aptly termed, with nothing solid back of it. This tendency crops out particularly in the younger generation, school and college boys diligently shedding the pleasant manners learned at home in favour of a swearing, bullying demeanour which they naively associate with manhood. While such an attitude may impress the gullible for the moment, it is a broken reed in time of stress. There is no sound core of true qualities within that puffed pretence of a Personality, and at the first test of circumstances it collapses abjectly.

Simplicity, Courtesy and Sincerity are the Fundamentals of attractive contacts with other people. They are what carry conviction and inspire liking. "Be yourself" is an axiom to be followed rigorously in all circumstances, because it is only through letting your own Real Inner Self emerge as it is that you can act in accordance with these three essentials. The more you diverge from your Individuality in the Personality you present to the World, the more you defer to outward forms at the sacrifice of your intrinsic qualities, the farther you slip from the object to which you aspire. Genuine Manliness is based, not on weaknesses, fear and shortcomings, but on true qualities alone.

Women, urging toward equality of rights with men on the great wave of modern Feminism, often fall victim to the same dismal error of imitating men's shortcomings instead of taking example from their strength of positive qualities. Faults always stand out strikingly by contrast, like the one discordant note in a powerful symphony, but theirs is a shameful prominence to be shunned and not copied. Profanity, brutality or any sort of vulgar conduct never helped make a man; it unmakes them. Distinction mounts only on positive attributes of character; notoriety is simply the advertisement of weaknesses. One cannot substitute for the other, and while women can command equal recognition on either score by equally asserting it, they can win their goal only by intelligent emphasis of the constructive side.

The qualities that men can contribute to the complementary sex are the aggressive ones such as Energy, Courage, Reason, Initiative, Sense of Responsibilities, Self Control, Generosity and Wisdom. These are what cluster dominantly under the heading of Male Gender and they point very clearly the road of development up which women must climb to equality with men.

Men, on the other hand, if they do not want to be completely outstripped by women, must cultivate within themselves those qualities which women have pre-eminently and which in men are usually left undeveloped. These are of the passive and receptive nature typical of the Female Gender, such as Love, Patience, Gentleness, Sympathy, Forgiveness, Intuition, Refinement, Sense of Beauty, Love of Music, Arts, etc.

At present, neither men nor women are complete Personalities; each sex borrows its Identity from a lack which the other supplies, and each requires the other for its completion. In proportion as both develop that completion out of themselves instead of looking to the other for it, they acquire the true Self Reliance and Independence which is their common aim. That is why men must be alert to take from the female exchequer of qualities the equivalent of what women are taking from their own, or else be content to see women rise superior to them by reason of more complete development.

Frequently men profess to abhor the idea of cultivating any of those refining qualities, lest it render them liable to the stigma of effeminacy. This attitude, if genuine, is a deplorable weakness, compounded in about equal portions of Fear of criticism and a perhaps well-founded mistrust of that Manhood whose integrity they are so jealous to preserve. If it is simply a habit caught from associates, it is a no less deplorable mistake. Real strength of character is tempered, not corrupted, by refinement; the contribution from the female catalogue of qualities is essential in bringing out the full richness of the male side. This fact finds its recognition and proof in the term selected to define the ideal of thorough Manliness — Gentle-man.

Aside from shaping your Personality consciously and intelligently, as described above, there is another aspect of even more vital importance to be considered — the composition. Just as a builder must take care that his materials — mortar, steel, cement, etc. — are of the best, as well as see that they are laid according to the plan of the architect, so you, in reconstructing the home of your individuality, must strain out of the stuff and fabric with which you work the impurities latent there. You must not only correct the structural flaws which your laxity has allowed to break out in your existing Personality, but you must purge the texture itself clean of the dry dust of evil left there by an endless sequence of Personalities from which it was derived.

Remember that although you have but one Individuality, a single living thread of the Eternal Fire, the number of Personalities through which it has pulsed and ebbed in its evolutionary progress up the Ages is legion. In each of the successive incarnations on which you climbed to your present stage of development, you wore a Personality more or less appropriate to the respective stages. through which you passed, just as you might wear a suit of clothes. But unlike clothes, each successive Personality is erected out of the stuff of its predecessor, and each partakes also of that one vast composite Personality of the whole of Humanity of which it is an integral part. In this lies the explanation of so-called Heredity and the complex influences of your environment.

There is thus the accumulated product of the Past both within you and outside of you, comprising the sub stance from which you are to fashion your present Personality. It mingles the good with the bad, the sound with the dry rot, and confronts you with the problem of doing the best you can under the circumstances to eliminate the undesirable and accentuate the positive qualities, in order to make your personality as perfect as possible. This is not an easy task; it is beyond your own limited human power to accomplish it; yet the whole tide of Laws and Forces of Nature sets in your favour and places at your disposal the means by which it can be done.

In Nature, the trend of all things is perpetually upward, from the existing condition into a better one and never from the better down into a worse. Evolution, or the Law of Eternal Progress, is the Fundamental Moving Principle which floods into expression through every Aspect of all Being, manifesting on the small scale through the individual as well as on the larger scale through the whole of the Race. Therefore Personality tends naturally to improve as Individuality, in its successive incarnations, unfolds more and more.

That improvement, however, can be very gradual and tedious, so slow that the amount of it in one ordinary lifetime is scarcely perceptible, or it can be very vigorous and rapid. If Personality is permitted merely to be dragged upward by the rising level of general Progress, responding only to the prod of hard experience, its advance will be at a correspondingly minute rate. But if it is given consciously the stimulus by which that improvement can be accelerated, the process of eliminating the negative and emphasizing the positive elements in it will jump quickly and energetically forward.

It is in this basic respect that Universal Life Energy becomes of invaluable assistance. That Force, the pure essence of the Positive, will reach the substance itself where you consciously are able to mold the form alone. However symmetrical and well proportioned may be the edifice you erect, it needs to be built of sound material if it is to stand without crumbling in the face of adverse circumstances. Temper those materials in the cleansing Fire of Life Force, so that the impurities are burned out and the good qualities enhanced, and the temple you raise from them, will endure and gather strength throughout the entire course of its existence.

With this in mind, make it a practice to use Universal Life Energy constantly in every activity and undertaking of your daily life. Let It serve as the direct connecting Ray between the object to be achieved and your Individuality, the Vital Current through which your real reactions are stamped indelibly into your environment without being warped and blunted by the intervening barrier of a wrong Personality. In that way you will bring your Individuality into forceful and accurate expression, knitting its harmonious impulses unchanged into an equally firm and vigorous Personality.

A well balanced Personality is primarily distinguished by four striking features—it is Strong, Intelligent, Sincere and Pleasant. In other words, it manifests dominantly the Four Aspects of Universal Life Energy, Life, Mind, Truth and Love. The more consistently and energetically you assert those Four Qualities in each act of yours, the more you adjust every phase of your Mental and Physical Existence to the Standard they imply, then the more perfectly you develop and stabilize the character behind those acts.

Complete harmony and equilibrium are intrinsic in the Individuality from which your conscious human life is derived, because it is One with Universal Life Energy;

complete harmony should and can be maintained in the expression of that Individuality. Invest every act deliberately with the same perfection inherent in its Source and you will automatically consume the negative taint in the Personality between.

Of the four essential Attributes which Personality must possess, the- greatest is its Power of Attraction. That is what draws things and people within the scope of the other three and affords them the opportunity to exert themselves. This Power of Attraction is in direct proportion to the amount of Universal Life Energy you are able to absorb and store within you. Like a magnet whose pull becomes more irresistible and far reaching in exact ratio to the electricity poured into it, so your varied qualities of Body, Mind, and Soul flush into more and more lustrous expression on the quickening surge of that Force through them. It is what lies behind the whole intricate assortment of human machinery and makes it work and live.

Many Personalities otherwise well equipped to serve their purpose admirably fail to impress simply because they lack this vital animating Power. Often you have come in contact with people of mildly pleasing presence whose memory vanished gently with their faces at the end of a casual conversation. They die across the field of your experience as charmingly as a cloud reflection in a quiet pool, and as completely. The World is sown with intellectual spectres, also, whose mental agility and attainments are the marvel of all who behold — until some more substantial interruption like lunch switch their attention into a really serious channel.

Such Personalities are like perfect brands carved on cold iron — an intricate and richly wrought pattern which needs only fire to stamp its impress indelibly into its environment.

Remember, all Mental Laws and Forces function only as the physical stream of Life Energy turns the wheels. That is the Central River of Power from which each Mental Mill must scoop its driving impulse, and if the current is weak all the multitudinous activities dependent on it will be weak also. First take care of your source of Power; once that is assured you will find little difficulty in adapting the machinery to get the most use of it.

Success in your Life Race and in the Life Race of everyone spells its secret in the word Strength. The whole purpose of human Existence is to OVERCOME; no matter what your occupation, no matter in what direction you turn your endeavours, the same problem presents itself to you — obstacles to be conquered by the exertion of your qualities. The one who is able to exert those qualities most strongly, who is able to call into play an extra margin of power over all the rest, is the one who forges into the lead and wins.

As long as Mankind continues to be born to this Earth there will always be competition, those who win and those who lose, because there will never be a time when the Law of Evolution ceases to function through Humanity just as through everything else in Nature. Even now, slow as that unfoldment is within the narrow limits of our concept of Time, its progress is measurable and can be proved beyond any question of doubt.

Modern statistics disprove with cold figures any argument to the contrary, showing that the Human Race as a whole is markedly taller, stronger and more intelligent than it has ever been before.

In the centuries to come an even wider gap will open up between what is now and what will then be. The weak and unfit will ever be ground into discard, a pathetic lower fringe of failures dropped unregarded out of the fierce Struggle for Existence, dross burned away in the incandescent heat of that battle in which they are no longer qualified to partake. Nations will rise and fall, peoples sweep forward to set new tidemarks for a succeeding wave to overlap, individuals tower to brief prominence and subside in the dust of years, and throughout the whole titanic combat the enfeebling elements will be gradually expelled to leave a stronger, finer, purer Race behind.

Yet this process does not mean that those who have been eliminated are doomed to wear their failure throughout Eternity — a theory once widely advertised in the conventional concept of Hell. In Nature there can be no stagnation, no permanent retrogression; every individual, however evil, weak and perverse, is compelled by the Law of Evolution working through him to sweat painfully out his composition the poison of negative in which it is steeped. Therefore the one brief span from birth to death, though it looms so big in our tiny vision, is in reality but one small step in a very long and involved refining process, a single stage in an interminable sequence.

Death is simply the introduction to a fresh start in Life, the shedding of an old burden of disharmonies, imperfections and wrongs in order to enter anew, free from handicaps, into the arena of mortal Existence. We are born again and again, reincarnated each time usually under better conditions, with our own strength of positive qualities a little greater and our load of negative correspondingly less. As the whole of Humanity improves, so do the circumstances into which we are born also improve, opening to us in the successive grades of our schooling here wider opportunities and revealing loftier goals for which to strive. We are taught piece-meal, a bit at a time, what is too vast to be gulped down in a single lesson.

Most people, not realizing this, believe that they live only once on Earth and that their whole Fate hereafter is spun inexorably out of the thin threads of the years here. Consequently they see in the natural process of Evolution a remorseless, crushing Force, a merciless tyrant holding up to them one chance alone to achieve the heights and ruthlessly stamping out once and forever the multitude who fail. This is an appalling mistake.

Life is simply one school session in the uncounted ages of a complete Education. Today a single task has been allotted, a single lesson to be learned, and between the dawn and dark of your Human Consciousness you will add the crumb of knowledge it contains to the store of your evolutionary experience. Tomorrow another task awaits you a different problem challenging your further advance and demanding the exercise of what you learned yesterday for its solution. But meantime evening entices to rest, and like a child returning home from school the individual steps out of the class room of his Physical Body, away from the atmosphere of the day's responsibilities and mistakes, and passes through the Gates of Death into the Realm of the Invisible.

There he remains for a recess of longer or shorter duration, gathering fresh forces against the morrow when he will be incarnated again, but with a different Personality, a fund of Experience richer by the measure of what he has learned before, and with correspondingly greater opportunities and tasks confronting him in this new day of his Human Career.

As it was explained in the First Lesson, every human being is born with the power to win, to succeed. All the elements of Success are latent there, waiting only to be developed into expression. Some may avail themselves of those possibilities within, some may not. Eventually they will have to do so, but if they neglect now to realize on the hoarded powers seeking expression through them, theirs is the fault and blame. They deliberately defer the end by refusing to bring forth the means when by applying themselves intelligently and whole-heartedly to it, they could develop out of the core of their being that which outlasts a thousand Deaths and attracts automatically from without the things that make Life worth living.

The ultimate end towards which Evolution tends is perfect equality, through the elimination of that Personality in whose differences inequality resides. Fundamentally, all human beings are equal and perfect, but no two Personalities transmit that basic perfection into a like degree of expression. Only as the flaws and imperfections existing in Personality are removed and it is made to coincide exactly with the Individuality behind it will it vanish and take distinctions with it.

That revision is your particular and specific problem, your contribution to the achievement of absolute equality among men. When all have first individualized themselves, then will emerge that Individualization of the masses referred to in the previous Lesson, the condition in which all attain an equal eminence of Freedom, Strength and Poise in the assertion of their respective arrays of qualities.

That state is yet an Ideal on the remote horizon of our Evolution, a far goal toward which Humanity is streaming blindly by many and devious paths. In the van, now some and now others forge into the lead; behind, the same fierce competition boils and seethes throughout the following masses; the travelled course is strewn with those who have fallen by the way. Always there is Leadership on the part of a few, rivalry among the many and strife between all, yet all converging towards one common distant end—the Equality of Perfection, the only Equality there is.

Understanding this, you will understand clearly the true nature of Leadership and its relation to your own Personality. For the time, Personality is the indispensable instrument through which your Individuality must express. Yet it exists as a Personality by reason of the flaws and imperfections which distort and corrupt that expression. In proportion as you eliminate those flaws from it, so that it reveals ever more accurately the Real Self within, you rise from the grey level of mediocrity into the prominence of Success.

To lead, therefore, does not mean primarily to dominate others. It means to improve yourself, to advance at a faster pace than others in the development of your own qualities. In so doing you will naturally draw ahead of the others and also draw them after you, helping and benefiting them; but you will never feel the impulse to misdirect your superior strength of qualities to their abuse. You will be too concerned with attuning yourself still further to the Law of Evolution on whose current you have attained your present elevation to waste your energies in a baser fashion.

In its final analysis, Leadership is simply the inevitable product of Growth. As your positive qualities fight free of the vicious negative passions which choke them, you are lifted into the open sunshine of the Success which breeds Success. You no longer look with envy or jealousy at those above you; their superiority becomes an inspiration and an example, a visible proof of what awaits you when you develop the strength to grasp it; but it does not arouse resentment and anger. You realize that you must grow to fit the position to which you aspire, both in vigour of Personality and unfoldment of Individuality, instead of hoping vainly to make the position fit you without shrinking from its present proportions.

No one can ever become a leader without paying the price for it. Only when you learn to obey whole-heartedly the instructions of those bigger in character than you, without malice, jealousy or false pride, will you qualify to lead in your turn. Only as you absorb experience from above can you put it into practice in a widening sphere below you. Only as you exercise your inner powers to a greater strength through matching them with the more powerful can you rise to a loftier height above the less capable ones around you and pull them upward also.

But you must first recognize and face frankly the fact that your Progress can be bought only by a corresponding burden of Responsibilities, a weight which increases with each forward step and exacts from you full recompense for your advance beyond the supporting level of the crowd. Unless you are willing to assume that burden and pay the price, it is better to give up any idea of becoming a leader and thus avoid certain disappointment of your hopes. But if you honestly desire to be among those whose heads are rising above the rest of Humanity, if you are ready to trade the sweat of your brain and heart and body for the glory that only real achievement brings, you have at your disposal the Power to drive you on to victory over every obstacle that may bar your path — Universal Life Energy.

EXERCISES TO LESSON TWENTY-TWO

Continue to practice as usual the Star Exercise morning and evening, Relaxation, Silence and the continual Contact with Universal Life Energy. Then to the sum of those specific EXERCISES TO which the above are the foundation, add the new Exercise for this week, called MAGNETIZATION.

The purpose of MAGNETIZATION is to attract, by the exertion through your intrinsic qualities of a sufficient Force, the elements for their material expression and realization. It is accomplished by pouring through your physical and mental channels a constantly increasing flood of Universal Life Energy, to flush forth in an ever more powerful radiation that contacts and draws within your reach from outside whatever is needed to embody in fact your ambitions and desires. For the performance of MAGNETIZATION, proceed as follows:

Relax, enter into Silence and make the Mental Contact with Universal Life Energy. When you feel the Force flowing, stand and extend your two hands straight forward in front of you, in a position of blessing, with the palms downward. In effect, you are genuinely blessing the World during this time, because the Physical Stream of Universal Life Energy soaking in through every cell and nerve of your body is concentrated into a real River of Power sent out from your hands into Space. That constructive and animating Force not only benefits with its stimulating touch the entire World, to whose limits the vibrations instantly penetrate, but it establishes also the physical connection you desire between your immaterial concepts and the corresponding material means for their realization. It gives first, richly and abundantly, and in the giving puts into operation the machinery of an inevitable equivalent return.

This machinery is the Law of Compensation, which determines that in proportion as you give out of yourself into the general pool of All Wealth, or Achievement, that wealth spills back on you in the specific form required by your qualities for their materialization. You become a Nucleus of Magnetic Force, a Centre of increasing Attraction from which, through the channels of all your varied positive traits and talents, a stronger and stronger current pours out to set up an equally strong flow in return. In the stream of that returning flow of Power, naturally, are carried to you the things you desire, the opportunities you need, the contacts with people which will open the way for you to your goal.

Your attitude during the performance of that Exercise of MAGNETIZATION should be one of serene and impersonal Love. Be glad to give the World your surplus of vitality; let the warm glow of that giving steal expansively through your whole Being; simply feel happy, harmonious, poised. The more you are able to invite further relaxation in this way, the wider you will open within yourself the channels for the flow of Universal Life Energy and the finer will be the tinge of your own Self which you impart to the outgoing current. This, because of the higher rate of vibration with which you thus invest it, will in response attract to you from without the best and finest also.

Do not try to localize the Power of Attraction you generate during that MAGNETIZATION to any single or particular object you wish to achieve. By limiting it to a specific thing you limit it also in its strength and effectiveness. When properly developed, it will attract anything and anybody with whom you come in contact; but just as one light needs the supporting radiance of many candlepower to make it brilliant, so one application of Magnetic Force needs the support of its own strength in every direction to make it in the highest degree efficient.

MAGNETIZATION should last only for from five to ten minutes each time it is practiced. Physical or mental effort of any sort must be avoided, as the keynote of the Exercise is thorough relaxation of the sort derived from complete poise. If your hands and arms feel tired in the beginning, do not try to keep them up, but drop them and raise them again when rested. As practice accustoms you to the position all fatigue will vanish and you will develop gradually the requisite ease and strength which it must be your aim to achieve.

QUESTIONS TO LESSON TWENTY-TWO

1. What is Personality?

2. How is Personality related to Individuality?

3. What practical results are obtained by adapting Personality to Individuality?

4. Where should this re-adjustment start?

5. What relative importance do material surroundings bear to this process?

6. What are the distinctive attributes of a real Gentleman?

7. What qualities must Women develop in order to attain equality with Men?

8. What qualities must be cultivated by Men in order not to be outstripped by Women?

9. In what vitally important respect does the use of Universal Life Energy help reconstruct your Personality?

10. What are the distinguishing features of a well balanced Personality?

11. To what single vital Fundamental do all the varied activities of human life finally reduce?

12. Define Leadership in its relation to the Law of Evolution and ultimate end toward which it tends.

ANSWERS TO LESSON TWENTY-TWO

1. **Personality is:**

   The manner in which you display to others the qualities comprising your Individuality.

2. **The relation of Personality to Individuality is:**

   The relation of an Effect to its direct Cause.

3. **The practical results obtained by adapting Personality to Individuality are:**

   Emergence into actual expression of that Individuality, with corresponding development of Strength, Poise and Power.

4. **This readjustment should start:**

   On the Physical Plane into whose terms all human activities must ultimately be fused for expression, and first of all on your nearest material environment, your physical appearance and your home.

5. **Material surroundings are important in this process:**

   Simply as foils to exercise and draw forth your inner harmony of qualities, and not for any poverty or worth attached to the material elements themselves.

6. **The distinctive attributes of a real Gentleman are:**

   Strength of qualities, gently but firmly expressed through their own natural channels of Simplicity, Courtesy and Sincerity.

7. **The qualities which Women must develop in order to attain equality with Men are:**

   The aggressive qualities of the Male Gender, such as Energy, Courage, Reason, Initiative, Self Control, Generosity, Wisdom and Sense of Responsibilities.

8. **The qualities that Men must cultivate in order to maintain an equal footing with Women are:**

   The receptive qualities of the Female Gender, such as Love, Patience, Gentleness, Sympathy, Forgiveness, Intuition, Sense of Beauty, Refinement, etc.

9. **The vitally important respect in which Universal Life Energy helps to reconstruct your Personality is:**

   In eliminating the negative inherent in the composition of your Personality, deposited there from the preceding incarnations of your Individuality.

10. **The distinguishing features of a well balanced Personality are:**

Strength, Intelligence, Sincerity and Pleasantness, representing the Four Primary Aspects of Universal Life Energy, Life, Mind, Truth (Law) and Love.

11. **The single Fundamental to which all the varied activities of human life reduce in the final analysis is:**

The Power of Life Itself, or Universal Life Energy.

12. **Leadership is:**

The natural result of a stronger and quicker unfoldment of qualities on the part of some, which carries them forward ahead of the rest on the spiral course of Evolution. Once this Perfection is achieved by all, Personality with its imperfections will be eliminated and the Absolute Equality which resides in Individuality alone will prevail.

Dear Friend:

In this Lesson you will make a broad survey of all the knowledge you have collected concerning Universal Life Energy in its action through the Three Planes of your Being, in order that you may gather the triple Branches of that Power into a single focus as one concentrated Ray, combining into one harmonious unit the forces respectively of Body, Mind and Soul. Once you are able to achieve this, you have at your command a Power invincible in whatever direction you may choose to turn it, whether for healing purposes, business or any other constructive work, because for every task to which you apply it you enlist the full strength of all your qualities instead of the limited strength of the few directly concerned.

Until each individual can break down the negative walls which bar some of his Soul Qualities from complete expression, that individual cannot experience the full freedom he is here to attain. The Life Lesson we are sent here to learn is Independence, the utter Self Reliance based on the enduring Strength of qualities within and not the precarious liberty that depends on the help of perishable material things, such as money, worldly power, human beings, even of friends. Only by attuning oneself to the Infinite and Eternal Power of the Universe, in Its Four Aspects of Life, Intelligence, Truth and Love, can such Independence be achieved, because only that Power is immune to destruction or to change.

That adjustment cannot be imparted to you by someone else. If you are sick, it is because of some fault of your own, some mistake which you have to search out and eliminate by yourself. You develop your Strength only as you exercise it, and in this Lesson you will be given the most advanced yet simple processes of self adjustment. Whether the prospect appeals to you or not, you must sooner or later experience it anyway in the course of your Evolution, so the sooner the better.

Cordially yours,
Eugene Fersen.

LESSON TWENTY-THREE

The first part of "Science of Being, dealing only with the Physical aspect of your Being, taught you the simplest methods of contacting Universal Life Energy and using It on the Material Plane to make your Body strong, clean and healthy. Next, you studied the subtler activity of that Basic Force on the Mental Plane, Its operation through complex Mental Laws and how to handle It in connection with the Concentrated Thought in order to remove the causes of most physical and mental ills. Finally, you analysed Its changing play through the quick and delicate machinery of your Emotions, the human instruments through which your Soul seeks its most direct expression.

Today you will enter upon the last and greatest step it is possible to achieve in your present State of Human Consciousness, the one for which your previous efforts were designed to prepare you — the fusion into a Single Ray of all the potent Forces of Body, Mind and Soul. Only if all three channels, the Physical, the Mental and the Emotional, through which your Individuality must unfold its qualities, are developed to the same pitch of absolute perfection can you expect to accomplish this blending of their respective powers. Therefore your Success now will be both the test and the reward of your work in the Past, placing at your disposal a Perfect and Infinite Power before whose radiance all darkness melts away, or revealing the flaws which still stand in the way of your realization of It.

This Power, derived from the combination of the vibrations of Life, of Intelligence and of Love, represents the Soul Vibrations, in whose terms are compacted all the specific powers relating to each member of the Human Trinity. Very few people are able to employ Soul Vibrations in their daily life, because very few ever attain that apex of complete and rounded development on every Plane which alone will render them fit channels for those Vibrations. In one respect or another the individual is almost certain to fall short, favouring perhaps some shortcoming not strikingly prominent in itself but of fatal significance so far as achieving the ultimate in constructive Power is concerned.

Soul Vibrations are the natural result of utter Poise. In diagram, they are represented by the exact central point to which the Four Aspects of Universal Life Energy converge when they are equally developed into expression. The individual, as a unit, must therefore conform unerringly to the Ideal embodied in the Four Square, which he can only do by conforming to it precisely in all departments of his Being separately. He is like a triple lens through which the clear Soul Ray holding his Identity must pass into manifestation; but the respective members of that lens must be in perfect alignment to permit unobstructed passage. A distorting weakness which throws even one a trifle off scale blurs the focus, introducing a flaw which, caught up and projected by the passing current, effectively cancels the perfection of the other two.

That is why this highest and finest harmonizing method is explained to you almost at the end of the Course, after you have devoted a certain period of exclusive training to each of the Three Aspects of your Human Existence in turn. You have been brought in a logical progression nearer and nearer to that state of complete Poise so vital for the transmission of Soul Vibrations. Conscientious practice during the past five months will have developed the Four Aspects of Universal Life Energy into equal and balanced expression on all Three Planes of your Being, producing that inner condition of Equilibrium, Peace and Harmony which attunes you to the Highest. But unless you have scrupulously eliminated all the imperfections, you will fail by just the margin of your neglect to secure that exact conjunction of all your powers and faculties on which this crowning Success depends.

There is no way to force Soul Vibrations. Like the single correct answer to a problem in Mathematics, they form the one and only perfect solution to that long and complicated problem of your life. If the problem has been solved rightly, the right result emerges naturally and inevitably, but there is no allowance for error. Even a fractional mistake in the preliminary working trails its widening length throughout the whole succeeding process and erupts in a gaping fault at the last. You cannot patch that crack together at the end and call it healed; the only recourse you have is to go back to the original mistake, the cause itself, and by eliminating that knit together the entire wrong sequence springing from it. Then, and then only, will the discordant elements resolve themselves into the thoroughly harmonious relation for which you strive.

In your progress thus far, you will doubtless have observed the change for the better within your own self, and studied along the traversed route you will perceive the mile-posts of certain immutable Truths by which you have clambered gradually upward. First among them will be the distinct realization that your own powers and forces cannot be unfolded by proxy, through the agency of someone else. Your personal development is in exact proportion to the personal, individual effort you put into it, and nothing else. You cannot let another person take the exercise for you and expect to gain strength from it yourself.

Therefore the responsibility of mending any flaws in your character devolves solely upon you. Into every desire you wish to see accomplished, every ambition you want to achieve, you must pour the utmost that Body, Brain and Heart can give. If all your faculties have been developed to the harmonious proportions of the Four Square, you will bring to bear on that task a positive flow of constructive action that no obstacles can thwart or hinder. If you still harbour weaknesses and shortcomings, those weak spots will show up with unmistakable clarity under the testing strain and invite your attention to their repair.

Another mile-post which will command your instant recognition will be the correlative growth of responsibilities with your own growing capacity to carry them. The higher you rise in the Scale of Evolution, the more important will become the duties you encounter and the greater the responsibilities which fall on your shoulders. You gather to yourself the threads of all the myriad lesser responsibilities strung across your path; with each step the burden increases; but each step challenges the exertion of greater Strength, the unfoldment of lustier Powers, to take it. That ever more imposing weight is the foil against which you whet your qualities to a keener and brighter edge, tempering them for the stiffer opposition to be cleft next.

You can never hope to dodge the refining process and yet acquire the finer temper, accomplish the harder aim. Whatever object you have in view, it commands an equivalent outlay of your own forces to win and hold it. Your concern is to steer a direct course for it, clinging stubbornly to that main purpose and marshalling every effort to drive you onward through the difficulties that clog your way. The farther you advance the larger and more complicated will be the load of responsibilities you accumulate; but as long as you pin your attention to the one dominant thing you will always find plenty of other people to take care of the details.

The Great Law Itself will supply those whose measure of ability is sufficient to embrace the small parts of the greater Whole; your job is to carry the load of that "Whole." For this most difficult work you must keep yourself free of entanglement in distracting petty details, while at the same time serving as the central hub which holds those details in order.

This is the reason why some people are able to draw to them hundreds and thousands of individuals and fit them snugly into their appointed places, each a working unit through which functions one fraction of a great coherent scheme, while others have to unravel their smaller problems alone. Those who work on the vaster scale have unfolded from within themselves the vaster Strength which qualifies them to do so; they are concerned with the big movements that exercise their superior ability and cannot afford to fret away their talents on the minute dependent reactions which must automatically fall into line.

Yet for the most part they started alone, on the little scale, cultivating their individual powers bit by bit from the very source and building up to their present position by a process of sound growth free from blemish, from beginning to end. The so-called "Captains of Industry," men who wield the authority crystallized in tremendous sums of money and to whom are tied the destinies of thousands of employees, usually started at the bottom in this fashion, poor in worldly goods, but rich in latent ambitions and qualities which they developed gradually, through struggle, into compelling expression.

What is true with relation to the pursuit of Wealth and Material Success is equally true with relation to the pursuit of Health. Physical disharmony is the reflection of disharmony within yourself. If you were at the top of your efficiency, with all your qualities equally developed on the three Planes, your Body would be an impregnable fortress against all the negative influences that might assail it. The perfect Harmony inside would constitute an unbroken wall of protection, innocent of any crevice through which negative influences might penetrate to corrupt it. In such a condition of utter Equilibrium, of Inner Poise, it would be impossible for you to express disharmony of any sort. You could not experience headaches, colds, sicknesses, etc., because you would be wholly immune to the discordant vibrations of which they are the result.

"Like attracts like" is a Natural Law, functioning alike through the Physical, Mental and Emotional channels of the individual. The disharmony that every human being more or less unconsciously fosters within himself is an open mouth to drink in destruction from outside. It attracts the corresponding negative vibrations and pours them into his Mind, there to grow and spill forth eventually in a rich variety of evil ways. Every negative condition you permit to exist, whether in. Mind or Body, acts as a vicious magnet to draw more trouble to you.

The cure of this lies exclusively in your own hands. Real adjustment can proceed only from within and never from someone else. Another individual can relieve you for the time being from some particular trouble which may afflict you and by so doing will appear to help you, but that help achieves no permanent cure. It lasts only as long as the helper chooses to extend it; when he ceases to substitute his strength for your own, the burden settles back on your shoulders with redoubled weight.

Only as you yourself put forth the necessary effort and develop in yourself the Strength to throw off that burden, instead of relying on outside aid to lighten it, can you rid yourself of it completely and finally. Others may bring to your assistance their support and various harmonizing methods to overcome physical or mental ills, but at best they simply aid you in a work that can actually be accomplished by only one person — yourself.

Very often people are led by circumstances to concentrate on the development of one side of their Triune Nature, to the neglect of the other two equally important sides. An individual will discover his greatest profit and pleasure in the exercise of his Mental faculties; consequently he will allow himself to be absorbed wholly into that single channel of expression, while his Physical and Emotional parts wilt unregarded about him. Another will find his greatest interest in the cultivation of Bodily strength, a pursuit in the rear of which his Mental development tags along in a casual and disinterested fashion. Still others live chiefly through their Emotions, a spectacular existence shot with warm contrasts but notoriously lacking in balance.

However striking may be the progress any of these make in a single specific direction, it is never enough to compensate for their backwardness in the others. The tragedy of one who has fought to the pinnacle of human power and worldly possessions, whose word perhaps swings the destiny of nations or reconstructs the entire social edifice from foundation to roof-tree, yet who topples from his throne of authority at the first passing breath of a cold or a contagious disease, is almost too general to excite comment. As long as people will house their most precious gifts in a weak and rickety vault of flesh, as long as they will provide for their sublime qualities a shabby, absurd, outworn material instrument to express through, they will deliberately place all they have won through a lifetime of painstaking struggle at the mercy of every destructive influence they may encounter.

Those who have experienced a serious illness, particularly if it happened during a critical period in their affairs, know the feeling of utter helplessness in those moments and the new perception of values they find looming out in stark relief against that empty ground. They are eager and willing to part with any amount of money, power and material goods, if in exchange they can buy back the Health they were accustomed to take for granted when they had it. The conditional nature of worldly advantages becomes more vividly apparent the more those advantages slip beyond reach; but frequently this viewpoint is attained too late. Doctors, with all their skill, are often helpless to prop the tottering wreck on its feet again and make it go as before. Such individuals owe their unhappy condition to their own neglect. If, instead of turning to drugs and medicines for the strength they need, they would repair and re-fuel their physical engine during spare moments through the use of Universal Life Energy, they would generate within themselves the necessary vigour to throw off any negative condition that might attach them. They would knit into their very Being a solid and permanent defence as well as an ample reserve of Power, and would increase that reserve every time they were called upon to use it.

As it is now, the cornerstone of many a far-flung enterprise is a medicine chest; but modern sentiment is beginning to set less and less faith in the man who draws his efficiency from a pill box. The demand is for genuinely strong individuals, sound to the core, whose executive efficiency is simply the direct expression of real Strength and Power within.

Business men of today are arriving gradually and instinctively at a realization of this. They devote a portion of their time to golf, tennis, and various other physical exercises whose benefits they are quick to perceive and appreciate. The next step is to take full advantage of an adjustment so auspiciously started and promote it still more vigorously by contacting the wonderful Power of Universal Life Energy all the time, flushing It through every farthest corner of their Triune Being, washing away discord, stimulating positive growth, coordinating Body, Mind and Emotions toward that harmonious relation which will blend into one invincible Soul Ray the individual qualities and powers carried into expression through them on the current of this Universal Force.

The bitter root which sprouts into evil blossom on any or all of the Three Planes of Human Existence draws its sustenance from the dark places of the Human Mind. There, in Ignorance, Fear and Apathy originate the perversions of constructive power that blight and ravage your normal channels of expression, choking back the very qualities whose development is essential for the Equilibrium you seek. Consequently it is in Mind first that you must light the lamp of Understanding, whose searching radiance will expose the hidden causes of the negative that break into evidence and will reveal to you the proper way to handle it.

Fortified with this Understanding, you will discover that the first actual step on the road to complete self adjustment is by way of moral sanitation. That is, you must eliminate the sudden and treacherous destructive passions which so often blow apparently out of nowhere to blur your faculties, upset your Poise and eat away the mental and physical foundation stones of your whole Being. They are of all harmful influences the subtlest in their nature and the most dire in their effects, hard to anticipate, easy to indulge, baffling in their variety, violence and uncanny accuracy in storming each vulnerable point; but as instantly vulnerable in turn to those who know how to meet their assaults.

So whenever you feel Anger, Jealousy, Envy, Pride or any other phases of so-called Evil Passion, do not fall into the specious course of trying to overcome them by sheer Will Power or persistent Mental Denial. Your humanly mental forces, while they may succeed for the moment, really accomplish in the long run the exact opposite of the desired results. They stamp back within you the very negative that your own Soul is endeavouring to throw out of your system. A more virulent self poisoning can scarcely be conceived, because that venom, accumulating more and more within you, will inevitably crop out at last in the form of all sorts of organic or mental troubles.

Your mode of procedure, when you feel the gust of ominous passions rising, is to recognize them frankly for what they are, understand the purpose behind them and set courageously and intelligently about the business of helping to eliminate them in the fashion Nature has decreed. Instead of closing yourself up through an abrupt exertion of Will, relax, make the contact with Universal Life Energy and admit ever more abundantly the healing current of Love. That energizing Power, in its Aspect of Love, will accomplish the miracle of transmuting the evil you are trying to expel, because it will pierce through the crust of negative vibrations to the core of Universal Life Energy imprisoned within them, the innocent source from which they borrow their vitality and power, and in liberating that positive nucleus will restore to their original harmonious condition the destructive vibrations comprising your wrong impulses.

Remember, the basic activity of Universal Life Energy, especially in its Highest Aspect of Love, is to establish harmony wherever It goes. Discord and negative are powerless to withstand Its positive influence and infinite harmonizing qualities. Therefore in all that It touches the bad is melted away just as the good is emphasized, and the distorted balance resumes gradually its normal state of Equilibrium and Poise.

However much of the Negative there is in an individual, it is nevertheless limited and must sooner or later be brought to the surface. The more you will use Universal Life Energy in transmuting it as it appears, the more astonishingly easy and efficient you will find yourself becoming in that respect. As you develop daily toward the Perfection required for the Attainment of the Soul Ray, the formidable surges of temper lose in power in proportion as you gain, dissolving magically at the touch of the Force you summon to encounter it. No other process of self adjustment could so thorough, quick and painless, and none so exactly satisfying, because no other could be so naturally right.

As the current of Universal Life Energy floods in through your Soul Itself, of course It sluices also into that sunken mental seat of most of the evil that you experience, your Subconsciousness. The negative stirred up there and flung to the surface for elimination is sometimes so great, because of the strength of the Power used, that it may cast you for the time into a torment of utter hopelessness and despair. All fine qualities and constructive thoughts seem swallowed in the murky torrent of Evil, abandoning you to a darkened world of selfishness, wrong and woe.

In such a predicament, one needs the raft of a sure Knowledge to keep him afloat. Armed with your Understanding, you are able to perceive the real significance of this unpleasant state and welcome it as an excellent sign. You know that the worse the outside tastes, the more thoroughly the inside is being scoured and cleansed, and that when all the dirt has been washed up and eliminated you will feel like a new Being, re-born to a finer State of Consciousness and a happier life.

If you wish to help others to a similar re-birth, remember that Universal Life Energy, recognizing no barriers of Time or Space, can be transferred to any distance by means of Absent Treatments. However far your patient may be, and however ignorant of his geographical location you may be, he is always instantly within your reach through the long arm of that Force. Simply concentrate your thought very strongly on him for a moment, even visualizing him as present before your face, and then release the healing current over that mental line.

If the individual will attune himself to the vibrations you send, proper adjustment will occur as the Negative is there transmuted into the Positive. Just as an electrical current of killing potency, when directed into a transformer, emerges merely as a stimulating and harmless flow on the other side, so the destructive power of Evil is strained of its ability to harm the individual

9. **Disharmony can be eliminated from married life:**

    By using Universal Life Energy to balance and reconcile the conflicting angles of your respective natures.

10. **The kind of child that will be born to prospective parents is determined:**

    By the attitude of the parents, the traits of character most strongly represented, during the few moments of their physical union.

11. **The importance of parents' attitudes during the few moments of their physical union:**

    Lies in the fact that the vibrations projected by them into Space at that time attract a Soul of a corresponding rate to be incarnated. Therefore if those vibrations represent the best of the prospective parents' natures, a correspondingly evolved Soul will respond, while if the lower side of their natures is represented, the Soul attracted will be of the same low level of development.

12. **Bad characteristics of children may be transmuted into good qualities:**

    By teaching them how to contact Universal Life Energy constantly in all their activities, and by directing that Positive Force into them yourself whenever they allow their negative traits to erupt into   evidence.

Dear Friend:

Love has always been hailed as the Great Ideal, the one Dominant and Supreme. Power which rules the Universe. Yet the exact manner in which it performs this stupendous task has never been compactly and clearly explained. In order to appreciate the tremendous Power of Love, it is necessary to understand what it really is, from whence it comes and what results it will achieve in its application in your own life.

The object of this Lesson is to give you a lucid idea of the Source and Nature of Love, not simply from the personal viewpoint of it as a peculiar and disturbing emotion, but from the scientific perspective of it as a stupendous magnetic Force which bowls the planets on their courses as easily as it bowls the hearts of men and women. Not only is it a Universal Power, but it is at the same time a Law, containing within itself all harmonizing qualities. Not only does that Force, carrying into effect its own Law, operate in the field of human relations with which it is generally associated, but it works constantly, tirelessly, throughout the whole broad range of human activities. In business, in art, in teaching, in the bringing up of children, in every occupation where Human Beings come in contact with Nature and with each other, the Law of Attraction functions and can be used with the greatest practical results.

Mankind creates its own worst enemies through the perversion of Love to its opposite extremes of Hatred, Jealousy, Selfishness and the like. Only through Love Itself can these destructive forces be eliminated.

Love is Attraction. Knowledge of how to employ it enables one to attract all things for Success in Life, in Friendship and in Marriage. Therefore its development within you is one of the greatest achievements possible to you in this Life.

Cordially Yours,
Eugene Fersen.

LESSON TWENTY-FIVE

Love has been designated in the beginning of this Course as the Fourth and Final Aspect of Universal Life Energy. Though last in logical order, it is nevertheless First in Importance among the Four Fundamentals from which all Existence is derived, because without it nothing could exist for a single moment. Deprived of Love, or the Power of Attraction, to hold its component particles together, the Universe itself would collapse, melting back into its original common Substance and vanishing in a whirl of electronic dust.

The Law of Attraction, or Love, is therefore the governing and sustaining Power which holds the entire Universe together in one coherent whole. Whatever Is, exists because of the Law of Love, manifesting through it. It continues to exist as that thing because the Law of Love prevents it from lapsing from its place in the harmonious Universal Scheme and invading the sphere of something else. Love is the basis of Eternal Harmony — the Law and also the Fulfilment of the Law. That is why it must be continually manifested in order to operate; the two acts are identical.

All constructive growth and progress achieves its increase from the Law of Love operating through it. At the impulse of that Law it proceeds unerringly along the ways which offer it the soundest development free from conflict with other Natural Laws. Disharmony is the result of going contrary to the Laws of Nature, a course which can only have its origin first in a violation of the law of Harmony itself. Love is Harmony, and because of its harmonizing qualities is able to smooth out discord, coordinate, adjust and strengthen wherever it is given the opportunity to emerge into expression.

Man, as a product of Nature, is a most complex, highly evolved and potentially powerful channel for the Law of Attraction to work through. On him converge, from one side, all the boundless Natural Forces and Laws, to be transmuted and built out into actual expression as the varied activities through which he projects his Individuality into evidence. If, in the Inner Self where the manner of that expression is conceived, the Law of Love is permitted to operate freely in connection with it, each act will shape itself rightly for the realization of whatever constructive aim prompts it, and each will constitute a perennial spring of harmony through which that Law wells into ever ampler evidence in his life.

Thus there is no department of human activities from which the Law of Attraction may be profitably withdrawn. Every daily act, however, trivial in itself, is like a twig on the spreading tree of your mortal life. As long as it is nourished by the same sap that feeds the massive trunk and branches, it flourishes as a useful, dependable harmonious unit in the life of the tree, contributing its tiny quota of strength to the whole and growing constantly to more important proportions of utility and service. But let the sap be diverted from the twig, the Law of Attraction shut out from the act, and it will wither to ruin and decay, becoming simply so much of a dead burden to be carried by the rest. For instance, if you are in business you naturally want that business to function smoothly, efficiently and successfully. Friction and trouble within the machine, or unnecessary difficulties in its path, are equally distasteful, for the very practical reason that they waste precious energy and retard progress. A new enterprise that goes to wreck for lack of cooperation between employer and employees, a plan of expansion that fails to secure the expected approval of customers, short sighted buying and selling, irritating transactions of every sort which tend to upset your poise and judgment and render you liable to successively greater mistakes in the future, form an increasing load of dead wood for you to carry or sink under. Yet the solution of all these difficulties lies constantly at hand in the proper application to them of the Law of Attraction, or Love.

Whenever you deal with employees, customers, or anyone with whom your business interests bring you into personal contact, take the trouble to make the contact first with Universal Life Energy. Relax and open yourself, Body and Mind, to the inflow of that Force. The result will be that Love, as an Aspect of that Universal Power, will pour into you and through you, restoring your lost Equilibrium, smoothing away the tension that dulls your faculties, clearing you're vision and your judgment and establishing a sympathetic channel between you and the other individual over which you will affect the most mutually satisfactory exchange.

In this connection remember that "Love" is referred to, not in its limited sense of a personal sentiment, but in its great impersonal Aspect as a Supreme Universal Power. To feel a personal attachment for a business rival whom you may not even know is neither practical nor, as a general rule, possible But to achieve an open and kindly attitude, unbiased by prejudice, which enables you to weigh all things justly, to perceive the bad without losing sight of the good, to meet all conditions with a calm understanding that proceeds from an impersonal Love of a larger nature, is not only possible but essential for your best advantage. Supplement Common Sense by the constant use of Universal Life Energy, particularly through its Fourth Aspect of Love, in your ordinary business transactions, and you will be astonished at the practical results it will achieve in promoting fairness and honesty from others, and Affluence and Success in every direction.

The real Power of Love cannot be misused. Like the Universal Life Energy of which it is one Aspect, it is superior to any effort to direct it into a negative channel for a wrong end. Constructive as it is when allied to a Positive Cause, just so destructive does it become when an attempt is made to pervert it. Therefore never think to take an unfair advantage of someone else with its help. It will destroy evil and discord without respect to persons, and will carry disaster to you with as little compunction as you sought its aid. You yourself are aware of what a blighting passion Hatred is, yet Hatred is but the perversion of Love to its other extreme. Often people with a narrow and twisted concept of Love only perceive it mirrored in reverse in this fashion. The most compelling Power in the Universe is corrupted in their understanding to a spineless sentimentality, which finds expression in a slavish catering to other people's desire, whims and impulses, whether good or bad. Such a diseased version of Love, substituting weakness for strength, shows the most abject ignorance of its real nature. Love is a Supreme Universal Power; therefore to use Love means above all to become powerful. Love is unalterably allied to Right, and the Individual' also must conform to the Right in order to experience its positive influence. To manifest Love, you must first be alert to discern, beyond all immediate consequences, the truly constructive course to follow, and resolute to decide on it. Then stand firmly by your decision, not in words but in actions, and at the same time temper that firmness with Fairness and Gentleness.

Such a Love will not win easy acceptance in the beginning, perhaps; it will touch to a boil the negative in others, who see their interest in swaying you from your purpose by their hostile clamour; but it will command Respect. Strength cannot do otherwise; and as the Right asserts itself behind the friendly and unaggressive firmness in which you persevere, opposition will simmer away to be replaced by a genuine responsive Love. Give Love to the World, and the World will sooner or later always return it to you with increase.

While Business is one limb of the many-branched tree of your interests, another, most important of all and most completely dependent on Love for its proper nourishment, is your Family. Especially in the upbringing of children should Love be the single recourse for guiding and developing the unformed character, because Love is a dominant trait in children and quick to respond to its call.

Yet even more firmly than with adults must that Love be exercised. Parents who are prone to indulge children in any and all circumstances, on the assumption that they thereby encourage the growth of spirit and independence, in reality simply indulge their own weakness at the child's expense. Children, who are very sensitive and observing, as well as far more direct and logical in their reasoning than adults, as a rule, are not slow to perceive weakness and take advantage of it. They delight in reversing the roles, and are such natural born adepts at doing so that few parents ever suspect the extent to which they are the dupes of their innocent offspring.

Moreover, do not imagine that you can successfully recommend one code of living to your children and practice another yourself. They pattern themselves after what you are, not what you say. Though they may not tell you so, for fear of punishment, they are all the time judging you with remorseless accuracy. Your acts are what set the seal of absolute conviction on your precepts, and it is only by being in your life an example of the Power of Love that you can bring forth the best in children.

One of the most regrettable features of modern existence is that everyone seems too busy to scatter among his fellow men many kind thoughts, words, looks or deeds. This is a great mistake. Love, like anything else, requires continual exercise in order to give its best service. Unexpressed, it merely stagnates.

Never fear to show kindness and consideration to others, under the mistaken impression that you. will lose something of your own dignity or expose yourself to the hurt of a rebuff. A rebuff cannot disturb a spirit of genuine. Kindliness, and a dignity too unsure of itself to stir into the open is scarcely worth preserving. The pleasantness and beauty of human relations spring from the degree of Love manifested in those relations, and as Love is by nature free from the taint of any selfish or unwholesome motives, it can never infringe upon the rights of another. Far from becoming a burden, it emphasizes Individual Freedom and promotes the unhampered growth of individual interests, bringing Happiness to all.

The negative passions, on the other hand, such as Selfishness, Jealousy, Hatred, Anger, etc., are as universally destructive as their positive counterparts are beneficial. Like a virulent acid, they scorch and burn wherever they touch; but the havoc they may wreak on the one against whom they are directed is mild compared with the destruction they work on the one who entertains them. Failure, ruin, and unhappiness travel in their wake; for success, the actual realization of constructive endeavour, cannot possibly survive where the Negative prevails.

It is not easy for most human beings to rid themselves of their Negative Passions, nor do they often perceive the full extent of the danger that resides in indulging them. Yet if they would study their aberrations, not in the false light of isolated occurrences, but as the ominous pulsations of a rising current of Evil which threatens to corrupt their whole character and abilities, they would suddenly appreciate the immense practical advantage of getting rid once and for all of such an enemy within.

Universal Life Energy is, of course, the certain corrective of these unbalanced states. Any access of Passion which breaks through your Self Control upsets your Equilibrium and drags you from the position of command over your faculties. To rely on Will Power or any mental forces to suppress them is unwise and usually futile, because their source is in Mind and their very existence proves that they have already stampeded precisely those mental forces with which you wish to combat them. Moreover, your chief aim is to eliminate the Evil itself rather than merely suppress a single manifestation of it, and this can only be accomplished by a Power greater than any which dwells in the afflicted Mind alone. Whenever you feel Jealousy, Envy or Hatred flare suddenly in your heart, or Selfishness invade with smothering vapours your better impulses, relax and make the contact with Universal Life Energy. Do not yield to the sudden impulse of Fear that prompts you to try to choke them back within you the enemy must be openly met to be vanquished. Let them come out in the natural manner, but be sure that you yourself make the contact each time with Universal Life Energy, either mentally or, if you are too much upset mentally, through the Star Exercise, or simply by turning one or both palms upward. You will discover, to your amazement, that you are no longer helpless in the grip of the storm that rages within, that you feel soothed, quieted, unafraid, until presently you are aware that the Evil Passion has vanished as traceless as a shadow, leaving a calm of perfect confidence in its place. Such is the miracle wrought by the harmonizing Power of Love, the Fourth Aspect of the Universal Force.

So simple and automatic is the process that one often finds it hard to credit the remarkable results. The condition it has to combat looms so impressively that the instinctive reaction is to anticipate an equally difficult struggle to contend successfully with it. But these difficulties exist chiefly in the victim's imagination, which magnify the whole thing to alarming proportions. The greater and more powerful the Force used, the simpler its operation, especially when the Force in question is a Natural one.

Every human being cherishes in his heart a longing for companionship, for the wholly disinterested exchange of affections with another. Yet few can ever affirm honestly to their Inmost Selves that this longing has been fully realized. Life is in this respect a great disappointment for the majority of people, who at the best are forced to admit secretly that they never attained real Happiness or a very generous measure of true Friendship. But life was not meant to be that way.

Every individual possesses as birthright the right to have friends and life companions. Through him as through all human beings the Law of Love is continually working out the Universal Brotherhood of Man, by its own Motherhood. It is only necessary to be an open channel for the Law to work through freely, in order to have friends who love you as you love them.

Guard against the mistake of envying others who are rich in Friendships. Such a course will never attract friends to you. Envy is one of the most common and potent of the negative influences to which Mankind are liable, and like all negative forces is distinctly repellent. It will drive back as nothing else could the very thing you want to attract. Understand that in order to be loved you must have in your own nature something worth loving. An ordinary piece of iron possesses nothing to distinguish it from any other piece of iron, until it is invested with a peculiar current of force. Then it becomes a magnet, drawing to it other metals. Similarly, you must radiate from yourself the Magnetic Power of Love which will draw a like response from those with whom you come in contact.

The importance of finding, not only the right sort of friends, but the Life Companion who should be the foremost friend, cannot be overestimated. Yet very often people devote all their attention to sifting out those whom they would like to establish in this relation, and complain with bitter melancholy when they find their proffered friendship ignored. Wholly blind to the supreme Selfishness of this course, they consider themselves abused and unappreciated, when in fact their trouble comes only from being truly appreciated at their real value. They look for the best, without giving any thought to what they themselves have to offer in exchange.

Start your career by wringing this foolish conceit out of your system. Forget the Success others may have had in obtaining ideal friends and life companions, and turn all your attention to developing Love within yourself. The more you exercise it, the more you manifest Love to everyone under all circumstances, the greater it grows. That is the Treasure you must heap up in yourself to attract the desire of others. Gold never glitters unnoticed for long amid the passing throng; it's worth strikes the most heedless eye and draws plenty of claimants.

Once having created the genuine value within yourself, your only difficulty will be, not how to attract those to whose friendship you aspire, but how to select the best among those who have been attracted. Use your own discrimination to single out as friend or life companion the one whom your own heart fixes on as a kindred spirit, the one whose Individuality blends most sympathetically with your own.

Age or physical appearance play a very minor role with respect to Love and its Power of Attraction. The gold is no less precious and desirable for the shape and texture of its container. That is why Beauty so frequently yields precedence to more homely virtues in the matrimonial field; the choice falls rather on a less ornate fleshly purse that is full of the coin of sound qualities than on the more handsome one that is empty.

Therefore if real Love glows in your heart and radiates throughout your whole being, do not doubt but what you will be loved in spite of the disadvantages of Age. People will no longer see the material shell when its chinks and crevices serve only to reveal the Treasure of inner qualities. They will love you for what you actually are, not for the transitory abode in which you live.

Youth commands Love, and Love itself is the very essence of Youth. Eventually even the physical evidence of Old Age must surrender to the transcendent Power of Love. If you want to be young in physical appearance, entertain constantly in your heart, and manifest constantly in your actions, the Love from which Youth springs. There is no better method of Rejuvenation than this.

Remember, your Physical Body is simply the expression of your inner activities, a statue moulded by your own Soul. In its lines are wrought all the changing play of those emotions and thoughts out of which your character erects itself. A positive and constructive way of thinking and feeling carves its touch of Health, Strength, Beauty and Youth on the image it inhabits. The negative passions that creep in, such as Hatred, Jealousy, Envy and Selfishness, chisel their ugly marks deep in the defenceless features.

Take advantage of this unceasing renewal of your Material Self and fashion it to a pattern of an Inner Self remodelled on lines of higher thinking and an improved standard of living. If you attend to the inner development you will have no cause to worry about its embodiment in outward form. Love, the Greatest Power, is a Master Sculptor, who will scrupulously translate in terms of flesh and form as much of your Soul as you will expose on the model's seat.

Therefore love truly and constantly, and leave the rest to the Law of Love. You will find that the unique assortment of qualities which constitute your Individuality, the distinctive Beauty of Soul which sets you apart from every other living Being, will soak through into material expression as sunlight soaks through clouds. The Individual YOU will glow forth arrestingly and strike you out from the mass of your fellows as original, interesting and lovable.

In conclusion, carry away with you from these pages a clear and vigorous concept of what Love actually is.

Understand it, not as a lonely and mysterious urge which roams only the narrow confines of your particular little life, but as the Measureless Tide of Universal Power which Science knows it to be. Identify your tiny candle flame of Love with relation to the blazing Sun of Love from which it was caught, and by perceiving its titanic works throughout the whole boundless expanse of rocks and firmaments, seas, stars and unseen worlds beyond the sweep of telescopic vision, obtain some idea of the nature of its Power and why it is such a compelling Force in your individual life.

Love is Attraction. Attraction is both a Force and a Law. The Law of Attraction, whose existence was perceived first by Newton, was called by him the Law of Gravity. This Force, operating in accordance with Its own Law, governs the entire Universe, functioning with an exactitude that never varies, on the greatest scale as on the smallest. Because of this precise and invincible Law manifest in its workings, Love is the basis of Eternal Harmony.

Human ingenuity has never been able to penetrate, either through the large or the small end of the scale, to a region where the working of the Law of Attraction, or Love, is not apparent. Celestial bodies small or vast in bulk, from meteorites to planets huge beyond the ability even of the imagination to embrace, float like bubbles through Infinite Space. Without visible support or impulse, they spin and hurtle through vacancy, each pursuing a regular orbit of its own with an amazing and mathematical precision. What prevents them from falling or erring from their course, so that they crash together in a common universal ruin? The Law of Attraction, within which resides all Order and Harmony.

The same Law asserts itself with the same marvellous precision within the microscopic walls of the, smallest particle of Matter. The Atom, resolved into its component parts, discovers itself as a tiny cosmos in which a swarm of Electrons repeat, on a scale below the farthest range of visibility, the identical evolutions which sketch themselves across the boundless sweep of the heavens in letters ages long. Everywhere the Force and the Law of Attraction operate to hold all things together, maintaining their proper relations, governing their activities.

Human beings, like everything else, are subject to that Law. It functions in the Electrons and Atoms of which their Physical Bodies are constructed, in the beat of their hearts, in the cycles of their thoughts. Every particle of their existence is threaded on it like beads on a string. To live in accordance with the Law of Attraction, or Love, to identify oneself with it in thought and wish and deed, is therefore to enlist the whole invincible Power of this Universal Force in one's behalf. To live against it is to oppose oneself to a juggernaut that will crush and destroy.

There can be no compromise with Love. It is an Impersonal Force, All-Pervading, All-Powerful, Supreme. No human Will can affect in the slightest the Power that holds the Universe in its grip. If you accommodate yourself to it, you will reap all the advantages that such a Strength can achieve. But if you violate it, you reap only destruction. A star which leaves its orbit, swerving aside from the course prescribed by the Law of Attraction, loses its equilibrium and presently encounters annihilation. That Law works through the life of the individual just as surely as through the life of the star. You have no choice but to be either with It or against It.

Let the Law of Attraction work through you and you will not fail to secure the Health, Success and Happiness to which you aspire.

EXERCISES TO LESSON TWENTY-FIVE

Continue to practice the Star Exercise morning and evening, together with Relaxation, Silence and the constant Mental contact with Universal Life Energy. In addition to these enter into the new EXERCISES TO this week, known as HARMONIZATION.

The purpose of HARMONIZATION is to adjust yourself with relation to the Universal Forces and Laws which seek expression through you. Sickness, Inefficiency, Poverty, Unhappiness, Discord, of any sort which impairs your rightful powers, exist in direct proportion to your own conscious or unconscious violation of Natural Laws. In proportion as you re-establish yourself in full accord with those Laws, the ill effect of your opposition to them will vanish and you will come to the peak of your vigour and efficiency in every direction. You will attain the perfect Poise which is the keystone of all Strength. To practice HARMONIZATION proceed as follows:

After you have relaxed, entered into Silence and made the Contact with Universal Life Energy, concentrate on the Love Aspect of that Force from which Peace and Harmony spring. Understand that Harmony is a fundamental condition of All Being, the norm of absolute Equilibrium toward which all things in Nature instinctively aspire. Realize that deep within you, as within everything, the core of that Harmony exists as true and uncorrupted as in the gigantic symphony of all Powers which roll the Worlds on their courses. Endeavour to feel it, to connect it once again with the

Harmony outside through the neglected human YOU which you have permitted to fall out of proper alignment. Let Inspiration, drawn from your Contact with the Love Aspect of Universal Life Energy, weld together the broken parts of that chain in which your Human Self has proved the faulty link.

This Exercise, more than any other, will build up within you that sense of Poise and instant command over all your faculties, Mental and Physical, which makes you master over every situation because it makes you master first over yourself. You will achieve the Peace which comes from consciousness of Strength, a calm and confident equanimity manifesting itself in steadiness of Mind and Emotions, which no circumstance even of the utmost danger can disturb. This is indeed a divine quality, and at the same time of the greatest practical value.

Remember in the performance of this Exercise to avoid any use of Will Power. Aside from the fact that such an attempt can only cut you off from contact with the very Force that you are trying to contact, it is clearly futile for you to exert a very limited human mental power in an endeavour to bend the Supreme Power to your ends. You cannot compel the Highest to resign Itself to your Will, but you can engage Its help by trustfully and lovingly delivering yourself into Its Arms.

QUESTIONS TO LESSON TWENTY-FIVE

1. What place does Love occupy in the Universe?

2. To what extent does it enter into the activities of Human Beings?

3. Of what practical advantage is Love in Business?

4. How is Love distinguished from weak Sentimentality?

5. Can Love and Discipline be reconciled in the rearing of children?

6. In what way are you directly responsible for the good or bad traits your children develop?

7. How will you profit from the exercise of Love in all your relations with the World at large?

8. What relation do the Negative Passions bear to Love?

9. How can they be eliminated?

10. What responsibility must you fulfil in order to attract the friends and the Life Companion you desire?

11. What part does Love play in physical Rejuvenation?

12. What, briefly, is the scientific explanation of Love?

ANSWERS TO LESSON TWENTY-FIVE

1. The place Love occupies in the Universe is:

That of the Governing and Sustaining Power which cements the entire Universe together in one harmonious whole.

2. The extent to which it enters into the activities of Human Beings is:

Completely, as there is no human activity which can proceed without it.

3. The practical advantage of Love in Business is:

That it constitutes the Power of Attraction on which all transactions depend, and by the Law of Harmony inherent in it determines the proper course for the greatest success.

4. Love is distinguished from weak Sentimentality:

Primarily, by its nature as the strongest Power it is possible to manifest, and by the fact that this Strength is unalterably allied to the Positive and Constructive side.

5. Love and Discipline:

Can and must be reconciled in the rearing of children, because real Love cannot tolerate a negative and destructive tendency.

6. **You are directly responsible for the good or bad traits in your children:**

   In that children pattern their character after your example, fully accepting your precepts only as you confirm them by your acts.

7. **You will profit from the exercise of Love in all your relations with the World at large:**

   By developing the Power of Love within you, thus making yourself constantly strong in every direction.

8. **The relation of the Negative Passions to Love is:**

   That Negative Passions, such as Hatred, Envy, Jealousy, etc., are the perversion of Love to its other extreme of destructive power.

9. **They can be eliminated:**

   By contacting Universal Life Energy, especially in Its Aspect of Love, and allowing that Harmonizing Current to flush Body, Mind and Emotions clean of the discord which manifests itself in Negative Passions.

10. **The responsibility you must fulfil in order to attract the friends or Life Companion you desire is:**

    That of developing within yourself something worth loving, a strength of Love that will merit the return of Love that you expect from them.

11. The part played by Love in Physical Rejuvenation is:

That Love is itself the essence of Youth and will be built out into harmonious and youthful physical expression in proportion as it exists within you.

12. The scientific explanation of Love is:

Love is the Power of Attraction, which is both a Universal Force and a Law of Harmony. It manifests itself throughout the entire Universe as a Magnetic Power, called by its discoverer, Newton, the Force and Law of Gravity. Its most commonly known expression through the Human Emotions is known as Love in its limited personal sense.

Dear Friend:

As the separate visions blend through the lenses of a glass, so the fields that have been covered in this Course are brought to a Focus in this twenty-sixth Lesson.

All the specific knowledge gathered in the previous Lessons tended toward a single Purpose—attainment of the full stature of Manhood and Womanhood. That knowledge is now to be correlated in order to give you a sweeping perspective of your Triune Being, showing you how to develop in unison Body, Mind and Soul for the achievement of this Purpose.

To see your way clearly it is necessary to know what your position is in the Universe. The Scientific Definition of Man will be to you as the daily observation is to the mariner, locating you in the vast Sea of Life, establishing your relation to the things about you and enabling you to chart your surest course to the haven you desire.

Understanding alone lends Worth to Knowledge. There is but one ground upon which a secure Understanding is based. Having attained it, certain salient facts stand boldly forth to point the right path for future progress. Foremost among these is the necessity for Soul Development as a fundamental of modern education. People today, appreciating Education as never before, dimly sense this, but do not yet clearly perceive it because they have not found that ground.

In this Lesson the ground you seek will be clearly defined in Five Statements of Being, which set forth concisely your relation to the Universe and to the Four

Aspects of Universal Life Energy. With this knowledge, and with the effective use of Inspiration as an aid to your more rapid unfoldment, you will advance quickly and confidently toward the goal of your most ardent aspirations.

Cordially yours,
Eugene Fersen.

LESSON TWENTY-SIX

The Science of Being has thus far dealt separately with the three basic parts of Man's Triune Being — Body, Mind and Soul. Yet in the individual himself there can exist no such separation. All three, while preserving intact their respective identities, are nevertheless merged in a union so complete that nothing short of death can entirely dissolve it. Each is fundamental to continued existence as a human entity, and each maintains its place in the human trinity through the support of the others.

Most important of the three, because it is the Source from which the rest proceed, is the Soul. The Soul alone is by nature perfect and immune to flaws. It represents the Ideal to be transmitted into expression through its own human instruments. But imperfections can and do abound in those instruments, with the result that only a distorted and unwieldy partial expression is usually achieved through them.

Both Mind and Body, including Emotions, must represent equally the Soul from which they are derived. To accomplish this, the imperfections which mil- them and stunt their growth must be kneaded out. A Body that is over-developed signifies a corresponding shortage in manifestation of Mind or, through the Emotions, of Soul. Similarly, if Mind dominates, it can be only at the expense of the other two. The same is true of Soul when it foams too lightly through a highly emotional nature. Any instance of one member of the human trinity outbalancing the others points to an absence of Poise which can be corrected simply by developing the weaker up to the level of the stronger. Without that correlative development to establish perfect balance between the three constituent parts of YOU, the Equilibrium from which Power and Harmony spring is absolutely unattainable.

The way to get the Best and Most out of your life is primarily to live in a clean, healthy and normal fashion. Give to both Mind and Body a wholesome environment in which to flourish and they will flourish accordingly. Plenty of exercise, as much out of doors as possible, simple and well prepared food, pleasant to the taste yet in quantity sufficient only to meet the needs of your Body, all the sunshine you can get, abundant fresh air, especially at night when you are sleeping, as little and as loose clothing as is consistent with comfort and the laws of the community and an intelligent interest in your own general well being are the commonest worth-while aids for sustaining the life current within you. Clean contacts outside will start a natural appetite for clean and stimulating mental foods also, and will help to rid you of whatever rubble may have collected in your Mind.

Never be afraid of physical effort. Your Body is a tool which requires use to keep it bright and in good working order. As long as you have it, give it the exercise it needs to keep it at its highest capacity to serve you. Make it the foil against which to whet your Will Power, also, whenever you feel a disclination to exert yourself stand in your way. And above all, contact and use Universal Life Energy constantly, making every instance of fatigue or reluctance to undertake physical work an occasion to call upon that Power.

Your desire, and the desire of everyone, should be to have a fine Physical Body, strong, healthy and beautiful in appearance as well as dependable and prompt in action. Work for it according to the instructions of this Course. Young or old, man or woman, it is within the reach of all who are willing to take the trouble of earning it. Then only, when you have made the best of physical attributes your own, will you fully understand the great practical advantage and joy of possessing real Health, Strength and Beauty. You will learn to appreciate your Body.

Your Mind responds richly to one excellent course of treatment — Action. Cultivate it intelligently; be both quick and deep in your thoughts, broad and at the same time one-pointed. Have the courage to recognize and weed out the negative trends in your thinking. Banish Fear and Worry and especially refrain from using your thought destructively against others. Remember that every thought comes back to you soon or late, vastly increased, and that for every wind of evil you sow, you will inevitably reap the whirlwind.

Universal Life Energy, with Its invigorating Power, is of inestimable value in developing to the utmost all your mental qualities. The more you use It, the more efficient and the more indispensable you become in the position you occupy in life. If you are at the bottom, It will lift you gradually to higher and higher levels as the inner growth and expansion qualifies you to function there. Power and Affluence will flow to you from without in answer to the increased Power within. If on the other hand you are at the top, the Universal Force will enable you to widen the scope of your activities, promoting stronger leadership, more efficiency, greater productivity and ampler benefit to others in proportion as you benefit yourself.

Finally, the proper development of your Soul qualities through the emotional side of your nature will be to you a crowning achievement, because it will open Life in its richest aspect for your use and enjoyment. Powers of Mind and Body are the nether links of the chain, but the weight they will lift, the tasks they will do, is determined by the strength of that ultimate third link, the noblest part of your Triune Being through which you find your connection with the Universal Source.

Release from the poverty of earthly existence lies in the development of this higher part of your Human Self. Lacking it, the wealthiest are poor, because they lack that which enables them to draw full satisfaction from their possessions; possessing it, the poorest are rich beyond measure, because the least yields them the most. It endows you with Success and Happiness, both of a material and individual sort, making you one of that rare company so necessary to the Progress of the Human Race, a Leader of Men.

Enhance your physical and mental forces by the cultivation of this most precious gift of yours. Then, with your Triune Being properly developed, you will find the dark vision of sorrows and struggles, suffering and failure which thickens over the mortal future of most people clear to a bright vista of sparkling action, shining with interest, tempting to live and conquer, marking the path of your progress with victories waiting to be won, and lifting the final goal of Success and Happiness in warm promise at the far end of your career.

The last chapter of your life on Earth is but the introduction to your life to come. Your development here determines the level at which you will enter upon the path of your further Evolution on the next Plane of your Existence. Therefore to be able to look back upon a busy history of constructive activity, of much attempted and much done, of Success and of Happiness, is an assurance with which you can step serenely and confidently through the doors that lead to another World, knowing that you but enter a field of broader scope where greater achievements invite to still greater enfoldment and still larger Happiness. All this you can attain, not by praying but by working, developing your Triune Nature by application of the principles explained in SCIENCE OF BEING and growing thus to the full stature of Manhood and Womanhood.

Seek Inspiration always, within yourself as well as outside of yourself. The World is teeming with marvellous things, great and small, which have a definite purpose with relation to you. They are there to awaken the corresponding wonders which slumber within you, touching to life a thousand unsuspected fibres of your Being which, once aroused, grow out to tap as many and more glorious new fields.

Prize Beauty as the Source of Inspiration. Love all things beautiful, whether they are of a physical, mental or spiritual nature. As long as Humanity's existence is cast in the Three Planes, there must be beauty also on those Planes to strike the corresponding note in your Triune

Human Nature. Look for that Beauty and you will find some everywhere and in everything.

Remember that Beauty is but another word for Harmony. It represents the very end you are striving to realize in the development of your Triune Being. The more you bring Body, Mind and Soul into harmonious accord, the more successful you are in living your human life. The more you eliminate discord from any one of these three, the nearer you come to that state of perfect Equilibrium to which you aspire. Everything, in the final analysis, reduces to a single factor within it which sets the measure of its worth—the Beauty, or Harmony, it contains.

Teach your children, your boys and girls, the value of Beauty and lead them to love it in every form and aspect. So many people, especially the intellectual, believe that Intelligence alone counts. They do not see that the thing they admire in Intelligence is first of all Harmony. Modern educators are beginning to perceive this truth and to lay more and more stress on the development of the Soul's qualities. Only when it is understood that this phase of Education should stand by right ahead of all the rest, setting the pace to which the development of Mind and Body must be correlated, will Humanity enter fully upon that Era of tremendous Progress which the Future holds for it.

Bear in mind also that children are such merely in terms of mortal years. As Souls, they are your equals, both in point of time and of intrinsic qualities. Their task is to unfold those Soul Qualities through their human incarnation. Help them to do so. Be their friends, revealing to them what Harmony is, their guides, to show them the way, their pals and confidants to accompany them on it. Encourage the Expression of Soul Qualities, for in proportion as Mankind learns to realize through their mortal selves the unbounded Harmony within will the Race grow toward that goal of Power it is placed here to achieve.

Man condenses within himself the Essence of all from which he sprang. He is the visible manifestation, the actual living proof of that Infinity of Power out of which he is derived and which is called Universal Life Energy. However much disharmony may mar the workings of his complex and curiously perverse Human Self, he holds deep within him the whole vast Perfection of that Harmony which constitutes his origin.

Therefore it is not necessary to struggle blindly toward the realization of that Harmony. Study your own Self. The more you will learn of it, the more you will know of the Eternal Source of which you are the emanation. Discover your own true nature and you will discover the truth of the statement, "Know thyself and thou shalt know All."

In the present stage of Evolution, called the Fifth Period or Cycle of Humanity's Evolution, the natural division into which things fall is Five. That is the dominant number. This planet is divided into Five Continents. There are Five Oceans. Five Elements form the Substance of Creation — Earth, Water, Fire, Air and Ether. Five Races people the Earth =White, Yellow, Red, Brown, Black. Human Beings have Five Senses through which they live,

Five Brain Lobes, Five Extremities, Five Fingers and Toes. In the vegetable kingdom Five is most commonly manifested in the structure of plants. Everywhere Five asserts itself; so does it also in your own Self, which it is the purpose of this Course to teach you to know.

SCIENCE OF BEING therefore crystallizes out into Five Statements of Being which summarize it completely. Each Statement is, so to say, one finger pointing to a central Fact that is the Focus of all. A single Lesson, the Lesson of Unity, is taught Five Times from Five different directions, in a sequence as logical as the points of the compass. They are as follows:

The sum of all lives, the One Universal and Eternal Life, is that Great Creative Power of the Universe called Universal Life Energy."

There is but One Life, of which you and all living things are a part. All individual manifestations of life, without distinction as to whether they be people, animals, minerals, or gases—everything which moves and vibrates—represents that Single Infinite and Eternal Life which is the First Aspect of Universal Life Energy. You are at one with that Life, an integral part of It, not simply for the brief term of your human incarnation, but for Eternity. It is in you as you are in It; you can never be separated from It, because It is YOU. The clearer your understanding is of this Eternal Fact, the stronger your realization of its truth, the greater will be its practical value in helping you to live your own life.

"The Sum of all Intelligences, the One Universal Intelligence, is that great Organizing Power of the Universe called Universal Life Energy."

The dimmest spark of intelligence which may glimmer in the dullest particle of Life, as well as the most luminous and comprehensive intellectual fire, every thought both small and great, of the Future as well as of the Past and Present, everything that will ever enter the Consciousness of Man, all Knowledge throughout Eternity, exists as part of one common Universal Ocean of Intelligence, the Second Aspect of Universal Life Energy. Just as your life is a Ray of the Eternal Life, so your Mind is a Ray projected from the Infinite Mind, eternally connected with It and tapping Its limitless resources of knowledge.

The reason Mankind do not take advantage of their connection with the Source of All Knowledge is because they have permitted Fear to stand in their way. As long as you believe yourself to be a separate intelligence, that delusion will set the limits of your knowledge. Though you are part of Infinite Mind, possessing all Its qualities of Infinite Knowledge and Infinite Intelligence, you will be able to tap those vast reservoirs only when you free yourself from the grip of Fear and become open and receptive.

Perceive your Unity with Universal Intelligence. Understand as an Eternal Truth the fact that your intelligence abides in It and expresses It. The two are one; they cannot be separated. Let the confidence derived from this understanding help you to dispel the Fear which has hitherto limited your Consciousness, and you will find your way open into the Treasures of Knowledge in the Universal Mind.

"The Sum of all truths, the one Great Truth, or Law, is that great Governing Power of the Universe called Universal Life Energy."

Truth Expressed is Law. All Truth is contained in the Great Law, the Third Aspect of Universal Life Energy, which, being eternally true to Itself, reflects that Truth through all Its myriad manifestations. Just as a single ray of sunlight, striking a fragment of glass, is splintered into countless varicoloured lesser rays, so the One Truth is refracted by the facets of every occasion, forming the infinity of laws and truths apparent throughout all the Universe. Thus the Physical Laws governing your Body, the Mental Laws governing your Mind and the Spiritual Laws working through your Soul are but fractions of the one Great Law which includes them all.

Whenever you are in accordance with the lesser laws inside, whether on the Physical, Mental or Emotional Plane, you are thus in accordance also with the Great Law outside which they represent. That is what is meant when it is said "Be true to your own Self," because your Real Self is identified with the Great Law from which it springs. The more true, honest and sincere you are, the greater will be the power you find yourself able to manifest in every direction, since you enlist in your behalf the whole Universal Power embraced in the Great Law to which you ally yourself.

Conversely, the more you violate the branches of that Great Law in your own nature, the more you shut yourself out from the one Source of All Power. Hypocrisy, Untruthfulness, Dishonesty of all sorts, are poisons which rob you of Strength far more valuable than any immediate advantage you may gain from them. To practice such Untruths is to make yourself the first and most pitiful victim of your ignorance of the great Worth and Power of Truth.

Realize the fact of your oneness with the Great Law, or Eternal Truth. It governs you, whether you will or no, penalizing violations as inevitably as It rewards observance, because It is the very stuff of which you are made. Live in truth, be Law Abiding, and you will gather to yourself the Strength of that Invincible Power. This, transmitted into expression in your daily activities, will command Success in everything you undertake and do, repaying you a thousand-fold for your effort.

"The Sum of all loves, the One Infinite Love, is that Great Sustaining Power of the Universe called Universal Life Energy."

Few people recognize in the tender emotion of Love, which dyes with its own stimulating and harmonizing hues all that it touches, a vast Universal Power, the Fourth Aspect of Universal Life Energy, holding in Itself all other Powers. Such unimaginable Strength is hard to reconcile with such exquisite delicacy in human understanding; yet the mysteriously compelling influence that weaves its subtle charm in human hearts is but one Ray of the Force which knits the Worlds together and hurls the planets in their courses.

Baron Eugene Fersen   626

Love is Attraction, and only through the magnetic pull of Attraction do all things, including the Universe itself, continue to exist. Withdraw the Force of Attraction from your Body, even for a moment, and the cells which comprise that Body will immediately fall apart, disintegrate, cease to exist as one coherent unit. In other words, your very Being is dependent wholly upon the Power of Attraction, or Love, to sustain it.

Unconsciously, you manifest this Love in every particle of your Being. It is apparent in the automatic functioning of your organs, in the clinging of cell to cell and atom to atom, and within the atomic walls in the ordered evolutions of those minutest elemental units called Electrons. Everything in your Body is kept in a condition of Harmony by the Power of Attraction, or Love. It is only when you come to the Conscious part of your Human Self that you find this Harmony lapsing into disorder.

Your human intelligence is that within you which must learn the lesson of love. You are saturated with Love, made up and sustained by It; Love is the Foundation on which you are based. But you must realize this, perceive it to be so, and by thought and action build up a superstructure of Love and Harmony on that very Foundation of Love which Nature gave you at birth.

You build the temple under whose dome you live your life on this Earth, as well as forecast the plan of that which you will inhabit on another Plane of your Existence. Make it a noble structure of Love and Power, of Harmony and Happiness. Every kind and constructive action is a stone added to its height, every friendly thought, word or deed is a breadth moulded into its proportions. And because it is natural to do this, in accordance with the Great Law, it is not difficult.

Summon to your aid the constructive Force of Universal Life Energy; then the more you practice it the more easy and pleasant it will become. What you desire to realize-in your conscious life is an integral part of that Universal Power, so by the very act of inviting It to help you and work with you, you identify yourself with that to which you aspire.

The more you live consciously, releasing into expression that fundamental love nature of which you are usually not aware, the more harmonious, the stronger, happier and more successful you will be. All loves, great and small, of planets and electrons no less than of human beings, and of every sort, whether of the needle for the magnetic pole or of one friend for another, are but trickles from the Limitless Ocean of Love of which all are an integral and eternal part. In proportion as you make yourself One with that Infinite Love, the Supreme Power of Attraction, It flushes into evidence through you as your own increased personal Power of Attraction. All future expansion, the greater Success and Happiness of Humanity as a whole as well as that of each individual in particular, is determined by the greater degree to which they are able to express Love in their lives.

"The sum of all Beings, the Infinite, Eternal and Supreme Being, A that One Great All, embracing the Universe, including every visible and invisible expression of Universal Life Energy."

Though you may believe that you are separate from the rest of Creation, that is not so. Your Body is but a cell in the Great Universal Body, the Visible Universe. Your Mind is but a ray of the Infinite Universal Mind. Your Soul is but an individualized projection from the Great Soul of the Universe Itself. In every way, through every finest filament of your Triune Being, you are intimately connected with and woven more closely into the vast scheme of the Universe, of Nature.

Body, Mind and Soul unite to teach you a single dominant fact—that Man is simply the conscious, individualized, compound, harmonious and eternal projection of Universal Life Energy into Its own Eternal Substance Proceeding from this One Universal Source, indissolubly connected with It, manifesting all Its Qualities and Powers, Man is indeed the "image and likeness" of that Power, coexistent and co-eternal with It.

The more you consciously realize this to be an actual fact, perceiving behind all the bewildering complexities of your human expression the Unity from which it is all derived, the more you will grow and develop in every direction. Then eventually, when you have fully welded yourself through your own Triune Nature to the Universal, you will attain the common goal of all human Aspirations—Power, Freedom and Happiness.

Baron Eugene Fersen

EXERCISES TO LESSON TWENTY-SIX

Continue as usual the Star Exercise morning and evening. Practice Relaxation, Silence and constant Contact with Universal Life Energy. Then proceed with the new Exercise for this week, which is known as LIBERATION.

The aim of this latest Exercise is to establish perfect Poise in the individual by establishing his Unity with the Universal Power through the three parts of his Triune Nature. This is accomplished by freeing the individual from whatever limitations may hamper his growth and unfoldment on any of the Three Planes. To practice LIBERATION, go on as follows:

After Relaxation, Silence and Contact with Universal Life Energy, concentrate your thought on your Oneness with the Universe which is the Great Expression of that Power. Drink in through every fibre the sense of its illimitable Vastness, its Strength and above all its Freedom. Extend yourself through the close horizon of limitations which crowds about your narrow conscious sphere and pierce for a time into the horizonless All beyond. Perceive the boundless sweep of the Great Law surging also through you, be absorbed into It and realize that, as a drop of water shares the power of the ocean into which it falls, so you partake of the free Immensity of the Universe in which you exist.

The more strongly you are aware of that sense of Universal Freedom, the more successful you will be in shaking off the limitations which divide you from It. All burdens, physical, mental and emotional, will gradually drop away. An extraordinary feeling of security, ease and power will spring up buoyantly in their place. You will look upon life with a new vision, a richer understanding, an equanimity serene and confident, beyond the power of any circumstance to balk or disturb. You will be FREE within yourself.

Once you have obtained this inner LIBERATION, the outside expression of it is bound to follow. Nothing and nobody can bind one who is really free within, because nothing can withstand the force of Natural Laws which demand corresponding recognition. Freedom is Man's birthright; nations and individuals war to the end for it; you can attain it alone, because you KNOW HOW.

QUESTIONS TO LESSON TWENTY-SIX

1. What relation does your Triune Human Nature bear to your own Soul?

2. How is Equilibrium to be achieved?

3. Define Beauty?

4. What role does Beauty play in the development of your Triune Nature?

5. Where do you look to obtain knowledge of your Universal Source?

6. Why are there exactly Five Statements of Being?

7. What is the Source of your life and the life of everything?

8. From what are all individual intelligences derived?

9. Define Law and its origin.

10. What is Love?

11. What is your relation to the Universe?

12. What single all-important Lesson is reiterated by each member of your human trinity, Body, Mind and Soul?

Lesson Twenty-Six

ANSWERS TO LESSON TWENTY-SIX

1. **The relation your Triune Nature bears to your own Soul is:**

   It is derived from your Soul for the purpose of affording physical, mental and emotional channels for the expression of your Soul Qualities.

2. **Equilibrium is to be achieved:**

   Only by the correlative development of these three parts of your Triune Human Nature.

3. **Beauty is:**

   Harmony.

4. **The role played by Beauty in the development of your Triune Nature is:**

   That you shape it to the proportions of Beauty in the measure that you bring its three aspects into harmonious accord. Beauty outside the individual acts as a stimulus to help that work of inner development along.

5. **The place to look to obtain knowledge of your Universal Source is:**

   Within your own Self, deep within which is the whole vast Perfection of the Harmony from which you sprang.

6. **There are exactly Five Statements of Being:**

    Because, as we are living in the Fifth Cycle of Humanity's Evolution, Five is the division into which all things naturally fall for the most clear and comprehensive expression.

7. **The Source of your life and the life of everything is:**

    The First Aspect through which Universal Life Energy expresses Itself, LIFE.

8. **All intelligences are derived from:**

    The Second Aspect through which Universal Life Energy expresses Itself, MIND.

9. **Law is:**

    Truth expressed. It has its origin in the Third Aspect through which Universal Life Energy expresses Itself, TRUTH.

10. **Love is:**

    The Power of Attraction, the Fourth and Greatest Aspect, embracing all the rest, through which Universal Life Energy expresses Itself.

11. Your relation to the Universe is:

That you are One with It, the conscious, individualized compound, harmonious and eternal projection of Universal Life Energy into Its own Eternal Substance.

12. The single all-important Lesson reiterated by each member of your Human Trinity, Body, Mind and Soul, is:

The Lesson of Unity.

Dear Friend:

This Lesson brings the "SCIENCE OF BEING" to an End, even as it brings you, its student, to a Beginning. You stand now at the threshold of a new life, a broader, richer, finer field of activity, which your greater development on the Three Planes of your Human Existence has opened out to you. It is but fitting that at this point on our journey together we should pause to survey the Future into which you are about to advance.

Therefore in this final Lesson the prospect will be brought into proper focus by a few general instructions. It is for you to handle details as you come to them, steering your course between the rocks and shoals that may lie in your way; but there are certain main currents the knowledge of which will give you a clearer perception of how best to meet your individual problems in relation to them.

One of these currents marks its direction most significantly in the recent rise of Womanhood. This movement illustrates compactly the great change which Humanity is experiencing at this stage of its Evolution. The present Human Race, occupying the Fifth Cycle of Evolution, is approaching the end of its course. A New Race, the Sixth Race, is about to emerge in its place.

This imminent change is perceived and heralded by many. Let us, through these closing pages, look to that coming Dawn when Man will awaken to the Realities of Eternal Existence and will see himself no longer as the

Slave, but as the Master. It is with that glorious Promise that this Course salutes you in farewell.

Cordially yours,
Eugene Fersen.

LESSON TWENTY-SEVEN

This final Lesson represents the lofty pinnacle of Self Development which you have achieved in the past six months of patient study and practice. Behind you unrolls the steep path up which you have climbed to a broad and sure knowledge of your own Triune Nature. Before you spreads the ample field of the Future in which you are to apply that knowledge. Let us hope that the work thus far has been a happy and successful one whose difficulties have but led to greater victories and whose rewards of added Strength, Health and Wisdom now fulfil their first function of helping you to survey this field.

Great changes are taking place today, both in Humanity and on this planet itself. Everywhere new movements are springing up, new avenues of thought opening out, new ideals beckoning to fruition. The wreckage of outworn concepts begins to strew our mental shores as the currents break from ancient channels and seek another direction. People fight for Freedom, not always wisely but at least energetically, and at this period their fighting is being crowned with a measure of Success.

Typical of the general trend is the Great Wave of Womanhood which has swept its members from their age-old bondage to a position of equality with men. There is a far deeper significance to this than the mere conflict between the sexes. The nature of women is love. Collectively they stand for Love, highest of human qualities because it is the Fourth and Greatest Aspect of Universal Life Energy. Yet throughout the centuries of Humanity's Evolution, women have been repressed and held in subjection by men, enslaved, bought and sold, at worst no better than cattle and at best scarcely more than servants of a higher degree.

Men, on the contrary, are keyed to the Second and lesser Aspect of Universal Life Energy, Mind. Their interest is in the active and aggressive phases of mortal existence. Just as women are by nature prone to manifest the gentle and receptive qualities chiefly characteristic of Love, so men derive their greatest satisfaction from the exercise of Power, Authority and Strength. Proud of their physical vigour and intelligence, it was inevitable that men should refuse to admit or tolerate that another Power, Love, could share the supremacy of Mind.

Today women are challenging this attitude. Though Civilization has carried its Torch to the darkest corners of the Earth, the old superstition of female inferiority still clings securely in the minds of at least half of Mankind. The rest, with a few exceptions, fight bitterly to prevent women from acquiring equal rights. Yet to the enlightened one who can perceive the fundamental merits of both sides, the eventual outcome is at once apparent.

Love, the Fourth Aspect of Universal Life Energy, is superior to Mind, the Second Aspect. These two numbers not only define the relation between men and women and their corresponding values in the Universal economy, but represent also their respective natures. "Two" signifies Duality, Strife, Restlessness, dominant traits of the male nature, while "Four" symbolizes Unity, Harmony, Peace, fundamental traits of the female nature. But "Four" embraces "Two" and is greater, whereas "Two" can never expand itself to the larger dimensions of "Four."

The reason "Two" has been able to assume dominion over "Four" in the relation between the sexes is because women have not made use of their full complement of powers to stop the aggression. Unaware of the fact that Love becomes strong in expression only through the equal development of other factors within it, notably Mind, they contented themselves with the passive and receptive side only and left to men the livelier field of active accomplishment. Men, on the contrary, finding the mental phase of their nature sufficient to maintain their supremacy under these circumstances, emphasized its development without troubling to cultivate the refining influences of their latent Love Qualities.

Now women are beginning to perceive their mistake and correct it by invading the field so long tamely abandoned to men. They are developing physical strength and energy, mental efficiency and power, qualities formerly claimed by men as attributes of the male alone. In schools and colleges, libraries and private homes, this training is rapidly going on, and in the business, political and artistic worlds its effects are becoming forcefully apparent. There is scarcely a department of male occupations that women have not successfully entered in modern times, and not one, from the subtleties of politics to the hard physical labour of farms and factories, where they have not demonstrated their ability to compete on even terms with men. Even in athletics their rising star rivals in brightness the masculine luminaries, while in matrimony the modern girl exercises her own selection instead of abiding the choice of parents or suitors.

The challenge has been carried directly to Man. He must meet Woman on her own ground or perish from his seat of power. Just as Woman has invaded his domain of Mind, so must he seek a compensating gain in her domain of Love. That is, he must develop out of his own nature the neglected Love qualities which he has hitherto considered the exclusive province of woman, in order to keep pace with the growth of women through their development of mental qualities formerly resigned to him alone. Otherwise he will soon witness a transfer of balance as deplorable as that which existed when the bulk of weight and authority were concentrated on his side of the scales. Women will outdo him in the very field where he has been accustomed to lead, and because he has acquired nothing to counterbalance the gain he will see himself reduced to a position of inferiority similar to that once occupied by women.

Such a shifting of the balance from the scale of Mind to the scale of Love would be a change devoid of profit. The same inharmony as before would still prevail, only turned end for end. The single condition productive of mutual Harmony and Happiness is one of Equilibrium, in which the two great divisions of Humanity enjoy an equal balance in development and power.

But to promote this condition Man must do his part. He must see the situation as it actually is and appreciate the problems which the growing Wave of Feminism brings up before him for solution. Once he clears his vision of the ancient prejudice which yet clings to obscure it, he will be in a position to gauge accurately the conditions and perceive intelligently the measures necessary to adapt himself to the new state of affairs introduced by the advent of this great World Factor, Love.

These measures are not outside ones. They are within the individual, where the shortcomings are. Men must realize the lack of development in their Love natures and supply that lack by cultivating such qualities as Honesty, Charitableness, Sympathy, Patience and Gentleness in their general human relation, even among their own kind. They must seek Beauty in Nature, Music, the Arts, to feed their higher interests, and not let their attention be wholly absorbed in the grosser pursuits of life, such as gathering money and power into their hands. And above all they must rid themselves of the false concept which prompts them to see harshness as strength and refinement as effeminacy.

Refinement is Strength enhanced and tempered by culture. It is one of the highest attributes of real Manhood. Effeminacy is simply weakness and shallowness, proceeding from absence of Strength, and is no less disgraceful and out of place in women than in men. A man who fulfils the demands of Manliness in the true sense of the word can never be afraid of appearing effeminate. Strong in Body, broad in Mind, high in Aspirations and energetic in Action, he will nevertheless be gentle and refined without dreading a possible misinterpretation of his attitude, because he is conscious within himself that he can never be less than a man. But the pretenders who try to dissemble their fear of appearing effeminate behind a harsh and uncompromising manner are merely hiding the shallowness and poverty of their natures under a mask of Arrogance, Roughness and Conceit.

Great men throughout History demonstrate the truth of this distinction. Wherever a reasonably impartial picture of their characters has been handed down, it reconstructs before our mind's eye the image of great souls, strong yet gentle, complete spheres manifesting equally both male and female qualities. Their might to vanquish enemies was no less amazing than their might to win the hearts of friends; but the secret of their influence over the rest of Humanity lay in the inner Equilibrium they possessed within themselves, where Mind and Love worked hand in hand for the common good.

Today the course of Evolution is lifting all Mankind a little nearer to the Greatness manifested by famed leaders past and present. The Power of Love, surging with a quickened beat through the whole Race, is beginning to eat away the discrepancies in their individual natures by which their lack of balance was measured. A fresh access of Life and Strength, like the first rays of the morning sun, writes on the dark horizon of their Consciousness its glowing promise of a New Day about to dawn, a Day of Power, of Knowledge, of Justice, Peace and Happiness.

When that Day will have risen the present Race will no longer reign supreme. It will have yielded place to the Sixth Race, the Race of Masters, who are the real lords of Creation and who will then rule also this planet.

At present Humanity is suffering the birth pangs of this new Era. Unrest of every kind pervades the Earth, domestic strife and troubles, wars and revolutions, famine, pestilence, earthquakes, storms and tidal waves. Nature itself seems to be severely infected with the discontent that agitates men and nations. Yet never in the history of Mankind has there been such a period of meteoric Progress in every constructive direction.

On the one hand, therefore, is a marvellous development and increase of the Good, while on the other hand Evil seems to multiply at an equally astonishing rate. Crime and destruction were never so rife as now. The entire movement of Humankind has been accelerated in both directions; events spin by with an extraordinary rapidity. The average individual lives more in a day in modern times than his not very remote ancestors lived in a decade. But if the Evil keeps pace with the Good in its growth, where does the advantage lie?

Evil does not keep pace with the Good. On the contrary, there is less real Evil today than ever before, because people are eliminating from their systems the Evil which in other times has been pent up within to breed and fester. Stirring up this latent deposit, bringing it to the surface and dumping it, has naturally brought more of it into evidence but leaves less of it in fact.

Do not be deceived and discouraged by the murky hue this process lends to the outlook for the time being. Humanity of today is incomparably better than the Humanity of days gone by and is becoming finer and nobler with each passing moment. Contrast the general conditions of life and Standards of living with those of the past generation, and you will realize how great has been the inner improvement, individually and collectively, of which those conditions are the outer expressions. Higher Standards in every direction, ampler Powers, greater Knowledge and finer Morals are the invaluable assets of Modern Humanity. If these results are won in• the face of darkness, what will the Future hold when the clouds have been dispelled and the night yields place to a clear New Day.

That this Day must arrive is inevitable. Progress is the Law of Eternal Evolution. All things, from the smallest to the greatest, are subject to that Law. Individuals and Nations, Electrons and Worlds, respond equally to its dominating influence. In this knowledge, so vividly proven in a comparison of Yesterday with Today, rests your assurance that Mankind cannot fail to achieve the Goal looming in prospect.

Throw off the despair that may assail you when conditions appear too hard to bear or the time too wearisomely long to wait. In the darkest hours of your life, when the stress of circumstance is at its crisis, you have a Light to guide you and a Strength to help you support the burden. Universal Life Energy, that wonderful Power vouchsafed to Mankind, is always ready at hand to answer your call, an Ever Present Help in time of trouble, an Ally never loath to come at your summons and lend Its invincible Strength to fight and win all your life's battles.

Do not forget It. Use It always. You need It. Especially NOW will you require It more and more every day in order to achieve Success in the midst of failures, to retain Confidence amid Discouragement, Strength amid

Weakness, Happiness and Poise amid Sorrow and Disturbance. It is the Aspect under which the Great Law of the Universe offers Itself to you, the Fount of Everlasting Waters, of Life, crying out to Humanity "Come unto me, all ye who are thirsty, and I will give you to drink."

The Great Law is never absent and never idle on this Earth or elsewhere. It is continually seeking new channels for Its expression, new mouths to carry Its Message to suffering Humankind. It speaks through the lips of Leaders of men, through scientific discoveries, through better laws, artistic achievements, the living word and the printed page. This Course is a printed medium through which It is conveying Its Message to the World, the Message of Life, Light, Liberty and Love. Wherever It finds an open mind and a receptive heart, there Its mission is fulfilled.

Humanity has for countless ages lost sight of its place in the Universal Scheme. It has believed in its own separation from the Universal Power. Yet Unity is the Law of the Absolute. The Universal is all there is, and you are ONE WITH IT.

This Lesson Humanity has to learn quickly. The time is not far off when a conscious knowledge of It will be essential to individual progress. It is not easy to recover an idea so long completely buried in forgetfulness, and the beginning is to bring about the reunion first through that part of our Being which now seems the most real and substantial to us, the Physical Body. By becoming consciously One with Universal Life Energy on the

Physical Plane, Humanity will pave the way for the next Great Step, the Mental Union, and finally for the last crowning Stage in the Progression, the realization as an Eternal Fact of the Spiritual or Soul Oneness with that Power. You who have taken this Course, who are able to apply now in your daily life the Knowledge imparted through these Lessons, who are able to become consciously One with All Power and who realize the immeasurable value of that Contact in helping you to achieve Health, Success and Happiness, do not selfishly keep the Knowledge for yourself alone. Open to others the glad way you have trod. Tell them of that Infinite Power which will refresh and renew their lives and amplify their powers as it has done yours, and of the Knowledge contained in these pages of how that Universal Force can be contacted and used practically in daily life.

This work is exclusively Humanitarian. Its object is to help Humanity come into its own. You, as a member of the Great Human Family, will help yourself only in proportion as you help others. Therefore carry out the purpose of this Lesson in its broadest humanitarian aspect by spreading these Teachings among your Friends and Fellow Beings. In so doing you will be seconding the efforts of the author, whose energy and knowledge are not alone placed thus at the service of his Fellow Men, but who is reinvesting in the Work its financial proceeds in order to spread its enlightening influence as far as possible among Mankind. As he is making a constant and personal effort to bring this Knowledge home to you, so must you make a corresponding effort to acquire it. Then teach others to do likewise.

This is a personal Course, not intended to be lent or given to others. Having been through it, you are aware of the necessity for acquiring it through your own efforts in order to value it and profit by it properly. You made the effort; let others do likewise. No one obtaining it without making the equivalent sacrifice will derive the benefit from it, nor will they escape paying the price in their own characters, though perhaps not in actual cash. They will have violated the Law of Compensation, and Laws of Nature permit no violation with Impunity.

The value you get out of anything is the value you put into it. All things in this World have a certain valuation, high or low in proportion to the effort and sacrifice you have to put forth to obtain them. It is a well known fact that the higher the price you have to pay for something, the greater the obstacle you have to overcome to possess it, the dearer it becomes to you and the more benefit and satisfaction you derive from it.

So for the advantage of those whom you wish to help and enlighten, tell them of this Course and what it did for you, but also impress on them the necessity for acquiring their own copy of it. Thus you will be benefiting both your Friends and Yourself by observing the Principles explained in these Teachings.

EXERCISES TO LESSON TWENTY-SEVEN

Continue to practice the Star Exercise regularly, morning and evening, ALL THE DAYS OF YOUR LIFE. This, with Relaxation, Silence, and the Mental Contact with Universal Life Energy, forms the vital foundation of all that you can hope to do in your life with the help of that Power. Then, whenever you feel the need of a specific Exercise, choose it from among the number given you and through it apply the Life Current to the strengthening of whatever part of your nature you think requires it most.

Bear in mind always that this Course is first and foremost a practical one. It is to be LIVED. Perform its Exercise daily, maintain a real living interest in the progress you are making through its help, and you will obtain real living results.

The special Exercise for this week, culminant one of the entire series, and for that reason most advanced of all, is SPIRITUALIZATION. In order to practice SPIRITUALIZATION proceed as follows:

After you have relaxed, entered into Silence and made the Contact with Universal Life Energy, concentrate your thought on SPIRIT, on the Supreme Ideal. Do not try to give it concrete form and outline in your Imagination. That is impossible. Perceive it only as the Ideal, as Spirit, an abstract concept personal to each individual, and feel your Oneness with It. Rise through Inspiration into complete identity with It, shedding all consciousness of your limited Human Self, your human desires and aspirations.

Then gradually release yourself even from thought itself. Let your whole nature dissolve into an exquisite atmosphere of feeling. Sense through every fibre of your Being the Supreme Power surrounding you, protecting, strengthening and refreshing you, pulsating with an ever quicker and fuller beat within you. Cast loose the last thread of remembrance connecting you with mundane things and entrust yourself wholly to the gentle tide of that Power.

Soon an extraordinary sense of wordless Happiness, Peace and Strength will flush with living light the inner darkness in which you dwell. Sorrow, Discontent, Discouragement, all the sombre shadows which thicken within the confines of your human life, will melt before the sun of utter Harmony which dawns in placid splendour upon you. You will have attained the Highest it is possible to attain in your present State of Human Consciousness. You will have become, for the time, consciously One with the Ideal, with Spirit, and you will have drawn into your life from each of those contacts such attributes of that Ideal as can be adequately suggested only by your own individual experience. Mind alone cannot convey any idea of them; it is too limited. They are of Spirit, and like Spirit they surpass all understanding.

QUESTIONS TO LESSON TWENTY-SEVEN

1. What is the motive responsible for the agitation and unrest among the people of today.

2. What movement most vividly illustrates this motive?

3. What is the deeper significance of the conflict between the sexes?

4. Why have women until now been held in a subordinate position by men?

5. How are women proceeding to do away with this distinction?

6. What will be the result if men fail to make the proper countermove?

7. What is the proper counter-move?

8. What is the difference between Refinement and Effeminacy?

9. Explain the alarming increase in Evil today.

10. How does modern Humanity contrast with the Humanity of the Past?

11. What infallible recourse have you amid the trying times in prospect?

12. Has your study of this Course carried to you a sincere conviction of your duty to others with reference to it?

ANSWERS TO LESSON TWENTY-SEVEN

1. **The motive responsible for the agitation and unrest among the people of today is:**

   Desire for Freedom.

2. **The movement that most vividly illustrates this motive is:**

   Feminism, lifting women to equal rights with men.

3. **The deeper significance of the conflict between the sexes is:**

   The conflict between the Love Principle, represented by women, and the Mind Principle, represented by men.

4. **Women have until now been held in a subordinate position by men:**

   Because they did not develop the mental side of their natures and were therefore unable to express strongly enough to compete on equal terms with men, in whom the mental side was over developed.

5. **Women are proceeding to do away with this distinction:**

   By developing themselves physically and mentally and successfully invading occupations formerly restricted to men alone.

6. **The result, if men fail to make the proper countermove, will be:**

 That the relations between men and women will be reversed, women dominating and men occupying an inferior position.

7. **The proper counter-move is:**

For men to develop the neglected Love qualities of their nature in proportion as women develop the neglected Mind aspect of theirs.

8. **The difference between Refinement and Effeminacy is:**

Refinement is Strength enhanced and tempered by Culture, while Effeminacy is Weakness proceeding from shallowness and poverty of Character.

9. **The alarming increase in Evil today:**

Is due to the fact that modern people stir up and bring to the surface to be cast off the latent Evil that used to be repressed.

10. **Modern Humanity contrasted with Humanity of the Past:**

Shows the vast improvement and progress of the Race in every direction, manifesting itself in better conditions of life, higher Standards, greater Powers, more knowledge and finer Morals.

Baron Eugene Fersen

11. Your infallible recourse amid the trying times in prospect is:

Universal Life Energy.

12. Has your study of this Course carried to you a sincere conviction of your duty to others in reference to it?